KYOTO AREA STUDIES ON ASIA
CENTER FOR SOUTHEAST ASIAN STUDIES, KYOTO UNIVERSITY
VOLUME 24

The End of Personal Rule
in Indonesia

KYOTO AREA STUDIES ON ASIA

Center for Southeast Asian Studies, Kyoto University

The Nation and Economic Growth:
Korea and Thailand
Yoshihara Kunio

One Malay Village:
A Thirty-Year Community Study
Tsubouchi Yoshihiro

Commodifying Marxism:
The Formation of Modern Thai Radical Culture, 1927–1958
Kasian Tejapira

Gender and Modernity:
Perspectives from Asia and the Pacific
Hayami Yoko, Tanabe Akio, Tokita-Tanabe Yumiko

Practical Buddhism among the Thai-Lao:
Religion in the Making of a Region
Hayashi Yukio

The Political Ecology of Tropical Forests in Southeast Asia:
Historical Perspectives
Lye Tuck-Po, Wil de Jong, Abe Ken-ichi

Between Hills and Plains:
Power and Practice in Socio-Religious Dynamics among Karen
Hayami Yoko

Ecological Destruction, Health and Development:
Advancing Asian Paradigms
Furukawa Hisao, Nishibuchi Mitsuaki, Kono Yasuyuki, Kaida Yoshihiro

Searching for Vietnam:
Selected Writings on Vietnamese Culture and Society
A. Terry Rambo

Laying the Tracks:
The Thai Economy and its Railways 1885–1935
Kakizaki Ichiro

After the Crisis:
Hegemony, Technocracy and Governance in Southeast Asia
Shiraishi Takashi, Patricio N. Abinales

Dislocating Nation-States:
Globalization in Asia and Africa
Patricio N. Abinales, Ishikawa Noboru and Tanabe Akio

People on the Move:
Rural–Urban Interactions in Sarawak
Soda Ryoji

Living on the Periphery:
Development and Islamization among the Orang Asli
Nobuta Toshihiro

KYOTO AREA STUDIES ON ASIA

CENTER FOR SOUTHEAST ASIAN STUDIES, KYOTO UNIVERSITY

Myths and Realities:
The Democratization of Thai Politics
TAMADA Yoshifumi

East Asian Economies and New Regionalism
ABE Shigeyuki and Bhanupong NIDHIPRABA

The Rise of Middle Classes in Southeast Asia
SHIRAISHI Takashi and Pasuk PHONGPAICHIT

Farming with Fire and Water:
The Human Ecology of a Composite Swiddening
Community in Vietnam's Northern Mountains
Trần Đức VIÊN, A. Terry RAMBO and Nguyễn Thanh LÂM

Re-thinking Economic Development:
The Green Revolution, Agrarian Structure and Transformation in Bangladesh
FUJITA Koichi

The Limits of Tradition:
Peasants and Land Conflicts in Indonesia
URANO Mariko

Bangusa and Umma:
Development of People-grouping Concepts in Islamized Southeast Asia
YAMAMOTO Hiroyuki

Development Monks in Northeast Thailand
Pinit LAPTHANON

Politics of Ethnic Classification in Vietnam
ITO Masako

The End of Personal Rule in Indonesia:
Golkar and the Transformation of the Suharto Regime
MASUHARA Ayako

KYOTO AREA STUDIES ON ASIA

CENTER FOR SOUTHEAST ASIAN STUDIES, KYOTO UNIVERSITY

VOLUME 24

The End of Personal Rule in Indonesia

Golkar and the Transformation of the Suharto Regime

by

MASUHARA Ayako

Translated by
Yuri Kamada

Kyoto University Press

First published in 2015 jointly by:

Kyoto University Press
69 Yoshida Konoe-cho
Sakyo-ku, Kyoto 606-8315, Japan
Telephone: +81-75-761-6182
Fax: +81-75-761-6190
Email: sales@kyoto-up.or.jp
Web: http://www.kyoto-up.or.jp

Trans Pacific Press
PO Box 164, Balwyn North, Melbourne
Victoria 3104, Australia
Telephone: +61-3-9859-1112
Fax: +61-3-9859-4110
Email: tpp.mail@gmail.com
Web: http://www.transpacificpress.com

Copyright © Kyoto University Press and Trans Pacific Press 2015.
Printed in Melbourne by BPA Print Group.
Cover photo: AP/AFLO

Distributors

Australia and New Zealand
James Bennett Pty Ltd
Locked Bag 537
Frenchs Forest NSW 2086
Australia
Telephone: +61-(0)2-8988-5000
Fax: +61-(0)2-8988-5031
Email: info@bennett.com.au
Web: www.ennett.com.au

USA and Canada
International Specialized Book Services (ISBS)
920 NE 58th Avenue, Suite 300
Portland, Oregon 97213-3786
USA
Telephone: (800) 944-6190
Fax: (503) 280-8832
Email: orders@isbs.com
Web: http://www.isbs.com

Asia and the Pacific (except Japan)
Kinokuniya Company Ltd.

Head office:
38-1 Sakuragaoka 5-chome
Setagaya-ku, Tokyo 156-8691
Japan
Telephone: +81-3-3439-0161
Fax: +81-3-3439-0839
Email: bkimp@kinokuniya.co.jp
Web: www.kinokuniya.co.jp

Asia-Pacific office:
Kinokuniya Book Stores of Singapore Pte., Ltd.
391B Orchard Road #13-06/07/08
Ngee Ann City Tower B
Singapore 238874
Telephone: +65-6276-5558
Fax: +65-6276-5570
Email: SSO@kinokuniya.co.jp

All rights reserved. No reproduction of any part of this book may take place without the written permission of Kyoto University Press or Trans Pacific Press.

ISSN 1445–9663 (Kyoto Area Studies on Asia)
ISBN 978–1–920901–19–6

Contents

Tables	viii
Figures	ix
Abbreviations	xi
Author's Biography	xvi
Preface	xvii
Introduction	1
1 Rethinking the Suharto Regime and the 1998 Political Change	6
2 The Suharto Regime as Co-opting-type Personal Rule	41
3 Golkar in the 1970s: Fumbling Its Way	77
4 The Consolidation of Golkar and Recruitment of Social Elites	94
5 Dilemmas of the Giant Ruling Party: The Struggle for Independence and Its Failure	129
6 The Rise of the Suharto Family and a Rift in Golkar	160
7 The Reformist Movement and the Fall of the Suharto Regime	188
Conclusion: The End of Personal Rule and Regime Change in Indonesia	235
Notes	242
Bibliography	258
Name Index	277
Subject Index	281

Tables

2.1:	Fluctuations in the defense-security budget in Indonesia (1972–1989)	54
2.2:	Political and administrative posts allocated to high-ranking military officers (1968–1989)	58
2.3:	Political and administrative posts allocated to middle-ranking military officers (1968–1989)	59
3.1:	Central Executive Board of Sekber Golkar (November 1967)	80
3.2:	Central Executive Board of Golkar at its establishment (July 1971–September 1973)	84
3.3:	Central Executive Board of Golkar (1973–1978)	86
3.4:	Central Executive Board of Golkar (1978–1983)	91
4.1:	Percentage of votes and number of seats won by Golkar in elections under the Suharto regime	95
4.2:	Central Executive Board of Golkar (1983–1988)	99
4.3:	Former student activists' membership history in the KNPI and AMPI	106
4.4:	Business and political careers of entrepreneur Golkar politicians	109
4.5:	Occupational backgrounds of DPR members elected from Golkar in the 1987, 1992 and 1997 elections	117
5.1:	Central Executive Board of Golkar (1988–1993)	133
5.2:	Competition and conflict between the Armed Forces and Golkar over Regional Representative Councils' chair posts in 1992	148
5.3:	Competition and conflict between the Armed Forces and Golkar over provincial governor and regent posts from 1992 to 1994	151
6.1:	Golkar legislators with past membership in the KNPI and AMPI	162
6.2:	Central Executive Board of Golkar (1993–1998)	167
6.3:	New and re-elected Golkar legislators under the Suharto regime	174
6.4:	Incidents over the selection of Golkar's legislative candidates for the 1997 election	176

Figures

1.1: Subtypes of personal rule 29
2.1: Proportion of defense spending to the total national budget (1972–1989) 55
3.1: Golkar's basic organizational structure 92

Abbreviations

ABRI (Angkatan Bersenjata Republik Indonesia): Armed Forces of the Republic of Indonesia
AMPI (Angkatan Muda Pembaharuan Indonesia): Indonesian Renewal Youth Generation
AMS (Angkatan Muda Siliwangi): Siliwangi Youth Generation
Aspri (Asisten Pribadi): Personal Assistant
BAKIN (Badan Koordinasi Intelijen Negara): State Intelligence Coordinating Agency
banpres (bantuan presiden): presidential assistance
Bappenas (Badan Perencanaan Pembangunan Nasional): National Development Planning Agency
BAPILU (Badan Pengendali Pemilihan Umum): General Election Controlling Body
BI (Bank Indonesia): Bank of Indonesia
BPK (Badan Pemeriksa Keuangan): Supreme Audit Board
Bulog (Badan Urusan Logistik): National Food Logistics
CBS: Currency Board System
CSIS: Centre for Strategic International Studies
DMI (Dewan Masjid Indonesia): Indonesian Mosque Council
DPA (Dewan Pertimbangan Agung): Supreme Advisory Council
DPD (Dewan Pimpinan Daerah): Regional Executive Board
DPK-EKU (Dewan Pemantapan Ketahanan Ekonomi dan Keuangan): Economic and Financial Resilience Council
DPP (Dewan Pimpinan Pusat): Central Executive Board
DPR (Dewan Perwakilan Rakyat): People's Representative Council
DPR-GR (Dewan Perwakilan Rakjat Gotong-Rojong): Mutual Assistance People's Representative Council
DPRD (Dewan Perwakilan Rakyat Daerah): Regional Representative Council
FBSI (Federasi Buruh Seluruh Indonesia): All-Indonesian Labor Federation
FKMIJ (Forum Komunikasi Mahasiswa Islam Jakarta): Communication Forum of Muslim Students of Jakarta
FKP (Fraksi Karya Pembangunan): Golkar Faction
FKPMJ (Forum Komunikasi Pers Mahasiswa Jakarta): Press Communication Forum of Students of Jakarta
FKPPI (Forum Komunikasi Putra-Putri Purnawirawan Angkatan Bersenjata Republik Indonesia): Armed Forces Son's and Daughter's Communication Forum

FKSMJ (Forum Komunikasi Senat Mahasiswa se-Jakarta): Communication Forum of Student Senates throughout Jakarta
GAKARI (Gabungan Karya Rakyat Indonesia): Indonesian People's Functional Union
GBHN (Garis-garis Besar Haluan Negara): Broad Guidelines of State Policy
GM-FKPPI (Generasi Muda Forum Komunikasi Putra-Putri Purnawirawan Angkatan Bersenjata Republik Indonesia): Armed Forces Son's and Daughter's Communication Forum Youth Generation
GMKI (Gerakan Mahasiswa Kristen Indonesia): Indonesian Student Christian Movement
GMNI (Gerakan Mahasiswa Nasional Indonesia): National Student Movement of Indonesia
Golkar (Golongan Karya): Functional Group
GP Ansor (Gerakan Pemuda Ansor): Ansor Youth Movement
GUPPI (Gerakan Usaha Pembaharuan Pendidikan Islam): Islamic Education Reform Endeavour Movement
HIPMI (Himpunan Pengusaha Muda Indonesia): Association of Indonesian Young Entrepreneurs
HIPPI (Himpunan Pengusaha Pribumi Indonesia): Association of Indonesian Indigenous Entrepreneurs
HKTI (Himpunan Kerukunan Tani Indonesia): Indonesian Farmers' Harmony Association
HMI (Himpunan Mahasiswa Islam): Islamic Students' Association
HNSI (Himpunan Nelayan Seluruh Indonesia): All-Indonesian Fishermen's Association
HWK (Himpunan Wanita Karya): Women's Functional Association
IAIN (Institut Agama Islam Negeri): State Institute of Islamic Studies
ICMI (Ikatan Cendekiawan Muslim Se-Indonesia): Association of Indonesian Muslim Intellectuals
IIP (Institut Ilmu Pemerintah): Institute of Government Studies
inpres (instruksi presiden): presidential instruction
IPB (Institut Pertanian Bogor): Bogor Agricultural University
IPKI (Ikatan Pendukung Kemerdekaan Indonesia): League of Upholders of Indonesian Independence
ITB (Institut Teknologi Bandung): Bandung Institute of Technology
KADIN (Kamar Dagang dan Industri): Chamber of Commerce and Industry
KADINDA (Kamar Dagang dan Industri Daerah): Regional Chambers of Commerce and Industry
KAHMI (Keluarga Alumni Himpunan Mahasiswa Islam): Alumni of the Islamic Students' Association

KAMI (Kesatuan Aksi Mahasiswa Indonesia): Indonesian Students' Action Front
KAMMI (Kesatuan Aksi Mahasiswa Muslim Indonesia): Indonesian Muslim Students' Action Front
KAPPI (Kesatuan Aksi Pemuda Pelajar Indonesia): Indonesian Youth Student Action Front
KBA (Keluarga Besar Angkatan Bersenjata Republik Indonesia): Great Armed Forces Family
KBG (Keluarga Besar Golkar): Great Golkar Family
Keppres 10: Presidential Decision Number 10
KINO (Kelompok Induk Organisasi): Basic Organizational Units
KKN (Korupsi, Kolusi, dan Nepotism): Corruption, Collusion and Nepotism
KNI-Reformasi (Komite Nasional Indonesia untuk Reformasi): Indonesian National Committee for Reform
KNPI (Komite Nasional Pemuda Indonesia): National Committee of Indonesian Youth
Kokarmendagri (Korps Karyawan Departemen Dalam Negeri): Corps of Officials of the Ministry of Home Affairs
Kopassus (Komando Pasukan Khusus): Special Forces Command
Kopkamtib (Komando Operasi Pemulihan Keamanan dan Ketertiban): Operational Command for the Restoration of Security and Order
KOPKKN (Komando Operasi Kewaspadaan dan Keselamatan Nasional): Operational Command for National Alertness and Safety
KORPRI (Korps Pegawai Negeri Republik Indonesia): Corps of Civil Servants of the Republic of Indonesia
KOSGORO (Kesatuan Organisasi Serbaguna Gotong-Royong): United Multipurpose Mutual Assistance Organizations
KOSGORO (when founded in 1957) (Koperasi Simpan Pindjam Gotong-Rojong): Mutual Assistance Cooperative Savings and Loans
Kostrad (Komando Cadangan Strategi Angkatan Darat): Army Strategic Reserve Command
KOWANI (Kongres Wanita Indonesia): Indonesian Women's Congress
KUKMI (Kerukunan Usahawan Kecil dan Menengah Indonesia): Indonesian Association of Small and Medium Entrepreneurs
LPU (Lembaga Pemilihan Umum): General Election Bureau
MA (Mahkamah Agung): Supreme Court
Malari (Malapetaka Limabelas Januari): Fifteenth of January Disaster
MAR (Majelis Amanat Rakyat): People's Mandate Council
MDI (Majelis Dakwah Islamiyah): Council for Islamic Dakwah
MI ((Partai) Muslimin Indonesia): Indonesian Muslims' Party

MKGR (Musyawarah Kekeluargaan Gotong-Royong): Mutual Assistance Families Association
MPR (Majelis Permusyawaratan Rakyat): People's Consultative Assembly
MPRS (Madjelis Permusjawaratan Rakjat Sementara): Provisional People's Consultative Assembly
MUI (Majelis Ulama Indonesia): Council of Indonesian Ulama
mukernas (musyawarah kerja nasional): national work conference
Munas (Musyawarah Nasional): National Congress
NASAKOM (Nasionalisme, Agama, dan Komunisme): Nationalism, Religion and Communism
NKK (Normalisasi Kehidupan Kampus): Normalization of Campus Life
NU (Nahdlatul Ulama): Awakening of Religious Scholars
Opsus (Operasi Khusus): Special Operation
Ormas Hankam (Organisasi Massa Pertahanan Keamanan): Defense and Security Mass Organizations
P 4 (Pedoman Penghayatan dan Pengamalan Pancasila): Guidance on Understanding and Implementing Pancasila
Parkindo (Partai Kristen Indonesia): Indonesian Christian Party
PDI (Partai Demokrasi Indonesia): Indonesian Democratic Party
Permen (Peraturan Menteri Dalam Negeri): Regulation of the Ministry of Home Affairs
Pertamina (Pertambangan Minyak dan Gas Bumi Nasional): State Oil and Natural Gas Mining Company
PERTI (Persatuan Tarbiyah Islamiyah): Islamic Educators' Association
PETA (Pembela Tanah Air): Defenders of the Homeland
Petrus (Penembakan Misterius): Mysterious Shootings
PGRI (Persatuan Guru Republik Indonesia): Teachers' Union of the Republic of Indonesia
PKI (Partai Komunis Indonesia): Indonesian Communist Party
PLN (Perusahaan Listrik Negara): State Electricity Company
PMI (Partai Muslimin Indonesia): Indonesian Muslims' Party
PMII (Pergerakan Mahasiswa Islam Indonesia): Indonesian Islamic Student Movement
PMKRI (Perhimpunan Mahasiswa Katholik Republik Indonesia): Union of Catholic University Students of the Republic of Indonesia
PNI (Partai Nasional Indonesia): Indonesian National Party
PPP (Partai Persatuan Pembangunan): United Development Party
PRRI/Permesta (Pemerintah Revolusioner Republik Indonesia/Perdjunangan Semesta): Revolutionary Government of the Republic of Indonesia/Total Struggle

PSII (Partai Sarekat Islam Indonesia): Islamic Association Party of Indonesia
PWI (Persatuan Wartawan Indonesia): Indonesian Journalists' Association
raker (rapat kerja): working meeting
rapim (rapat pimpinan): leadership meeting
RCD (Rassemblement Constitutionnel Démocratique): Democratic Constitutional Rally
REI: Real Estate Indonesia
SARA (Suku, Agama, Ras, dan Antargolongan): Ethnicity, Religion, Race and Inter-group Relations
Satkar Ulama (Satuan Karya Ulama): Ulama Functional Union
SAVAK (Sazeman-e Ettelaat va Amniyat-e Keshvar): Organization of Intelligence and National Security
SBSI (Serikat Buruh Sejahtera Indonesia): Indonesian Labor Welfare Union
SDSB (Sumbangan Dermawan Sosial Berhadiah): Social Philanthropists' Donation with Prize
Sekber Golkar (Sekretariat Bersama Golongan Karya): Joint Secretariat of Functional Groups
Setdalopbang (Sekretariat Pengendalian Operasional Pembangunan): Secretary for Operational Control of Development
SIT (Surat Izin Terbit): Publishing Permit
SIUPP (Surat Izin Usaha Penerbitan Pers): Press Publication Enterprise Permit
SOBSI (Sentral Organisasi Buruh Seluruh Indonesia): All Indonesia Center of Labor Organizations
SOKSI (Sentral Organisasi Karyawan Swadiri Indonesia): Central Organization for Indonesian Independent Workers
Spri (Staf Pribadi): Personal Staff
SPSI (Serikat Pekerja Seluruh Indonesia): All-Indonesia Workers' Union
Supersemar (Surat Perintah Sebelas Maret): Order of March the Eleventh
TGPF (Tim Gabungan Pencari Fakta): Fact-Finding Combined Team
TSSB (Tanda Sumbangan Sosial Berhadiah): Testimonials for Social Donation with Prize
UIN (Universitas Islam Negara): State Islamic University
Wanbin (Dewan Pembina): Advisory Board
Wanbinda (Dewan Pembina Daerah): Regional Advisory Board

Author's Biography

Ayako Masuhara is an associate professor in the Faculty of International Relations at Asia University. She began researching Indonesian politics from the perspective of comparative politics while a student of international relations at the University of Tokyo. She lived in Jakarta from June 2000 to October 2002 to conduct research for her PhD thesis. In 2007, she submitted her PhD dissertation to the Graduate School of Arts and Sciences of the University of Tokyo, which was published by the University of Tokyo Press in 2010. This book received the Ōhira Masayoshi Award in 2011. Recently, she has published papers on Indonesian politics and democratization focusing on civil–military relations and social security policy.

Preface

This book is an English version of my book published in Japanese by the University of Tokyo Press in 2010. The original version, *Suharuto Taisei no Indonesia: Kojinshihai no Henyō to 1998 nen Seihen*, was based on my PhD dissertation submitted to the University of Tokyo in 2007. After this original version was published, countries of the Middle East experienced the Arab Spring. In this new book I have added a few sentences outlining my interpretation of the condition of Syria according to my analytical frame. Regarding Indonesia, the main focus of this book, I have made a few small corrections to the original version.

Many people supported me during my research for this book. I am grateful for their assistance, criticism and feedback over many years. Firstly, I would like to thank Motoo Furuta and Susumu Yamakage for being the best advisors while I was writing my PhD dissertation. Their patient and thoughtful advice supported me always. Seniors and friends participating in their seminars, in particular Masako Ito, Hiroyuki Yamamoto, Kazuto Ikeda, Satoshi Miyawaki, Kaoru Kōchi, Yoshimi Nishi, Kaori Shinozaki, Yūko Ogawa, Hiroko Furuya, Katsuma Mitsutsuji, Terue Okada, Kumiko Makino, Nana Yamamoto, Sanae Suzuki, Ayame Suzuki, Hidekuni Washida, Hiroshi Hoshiro, Kazutoshi Suzuki and Taku Yukawa gave me critical and valuable feedback.

I also owe a debt of gratitude to Noriaki Oshikawa, Hiroyoshi Kanō, Takashi Shiraishi, Kiichi Fujiwara, Keiichi Tsunekawa, Akira Suehiro and Keiko Sakai. They have strongly influenced my studies since I began researching Indonesian politics and comparative politics twenty years ago. I am very fortunate to have received their insightful comments and constructive criticisms. Of course, many researchers who study Indonesian politics, in particular Yuri Satō, Jun Honna, Masaaki Okamoto, Ken Miichi, Kōichi Kawamura and Sachiko Imamura have also given me invaluable comments and influenced my studies.

A great number of Indonesians helped and supported me while I was researching in Indonesia. I would like to thank former Golkar Central Executive Board members and legislators, particularly Abdul Gafur, Cosmas Batubara, Rachmat Witoelar, Ade Komaruddin, Ibrahim Ambong, Ary Mardjono and other politicians and retired generals. Their interviews made a significant contribution to this book. I collected a lot of documents and periodicals from the many libraries I visited in Jakarta: the National Library and the libraries of the DPR, the MPR, the National Election Commission, the head office of Golkar, the Department of Home Affairs, the Department of Religion, the museum of the Armed Forces, the CSIS, the Kompas-Gramedia Documentation Center, the Idayu Foundation, the University of Indonesia (UI), Syarif Hidayatullah Jakarta of the National Islam University (UIN) and the Istiqlal Mosque. Library staff assisted me very kindly and the documents and periodicals I collected made a major contribution to my research. I would like to thank all of them. I would also like to express my gratitude to the Indonesian Institute of Science (LIPI) for permission to conduct research in Indonesia and the University of Indonesia for supporting my research. Former head of the Centre for Japanese Study (PSJ) of the University of Indonesia, Bachtiar Alam, provided indispensable support to my research in Jakarta. At the University of Indonesia, Padang Wicaksono, Asra Virgianita and Sri Budi Lestari have helped and advised me. Discussions with them provided a profound understanding of Indonesia and made a significant contribution to my study.

I would like to express thanks to Yōko Hayami and Narumi Shitara of the editorial office of the Centre for Southeast Asian Studies (CSEAS), Kyoto University. I am also indebted to referees for recommending the publication of my book as part of the Kyoto Area Studies on Asia, CSEAS, series. I am grateful to Yuri Kamada who translated my book into English and to Miriam Riley who edited this book. I wish to thank the Executive Director of Kyoto University Press, Tetsuya Suzuki, who supported me through the editing process. Former editor of Kyoto University Press, Itaru Saitō, provided advice about publication and translation in English. I want to thank him too. I am indebted to Hideki Yamada of the University of Tokyo Press, who edited my original book. Any mistakes and errors that remain in this book are my own.

This book was supported by the Japan Society for the Promotion of Science (JSPS) Grant-in-Aid for Publication of Scientific Research Results. I am grateful to the JSPS for the financial support to aid in the translation and publication of my book. I would also like to express my gratitude to the Fuji Xerox Foundation Setsutarō Kobayashi Fellowship, Matsushita International Foundation, Resona Asia Oceania Foundation and JSPS Grant-in-Aid for Young Scientists (B) for their financial assistance for my research.

I am indebted to my parents, Gyoh and Hide Masuhara. I have been able to continue my studies due to their tolerant support. I also wish to thank my husband Takahiro Hasuike whose constructive feedback always provided encouragement and inspiration.

Since 1998, Indonesia has been changing. I am not so pessimistic about the future of this democratizing country. I believe that this change is leading Indonesia to become a more liberal, democratic and open society. I would like to dedicate this book to all the people who have worked and are working toward democratizing Indonesia.

Introduction

Indonesia's Suharto regime that ruled the country for thirty-two years collapsed during the political change that occurred in May 1998. When financial crisis hit Indonesia in July 1997, Suharto's rock-solid dictatorial rule began to crumble. Although society was suffering from ever-worsening economic uncertainty caused by the sharp depreciation of the rupiah, Suharto was yet again elected to the presidency for a seventh term in March the following year. The new cabinet formed by Suharto included his eldest daughter and his cronies, inciting the criticism that this was palpable nepotism. Cries for 'reform' (*Reformasi*) grew louder and the reformist movement led by students and intellectuals spread rapidly as people were dismayed at the President's failure to share the sense of crisis that gripped the nation in the face of unprecedented national emergency. Then, in May, amid widespread demonstrations, the shooting of student protestors by Armed Forces security troops occurred, triggering large-scale riots in Jakarta. The reformist forces calling for the resignation of President Suharto successfully formed an alliance with members of parliament, the People's Representative Council (DPR), who feared that the political crisis might spin out of control. Eventually, on May 18 the DPR recommended that President Suharto resign and on May 20 the cabinet's economic ministers followed the DPR's lead by submitting their resignations en masse. Finally convinced that he was no longer capable of sustaining the government, Suharto declared his resignation on May 21, bringing an end to the Suharto regime.

We are faced with the following questions. Why was Suharto's supposedly stable rule so easily put on a path toward collapse by the financial crisis? How were the reformist forces that were underdeveloped in terms of leadership and mass mobilization capability able to drive Suharto to resignation? What lay behind the 180 degree turn taken by the ruling party and the parliament that had been supporting the Suharto regime for thirty years to demand that Suharto resign on the back of cooperation with the reformist forces? What did the end of Suharto's rule mean for Indonesia?

Despite a considerable amount of discussion on Indonesia's political change, there are few studies that have offered a coherent answer to these questions, and even less have analyzed the regime change in Indonesia from the perspective of comparative politics. In this book, I try to provide a coherent explanation of the nature of Suharto's regime as personal rule that lasted for over thirty years, its transformation and collapse while bringing into light the political dynamism that existed within it.

The first and foremost issue in analyzing the Suharto regime and the 1998 political change is to determine what theoretical framework should be employed to understand the characteristics of the regime. In comparative politics, the Suharto regime is usually described as an 'authoritarian regime'. However, since 'authoritarian regime' is a general concept and cannot adequately account for the attributes and political transitions of various nondemocratic regimes, subordinate concepts are often placed under authoritarian regime when conducting case studies. Among the subordinate concepts commonly used are those developed on a ruling actor basis, such as 'military regime', 'one-party system' and 'personal rule'. The Suharto regime has often been described as personal rule, or sometimes as 'intermediate categories' between personal rule and military regime (Geddes 1999: 124).

Unlike military regimes and the one-party system, thorough research has not been conducted on personal rule. In comparative politics, the 'sultanistic regime' proposed by Juan Linz (1975 and 2000) was the first serious analytical concept regarding personal rule. However, as described later, Linz's sultanistic regime points to an unstable political regime with a vulnerable support base and pronounced arbitrariness and violence by the ruler. Thus, it is too narrow to encompass the diverse forms of personal rule that exist around the world. In fact, this concept cannot be applied to the Suharto regime as is. This is because Suharto managed to develop a broad support base through patronage distribution and ensured long-lasting stable rule while keeping power to himself.

Now I offer the following questions. What theoretical framework can best capture the Suharto regime and the diverse array of other cases of personal rule and better explain the characteristics of each type? How can we analyze instances of personal rule that end with a more peaceful transition of power rather than through revolution or violent coup, as is often the case in situations described by Linz's sultanistic regime? This book aims to address these questions by proposing four subtypes of personal rule. Especially, I propose 'co-opting-type personal rule', one of the four subtypes, which will help us analyze Indonesia's regime change as a result of the political dynamism under the Suharto regime.

The structure of the book is as follows.

The first chapter examines the key studies on the Suharto regime. The patrimonial nature of Suharto's rule remained unchanged for thirty years, coexisting with a 'pragmatic' development policy. Some researchers argue that the arbitrariness of Suharto's rule became increasingly noticeable in the 1990s and this was one of the factors that caused its downfall (Shiraishi 1999; MacIntyre 2003). However, demonstrating the increased arbitrariness of Suharto's rule alone does not provide sufficient explanation as to how the political change was brought to an end by the cooperation and consensus formed between reformist forces and groups within the regime. Reviewing the analytical framework of personal rule from the perspective of comparative politics and proposing the analytical concept of 'co-opting-type personal rule' will help provide a more systematic and comprehensive explanation.

In the co-opting-type personal rule proposed in this book, the distribution of political patronage (political and administrative posts) and economic patronage (economic concessions) used by the ruler to appease the ruled plays a significant role. In addition, the existence of a ruling party is crucial as it acts as a channel to distribute patronage to the wide expanse of public and co-opts elites who are critical of the government into the ruler's patron-client network. The ruling party can become the ruler's instrument for control on one hand, while on the other hand it can also play the role of 'host' (*wadah*) to accommodate elites who used to be in the opposition. The ruling party thus has the potential to undermine the regime from within, depending on the development of political circumstances. This was exactly the case for the Suharto regime in Indonesia, where the ruling party 'Golkar' eroded the regime from within. One of the objectives of this book is to examine through empirical analysis the dynamism within Golkar (co-opting of social elites and competition among elites) and the role played by Golkar in the political change (regime collapse from within). The first chapter provides an explanation of the logic of why and how such situation could occur in the context of co-opting-type personal rule.

The second chapter illustrates the basic structure of the Suharto regime as co-opting-type personal rule. Suharto tactfully controlled governing elites such as the Armed Forces and bureaucrats using a 'divide and rule' strategy while ensuring he had authority over personnel affairs for important posts and leveraging distribution of political and economic patronage. By such means, he secured support and loyalty and at the same time manipulated politics to prevent the emergence of a formidable rival. Having done that, he ruled the public by resourcefully switching between violent and paternalistic attitudes. The objective of this chapter is to examine in detail the means and mechanisms of the type of rule employed by Suharto.

The third chapter describes Golkar's organizational structure in the 1970s. Golkar was established with the purpose of gathering votes in elections ahead of the restructuring of the political party system by the Suharto regime. Golkar was merely an agglomeration of various organizations created by the Armed Forces and therefore notably lacked internal unity in the first ten years. Military officers involved in the establishment of Golkar were preoccupied with competition over leadership within the party and the drive to recruit executives and members did not deliver much success. The chapter depicts how Golkar remained largely inoperative during the Suharto regime's period of instability as it drew strong criticism from the public for corruption and heavy-handed tactics.

The fourth chapter presents a discussion on the way Golkar underwent a significant expansion in the 1980s under Chairman Sudharmono who carried out a full-scale restructuring of the organization and launched the membership and executive recruitment systems. This restructuring encouraged student activists, entrepreneurs and members of Islamic organizations who used to be vocal critics of the Suharto regime to join Golkar, diversifying its executive team that until that time consisted of military officers and bureaucrats. As Golkar started to function as a 'host' for incorporating social elites who used to be in the opposition into the regime, anti-regime voices gradually diminished. Then, over the period from the second half of the 1980s to the early 1990s, Indonesia entered an era of political stability.

The fifth chapter provides an analysis of the political impacts of the internal changes in Golkar. With social elites increasingly composing the party executive, an independent attitude among them aimed at ending the dependence on President Suharto and the Armed Forces emerged in Golkar in the early 1990s along with a growing expectation for political openness. However, this attitude caused friction with Suharto. As for the relationship with the Armed Forces, it resulted in intensified competition over posts. As a consequence, Golkar's move toward independence was eventually discouraged.

The sixth chapter explains the process of the increasing influence of the Suharto family within Golkar. Competition over party executive and parliamentary posts between members of the Armed Forces Son's and Daughter's Communication Forum (FKPPI) coupled with Suharto family and social elites-turned members within Golkar became intense. In 1993, President Suharto gave key posts in Golkar's Central Executive Board (DPP Golkar) to his eldest daughter and second son with the succession of power in mind as he became elderly. Retired military officers as well as FKPPI executives who were close to his eldest daughter and second son were also promoted to important posts within Golkar and the government. As a result, social elite groups within Golkar gradually lost their position and power in the party. This change in the distribution of political patronage implemented by Suharto created a rift among the elites in Golkar and this eventually gave rise to groups that turned against Suharto with the onset of the reformist movement.

The seventh chapter focuses on the process of political change leading up to the resignation of Suharto. The currency crisis of July 1997 not only caused serious economic damage to Indonesia but also brought about a political crisis. The reformist movement expanded in and after March 1998 when Suharto was elected for a seventh term. The reformist forces led by students and intellectuals engaged members of the government, the Armed Forces and parliament in dialogues and debates, in addition to holding demonstrations and gatherings, to press for political reform. During the process of these discussions, DPR members who were willing to cooperate with the reformist forces to promote political reform emerged in the ruling party. They had been increasingly marginalized in Golkar due to the change in Suharto's patronage distribution policy, and chose the path of survival by forming an alliance with the reformist forces and turning against Suharto. Amid deepening political crisis, these DPR members under strong pressure from the reformist forces seized the initiative in the party and parliament and recommended that Suharto resign. Their intention was to force an early resolution of the political crisis by the immediate resignation of Suharto. This call for Suharto's resignation by the DPR caused him to finally step down.

The final chapter returns to the perspective of comparative politics and reviews the end of the Suharto regime in Indonesia through the framework of co-opting-type personal rule. The regime change took the form of a peaceful transition of power through the resignation of the President rather than an overthrow of the government by mass mobilization, even though it did involve mass mobilization. The chapter concludes this book by outlining the reasons that enabled such form of regime change and the political implications of the transition.

1
Rethinking the Suharto Regime and the 1998 Political Change

The Suharto regime in Indonesian studies

An uncharismatic president and patrimonial regime
After the declaration of independence on August 17, 1945, Indonesia fought the war for independence against the Dutch imperial power over four years. Sovereignty was formally transferred to Indonesia in December 1949. Sukarno, who was hailed as a national hero and received enthusiastic support from the masses, assumed the first presidency in 1945. However, it was the prime minister, not the president, who held executive powers from 1950 through to 1959 since the country was run under a parliamentary system introduced under the Provisional Constitution of 1950. Nevertheless, this parliament failed to operate effectively due to conflicts between political parties. The Cabinet often fell and policy-making stalled.

The first general election held in 1955 resulted in four political parties winning a similar number of seats and did not put an end to the strife. As the central government became increasingly dysfunctional, rebellions erupted in Sumatra and Sulawesi one after another, intensifying the political chaos[1]. In 1959, in order to subdue the political turmoil, President Sukarno declared the reinstatement of the Constitution of 1945 that provided the president with the authority to govern. Accordingly, the liberal parliamentary democracy was abolished and replaced by so-called 'Guided Democracy' (*Demokrasi Terpimpin*), under which President Sukarno held supreme authority.

Guided Democracy placed President Sukarno at the head of four political actors; namely nationalist parties, religious parties and the Communist Party (collectively referred to as NASAKOM[2]) as well as the Armed Forces. In the early 1960s, President Sukarno raised a series of political slogans and mobilized the masses to become involved in politics. In terms of foreign policy, Indonesia withdrew from the United Nations denouncing the neo-imperial and neo-colonialist West while deepening relationships with communist states such as China and North Korea. As for internal affairs, the Indonesian Communist Party (PKI) was building up overwhelming mass mobilization capability. This escalated the anti-communist hostility among the Armed Forces and Muslim groups who were alarmed about the expansion of the PKI. Sukarno tried to maintain his prerogative status by ensuring the balance of the pro- and anti-communist groups, but it was his own health concerns that heightened the leadership struggle between these forces that now saw their chances beyond the end of Sukarno's rule. The battle over leadership had reached a point of no return.

Under such unstable political circumstances, an event that served as the catalyst for the establishment of the Suharto regime took place—the September 30th Affair (*Peristiwa September Tiga Puluh*) of 1965. This incident occurred from the late hours of September 30 through to the early hours of October 1, 1965. A group calling itself the 'September 30th Movement' consisting of mid-level military officers mainly from the presidential bodyguard unit kidnapped and murdered six senior officers including the Minister/Commander of the Army, Ahmad Yani, and declared the foundation of the Indonesian Revolutionary Council (Anderson and McVey 1971; Notosusanto and Saleh 1987; Crouch 1988: 97–157; Shiraishi 1997: 98–105). The annihilation of senior officers who occupied the top positions within the Armed Forces put then Major General Suharto[3], who was in command of the Army Strategic Reserve Command (Kostrad), in a favorable position to seize power within the military. This command was the Army's top elite unit at that time, and this put Suharto in a position to take command of the suppression of the September 30th Movement regardless of the fact that the main force of the unit was away in Kalimantan Island on an assignment as part of the policy of confrontation against Malaysia[4]. Four days after the outbreak of the incident, he seized the rebel base with a special unit commanded by Major General Sarwo Edhie and successfully restored order in Jakarta.

On the grounds that the leaders of the incident included officers known as communist sympathizers, Suharto proclaimed that the mastermind of the September 30th Movement was the PKI and directed a purge of communists that received strong support from anti-communist Muslims and student activists. During the purge the presidential bodyguard unit who carried out the kidnappings and murders as well as left-wing military officers who supported President Sukarno, serving in Regional Military Commands of Central Java and East Java, were arrested. In cities and rural areas alike, in addition to PKI members, anyone deemed a communist sympathizer was arrested, killed or executed. The Operational Command for the Restoration of Security and Order (Kopkamtib), established in the wake of the September 30th Affair, led to the arrest and killing of anyone affiliated with the PKI. In rural areas, Islamic organizations and anti-communist groups voluntarily organized militias that assisted the Armed Forces units and Kopkamtib in arresting and killing those involved in the PKI. The total number of victims nationwide, from 1965 to 1969, is said to amount to 500,000 in one study and one million in another; an accurate figure has not been determined.

From 1965 through to 1968, Suharto continued the annihilation of communist organizations and, backed by support from anti-communist political leaders and student activists, gradually amplified his political power. On March 11, 1966, Suharto received the 'Order of March the Eleventh' from President Sukarno, also known as *Supersemar*, authorizing him to restore security and order and rendering the PKI illegal[5]. In March 1967, Suharto was named Acting President by the Provisional People's Consultative Assembly (MPRS) upon the dismissal of Sukarno and formally appointed President one year later in March 1968. Suharto with his 'New Order' vision, or *Orde Baru*, was well received by student organizations and Islamic groups and gained support from the MPRS. The MPRS then unanimously appointed him President.

Suharto reorganized the structure of the Armed Forces in 1969 to reinforce his power base giving his immediate subordinates important positions through a drastic reform of personnel affairs (Shiraishi 1997: 146). Meanwhile, Suharto himself acted as both President and Minister of Defense and Security and further took on the position of Commander of Kopkamtib, successfully concentrating military powers in his hands. Although there was no viable rival threatening Suharto's authority, he did not hesitate to remove the officers that he deemed did not align with his views from their posts and eliminate them from the chain of command of the Armed Forces.

Suharto established his power base within the Armed Forces by restoring security and order through the successful suppression of the September 30th Affair and seizing political authority. However, he did not have a significant support base outside the military. His predecessor Sukarno was recognized by every Indonesian as the leader of the nationalist movement as well as the hero of Indonesian independence. His charisma enchanted the entire nation and people were enthralled by his speeches broadcast on radio—Sukarno was that kind of leader. On the other hand, in addition to the fact that Suharto was almost unrecognized outside the military prior to the September 30th Affair, he was often criticized for his lack of quality as a political leader even after the presidential inauguration. Particularly his speeches, which were read straight from a script with no intonation, were constantly compared unfavorably with those of Sukarno.

Without the charismatic qualities of Sukarno, Suharto tried to ascertain the legitimacy of his rule through 'patronage' and 'development'. In contrast to Sukarno who received support from the public through his charisma and enthusiasm, Suharto attempted to gain support by providing materialistic satisfaction. This naturally contributed to the formation of the patrimonial aspects of the Suharto regime.

Benedict Anderson and Harold Crouch have noted that the patrimonial characteristics of the Suharto regime were already apparent in the beginning of the New Order (Anderson 1990; Crouch 1979). Anderson revealed the resemblance between the Suharto regime and the political structure of early kingdoms in Java prior to colonization and pointed out the similarity of these structures to Max Weber's patrimonialism model (Anderson 1990: 46–48). Weber's patrimonialism (*patrimonialismus*) is a concept based on Karl Ludwig Haller's patrimonial state (*patrimonialstaat*) (Weber 1978: 237). In Haller's definition, a country in which the state is viewed as the patrimony (*patrimonium*) of the ruler is a 'patrimonial state'. Weber, despite having pointed out that there had never been a pure patrimonial state in history, created a patrimonialism model based on systems of governance that are highly patrimonial—characterized by the absolute power of the ruler who rules the state as his personal possession (Weber 1978: 231–232). Building upon Weber's patrimonialism, Anderson identified Suharto's regime as having patrimonial characteristics, pointing out the existence of the President's personal staff, behind the legitimate and legal bureaucratic system from the colonial legacy. He also identified an informal source of capital based upon the patron-client relationship, or a corruption structure outside the formal remuneration system of bureaucratic institutions (Anderson 1990: 50–60).

While Anderson outlined the patrimonial characteristics of the Suharto regime focusing on the historical context, Crouch conducted his characterization paying attention to political relationships among the ruling elites (Crouch 1979: 571–573). According to Crouch, at the core of Suharto's rule lay the distribution of patronage. Suharto granted rewards such as political or administrative posts (political patronage) and economic concessions (economic patronage) to officers loyal to him. Crouch claimed that this distribution of patronage was an important factor that enabled Suharto to maintain the support of the Armed Forces (1979: 577).

Behind the emergence of such arguments that characterized the Suharto regime as being patrimonial was the issue of the closed policy-making process within the regime and the corruption of officers who came to power. Suharto, who did not have deep connections with party politicians when he seized political power, organized an informal team consisting of military personnel and technocrats, aside from formal government institutions such as the Cabinet, and had this team design policies and manipulate politics. Although the terms used to refer to this body changed over time from 'personal assistants' (Aspri) and 'personal staff' (Spri) to 'special operation' (Opsus), it always comprised about five to ten military officers whom Suharto trusted the most. Each specialized in the political, financial and economic or information and intelligence sectors and important policy decisions were made by consultations between Suharto and members of this group. Furthermore, the top positions of government agencies capable of raising a large amount of capital such as the state-owned oil company (Pertamina) and the National Food Logistics Agency (Bulog) were filled with military men and these agencies started to supply unofficial funds to the Armed Forces. This gave rise to criticisms from the public that military personnel were abusing public authority. It can be said that it was this mode of ruling in which a handful of military men sometimes referred to as political or business-oriented military officers acquired as much wealth as they wished, thus substantiating the patrimonial characteristics of the Suharto regime.

Duality of patrimonial and rational rule

Another distinct characteristic of the Suharto regime in addition to patrimonialism was the concept of 'development'. While Sukarno's approach to politics was to mobilize the public under the slogan 'revolution' (*revolusi*), Suharto introduced 'development' (*pembangunan*) in an attempt to depoliticize a public politicized during the Sukarno era and make them focus on the development targeted by the state. In 1969, the First Five-Year Development Plan was launched and from then on the word 'development' was added to the names of Suharto's Cabinets, as in the 'First Development Cabinet'. All this was because Suharto believed that development and economic growth would assure the nation of the legitimacy of his rule.

'Developmental dictatorship'—a system that aims for state-led development under the national goal of economic growth while bringing the public under control by depoliticizing them—was a state development model experimented with not just in Indonesia but in neighboring Southeast Asian countries as well. Ikuo Iwasaki defined 'development-oriented authoritarian regime' as a system in which economic development is used as the principle of legitimacy and state-led development policies are implemented under a centralized administrative system. He positioned the Sarit government of Thailand, the Lee Kuan Yew government of Singapore, the Suharto government of Indonesia, the Marcos government of the Philippines and the Mahathir government of Malaysia as development-oriented authoritarian regimes (Iwasaki 1994: 8–9). Under such regimes, the legitimacy of the political authority depends on developmental success and economic growth. Political power was thus held exclusively by a handful of senior officers of the Armed Forces, bureaucratic institutions or top party officials. Public administration based upon the principle of rationalism and efficiency was carried out by bureaucratic elites and technocrats, resulting in the elimination of social forces from the policy-making process (Iwasaki 1994:19–29). Moreover, as preservation of the public order was given top priority, political participation and civil liberties were heavily restricted.

As Iwasaki pointed out, in order to promote economic growth driven by development policies, there must be rational policy-making by technocrats coupled with efficient bureaucratic mechanisms capable enough of actually implementing the policies (Iwasaki 1994: 8). In relation to this point, Dwight King argued that it was not President Suharto who possessed the ultimate power under the Suharto regime but rather the 'military as institution' held sway. King, based on Juan Linz's Bureaucratic Authoritarian Regime theory, emphasized the presence of the Armed Forces and technocrats within the Suharto regime and asserted that consultations within this ruling group took precedence above all else as far as policy-making was concerned and were carried out through a rational and bureaucratic decision-making system (King 1982: 109–110).

Behind King's emphasis here was a change in the policy-making process of the Suharto government. At the beginning of the Suharto regime, a group of Suharto's personal staff, which may be called a 'shadow cabinet', controlled the policy-making process while military officers close to Suharto fought each other for economic concessions. However, when lax management put Indonesia's state-run oil company, Pertamina in danger of bankruptcy in 1975, Suharto listened to the opinions of technocrats and dismissed the president of Pertamina, Ibnu Sutowo who was highly criticized as being a business-oriented military officer. This was viewed as a victory for the technocrats who made political decisions based on rationalism[6].

In addition, from around the mid-1970s, corporatist organizations such as those of farmers, fishermen, women, laborers, teachers and entrepreneurs started to be formed one after another. This was considered as an indication that the Suharto regime was attempting to shift to rationalistic rule through institutionalization—that is, the government was trying to regulate society and reconcile competing interests through these organizations. William Liddle argued that non-government forces were not necessarily prevented from playing certain roles in the policy-making process in Indonesia's military-bureaucratic authoritarian regime, and in fact the public had means of communicating with the government via a direct or indirect route (Liddle 1987: 127–146). Andrew MacIntyre has also pointed out that corporatist organizations began gaining the power, albeit limited in scope, to participate in policy-making processes throughout the 1980s as total control of the political system by the state was gradually becoming relaxed (MacIntyre 1990: 259).

Discussions that argued the presence of institutionalization and political diversification in the policy-making process were also encouraged by the expectation that the modernization policy promoted by the government would increase social demands, changing the relationship between the state and society, and inevitably give rise to a situation where the government was compelled to address society's demands. Furthermore, as if to substantiate this expectation, the beginning of the 1990s saw a period of 'openness' (*keterbukaan*), albeit for a short while only. In and after the late 1980s, the Suharto regime enjoyed stability and this was regarded as a successful outcome of development policies. As the recognition that the development strategy had succeeded and the political situation was now stable spread across society, Suharto eased press controls on mass media and permitted social discussions on a variety of political topics including the issue of his successor. Having witnessed this phenomenon, many researchers concluded that Indonesia had gained the momentum for democratization from above.

Nevertheless, the promotion of national development by the Suharto regime did not in any way signify a transformation from patrimonialism to bureaucratic rationalism. Rather, the Suharto regime's patrimonialism and rationalism were always two sides of the same coin.

Takashi Shiraishi noted that under the Suharto regime, the 'bureaucratic state' principle driven by instrumentally rational logic and the 'family state' principle coexisted (Shiraishi 1992: 10). An extensive network of personal relationships in the form of 'father/leader' (*bapak*) and 'children/followers' (*anak buah*) was built from President Suharto through to the very bottom of the bureaucracies and people received their due share according to such relationships (Shiraishi 1992: 81–84; 1997: 158–163). Misappropriation of funds by bureaucratic agencies and the Armed Forces was a widespread practice and was functioning as an allocation mechanism justified by the principle of 'familism' (*kekeluargaan*). A fraudulent diversion of funds or requests for 'commissions' and 'donations' would be considered corruption if one person took it all for himself, but if shared among everyone it would be justified as an act in line with the spirit of familism (Shiraishi 1992: 10). Another important point Shiraishi emphasized was Suharto's use of 'public' and 'private' in the decision-making process. Suharto managed to control both the 'bureaucratic state' and the 'family state' by tactically switching between formal authority as president and informal authority as the father of the nation as required (Shiraishi 1992: 83–84; 1997: 163–166).

Richard Robison and Vedi R. Hadiz, while emphasizing the patrimonial aspect of the Suharto regime, posed that the regime was an oligarchy (Robison and Hadiz 2003). This is because the extremely complex and extensive patronage ('rent' in their terms) distribution system Suharto had created formed a political-economic oligarchic ruling class around him (Robison and Hadiz 2003: 43). While Paul Hutchcroft who studied the Marcos regime in the Philippines claimed that Indonesian bureaucratic technocrats succeeded in driving an economic reform unlike their counterparts in the Philippines[7] (Hutchcroft 1993, 1998), Robison and Hadiz, on the contrary, highlighted that administrative rules and rationality in Indonesia were subject to patrimonial rent seeking by the oligarchic ruling class (Robison and Hadiz 2003: 42).

Concerning the Suharto regime, Shiraishi highlighted the 'coexistence' of formal bureaucratic rationality and informal familism whereas Robison and Hadiz interpreted it as a capitalistic oligarchy formed by a 'fusion' of formal authorities and informal interests (Robison and Hadiz 2003: 43). Their perspective plays an important role in allowing us to understand the nature of the Suharto regime.

Consolidation of personal rule

In the 1990s, increasing emphasis was placed on the personal rule aspect of the Suharto regime. Behind this were a number of changes in practical politics. One of the shifts was the diminishment of the influence of the Armed Forces in the policy-making process and another was the rapid expansion of business groups owned by the Suharto family, particularly his children.

In the 1990s, Suharto, who used to staff key political posts with powerful military men, started to appoint civilian cronies such as Baharuddin Yusuf Habibie, a technologist bureaucrat-turned politician, to key posts. Civilian politicians began to play greater roles in the decision-making process. What became clear from this was that whether it be military personnel or civilian, decision-making power would be allocated to a person trusted by the President, and the President had free will in terms of the policy-making process and was not bounded by the 'military as institution'.

Another point was that the Suharto family's businesses expanded rapidly as they were given advantages in winning large-scale projects and acquiring import licenses, and eventually grew to become one of the largest conglomerates in Indonesia. Although it was an undeniable fact that technocrats played major roles in the economic decision-making process, they had almost no influence at all in regards to matters that directly concerned the interests of the President and his family. It was mandatory to consult with the President and gain his approval on any issue; even the most powerful economic technocrats and high-level military officers were not allowed to make any important policy decisions without permission from the President. Opportunities for rationalistic policy makers to correct economically deviant behaviors involving the President's family were almost non-existent. This shows that it was the military, bureaucrats and technocrats who had restrictions imposed, not Suharto.

At the same time, the expectation of the gradual progression of liberalization and democratization disappeared in the mid-1990s. It became clear to everyone's eyes that democratization from above was unlikely under the Suharto regime, as anyone who did not conform to his view became the target of radical oppression as exemplified by tightened controls on the press and blatant oppressive measures against the Indonesian Democratic Party (PDI). The Suharto regime's arbitrary and violent aspects came under the spotlight once again and emphasis was given to the fact that Suharto's rule was increasingly assuming the form of personal rule not restricted by any institution or organization.

Andrew MacIntyre has stressed the absence of limits on Suharto's decision-making authority in Indonesia's political system and the arbitrary nature of his decisions. He compared the degree of the dispersal of decision-making power in Thailand, the Philippines, Malaysia and Indonesia in terms of their responses to the currency crisis that hit the Southeast Asian countries in 1997 (MacIntyre 2003). He argued that the impact of the economic crisis was more severe in Indonesia and the Indonesian Rupiah continued to fall for a prolonged period due to the 'volatility' of the government's economic policies determined purely by swings in Suharto's opinion and attitude, as there was virtually no institutional constraints on the President from parliament and political parties in the decision-making process (MacIntyre 2003: 48–50, 91–100). We can understand through MacIntyre's argument that the patrimonial or personalistic character of the Suharto regime was reinforced in the 1990s.

Shiraishi's explanation for this is that Suharto, who had tactically been controlling the principles of the 'bureaucratic state' and the 'family state', began prioritizing the 'personal' over the 'public' position. With the succession of power in mind, Suharto adopted personnel policies that gave important posts to Armed Forces officers close to the Suharto family. According to Shiraishi, the desire to change the political situation increased as Suharto's inclination to his personal interests accelerated the public's loss of trust in him. In addition, the generation without direct knowledge of the horrors of the oppression of the Communist Party after the September 30th Affair now accounted for the majority of the population (Shiraishi 1997: 168–169; 1999: 19–23, 45–51).

Edward Aspinall claims that the Suharto regime was increasingly displaying the characteristics of the sultanistic regime proposed by Juan Linz. According to him, although such characteristics became more prominent in the 1990s, they were already present from the very beginning of his rule albeit moderated by the existence of the military and bureaucracy (Aspinall 2005: 4, 204–205). Nevertheless, the Suharto regime differs from classic sultanistic regimes such as the Batista government of Cuba and the Somoza government of Nicaragua. There were more diverse actors within the Suharto regime and the 'gray area' that existed between state and society was providing dynamism to its politics. Aspinall concluded that, despite this, the Suharto regime was turning into a 'personalist dictatorship' due to the 'sultanization' of the system that rapidly took place from the mid-1990s, narrowing the gray area between state and society, and this ultimately led to 'a more dramatic struggle between state and society in 1998' (Aspinall 2005: 2–4).

Fall of Suharto in 1998

There are many studies featuring the political change of May 1998[8]. These studies indeed cover a broad range of topics, from the chronological description of the series of events from the economic crisis to the resignation of Suharto to the deep analysis of specific political actor's involvement in the political change. The Armed Forces was the second powerful actor under the Suharto regime next to Suharto himself. It is needless to mention the importance of actions taken and roles played by the Armed Forces in the process of the political change. Takashi Shiraishi (1999), Jun Honna (2002, 2003) and Marcus Mietzner (2009) have explained the political change with a focus on the behavior of the Armed Forces.

According to Shiraishi, in addition to the fact that Suharto had already started losing the public's trust via biased personnel policies and preferential treatment given to his family businesses (Shiraishi 1999: 19–23, 45–51), he intended to overcome the political crisis using violence rather than implementing the reform the public expected. Specifically, the plan was to take advantage of the occurrence of the rioting and establish a powerful security apparatus, and then assume total authority over the restoration of law and order (Shiraishi 1999: 55–80). However, the establishment of this apparatus did not go as Suharto had planned; it was obstructed by rivalry and conflict within the Armed Forces. It can be said that the 'divide and rule' policy Suharto himself implemented in the Armed Forces prevented it from taking unified action at a critical moment, breaking Suharto's will. Suharto, faced by the failure of the formation of the security apparatus, chose resignation fearing that the Armed Forces would undergo a schism (Shiraishi 1999: 93–102).

Honna's explanation focuses on internal conflicts within the military, identifying two key actors—those who sought dialogue and those who sought terror. The dialogue promoters needed to pursue communication with reformists in order to compete with their terror-minded counterparts and eventually brought Suharto over to their side and won the power struggle within the Armed Forces (Honna 2003: 159–162). Mietzner also noted the significance of the rivalry within the Armed Forces. He illustrated that the soft-liner officers within the military defeated the hard-liners and negotiated the handover of authority from Suharto to Vice President Habibie (Mietzner 2009: 125–138).

Shiraishi, Honna and Mietzner draw attention to the fact that there was an intense power struggle within the Armed Forces behind the political crisis.

According to them, this conflict played a certain role in the soft landing of the political change by hindering the formation of a new security apparatus and by linking some groups within the military to the reformists. While these discussions place strong emphasis on the behavior and roles of the military during the political change, there are, however, some researchers who are skeptical regarding the role of the Armed Forces during this time. Liddle and Aspinall made the point that the Army was reluctant to take political action in the last phase of the political turmoil and argued against the idea that the Armed Forces played an active role in the resignation of Suharto (Liddle 1999: 104; Aspinall 2005: 236–237). In addition, Michael Vatikiotis described that the mainstream military officers distrusted the Muslim reformist groups and that the dialogue between the Armed Forces and the reformist groups was not necessarily effective (1999: 162–163).

Certainly, there were a few officers within the military who showed receptive attitudes towards the reformist movement and participated in dialogues with them. However, they never took any decisive action of the kind that would dictate the direction of the political change. They neither oppressed the reformist movement nor staged a coup. Their inaction itself played a positive role; however, this does not necessarily account for the fall of the Suharto regime.

Aspinall, who conducted an analysis focusing on the opposition forces—especially NGOs, lawyer organizations, students and the Megawati supporters within the Indonesian Democratic Party—stressed the role played by the opposition forces in the reform movement and the political change in 1998. However, as Aspinall himself pointed out, the opposition forces were fragmented and ineffectual (Aspinall 2005: 242). Vincent Boudreau, who compared the scale and characteristics of the democratization movements of the Philippines in 1986 and Indonesia in 1998, argued that opposition forces were disintegrated in the Indonesian case, unlike the people power of the Philippines in which the opposition parties, military and mass organizations publically voiced 'anti-Marcos' sentiment and the movement was highly organized (Boudreau 1999: 14–16).

Why and how did the reformist movement in Indonesia, which was inadequate in terms of scale and organization and also lacked efficiency and unification, manage to achieve regime change? Aspinall suggested that a group that would compromise with the movement—the soft-liners—emerged from within the regime (Aspinall 2005: 233–238). His study did not, however, explain the soft-liners in detail. In reality, from the very initial stage of the reformist movement, the soft-liners had already emerged and engaged in numerous conversations with the reformists and were looking to cooperate with them. The parliament's call for Suharto's resignation was not a sudden, unexpected event, but rather the result of a long succession of dialogues that accumulated between the soft-liners and the reformist forces.

As discussed so far, we can see that many studies that analyze the Indonesian political change have constructed their arguments focusing on the power struggle that occurred in the process of the political change. While so much attention has been given to the power struggle, what has been overlooked is the fact that behind the power game there were continuous attempts to engage in dialogue and negotiation to resolve the political crisis. The reason that the political change was able to end in a 'soft landing' with Suharto's resignation cannot be explained without the fact that the dialogues carried out between the reformist forces and the soft-liners within the regime came to fruition and successfully established an alliance against the President and built consensus regarding his resignation. Without examining their negotiation, cooperation and consensus building, which progressed in parallel with the power struggle, it is impossible to provide a relevant explanation for the regime change in Indonesia.

This raises the questions as to how the soft-liners emerged in the process of the political change and how they managed to advance the negotiations and form an alliance with the reformists. These questions not only give an account of the regime change in Indonesia but also have very important implications from the perspective of comparative politics. This is because a commonly accepted thesis in comparative politics has been that, in regimes characterized by personal or sultanistic rule, there is an extremely small possibility that soft-liners that may cooperate with opposition groups could arise from within the regime. According to this thesis, the Suharto regime as personal rule was one in which the appearance of soft-liners was highly unlikely. However, in fact, soft-liners appeared from within the Suharto regime in the process of political change. The question is, given this, how can one explain the appearance of soft-liners and their successful cooperation with the reformist forces in the case of personal rule. The following section will examine this problem by presenting a discussion of comparative politics on personal or sultanistic rule, leaving Indonesian politics aside for the moment.

Subtypes of personal rule

History of conceptualizing personal rule
'Personal rule', or 'personal rulership', is one form of the many existing nondemocratic political regimes. It is sometimes called 'personal dictatorship', 'neopatrimonial dictatorship' or 'sultanistic regime'. The following two characteristics can be commonly found in all these regimes: (1) state power

and political decision-making authority are concentrated in one ruler and (2) the ruler, who runs the state based on patron-client relationships, monopolizes and misappropriates state power and wealth.

These concepts are derived from patrimonialism and sultanism outlined by Max Weber. Weber formulated patrimonialism as one type of traditional domination that is antithetical to rational-legal domination. For Weber, patrimonialism was an advanced form of gerontocracy and patriarchy, which are forms of primitive traditional domination. The transition to patrimonialism occurs when comrades of the master become his subjects and the master who has been strictly restrained by tradition is released from such bonds (Weber 1978: 231–232). Patrimonialism transforms into sultanism, which Weber refers to as patrimonialism in which the ruler is 'completely unrestrained by tradition' and 'where it indeed operates primarily on the basis of discretion' (Weber 1978: 232).

Guenther Roth was the scholar who introduced the above-mentioned Weberian concepts of patrimonialism (*patrimonialismus*) and sultanism (*sultanismus*) to the field of comparative politics in the 1960s and identified them as characteristics of regimes frequently found in newly developing countries. In Roth's definition, personal rulership occurs 'on the basis of loyalties that do not require any belief in the ruler's unique personal qualification, but are inextricably linked to material incentives and rewards' and it 'differs from charismatic rulership in that the patrimonial ruler need have neither personal charismatic appeal nor a sense of mission and differs from legal-rational bureaucracies in that neither constitutionally regulated legislation nor advancement on the basis of training and efficiency need be predominant in public administration' (Roth 1968: 195–197). Roth's definition laid the groundwork for defining forms of regimes that would later be known as personal rule, personal dictatorship, sultanistic regime and neopatrimonial dictatorship.

Juan Linz built upon Roth's definition of personal rule, and introduced Weber's sultanism into comparative politics. Linz included a short chapter titled 'Traditional Authority and Personal Rulership' in an article published in 1975[9] in which he formulated totalitarian regimes and authoritarian regimes and explained the concept of 'sultanistic regime' (Linz 2000). Linz wrote that the sultanistic regime is founded on 'loyalty to the ruler based not on tradition, or on him embodying an ideology, or on a unique personal mission, or on charismatic qualities, but on a mixture of fear and rewards to his collaborators' (2000: 151). He went on to argue that 'the ruler exercises his power without restraint at his own discretion and above all unencumbered by rules or by any commitment to an ideology or value system' and 'the binding norms and relations of bureaucratic administration are constantly subverted by personal arbitrary decisions of the ruler', stressing the significance of the discretion of the ruler (Linz 2000: 151).

Such a violent aspect resembles totalitarianism, but the major differentiating factor between sultanistic and totalitarian regimes is the fusion of public and personal interests in the former. Linz describes how in a sultanistic regime, 'the personalistic and particularistic use of power for essentially private ends of the ruler and his collaborators makes the country essentially like a huge domain... The boundaries between the public treasury and the private wealth of the ruler become blurred. He and his collaborators, with his consent, take appropriate public funds freely...The family of the ruler often plays a prominent political role, appropriates public offices, and shares in the spoils' (Linz 2000: 152). Support for the regime 'is based not on a coincidence of interest between preexisting privileged social groups and the ruler but on the interests created by his rule, the rewards he offers loyalty, and the fear of his vengeance. In this regime, the patron–client network extends into the military and bureaucratic apparatuses, gradually destroying their institutional autonomy until they finally become tools to help the ruler abuse authority for private gains' (Linz 2000: 152–153).

Because this conceptualization of sultanistic regimes published in 1975 was only a short discussion primarily based on case studies from the Caribbean countries, in particular, the Dominican Republic under Trujillo, Haiti under Duvalier and Cuba under Batista, Linz co-edited *Sultanistic Regimes* with H. E. Chehabi in 1998 to once again better formulate such form of rule (Chehabi and Linz 1998a). While leaving the original definition of the system itself unchanged, this time they incorporated the results of their worldwide case studies from Africa (Zaire), Asia (Iran and the Philippines) and Europe (Romania) and identified common characteristics such as a cult of personality, hereditary succession, lack of the rule of law, weakness in the social support base, economic exploitation and widespread corruption (Chehabi and Linz 1998b: 10–23).

The term 'sultanistic regime' that includes the word 'sultan' could be criticized for cultural bias. Thus, many researchers tend to use personal rule, personal dictatorship or neopatrimonial dictatorship instead. This book also uses 'personal rule', notwithstanding acknowledgement of the great contributions of Linz in conceptualizing this form of regime.

Weber's patrimonialism and sultanism, which gave birth to the concept of personal rule, were originally formulated as one type of traditional authority. Weber positioned the 'rule of men' based on traditional authority in which the ruler's arbitrariness is easily reflected in their governance in opposition to the 'rule of law' based on rational, legal authority relying on bureaucratic institutions. Similarly, Linz, who analyzed the structure and characteristics of nondemocratic regimes founded on Weber's argument also regarded the sultanistic regime as a form of traditional patrimonial rule and hence formulated it as something qualitatively different from the authoritarian regime derived from Weber's rational-legal rule. However, patrimonialism does not always contradict rational, legal rule but may well coexist and be combined with it. Eisenstadt called the patrimonial regime that coexists with bureaucratic rational rule 'neopatrimonialism' (Eisenstadt 1973).

Political transition in personal rule
In his book *The Third Wave*, Samuel Huntington categorized authoritarian regimes into groups based on actors, namely the one-party system, military regime and personal dictatorship, and depicted typical manners in which regimes undergo transition in each group (Huntington 1991). Having analyzed a great number of cases of democratization all over the world, he presented the following findings. In military regimes and one-party systems, 'transformation' (democratization from above) or 'transplacement' (transition by pact) are likely to occur, while in personal dictatorships, 'replacement' (the overthrow or collapse of the government) is the typical outcome (Huntington 1991: 110–121). Huntington's explanation for the high likelihood of regime change by overthrow or collapse of the government in a personal dictatorship was that dictators 'usually tried to remain in office as long as they could' and 'this often created tensions ... and also led on occasion to the violent overthrow of the dictators' (Huntington 1991: 120).

Michael Bratton and Nicolas van de Walle, who reviewed democratic transitions in African countries, also argued that there was hardly any chance of both 'democratization from above' and 'pacted democratization' in neopatrimonial regimes given the ruling group would never voluntarily initiate political liberalization and the chance of the emergence of soft-liners is very unlikely (Bratton and van de Walle 1994: 460–466). Negotiation is not possible in neopatrimonial personal dictatorships, as the ruling group establish 'few institutional channels for negotiation over rules and power sharing' and 'personal rule instead gives rise to all-or-nothing power struggles' (Bratton and van de Walle 1994: 474–477).

Likewise, Juan Linz and Alfred Stepan claimed in their discussion on democratization in the post-communist countries of southern Europe and Latin America that under a nondemocratic sultanistic regime, elites within the regimes were no more than personal staff of the ruler and soft-liners that could have engaged in negotiation with anti-government forces were absent (Linz and Stepan 1996). Furthermore, under this regime, the autonomy of civil and political societies is still vulnerable and thus moderates capable of negotiating with the government do not develop within the opposition. Hence, pacted transition enabled by negotiation between regime and anti-government forces cannot occur (Linz and Stepan 1996: 57–65). In light of this finding, Linz and Stepan concluded that rulers of nondemocratic sultanistic regimes are characteristically overthrown by mass movements, assassinations or armed revolts, if not through death by natural causes (Linz and Stepan 1996: 70).

Similarly, the discussion on sultanistic regimes by Chehabi and Linz also argued that such regimes tended to 'end in a more or less chaotic way' such as through anti-government mass movements or military coups, due to the difficulty of voluntary political liberalization by the ruler (1998c: 37–45).

As revealed through the above studies, it is believed that soft-liners—a group that may take a lead in liberalization and democratization and is capable of negotiating and making concessions and compromises with anti-government forces within the regime—are almost never going to emerge under personal rule. Therefore, the end of personal rule is most likely to be caused by the death of the ruler or forced overthrow by anti-government forces or a foreign power. Meanwhile, in other nondemocratic regimes such as military regimes and the one-party system, internal ties among the ruling group are not always strong, providing ample possibility for the disintegration of the ruling group from conflicts over interests and policies and the emergence of soft-liners within them. In contrast to this, under personal rule, the ruling group consisting of the ruler and a handful of his cronies not only has strong internal ties but also completely refuses negotiation and compromise with the opposition from the perspective that any political concession may lead to the collapse of their authority. Moreover, the lack of negotiation channels makes dialogue with the opposition simply impossible. This leads to the conclusion that democratization from above where the ruler voluntarily initiates liberalization and democratization as well as pacted democratization based on agreement between the soft-liners within the regime and anti-government moderates are unlikely to occur. However, the credibility of this argument is somewhat questionable. Like military regimes and the one-party system, in personal rule, ruling groups may not necessarily be monolithic. Richard Snyder also noted the possibility of the appearance of soft-liners in sultanistic regimes (Snyder 1992; 1998).

Personal rule has often been positioned as an unstable political regime with a narrow support base as in Linz's sultanistic regime and researchers have tended to focus on regimes vulnerable to collapse through revolution or subversion by large-scale mass mobilization (Goodwin and Skocpol 1989: 498–500). In this context, stable personal rule under which a revolution or insurrection would not take place has been excluded from analyses.

Personal rule needs to be reconceptualized within a more comprehensive analytical framework that includes more stable types of personal rule with a broad support base. In fact, the personal rule that existed in Indonesia was stable and ended in pacted transition by consensus between soft-liners within the regime and moderate opposition groups. In order to explain Indonesia's case more deeply and understand other cases of personal rule more comprehensively, we need to reconsider the analytical framework on personal rule. The following section will propose a typology to capture personal rule that will allow us to analyze Indonesia's and other cases of personal rule and identify its political transitions.

Categorizing personal rule

Definition and characteristics of personal rule

I would like to provide a definition of personal rule and outline its characteristics before categorizing the concept. The definition here does not substantially differ from those of personal rule and sultanistic regime formulated by Roth and Linz.

Firstly, state authority and governmental decision-making powers are concentrated in the ruler rather than the internal group of an organization or institution such as a military or a political party. The ruling group consists of the ruler and cronies who pledge their loyalty to the ruler and this differs from an institution such as a military council under a military regime or the central committee of a one-party system. The ruler is never bound by the rules and conventions of an organization or institution. Cronies comprising the ruling group are chosen to their respective posts based on loyalty. Joining the ruling group means their actions are no longer restricted by the organization to which they previously belonged, such as a political party, bureaucratic institution or military; instead they start acting in accordance with the ruler's intentions. Proximity to the ruler determines the extent of each crony's power.

Secondly, the ruler executes patrimonial control over the state. In personal rule, the distinction between state property and the ruler's private property is vague and the ruler misappropriates state funds and resources for their personal ends. The ruler also abuses their power to appoint personnel and to give permissions, taking advantage of their position as the head of the government. The ruler is not subject to any restrictions, legally or institutionally, and the 'rule of law' cannot be expected in personal rule. In addition, the ruler builds patron-client networks in which they are at the center and provides rewards to their supporters based on such relationships. On the other hand, the ruler takes vengeance against those who disobey or oppose their will. The ruler appropriates state authority and properties to use in dealing out rewards to their supporters and punishments to their noncompliants.

Lastly, another characteristic of personal rule is that succession of power is not institutionalized. The ruler in some cases appoints a family member or crony as successor but they often do not openly announce a successor fearing usurpation of authority during their rule. In any case, it is different from a military regime or one-party system, which have certain rules in place regarding succession of supreme power, such as hierarchy and consultation among the top executives. Even when a child of the ruler uncomplicatedly inherits power, it is not the child's quality and capability as a leader that gives legitimacy to the succession of power but it is, in fact, only the authority and power of the predecessor—their parent. Hence, the successor must build their own client network after assuming office.

Notwithstanding the possibility of hereditary succession, personal rule is substantially different from monarchism. Monarchism has rules that stipulate succession of power in great detail and even a king himself is not allowed to deviate from or change those rules. Moreover, the legitimacy of the king's authority is founded on tradition as well as institution in the monarchy. The king is restricted by tradition, institution and royal family rules. In contrast to this, the ruler in personal rule is never bound by either tradition, institution or family rules. However, to put it another way, tradition and institution do not legitimize their reign, as is the case in monarchism, leaving the ruler no choice but to depend on the distribution of patronage and the exercise of violence, so as to establish and maintain their own power base.

Personal rule tends to gradually form, unlike in military regimes and one-party systems where the military or a party often rises to power through a military coup or the usurpation of power by a party. In some cases, a prominent military officer or member of a political party ascends to the position of ruler by beating rivals and after attaining the top position, gradually solidifies their power by nipping new rivals in the bud and stripping autonomy from the military or party. In other cases, a political leader elected democratically later falls into dictatorship when faced with the struggle to maintain their power.

Although Chehabi and Linz mention the narrow social base as one of the characteristics of a sultanistic regime (1998b: 19–21), this is not always the case. This is because even in personal rule, the ruler can establish a social support base through patronage distribution. Chehabi and Linz remark that the rulers substitute foreign superpowers for domestic social bases (1998b: 21). However, there are a number of cases of personal rule in which the rulers were not dependent on foreign powers.

Criteria of categorization: vengeance and rewards

As mentioned above, in personal rule, the ruler's means of ruling manifest through vengeance meted out against dissidents and rewards bestowed on supporters. Differences in respective ruler's usage of these two means add variations to personal rule. For the purpose of this discussion, I define vengeance against dissidents as 'surveillance and violence' and rewards for supporters as 'patronage distribution', and categorize personal rule into four subtypes based on these two criteria.

There are two reasons for using these as the criteria for categorization that are worth mentioning here. One is that surveillance and violence and distribution of patronage as means of control are not specific to certain regions and times. This means that they may be common criteria in comparative politics. Adopting the common criteria that are invariably associated with personal rule will allow discussions on variations of personal rule with extended scope for analysis. Another is that using these criteria provides dynamism in terms of the typology. In other words, subtypes of personal rule will not be fixed, but one subtype is able to transform into another. This allows examination of changes in the nature of personal rule caused by fluctuations in the level of violence and the range of patronage distribution.

Vengeance: level of surveillance and violence
The first criterion is the 'level of surveillance and violence'. The ruler uses vengeance or fear of vengeance to force everyone, from cronies to the public, into submission. Vengeance mostly takes the form of concealed surveillance and unlawful violence by security apparatuses rather than the enactment of laws and penalties for infringements of those laws. Security apparatuses, secret police and surveillance devices are set up to efficiently carry out vengeance against dissidents or effectively instill the fear of vengeance in the public. Aside from anti-governmental activists and opposition party-related groups, even civilian activists who are not necessarily engaged in anti-government activities, including labor unions, leaders of student movements, religious organizations, NGOs and representatives of other associations, are often placed on the watch list by the security authority and become potential victims of detention, arrest, abduction, torture and murder. Meanwhile, in personal rule where the ruler monopolizes wealth and power, the public tends to develop dissatisfaction and hatred towards them. The more dissatisfaction and hatred the ruler feels from the public, the more dependent they become on surveillance and violence to suppress them. The ruler is also always wary of traitors within the regime, meaning the most loyal cronies and even family members could become targets of surveillance and violence. Feeling anxious about the possibility of a coup, the ruler thoroughly monitors the military. In fact, the military is in many cases the primary target of surveillance.

In personal rule, the degree of the use of violence is on a higher scale even when compared to other nondemocratic regimes. However, the effect of containment of anti-government movements varies depending on whether the surveillance and violence are systematic and continuous in nature or unsystematic and temporary. Whether a systematic and efficient surveillance network and apparatus of violence are in place or not is one of the criteria in determining whether the level of surveillance and violence are 'relatively high' or 'relatively low'.

Examples of 'relatively high' levels are: SAVAK under the rule of Mohammad Reza Pahlavi of Iran, Securitate under the rule of Nicolae Ceauşescu of Romania, Tonton Macoute under the rule of François Duvalier of Haiti and Mukhabarat under the rule of Hafiz al-Asad of Syria. That these organizations played effective roles as secret police and surveillance institutions to plant fear among the public in their daily lives has been shown in many studies (Katouzian 1998: 197–198; Tismaneanu 1989: 190; Snyder 1998: 63; Aoyama 2001: 15). The Public Safety Unit under the rule of Idi Amin of Uganda was widely known as Amin's personal killing squad, along with the presidential guards and military police (Jackson and Rosberg 1982: 258). Iraq under Saddam Hussein had secret police and spy surveillance networks spread over multiple layers in the public's everyday lives, imposing physiological coercive force in addition to physical violence (Sakai 2002: 73–74). Many of these organizations were directly positioned under Hussein and acted specifically under his orders. In the above cases, the ruler conducted strict surveillance on not only the public but also the military and created comprehensive surveillance networks and apparatuses of violence in order to contain any movement that may pose a challenge to his rule.

On the other hand, examples of 'relatively low' levels of surveillance and violence include the Armed Forces, Kopkamtib and BAKIN in Indonesia under the Suharto regime. Although these security agencies played a major role in the arrest and massacre of Communist Party members immediately after the September 30th Affair, they were neither so efficient nor continuous in terms of planting fear in the everyday lives of the public (Tanter 1990: 267–269). The use of violence was not consistent but rather sporadic and temporary in Indonesia. In some cases, they tried to scare people by reminding them of the massacre after the September 30th Affair or resorted to violence purely to instill fear in others. Never was the entire nation surrounded by fear and a network of surveillance, except for conflict areas such as Aceh and East Timor. Therefore, the Suharto regime can be categorized as employing a 'relatively low' degree of violence and surveillance in this sense.

Another criterion for determining the level of surveillance and violence is whether the ruler wreaks relentless vengeance for disobedience and misconduct carried out by the ruling elites, especially those significantly close to the ruler such as family members and cronies. In the Suharto regime of Indonesia and the Félix Houphouët-Boigny regime of Ivory Coast where the level of violence was 'relatively low', no strict vengeance was sought against the disobedience and misconduct of elites close to the ruler, and even some once-ousted elites were allowed to make political comebacks (Satō 2004: 78). In contrast, in regimes where the level is 'relatively high' such as Iraq under Hussein, even ministers or family members of the president himself could be executed or murdered if their disobedience and misconduct were considered betrayals and as for the military too, discharges, arrests and killings of senior and mid-level officers were common (Tripp 2000: 236, 249–250, 267–269). This kind of draconianism against elites within the regime is considered highly effective in the sense that it prevents elites from initiating any potential movement to challenge the ruler or change the status quo.

Rewards: range of patronage distribution

I now provide an explanation on another criteria for determining subtypes of personal rule, namely the 'range of patronage distribution'. Here the ruler tries to maintain supporters' loyalty by granting rewards to them in the form of political and economic patronage. This exchange of rewards and loyalty takes place within the scope of a network built upon the patron-client relationships of the ruler. By distributing patronage, the ruler attempts to stabilize the support base, increase loyal supporters, co-opt opposition elites, hamper the emergence of formidable counter-elites and keep much of the public under control.

Political patronage includes a broad range of posts such as ministers in the cabinet, senior offices in ministries and agencies, positions in the parliament, executive posts in the ruling party, senior posts in state-run enterprises, ambassadors, governors of provinces, regents of regencies, mayors of cities, local government offices, positions in the regional parliament and executive posts in the ruling party's local offices. In addition to these statuses and posts, political patronage includes authority over personnel affairs and authority to grant approvals and permissions accompanied by a variety of rewards and benefits. Through such distribution of patronage, the ruler conciliates political and social elites so as to prevent them from becoming oppositions or to co-opt them into the regime side. Borrowing Akira Satō's expression of this type of political patronage, these posts can be called 'conciliatory resources' (Satō 2004: 75, 80). Increases in the number of members of parliament and the ruling party, although personal rule severely restricts political participation, are intended to increase these resources. The more posts that are added, the more people who seek posts can be co-opted into the regime, which in turn means a rise in the number of the ruler's supporters.

Along with political patronage, economic patronage is also an important resource for securing support for the ruler. Entrepreneurs and business owners that are family members of the ruler and their cronies are prioritized when distributing business concessions such as import and export licenses, business permits, mineral resource mining permits and logging permits. These concessions exert significant effects when the ruler wants to seize control over the economic sphere, as they will be able to allure influential entrepreneurs who seek concessions to their side. For the entrepreneurs, they can enjoy substantial business benefits by collaborating with the ruler and their family's businesses through providing financial assistance or making investments. By doing so, the government becomes more favorably inclined to grant a variety of permits to them.

Economic patronage for the public is granted in the form of development projects and infrastructure works such as the construction and repair of housing, schools, hospitals, roads and religious facilities and in the form of a variety of subsidies for food, kerosene and daily essentials, or for education, medical or health care. These can be seen as part of a conciliation policy to relieve the public's dissatisfaction with and criticisms of the government. Sometimes projects and subsidies are provided as though they are 'gifts from ruler to subject'. In addition, economic patronage includes the 'acceptance of misdeeds' such as illegal businesses including contraband, drug trafficking and gambling or leaving corruption and the misappropriation of public funds unaddressed. The ruler exploits every available 'resource' that can be diverted to economic patronage.

Personal rule with widely distributed patronage is more easily formed in countries that have rich natural resources and are major producers of primary products for export. This is because enormous profits generated from the mining, production and export of such raw materials can be utilized by the ruler through state-owned companies as resources for economic patronage. In Indonesia where 'inclusive' patronage distribution was in place, large-scale development projects and infrastructure works as well as religious and educational subsidies began to be carried out, often under the banner of presidential instruction (*inpres*) and presidential assistance (*banpres*) since the mid-1970s due to the increase in revenue from petroleum exportation. Similarly in Iraq, after the seizure of power by Hussein, major construction of roads and housing as well as mosques began, funded by revenue from petroleum (Sakai 2002: 79). As exemplified by the launch of a sizable housing development plan immediately after the deadly oppression of anti-government forces in the northern Kurdish region and the southern Shia-dominated region (Sakai 2003: 242–244), the distribution was portrayed as though Hussein was 'sharing with the nation' the wealth of petroleum (Sakai 2002: 79; Tripp 2000: 214)[10]. Likewise, it has also been noted that in Ivory Coast under Houphouët-Boigny's rule, socioeconomic redistribution policies including but not limited to large-scale regional development projects, government guarantees on the purchase price of agricultural products and the improvement of primary education played key roles in securing support from the public (Satō 2004: 79).

In comparison, when patronage distribution is 'exclusive' in personal rule, the ruler and a handful of ruling elites dominating important political posts and economic privileges do not pass the wealth on to the public. As a result, prominent players in the society turn against the government and most of the public becomes dissatisfied with the ruler. If the ruler tries to suppress this dissatisfaction by excessive violence, personal rule evolves into a 'terrorizing type'. Personal rule with inclusive patronage distribution does not limit distribution to certain groups only but extends it to key social forces within the country. Personal rule that appeases social forces by providing patronage is different from that which relies on violence excessively. The former mitigates fear and hatred of the public and social elites towards the ruler and ensures a certain degree of support from them, creating a situation where organized anti-government movements are unlikely to occur. If not only oppression, but also effective appeasement measures through providing posts and concessions towards the anti-government forces are carried out, this may divide the social force, eliminating the possibility for them to organize a large-scale anti-government alliance. In this sense, distribution of patronage largely defines relationships between the ruler and elites as well as the ruler and the public.

Personal rule based on material rewards and vengeance is, essentially, in comparison to other regimes, 'expensive'. Rules based on ideology, charisma, tradition and legality do not incur as much material costs as personal rule, particularly when considering costs associated with the establishment of sophisticated apparatuses of surveillance and violence and the distribution of patronage to the public. It is so costly that it could even be suggested that the reason rulers of personal rule continue to exploit the nation even after having monopolized as much state power and assets as possible is to compensate for the costs associated with rewards and vengeance. There are many examples of personal rule regimes where the ruler drains the state's fortune and impoverishes the nation in order to maintain their rule, eventually driving the country to the brink of collapse.

Personal rule often ends in the overthrow of the government by a military coup or mass mobilization or defeat in a war against foreign powers because there are no institutionalized rules and procedures to end the rule. The ruler continues to reign until the political and economic impasse reaches breaking point giving rise to a situation where some other party must remove the ruler by physical force. However, although political transitions forcefully initiated by others—that is, the overthrow of the government or a revolution—may at a glance appear as though significant political changes have occurred, this does not guarantee the beginning of the rule of law or democratic governance. Moreover, even when significant political changes do take place upon the fall of a case of personal rule, political chaos may continue. This is because the lack of control based on institutions and laws, one of the characteristics common in personal rule, affects the subsequent political process to a large degree.

Four subtypes of personal rule

Figure 1.1 depicts the categorization of personal rule into four subtypes. The vertical axis represents the level of surveillance and violence, from 'relatively low' to 'relatively high', while the horizontal axis plots the range of patronage distribution, either 'inclusive' or 'exclusive'. Based on the combination of these, I have categorized personal rule into four groups, (i) isolated-type, (ii) terrorizing-type, (iii) dividing-type and (iv) co-opting-type, and included the names of the rulers with some of the characteristics of each subtype. Inside the

Figure 1.1: Subtypes of personal rule

Level of surveillance and violence by state
(Relatively low)

	(i) Isolated-type	*(iv) Co-opting-type*	
	Batista of Cuba (1933–1958, overthrown by anti-government forces)	Bourguiba of Tunisia (1956–1987, ousted by coup)	
	Marcos of the Philippines (1965–1986, overthrown by anti-government forces)	Houphouët-Boigny of Ivory Coast (1960–1993, natural death)	
Range of patronage distribution (Exclusive)		Suharto of Indonesia (1966–1998, resignation)	**Range of patronage distribution (Inclusive)**
	M. R. Pahlavi of Iran (1941–1979, overthrown by anti-government forces)	F. Duvalier of Haiti (1957–1971, natural death followed by hereditary succession)	
	Ceauşescu of Romania (1965–1989, overthrown by anti-government forces)	H. Asad of Syria (1971–2000, natural death followed by hereditary succession)	
	Amin of Uganda (1971–1979, defeated in war)	Hussein of Iraq (1979–2003, defeated in war)	
	J. -C. Duvalier of Haiti (1971–1986, overthrown by anti-government forces)		
	(ii) Terrorizing-type	*(iii) Dividing-type*	

(Relatively high)
Level of surveillance and violence by state

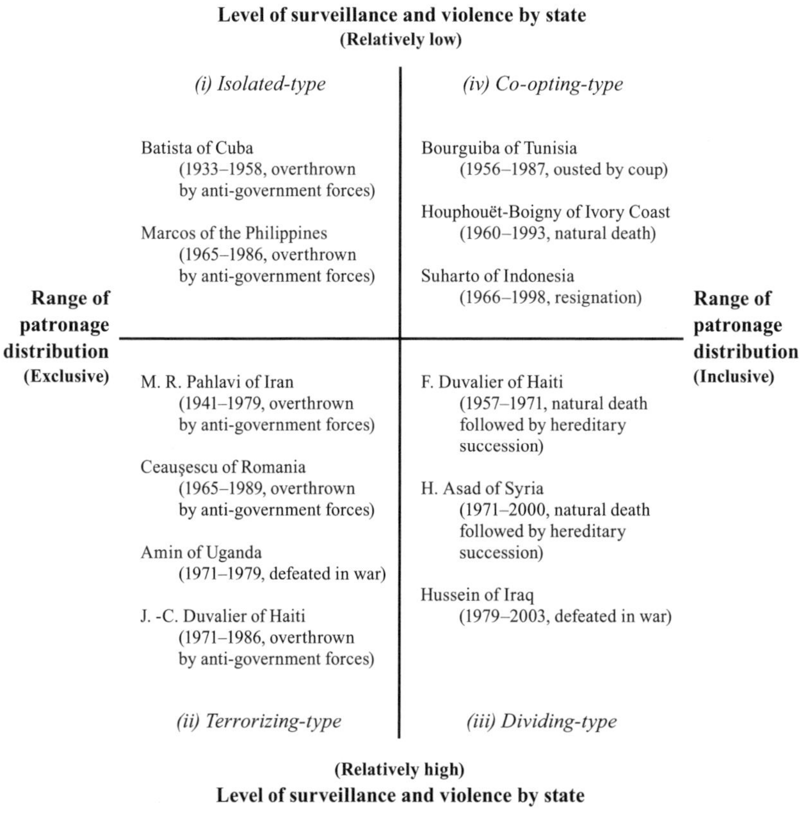

brackets are respective ruler's terms in office and details regarding how their personal rule came to an end.

(i) Isolated-type
In isolated-type personal rule, both the establishment of systematic, exhaustive apparatuses of surveillance and violence and patronage distribution are limited in scope. Wealth and authority are concentrated in a ruling group consisting of the ruler and a few cronies who try to monopolize state assets; hence most of the public and social elites are excluded from the benefits of distribution. This isolates the ruling group as discontent brews among the majority of the public who are not part of the distribution. Relatively low levels of surveillance and violence may give way to the development of anti-government forces, which could, absorbing the dissatisfaction of the masses, form a wide-ranging anti-government alliance. It is highly probable that the dissatisfaction of the masses would result in huge anti-government movements and eventually lead to the overthrow of the government, as neither democratization from above nor compromises can be expected from a cohesive ruling group consisting of a handful of people.

The Batista regime of Cuba and the Marcos regime of the Philippines can be considered as possessing these characteristics. In both regimes, the ruling groups progressively became isolated as the ruler and their family members as well as cronies exploited and dominated state wealth. In addition, both rulers' support bases weakened due to the limited range of patronage distribution. Inconsistent violence by the state and the absence of efficient and systematic security agencies and surveillance apparatuses left room for anti-government movements to be organized. Furthermore, surveillance on the military was relatively weak and favoritism-based personnel affairs resulted in a loss of professionalism within the military. This was the very reason why the military was routed when confronted by guerrilla soldiers led by Fidel Castro in Cuba, despite the relatively small size of the guerrilla army (Domínguez 1998: 129–131), and that gave rise to the group of military officers who plotted the coup against President Marcos and created a catalyst for the mobilization of the 'people power' movement in the Philippines (Thompson 1998: 227). In both Cuba and the Philippines, the rulers who were odious to the public had no choice but to flee into exile as a result of huge anti-government movements.

(ii) Terrorizing-type
The factor that differentiates the isolated-type from the terrorizing-type is the presence of extensive systems of surveillance and violence in the latter. In this type of personal rule, the state assets plundered by the ruler are spent on vengeance for disobedience through the establishment of powerful apparatuses

of surveillance and security. Sultanistic regimes as defined by Linz—that is, personal rule predominantly dictated by a ruler's arbitrariness and violence— can be considered as this type. The subjects of surveillance and violence include the ruler's cronies and even family members. Fear of vengeance prevents any initiative to change the status-quo as well as any dialogue or compromise with anti-government forces from emerging within the ruling group. The ruling group can be said to be almost monolithic, leaving no room for anyone to lead an initiative toward democratization and liberalization against the ruler's will. At the same time, anti-government movements are often carried out by defectors living abroad, since it can be enormously difficult for organized anti-government movements to operate within national borders.

Nevertheless, when the public's anger against oppression that uses intense violence surpasses their fear, a spontaneous large-scale mass mobilization could occur. Those that took place in Iran, Haiti and Romania are of this kind where vast, barely organized anti-government movements led to the collapse of the respective governments (Snyder 1998: 73, 78). Chehabi and Linz remarked that in terms of sultanistic regimes, 'most end in a more or less chaotic way' (Snyder 1998c: 37). This is because leaders and organizations that could control the situation do not emerge early enough when mass mobilization occurs due to day-to-day surveillance and violence prohibiting domestically organized anti-government movements. Without leaders and organizations, large-scale mass mobilization may fall into chaos and this situation may invite military intervention. In the cases of Romania and Haiti, the military coup took place upon the overthrow of the respective government and the military took advantage of the confusion to temporarily assume control, but they did not take initiatives toward democratization (Snyder 1998: 78; Nicholls 1998: 169). Amin of Uganda was forced to flee in exile after defeat in the war against neighboring Tanzania. In any case, it can be argued that a terrorizing-type ruler who depends on violence tends to be removed violently.

(iii) Dividing-type
In contrast to the isolated-type and terrorizing-type in which discontent is widespread among the public due to the narrow range of patronage distribution, the rulers of dividing-type and co-opting-type personal rule distribute patronage more extensively. The establishment of a certain amount of support for the ruler among the public through patronage distribution means that vast, sizeable anti-government movements are less likely to occur, enabling a more stable and long reign compared to the isolated-type and the terrorizing-type.

One characteristic of the dividing-type is that it goes beyond simply relying on violence to expand the support base by widely distributing patronage. The ruler divides prominent social groups within the country by tactically using both oppression and appeasement in an attempt to prevent these groups from organizing into unified anti-government forces. Moreover, the harshness of vengeance for dissent and betrayal lowers the motivation within the ruling group to embark on political transition. Therefore, in cases of dividing-type personal rule, it is possible for the child of a ruler to inherit power after their death by natural causes, as evident in the François Duvalier regime of Haiti and the Hafiz al-Asad regime of Syria.

François Duvalier of Haiti is said to have managed to extend his control over the population by gaining support from the black middle class in city areas as well as middle class farmers from rural areas while silencing opposition and potential opposition using a security apparatus called Tonton Macoute (Nicholls 1998: 158–159). Following François Duvalier's death in 1971, his authority was inherited by his son Jean-Claude Duvalier. However, Jean-Claude Duvalier started to skew allocation towards mulattos at the expense of distribution to the black middle class after his marriage to a wealthy mulatto and slowly lost the support his father François had gained from the black middle class (Snyder 1998: 71–72). Jean-Claude Duvalier thus gradually became dependent on violence. One can observe that Duvalier's personal rule transformed from the dividing-type to the terrorizing-type. Subsequently, a huge mass movement led to the collapse of the government, forcing Duvalier to flee in exile.

In Iraq, lucrative revenue from petroleum enabled Hussein to tactfully leverage patronage distribution (Sakai 2002: 79–80; Tripp 2000: 214–219) and this, in combination with instilling fear by radical violence and surveillance against anti-government forces (Sakai 2002: 71–75), stabilized Hussein's rule. However, the prolonged Iran–Iraq War, the outbreak of the Gulf War and economic sanctions by the international community quickly diminished Iraq's state assets, which had been enabling the distribution. Consequently, in and after the 1990s, the violent nature of the Hussein regime started to be exposed. Anti-government movements spread rapidly all over Iraq but became victims of brutal crackdowns. Hussein's personal rule can also be considered to have undergone a transformation from the dividing-type to the terrorizing-type similarly to that which occurred in Haiti. Hussein's personal rule finally ended in 2003 upon defeat in the war against the United States.

Mukhabarat, a Syrian security apparatus, comprises over ten intelligence and security organizations. These are roughly classified into two categories: intelligence agencies and security police organizations whose roles include monitoring and detaining internal and external insurgents, and armed security organizations whose duties focus on suppression by force. These forces are said to 'secretly pervade every tiniest detail of socio-political circumstances behind public life and activities' (Aoyama 2001: 15). Asad's reliance on violence was clearly displayed in the 1982 massacre in Hama, in which members of the Muslim Brotherhood and their families were killed en masse (Brownlee 2002: 43).

Meanwhile, Volker Perthes argued that along with this recourse to violence, 'Asad's personal rule over the system has, in addition, been secured by the deliberate employment of patrimonial instruments such as, in particular, personal loyalties and patronage' (Perthes 1995: 180). Perthes criticized the popular belief that Asad was extremely dependent on the Alawites—a religious minority of Shia Islam—to which he belonged, who account for about ten percent of the Syrian population, and explained that appointment of political posts was not based on religious branches but only on closeness and loyalty to Asad (1995: 182). In addition to patronage distribution, Asad also appointed some influential men from the Sunnis, who comprise the majority of the population, to key posts in his government and tried to build strong relationships with Sunni religious leaders in order to secure support from that community (Perthes 1995: 181–185). This combination of intense surveillance and violence and broad distribution of patronage divided the Syrian religious, ethnic and socio-economic communities respectively into pro- and anti-government groups and prevented them from building a vast anti-government alliance (Aoyama 2012: 22–25). As a result, this ensured the longevity of the Asad regime, leading to the succession of presidential authority to his second son Bashar al-Asad following his death in 2000.

However, the policy of the Asad regime that divided society through violence and distribution brought a destructive result to Syria—civil war. After the Arab Spring spread to Syria, anti-government movements occurred in various parts of the country, but the leaders of these movements could not efficiently form an alliance because of the divisive policy of the Asad regime. Patronage distribution by the government over an extended period of time had created a large cohort of loyalists within each religious and ethnic community in Syrian society. According to Thomas Pierret, attitudes of Islamic communities toward the government were ambiguous or divided along the lines of loyalists and dissenters (Pierret 2013: 217–234). This is thought to be one of the reasons behind the fragmentation of anti-government movements.

Moreover, the severity of punishment for defection prevented the ruling elites, including military officers, from betrayal. Joshua Stacher pointed out that there were no key defections in the Alawi and Sunni communities, or from state institutions (Stacher 2012: 17). Hiroyuki Aoyama also mentioned that almost no key troops or high and middle ranking officers defected, although many in the rank and file defected from the military (Aoyama 2012: 109).

In the Asad regime there are no channels for dialogue and the possibility of negotiation and concessions between the government and the opposition groups is non-existent because of a lack of mutual confidence. Deep hatred of the opposition groups had been generated by the government's draconian policies. If the government were to be defeated in the civil war, the ruling elites, not only President Asad and his cronies but also most of his supporters and the military, would lose everything including their lives. The opposition groups would also suffer the same fate if they were to be defeated.

Fear of vengeance, mutual hatred, and the fragmentation of the opposition groups that results from the characteristics of dividing-type personal rule, are the reasons why any means and efforts toward mediation have failed to develop, despite the fact that the civil war is destroying the country. Severe civil war created chaos in Syria and allowed the rise of more radical groups such as ISIS (Islamic State of Iraq and Syria), which eroded the territory. Although the state is on the point of dissolution, the Asad regime is still alive.

(iv) Co-opting-type
Personal rule that falls into the co-opting-type category relies on the approach that appeases anti-government forces and potential opposition by widely distributing patronage to turn dissenters into active or passive supporters. Although apparatuses of violence and surveillance are indispensable in this type, unlike in the terrorizing and dividing types, instilling fear by violence into the public is not systematic or continuous. Instead, violence is employed transiently and unpredictably, sometimes merely as a warning to others. As long as patronage is distributed smoothly, criticisms and oppositions against the government are unlikely to develop into a large anti-government movement potentially capable of overthrowing the government.

In personal rule of the dividing and co-opting types, the growth of national income and the establishment of the ruler's authority often progress simultaneously. For example, in the Hussein regime of Iraq and the Suharto regime of Indonesia, both of which possessed rich natural resources such as petroleum, a sharp rise in oil prices from the mid-to-late 1970s substantially contributed to the capital accumulation of the states and helped the rulers establish their respective power bases (Tripp 2000: 214–219). Research on the Ivory Coast also shows that the export of agricultural goods, particularly cacao and coffee, delivered strong economic growth in the period between the 1960s and late 1970s (Crook 1989: 205) and made a significant contribution to the consolidation of Houphouët's regime. As for Tunisia, the steady rise in income from petroleum in and after the late 1970s, although this timeframe does not exactly parallel the establishment of Habib Bourguiba's rule, became an important capital resource for the state-led development policy (Murphy 1999: 85–86). Likewise in Syria, the stabilization of its economy due to its transformation into a net exporter of petroleum following the discovery of a new oilfield in the late 1980s can be considered to have contributed to the endurance of Asad's rule.

Political parties are also of great importance as an instrument for the ruler to distribute political and economic patronage in dividing- and co-opting-type personal rule. Examples of such political parties include the Ba'th Party in Iraq and Syria, the Destourian Socialist Party of Tunisia, the Ivory Coast Democratic Party of the Ivory Coast and Golkar of Indonesia. Such parties act as bidirectional channels that enable the ruler to distribute political and economic patronage as far as the regional ends of the network and at the same time recruit social elites into the regime. A whole network of cells in the party was important in the above cases in terms of allowing the ruler to more easily form patron-client relationships and at the same time penetrating through and controlling the population.

The Ba'th Party of Syria widely opened its doors in and after the 1970s when Hafiz al-Asad assumed the presidency, welcoming even ex-members of the Muslim Brotherhood as well as local influential figures, and this resulted in a sharp rise in the number of civilian members in the party from 160,000 in 1974 to 530,000 in 1984 (Perthes 1995: 154–155). As Asad established his authority, the Ba'th Party started to lose its autonomy from the President as well as ideological leadership and began functioning, increasingly, as a channel through which the President distributed patronage and as an instrument for social control (Perthes 1995: 156–158). The Ba'th Party's local offices (regional commands) had a decisive influence over the personnel affairs of their regions (Perthes 1995: 159–160) and local strongmen absorbed by the party, in turn for receiving resources to guarantee benefits for their family members and clients, were expected to implement government programs in their regions and to mobilize clients to back the party and the President during elections (Perthes 1995: 188–189).

Indonesia's Golkar under the Suharto regime also played an important role as a channel for patronage distribution as well as a vehicle for recruiting social elites. When party executives, who also acted as the top government officials, visited regional areas for election campaign activities, they often provided residents of the areas with food and clothing and promised subsidies and projects such as payments for repairs of roads and mosques.

In cases of personal rule, the political party plays another role as a ruling party loyal to the ruler. They have an absolute majority in parliament and declare unanimous support for the ruler as the 'representatives' of the nation. For the ruler who seeks support from the nation and willingly tries to act in the role of 'father of the nation' respected by the public, such a ruling party is indispensable not only for mobilizing the public at the time of elections and referendums but also for playing a role in legitimizing the ruler's authority in parliaments recognized at home and abroad. The party leaders diligently attempt to make the parliaments stages on which to exhibit their loyalty to the ruler, knowing that such performances would please the ruler.

It is difficult for the ruling party under personal rule to maintain autonomy from the ruler. This is one of the major differences from the one-party system. Party leaders under personal rule are ever loyal to their ruler and almost never express objections to the ruler's policies. Even if the party tries to formulate a policy or law under their own initiative, whether it will or will not be adopted is entirely up to the ruler. In many cases, the role given to the ruling party is to echo the policies of the ruler.

In both dividing- and co-opting-type personal rule, the ruling party becomes a channel for patronage distribution as well as a vehicle of socio-political control for the ruler. Unlike the dividing-type where even elites within the regime are exposed to fear of violence and surveillance, elites of the co-opting-type who have been absorbed into the regime can act at their own discretion to a certain extent without fear of violence and surveillance. This freedom of action in turn creates diversity and fierce competition among the ruling elites, which generally manifest in the form of conflicts over posts and privileges. Although this could possibly cause schisms within the regime, such conflicts rarely surface while the rulership is in a stable condition.

In the co-opting-type personal rule where the degree of the ruler's dependence on violence is comparably low and state wealth is returned to the nation to some extent, the rule is relatively stable and an overthrow of the government by anti-government movements is less likely. The rulers of personal rule in Tunisia, the Ivory Coast and Indonesia, that is Bourguiba, Houphouët and Suharto alike managed to maintain their regimes for almost thirty years. Moreover, none of these regimes ended in the overthrow of the government by mass mobilization, events that have been observed in cases of isolated- and terrorizing-type personal rule where the distribution of patronage was limited in scale.

Potential causes of the end of the rule for regimes that rely on patronage distribution include a reduction or depletion of patronage resources and stagnation or biases in distribution. The more reliant the rule is on the distribution of patronage, the greater the impact of a reduction in patronage resources owing to an economic downturn or the saturation of political posts. A drastic decline in economic patronage, for example the abolishment of subsidies for food and necessities due to an economic crisis or cancellation of socioeconomic redistribution policies, turns the public away, resulting in the rapid spread of anti-government sentiment. In Tunisia, the Ivory Coast and Indonesia, an economic slump was one of the factors that destabilized the regime (Murphy 1999: 65–66; Satō 2004: 80).

While economic downturn reduces the distribution of economic patronage, a decline in the distribution of political patronage can be caused by a saturation of political posts provided by the ruler to their supporters (Satō 2004: 80), or by the appearance of partiality in the distribution of posts. In co-opting-type personal rule, the ruler tries to stabilize the system by absorbing numerous social elites into the regime to keep anti-government forces to a minimum. However, such absorption of a great number of elites naturally intensifies the competition for posts within the regime. If the ruler fails to coordinate the distribution of posts, the rivalry among the elites becomes a major cause of schisms within the regime. This is because a group of dissatisfied members who were overlooked in the distribution could potentially turn into soft-liners open to negotiation with anti-government forces. Furthermore, rulers in co-opting-type personal rule are not willing to go to the extent of resorting to violence to suppress the elites within the regime who have become dissatisfied with the distribution. If a ruler ever employs violent sanctions as a method of controlling elites within the regime, who are essentially the ruler's supporters, the regime is showing signs of transforming into dividing-type rule. Nevertheless, the control of elites within the regime is limited in scope in co-opting-type personal rule and this gives way to the emergence of soft-liners—a phenomenon hardly observed in other types of personal rule.

Research objectives

Hypotheses

Discussions after Chapter Two will focus on the political dynamism observed in Indonesia's Suharto regime as co-opting-type personal rule. As mentioned above, comparative politics researchers have argued that in personal rule or sultanistic regimes soft-liners are unlikely to surface. On the contrary, this book will suggest that co-opting-type personal rule can give way to the emergence of soft-liners as it differs from other types of personal rule such that the ruling elites within the regime are pluralistic to some extent and the violence the ruler exercises against them is limited. In the Suharto regime, which falls into the category of co-opting-type personal rule, the political change of 1998 gave rise to the emergence of soft-liners within the regime and this largely dictated the political transition that followed. Based on this notion, the primary focus of the empirical analysis after Chapter Two will be to reveal the mechanism of patronage distribution and its transformation and outline the emergence of soft-liners as a result of this process. This book's other aim is to explain how soft-liners negotiated and built consensus with anti-government forces in the 1998 political change, contributing to the soft-landing of the political crisis in personal rule.

The two hypotheses are as follows:
1. The political change of 1998 was a pacted transition based on consensus-building between the moderate reformist forces and soft-liners within the regime.
2. Secondly, the soft-liners within the regime which enabled such pacted transition based on consensus-building emerged as a consequence of political dynamism founded on patronage distribution practiced under the Suharto regime as co-opting-type personal rule.

Golkar as a ruling party in co-opting-type personal rule
Changes in Suharto's distribution of political and economic patronage will be one of the focal points in verifying the above-mentioned hypotheses. The changes in patronage distribution brought dynamism to politics under the Suharto regime. In the 1970s, as patronage distribution prioritized the Armed Forces and Chinese business groups, the regime was unstable in terms of a surge of dissatisfaction and criticism coming from most social forces as well as the public who were not allocated patronage. After entering the 1980s, as a measure to curb such dissent and ensure political stability, Suharto began extending the distribution of patronage to more diverse social forces and the public. This successfully diminished anti-government movements and criticism and the Suharto regime enjoyed stability from the late 1980s to the early 1990s.

However, the vast incorporation of social elites into the regime meant that political posts traditionally occupied by military personnel were now being distributed to civilians. This led to competition and conflict over posts, this time between the military and civilians within the regime. Furthermore, in the mid-1990s, Suharto's patronage distribution started to show biases, partly due to the issue of presidential succession. Distribution started to skew notably in favor of groups close to Suharto's eldest daughter who was considered the President's successor at the time. This kind of bias bred discontent among other groups in the ruling party and created a rift within the regime. The rift that arose just before the 1998 political change can be regarded as a consequence of changes in the distribution of patronage—expansion in the 1980s and partiality in the 1990s.

In order to capture such changes in patronage distribution and the political dynamism caused by them, the main object of empirical analysis here is the ruling party, Golkar.

Under the Suharto regime Golkar did not have much presence as a political actor, especially when compared to the Armed Forces, thus did not gather much attention from researchers. Well-known examples include studies by Julian Boileau and David Reeve which analyzed the corporatist nature of Golkar (Boileau 1983; Reeve 1985), the study by Leo Suryadinata which explained Golkar as the party of the *abangan*, or nominal Muslim, competing against Islamic parties (Suryadinata 1989), and that by Toshiyuki Ōgata which investigated the shift in the trilateral relationship between Golkar, Suharto and the Armed Forces (Ōgata 1995). However, many Indonesians and scholars studying Indonesia regarded Golkar as a mere vote-gathering machine to help win elections. This is accounted for by the fact that Golkar, despite being the ruling party holding parliamentary majority, had almost no influence at all in either legislative or policy-making processes.

This raises the question as to why Golkar, which has been regarded as quite insignificant thus far, should be the center of empirical analysis here. As mentioned in the previous section, a ruling party under co-opting-type personal rule becomes a channel for patronage distribution and a tool for augmenting social support for the regime. The role played by Golkar under Suharto's rule was precisely that. As Suharto broadened the range of patronage distribution in the 1980s, Golkar became the distribution channel as well as the host for accommodating diverse social elites into the regime. It was by virtue of Golkar that the Suharto regime, which lacked public support in the 1970s, was able to substantially expand its support base in and after the 1980s.

I regard Golkar as a place where a vast number of social elites drawn to patronage flock and compete against each other for larger shares. This competition within the regime, in other words, interplays among the elites, ultimately giving way to the rise of soft-liners within the regime who sympathized with the reformist movements[11]. In sum, Golkar created political dynamism under the Suharto regime.

Concerning the political change of 1998, most researchers have not made much of the role of Golkar and the parliament where Golkar held a majority. This was because they thought that both Golkar and the parliament were peripheral political actors loyal to Suharto, and hence no political action could be expected from these organizations. The reality was, on the contrary, that a number of Golkar members instigated dialogue and cooperation with the reformist forces and demanded Suharto's resignation. The victory of the reformist forces, underdeveloped in both leadership and mobilizing power, in forcing Suharto to step down after only a little over two months, cannot be explained without the defection of members of Golkar. Without cooperation with the ruling party, reformist forces could not have realized Suharto's immediate resignation through moderate means. Without compromises between the ruling elites and the reformist forces, it is highly likely that the reformist forces may have radicalized, further compounding the confusion, which would then have resulted in heavy-handed suppression of the movement or possibly a coup by the Armed Forces. In any case, the chance of a soft-landing of political change would have been next to nothing. The Indonesian political transition was settled upon Suharto's resignation because a constitutionally sound path for Suharto's exit from politics was prepared by an alliance of civilian groups within the regime, especially Golkar members and the reformist forces.

The reformist forces were well aware of the weakness of their movement and vigorously sought dialogue and cooperation with groups within the regime in search of a constitutional and moderate resolution. Meanwhile, groups that could potentially turn into soft-liners happened to exist within Golkar before the beginning of the reformist movement. This is because those who had been recruited to Golkar as social elites since the 1980s were disaffected by Suharto's biased patronage distribution that gave important posts of both the government and the ruling party to groups close to the Suharto family.

It can be assumed that, in the words of Guillermo O'Donnell and Philippe Schmitter, who analyzed pacted transition (O'Donnell and Schmitter 1986), the regime's soft-liners and the reformist forces were 'interdependent'. They explained that for a negotiation on a pact to take place, there must be 'a situation in which conflicting or competing groups are interdependent, in that they can neither do without each other nor unilaterally impose their preferred solution on each other if they are to satisfy their respective divergent interests' (O'Donnell and Schmitter 1986: 38). Indonesia's reformists required the support of groups within the regime due to the weakness of their own movements, while groups within Golkar needed to form alliances with the reformists to turn around their own political positions that were beginning to be marginalized. These two parties' interdependent relationship and shared sense of urgency drove the consensus building around a core issue—that is, 'Suharto's immediate resignation'.

2
The Suharto Regime as Co-opting-type Personal Rule

Control through patronage distribution

Basic structure of the Suharto regime

The Suharto regime constituted personal rule with all state power concentrated in President Suharto. In terms of its legal structure, on the contrary, the President was not necessarily the highest organ of the state. Rather, the People's Consultative Assembly (MPR) was designated as the supreme body of state power under the 1945 Constitution. The following five organs were placed in parallel under the MPR: the President, Supreme Advisory Council (DPA), People's Representative Council (DPR), Supreme Audit Board (BPK) and Supreme Court (MA).

The MPR had the authority to select a president and vice president and decide on a five-year Broad Guidelines of State Policy (GBHN) in general sessions held every five years and was also able to dismiss a president in special sessions summoned on an ad hoc basis. The President was responsible for the MPR, and exercised administrative authority. He worked together with the DPR to formulate laws, appoint ministers and command ultimate power in the three military forces, namely the Army, Navy and Air Force and the National Police. The DPA was an advisory institution that provided advice to the President, the DPR had the authority to enact laws and budgets, the BPK had rights and responsibilities for financial monitoring and the MA possessed power in the judicial domain.

Although under the 1945 Constitution the MPR stood above the President, from 1959, the President started to control supreme state power. President Sukarno created appointed seats in the DPR in 1960 and took advantage of the appointive system to control the parliament. President Suharto not only preserved this appointive system but also took it further by increasing the number of appointed seats in the DPR and newly designating half of the seats in the MPR as appointed seats while ensuring he had ultimate decision-making power in assigning such seats.

Another legislative institution that Suharto sought to bring under his control was the DPR. In an effort to achieve that, Suharto decided to take advantage of

Golkar. He used the Ministry of Home Affairs to engage in vigorous manipulation to help the ruling party Golkar win the 1971 election, which was the first general election conducted under the Suharto regime. Public servants were instructed to vote for Golkar, while strict screenings, interference in election campaigns and threats were carried out against the opposition candidates. As a result, opposition party candidates performed poorly, enabling Golkar to achieve victory with over sixty percent of the vote.

Having strengthened its confidence through this victory, in 1973 the government boldly implemented a reorganization of political parties transforming the nine opposition parties to just two through mergers. More specifically, they created the United Development Party (PPP) by merging four Islamic parties—the Nahdlatul Ulama (NU), Indonesian Muslims' Party (PMI), Islamic Association Party of Indonesia (PSII) and Islamic Educators' Association (PERTI)—while creating the Indonesian Democratic Party (PDI) by combining five nationalist and Christian parties—the Indonesian National Party (PNI), League of Upholders of Indonesian Independence (IPKI), Murba Party (Partai Murba), Indonesian Christian Party (Parkindo) and Catholic Party (Partai Katholik). Suharto specified that only Golkar, the PPP and the PDI were allowed to participate in elections and heavily restricted political activities in rural areas[1]. In the course of a total of six elections held under the Suharto regime, in 1971, 1977, 1982, 1987, 1992 and 1997, Golkar's victory formed a pattern. Golkar would win with about sixty to seventy percent of the vote on the back of unwavering support from the government, while the remaining thirty to forty percent of the vote would be shared among the two opposition parties.

Out of 460 seats in the DPR (or 500 seats from 1987), the appointed seats amounted to 100 (all of which were appointed from the military in and after 1986; the number was reduced to seventy-five in 1997), and sixty to seventy percent of the remaining seats were filled by members elected from Golkar. This meant that government-affiliated members occupied approximately eighty percent of the seats in the DPR. In such a parliament where government-affiliated members always held the majority, bills and proposed budgets submitted by the government were almost always passed with no significant amendments whatsoever. As a result, the public criticized the DPR on the grounds that it no longer functioned as a legislature and failed in supervising the government. The members of the parliament were often sarcastically described as 'D4'—*daftar*, *duit*, *duduk*, *diam*, meaning 'attend, get money, sit down, be quiet'.

The 1945 Constitution stipulated that the president be elected in a general session of the MPR. The MPR, which had double the number of seats than the DPR, consisted of a combination of members of the DPR and appointed members, and its majority was held by government-affiliated members as was the DPR.

Suharto's election must thus have been indisputable even if other presidential candidates had run for election and voting had taken place. Nevertheless, Suharto insisted on being the only presidential candidate and being elected by unanimous consent rather than via ballot. In addition, he wished to become the only presidential candidate through nomination by all factions of the MPR including opposition parties, rather than announcing his candidacy himself. For this reason, all the representatives of Regional Representative Councils (DPRD) and various organizations visited the MPR ahead of a general session, which was held one year after a general election, to submit a petition calling for the nomination of Suharto as president for the next term. Golkar would then lead a 'consultation' involving all factions in the MPR to nominate a president and vice president. Following this all factions would unanimously nominate Suharto as the only presidential candidate and name a vice president as per Suharto's request. This procedure was repeated every general session of the MPR held every five years, and Suharto continued to be reelected by unanimous consent on the back of support from all factions.

This was the so-called 'consultation and consensus' or *musyawarah dan mufakat*, that operated during the period of the Suharto regime. Presidential election through the above-described procedure was viewed as a product of 'consultation and consensus' by the MPR, which comprised members of the DPR elected through popular vote and appointed members such as local representatives. For Suharto, being chosen by unanimous consensus in this way justified his legitimacy as president. Hence, Suharto placed great value on this procedure and ensured this election process would be in place for every presidential election.

Bureaucratic institutions supported Suharto in planning and implementing policies. Although the ultimate authority pertaining to policy decisions rested in the hands of Suharto, bureaucrats were granted a certain degree of autonomy. In particular, economic technocrats were entrusted with the planning of economic policies by Suharto and provided with opportunities to showcase their abilities. This was simply because they could not pose a political threat to Suharto as they did not have any political power. Nonetheless, this autonomy did not necessarily mean that their freedom was promised in relation to policy planning. When the interests of the President's family members, cronies or business partners were involved, technocrats' opinions were often accorded secondary importance and the economic rationality sought by these technocrats was repeatedly distorted.

The role bureaucrats played was not limited to the administrative domain. During the Sukarno era, bureaucratic institutions used to be a strong power base for the Indonesian National Party (PNI), however, Suharto detached them from the PNI and, with the Ministry of Home Affairs' lead, enforced the concept of 'monoloyalty' or *monoloyalitas*, to turn them into a power base for the ruling party Golkar (Ōgata 1994: 160). Consequently, all public servants were banned from engaging in any political activities or joining political parties. A change came with the enactment of the law on political parties and Golkar of 1985, which allowed public servants to join a political party and Golkar with permission from their superior at their workplace. Under this law, public servants were now strongly urged to join Golkar (Umezawa 1992: 156; Kanō 1996: 33). In short, public servants were not only directed to vote for Golkar but also half-compelled to join. Public servants helped reinforce the Suharto regime in this sense as well. Some senior central government officers and local public servants were even elected as members of the DPR or DPRD from Golkar. It was possible for a public servant to hold a seat in the DPR or DPRD, while they temporarily left their current government job, or even while remaining an active public servant, since there was no regulation which barred public servants from having more than one job in Indonesia and the boundary between the executive and legislative bodies was blurry (Kanō 1996: 31–33). Therefore, many of the members of the ruling party came from bureaucratic backgrounds, contributing to the creation of an environment where the executive branch could easily control its legislative counterpart.

The judicial branch also failed to maintain its independence and was reduced to a partisan tool under the Suharto regime. The Supreme Court did not have judicial review rights to determine the constitutionality of laws but instead was only given the role of presenting legal advice or assessment for the President and other state agencies. Furthermore, under the Suharto regime, the Chief Justice of the Supreme Court was essentially appointed by the President and personnel affairs of other justices of the Court were also substantially influenced by the President and the Ministry of Justice (Pompe 2005: 354–355). The DPR used to have a substantive influence on the review of personnel affairs of the Supreme Court at the very beginning of the Suharto regime when the DPR still maintained its independence, but the legislature's function to check on the judicial branch dwindled in the process of the gradual erosion of the independence of the legislature by the government (Pompe 2005: 356–360).

In addition, the law on public servants introduced in 1974 defined judges of lower courts as public servants and the 'monoloyalty' thus far required for public servants was now expected from judges too (Pompe 2005: 128–129). Essentially, courts were increasingly forced to support and show loyalty to the government. The judicial branch, which had come under the executive branch's control, often attracted government intervention in actual court cases. Especially for cases involving Suharto's family members or prominent military officers, heavy pressure was placed on the judge responsible for the trial by the

Ministry of Justice and judicial decisions were manipulated to suit the intention of the person in power (Kingsbury 2002: 192–194; Pompe 2005: 126–128). The problem was that it was not just court decisions that were politically twisted. The judicial branch, which was in a position to take a hard line against corruption, became the very source of serious corruption. From the lower courts through to the Supreme Court, the bribery of judges by parties involved in litigation became commonplace. Anti-corruption campaigns carried out by the government delivered almost no improvement and the courts' authority as well as the people's trust in them declined markedly (Pompe 2005: 413–417). Corruption of the judicial branch and its submission to the executive branch made a fatal impact on the establishment of the 'rule of law' in Indonesia.

Distribution of political patronage and personnel policy

It is no exaggeration to say that the source of Suharto's power as a ruler stemmed from his extensive authority over personnel decisions. Suharto recruited highly loyal and competent persons and relegated those who began to show signs of weakening loyalty through the allocation of political and administrative posts—in other word, political patronage. By doing so, he wanted to control ruling elites and have his intentions reflected in policy decisions.

First of all, Suharto's presidential status gave him the authority to appoint his cabinet members. The cabinet included the Attorney General, a position equivalent to the rank of minister. Suharto also played a critical role in the selection of the Chief Justice of the Supreme Court. Indeed, he spread his power over the entire judicial branch by securing the authority to dictate personnel decisions on the positions of Minister of Justice, Attorney General and Chief Justice of the Supreme Court. In addition, the President also possessed the authority to appoint ambassadors and ministers for diplomatic posts abroad.

Regarding the central bureaucracy, the positions of secretary general (*sekjen*), directorate general (*dirjen*) and inspector general (*irjen*), existed below the ministry level (Kanō 1996: 19). Appointments to these director-level positions were also performed under presidential regulations. Furthermore, in the 1970s, heads of regional governments such as governors and vice governors of provinces were essentially determined by presidential appointment based on consultation with the Minister of Home Affairs (Fukao 1999: 99). In and after the 1980s, the selection of governors of provinces still required instruction or permission from Suharto. As was the case for senior government officials above the director-level, formal designation of both governors and vice governors was also made under presidential regulations.

Suharto was the Chair of Golkar's Advisory Board (Dewan Pembina), the highest supervising and decision-making body of the ruling party. This provided

Suharto with the power to supervise personnel selection for Central Executive Board (DPP) members including the Chairman of Golkar, suspend activities of the Central Executive Board in the event of any problems and overrule decisions made by them. Additionally, the President was able to use his influence in the appointment of half of the members of the MPR and in removing those who did not conform to his views from the nomination list. This control over choice of personnel for both appointed members in the parliaments (DPR and MPR) as well as DPR and MPR members of Golkar, who accounted for the majority, enabled Suharto to hold sway over the legislature in every practical sense.

Since Suharto as President also held the post of Commander in Chief of the Armed Forces (ABRI), he was able to appoint the Armed Forces Commander, which was the supreme position in the Armed Forces, as well as the Chief of Staff, who headed the four forces consisting of the Army, Navy, Air Force and Police. He also appointed Army posts that were strategically important—in particular, commanders of combat units including the Army Strategic Reserve Command (Kostrad), Special Forces (Kopassus) and Jakarta Regional Military Command. In addition, the President had the authority to grant permission for the promotion and postponement of retirement of general-class military officers and this added, on top of appointing to posts, another dimension from which the President could exert control over high-ranking officers of the Armed Forces.

A common remark that has often been made in Indonesian studies on Suharto's personnel policy was that he placed a high value on a particular ethnic group—specifically Javanese—and certain religious groups—Catholic and nominal Muslims (Jenkins 1984: 29). Javanese Muslims are often represented as belonging to either *santri* (devout Muslims), or *abangan* (nominal Muslims). Since Suharto was regarded as *abangan* in terms of his religious affiliation on the grounds that he followed *Kebatinan*, traditional beliefs indigenous to Java, the predominant view has been that Suharto distrusted and kept a watchful eye on the *santri* and that he tended to favor *abangan* in personnel recruitment. However, some non-Javanese and *santri* elites were also given important posts by Suharto and it cannot be concluded that his personnel affairs were biased toward a specific ethnic group or religious inclination.

I have outlined some of the characteristics of Suharto's personnel policy below.

Firstly, Suharto placed the greatest value on loyalty when recruiting elites. Those deemed to be highly loyal and trustworthy by Suharto were kept in their posts for a lengthy term. Conversely, those considered as displaying signs of failing loyalty or starting to act according to their own political ambitions and interests were removed from their positions. The degree of loyalty was of utmost importance to Suharto when recruiting elites.

The second characteristic was his emphasis on vocational competence and aptitude. Especially in terms of personnel selection for bureaucratic posts and key Armed Forces positions, candidates' suitability for the role and their competency to achieve objectives were important considerations to Suharto. The appointment of an intelligence officer, Ali Murtopo, to key positions from the late 1960s to the late 1970s was purely because Suharto recognized his skills in intelligence operations and political manipulation. Suharto's trust in Murtopo rapidly declined in the late 1970s, when Murtopo's political manipulation skills began to show signs of limitations. Moreover, Suharto's recruitment of Sudharmono, then an Army legal officer, as Chief State Secretary for a lengthy period from the late 1960s to the late 1980s was based upon Sudharmono's extraordinary policy planning and adjustment skills.

In order to rise to the position immediately under Suharto, in addition to the above-mentioned competence, the ability to render an accurate understanding of his intentions from very few words was also essential. Most of the time Suharto's instructions were ambiguous, to the extent that even his fellow Javanese often had difficulty understanding his words. Those who could correctly interpret the President's will, convey this to relevant individuals and implement policies in line with his vision were entrusted with and appointed to important posts for an extended term.

Thirdly, political influence was also an important consideration in personnel selection. Not surprisingly, Suharto did not want anyone to have political influence that was of a similar size to, or more extensive than, his own and those he recognized as having too much political power were thus relegated. Throughout the Suharto regime, a 'number two' never existed on a long-term basis. There was no exception to this rule, even in the cases of intelligence officer Ali Murtopo, Minister of Home Affairs Amirmachmud who rose to political power in the 1970s, Commander of the Armed Forces Benny Murdani or Chief State Secretary and Chairman of Golkar Sudharmono who possessed profound influence in the 1980s. They were all duly removed from strategic posts and disappeared from the political scene.

Finally, in many cases, Suharto prepared posts to accommodate relegated elites that were ostensibly high level but were actually of lesser importance. The appointment of Murtopo of the State Intelligence Coordinating Agency (BAKIN) to the position of Minister of Information, Minister of Home Affairs Amirmachmud to the Chair of the DPR, Commander of the Armed Forces Murdani to the Minister of Defense and Security and Chief State Secretary Sudharmono to the position of Vice President, all appeared to be promotions, but in fact Suharto's intention was to isolate them from their original political bases. Posts to diplomatic institutions abroad such as that of ambassador and minister were also used to demote elites. The reason for this was that no matter how strong an elite's power base was in a specific organization, their political power would virtually cease to exist after they had been overseas for a number of years.

As described above, Suharto used his power to allocate posts to recruit desirable personnel while eliminating those who were no longer needed, those who gained too much power and those who acted against his will. Nevertheless, Suharto gave considerable discretion to those he trusted and kept them in their positions for long terms. This provision of discretion led to the abuse of authority by the ruling elites.

Recruitment of elites was always controlled by Suharto's personal connections, in other words, patron-client relationships, and Suharto was invariably at the center of such networks. An anti-Suharto alliance was never formed among elites in Suharto's inner circle. Although Suharto did not put his political elites under surveillance or impose severe punishments on them, what he did was take advantage of rivalry relationships between them. There were always contentions and disputes among elites in the innermost circle of Suharto, as exemplified by rivalries of different generations, such as that between Murtopo of Opsus and Commander of Kopkamtib Sumitro in the early 1970s, between Commander of the Armed Forces Murdani and Chief State Secretary Sudharmono in the 1980s and between Minister of the Agency for Assessment and Application of Technology Habibie and some senior officers of the Armed Forces in the 1990s. However, Suharto managed to avoid being involved in such contentions and conflicts and, in fact, took advantage of such rivalries to create a situation where both parties had to depend on him. Suharto, having built the patron-client relationship networks around him through patronage distribution, leveraged the conflicts and disputes erupting around him to maintain his superiority. This is how Suharto continued to control high-level political elites.

Concessions as economic patronage

In addition to the distribution of political patronage based on extensive power in terms of personnel policy, Suharto leveraged economic patronage as another source of power. Since his time as the Commander of the Central Java Regional Military Command, Suharto had been securing funds in a variety of ways including illegal means such as smuggling to make up for a budget shortfall at the command center and he further expanded this practice on a national scale upon assumption of the presidential office (Shiraishi 1997: 121–122).

In 1968 when Suharto formally assumed the presidency, the Indonesian economy was on the verge of bankruptcy and in order to receive economic aid from international institutions such as the IMF and western developed countries, Indonesia needed to demonstrate to the international community they were heading in the direction of revising their radical economic policies and leftist diplomacy and replacing them with rational economic management based on liberal capitalism. Suharto recruited economic technocrats who had returned from studies in the United States as a 'team of economic experts' (*tim ahli ekonomi*), and had this team develop an economic package to promote development policies incorporating advice from international institutions and western developed countries. A series of economic recovery measures led by these technocrats from the late 1960s to early 1970s—macro-economic stabilization, inflation control, trade deregulation, the introduction of foreign capital and an increase in food production—delivered much success, helping Indonesia to overcome the economic crisis it was suffering at the beginning of the Suharto regime and even spurring the economy into growth. Economic technocrats who played major roles in these initiatives, such as Widjojo Nitisastro, Ali Wardhana, Mohammad Sadli, Radius Prawiro and Emil Salim gained trust from Suharto and worked under him for an extended period. Especially, Widjojo Nitisastro, Ali Wardhana and Radius Prawiro all served as economic minister from the end of the 1960s and continued to be involved in the economic policy decision-making process as advisors to the President until Suharto's resignation. Technocrats like these played a role in instilling economic rationality in the Suharto government to some degree.

However, on the other hand, economic management completely contrary to economic rationality was simultaneously carried out under the Suharto regime.

Public agencies capable of raising a large amount of capital such as the state-run oil company Pertamina and the National Food Logistics Agency, Bulog, were exploited by Suharto and his cronies as well as the Armed Forces. Particularly, Pertamina was exempted from government audit until 1975 as Suharto wrested it from the control of the Department of Mines and Energy and instead placed it under his direct control. Ibnu Sutowo, who had acceded to the position of President-Director of Pertamina from being a medical officer in the Army, not only made a substantial investment in major heavy industrial projects but also appropriated a large amount of income from petroleum derived from an increase in the petroleum price in order to compensate the Army's budget that was facing a funding shortfall. Furthermore, he obtained short-term loans overseas to fund major projects he was promoting and to purchase tankers to transport petroleum. Technocrats voiced strong opposition against Sutowo, who misappropriated a vast amount of funds that should really have been deposited in the national treasury and took out high-risk loans from foreign countries at his discretion. Subsequently Sutowo was dismissed from the position of President-Director of Pertamina, which by then had become nearly bankrupt due to massive debt and reckless management. This became a precedent for the undesirable practice of misappropriating large sums of off-budget funds (Robison 1986: 233–247; Prawiro 1998: 176–193).

Meanwhile, Suharto and his family established many foundations in the name of philanthropy and used them for business and wealth-building purposes. Businesses run by foundations created by the Suharto family were connected with entrepreneurs of Chinese descent as business partners were provided with economic concessions such as import licenses, exclusive rights to markets and logging permits. Chinese-Indonesian entrepreneurs who became Suharto family business partners grew to be one of the largest conglomerates in Southeast Asia and bestowed a large sum of funds on the Suharto family in return for economic concessions (Shiraishi 1997: 156–162). This kind of funds spirited into foundations controlled by the Suharto family were not only used to expand their businesses but also served as a resource for economic patronage that could be distributed to the public in the form of 'presidential assistance', which will be described in more detail later in this chapter.

There were at least thirteen foundations that Suharto himself chaired (Aditjondro 1998: 4). The ostensible purpose for the establishment of such foundations was charity, but the reality was that a massive amount of the funds collected were used to purchase shares in private banks and companies and further expand Suharto family businesses from profits made through these investments. Public servants were obliged to make donations to the Suharto family's foundations and a certain amount was withheld from their salaries depending on their rank (Dwipayana and Ramadhan 1989: 285). Moreover, a portion of revenue from state-run businesses and taxes collected from high-income taxpayers was also diverted into the foundations (Murai et al. 1999: 54). Private corporations that had a connection to the Suharto family were making a large amount of donations to their foundations. For instance, flour importer Bogasari, one of the companies owned by Liem Sioe Lion, a long-term business partner of Suharto, stipulated in its article of incorporation drawn up at the time of foundation that twenty-six percent of its profits, or twenty percent from 1977, would be shared with the Harapan Kita Foundation owned by Suharto's wife, Tien Suharto and the Dharma Putra Foundation linked with Kostrad (Robison 1986: 232; Y. Satō 1992: 82; 2003: 91). The funds gathered by the foundations would be invested in the Suharto family and his business partners' businesses and this would deliver profits and help expand these businesses, which would in turn circulate money back into the foundations.

Foundation owners were not just Suharto and Mrs. Suharto. Suharto's brother-in-law Sudwikatmono, his paternal half-brother Probosutedjo, his children and even grandchildren chaired many foundations. Tien Suharto chaired nine foundations, Suharto and Tien's brothers and cousins chaired thirteen and Suharto's children and grandchildren and their spouses chaired thirty-three; in total there were sixty-seven Suharto family-affiliated foundations (Aditjondro 1998: 3–77). The total assets of the Suharto family's foundations were said to be anywhere between fifteen and forty billion dollars[2].

Many entrepreneurs who collaborated with the Suharto family in raising funds and formed partnerships with their businesses were of Chinese descent. In particular, the Salim Group owned by Liem Sioe Lion, also known by his Indonesian name Sudono Salim, and the Nusamba Group owned by Bob Hassan expanded and diversified their businesses to form huge conglomerates or corporate groups. Both Liem Sioe Lion and Bob Hassan had been Suharto's business partners since he was Commander of the Central Java Regional Military Command and hence received a variety of concessions from the government such as exclusive rights to import or market as well as the award of government projects on the back of full support from Suharto (Robison 1986: 259–260, 296–315; Y. Satō 1992, 2003)[3]. Corporate groups owned by the Suharto family were closely linked with Chinese-Indonesian corporate groups, such as those mentioned above, through investment, collaborative businesses and joint shareholding. A complete system of coexistence and mutual prosperity had been established between the two stakeholders. The Suharto family's foundations would provide funds and business concessions to Chinese-Indonesian companies and this helped those groups to expand their businesses. This meant increased income for Suharto family companies that held shares and engaged in joint enterprises with those Chinese-Indonesian companies, enabling both parties to prosper and transform into conglomerates together (Murai et al. 1999: 82–92).

However, excessive preferential treatment of Chinese-Indonesian companies became the target of a great deal of frustration among the public, of which the majority was of Malay descent, and this caused anti-Chinese riots to break out every so often during the Suharto regime. Anti-Chinese riots were often left unaddressed by the relevant authorities to allow the public to 'let off steam' in terms of their anti-Chinese sentiment, which was the underlying cause of such disturbances. Most of the actual targets of the riots were not the huge conglomerates that had a back-scratching alliance with the Suharto family but instead small-sized stores run by Chinese-Indonesians. Although Suharto gradually corrected his bias for Chinese-Indonesians and began giving consideration to the growth of indigenous capital such as that of *pribumi* (indigenous people of Malay descent) entrepreneurs from the mid-1980s (Y. Satō 2003: 127), Chinese-Indonesian corporate groups maintained dominance as the top private businesses in Indonesia until the very end of the Suharto regime[4].

'Institutionalized' corruption

While business concessions were primarily given to the Suharto family and Chinese-Indonesian corporate groups, Indonesian society was increasingly riddled with corruption and collusion. In central and regional offices alike, anyone who assumed a political or administrative post such as those in government agencies, the Armed Forces or parliament abused the authority to give permits associated with their posts and received a large amount of informal service fees and gratuities. Furthermore, some influential figures were given executive posts in private companies in exchange for political backing. Companies invited people who had nothing whatsoever to do with their business to become company executives in order to build connections with powerful figures to gain business advantages or use as 'insurance' on which they could rely should they become involved in any trouble. Those who became company executives could receive executive compensation packages without doing much work at all. Political and administrative posts played the role of extending patronage to secure economic profits.

This kind of corruption and collusion was not a newly introduced practice but had already been an issue even before the beginning of the Suharto regime; however, such practice clearly became 'institutionalized' during the Suharto regime and became prevalent throughout Indonesian society. The number of public servants skyrocketed as it was compulsory for them to vote for Golkar in elections and hence an increase in the number of public servants directly resulted in an increase in the vote for Golkar. The number of public servants, which was 1.9 million in 1980, doubled in just over a decade to 3.95 million in 1992 (Kanō 1996: 37). However, wages for public servants did not rise significantly but in fact remained considerably low—to the point that public servants could not make ends meet despite receiving benefits in kind such as rice and kerosene and often had to take on a second job (Kanō 1996: 34–35). It has often been suggested that this low pay was the cause of the proliferation of corruption. Nevertheless, Suharto increased the number of public servants knowing that they would receive little remuneration. In other words, Suharto tacitly permitted public servants to 'self-fund' through corruption to supplement their low income (Shiraishi 1992: 81–82; 1997: 159–160).

Besides public servants, Suharto also boosted the number of members of the DPR and MPR as well as members and executives of Golkar. He maintained a policy to include as many members as possible in the regime and at the same time connived with self-funding through bribes and misdeeds that were prevalent in each and every organization. Consequently, along with bureaucratic bodies, the legislative and judicial branches as well as the entire economic sphere became infested with illegal dealings, corruption and collusion across all levels. At the pinnacle of state power, Suharto created foundations using his authority and power as President to raise a huge amount of capital. Low-level public servants extorted informal processing fees from the public at the service counters of local government offices to supplement their low income. The presence of these practices meant that it was considered natural that one should be entitled to economic benefits befitting the various posts and positions and it was acceptable to abuse the authority associated with posts for unfair profiting throughout society. Furthermore, such economic benefits were justified on the grounds that they were indeed unavoidable because workers in low-level posts needed to compensate for low pay, officials in higher positions needed to look after their subordinates or organization and the head of state needed to cover budget deficits to ensure the welfare and well-being of the nation (Shiraishi 1992: 81–82; 1997: 159–160). This is how the system of highly routinized corruption developed under the Suharto regime.

Suharto and the Armed Forces

Patronage distribution to the Armed Forces
Even though President Suharto started his career in the Armed Forces, it was certainly not an equal partner to him. Although the Armed Forces constituted Suharto's support base and there were some senior officers within the organization who were able to voice their opinions to him, the influence of the Armed Forces on Suharto was limited in terms of both personnel affairs and budget and policy planning.

When considering the bilateral relationship between President Suharto and the Armed Forces, the most striking facet is the enduring loyalty of the Armed Forces to Suharto. Suharto's assumption of the top position in the government did not result in a significant increase in the defense budget. Quite the contrary, the defense budget was considerably small, especially taking into consideration the geographical size of Indonesia and its population (Shiraishi 1992: 124–126).

The budget in Indonesia is posted under two major categories: ordinary budget and development budget. Table 2.1 shows that defense spending continued to rise in both budgets while Figure 2.1 illustrates that the proportion of defense spending to the total national budget fell from a little over twenty percent to a little over seven percent over almost twenty years from the beginning of 1970 to the end of 1980.

This trend remained unchanged in the 1990s. International comparisons have revealed that Indonesia's defense budget is extremely small given the size of the country and its population. The 1995 figure shows the number of military personnel was 300,000 and defense spending was 4.4 billion US dollars in

Table 2.1: Fluctuations in the defense-security budget in Indonesia (1972–1989)

FISCAL YEAR	ORDINARY BUDGET			DEVELOPMENT BUDGET			PROPORTION OF DEFENSE-SECURITY SPENDING TO THE TOTAL BUDGET (%)
	TOTAL ORDINARY BUDGET	DEFENSE-SECURITY SPENDING	PROPORTION OF DEFENSE-SECURITY SPENDING TO THE TOTAL ORDINARY BUDGET (%)	TOTAL DEVELOPMENT BUDGET	DEFENSE-SECURITY SPENDING	PROPORTION OF DEFENSE-SECURITY SPENDING TO THE TOTAL DEVELOPMENT BUDGET (%)	
1972/73	437,500,000	144,976,462	33.14	231,100,000	6,000,000	2.60	22.58
1973/74	518,375,331	180,439,927	34.81	261,100,000	7,225,000	2.77	24.08
1974/75	961,600,000	276,140,330	28.72	615,700,000	18,000,000	2.92	18.65
1975/76	1,466,300,000	434,199,309	29.61	1,268,400,000	26,023,000	2.05	16.83
1976/77	1,600,300,000	480,468,177	30.02	1,920,300,000	42,500,000	2.21	14.85
1977/78	2,079,400,000	572,091,400	27.51	2,167,900,000	56,000,000	2.58	14.79
1978/79	2,371,600,000	586,324,000	24.72	2,454,747,000	115,633,900	4.71	14.54
1979/80	3,445,900,000	662,316,800	19.22	3,488,050,000	254,300,000	7.29	13.22
1980/81	5,529,200,000	939,315,800	16.99	5,027,700,000	386,890,000	7.70	12.56
1981/82	7,501,100,000	1,246,288,000	16.61	4,838,100,000	337,500,000	6.98	12.84
1982/83	7,001,500,000	1,272,019,000	18.17	8,605,800,000	568,678,300	6.61	11.79
1983/84	7,275,100,000	1,318,116,000	18.12	9,290,250,000	573,957,000	6.18	11.42
1984/85	10,101,100,000	1,362,468,000	13.49	10,459,300,000	697,761,000	6.67	10.02
1985/86	12,399,000,000	1,600,392,500	12.91	10,647,000,000	714,064,000	6.71	10.04
1986/87	15,026,500,000	1,678,351,736	11.17	7,756,600,000	510,000,000	6.58	9.61
1987/88	20,066,000,000	1,763,980,114	8.79	8,897,600,000	555,000,000	6.24	8.01
1988/89	26,648,100,000	2,032,324,093	7.63	16,225,000,000	981,600,000	6.05	7.03

Unit: 1,000 Rupiah
Source: Each year's edition of *Nota Keuangan dan Rancangan Anggaran Pendapatan dan Belanja Negara.*

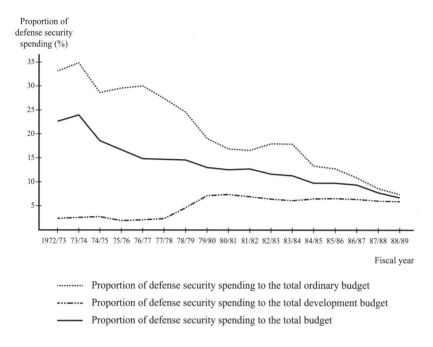

Figure 2.1: Proportion of defense spending to the total national budget (1972–1989)

·········· Proportion of defense security spending to the total ordinary budget
- - - - - - Proportion of defense security spending to the total development budget
——— Proportion of defense security spending to the total budget

Source: Each year's edition of *Nota Keuangan dan Rancangan Anggaran Pendapatan dan Belanja Negara*.

Indonesia with a population of almost 200 million. Malaysia had 115,000 military personnel and 3.5 billion in defense spending and Singapore approximately 50,000 and 4 billion in the same year. According to those figures, Indonesia's defense spending was not much greater than that of Malaysia with a population of 24 million and Singapore with 3 million (*Military Balance* 1996–7: 190, 195; 1997–8: 179, 181).

The budget allocated by the government to the Armed Forces is often said to have been about half or even one-third of the required amount. Such budgeting put the Armed Forces, especially regional military commands, in a situation where they were poorly equipped and could not even carry out proper combat training. Consequently, while regional military commands which accounted for roughly half of all military manpower were established for the purpose of maintaining security in their respective regional areas, they were not sufficiently trained for combat and many officers instead engaged in bureaucratic work due to budget shortfalls (Widoyoko et al. 2003: 91–92).

In spite of this, the Armed Forces remained organized and their loyalty to Suharto was constant. This is evident in that no active military officer made public criticisms of President Suharto, let alone plotted a rebellion or coup. This, then, gives rise to the question as to why the Armed Forces, despite receiving a minimal budget, remained obedient to Suharto. It was not because the ruler enforced exhaustive surveillance throughout the military, as is commonly observed in personal rule. Indonesia's security and intelligence agencies do not appear to have been functioning as surveillance apparatuses overseeing the Armed Forces, since most of those that held key positions in security and intelligence agencies such as Kopkamtib and BAKIN were generally military personnel transferred from the Armed Forces.

Shiraishi's explanation for the strategy Suharto employed to control the Armed Forces was structural reform coupled with tactful personnel policy, as well as the widely-spread practice of familism—in other words, self-funding of capital (1992: 135–144; 1997: 158–162). Suharto took full advantage of his authority over personnel matters in military organizations to govern the Armed Forces. In particular, Suharto made sure to appoint officers whom he trusted highly to key posts such as the Commander of the Armed Forces, Army Chief of Staff, Commander of Kostrad and Commander of the Jakarta Regional Military Command which had a major responsibility in maintaining security in the capital city. During the period from the 1970s to 1980s, he assigned his immediate subordinates to these important posts. Subsequently, in and after the 1990s, when these subordinates were to retire from the military, he promoted presidential adjutants to these Armed Forces top posts. Presidential adjutants were posts to which only young officers who had achieved excellent results at the military academy could be assigned and their array of responsibilities included bodyguard duties and attending to the everyday needs of Suharto. Suharto knew these officers very well, even their personal qualities.

In addition to personnel policy in the military, the allocation of political posts for military personnel also played a significant part in dictating the Armed Forces. Especially, mid- to high-level officers who played central roles in the Armed Forces had political or administrative posts arranged for them and such posts came with economic benefits. During the Suharto era, the Armed Forces repeatedly underwent a major personnel shuffle in relatively short intervals of one to five years (Masuhara 1998: 35–38). The term of the Commander of the Armed Forces, the top post in the Armed Forces, was set at five years and no one who reached this post held their office for longer than that period. The retirement ages were fifty-five for high-level officers and fifty for any officers below them, and even the highest-level officers equivalent to the Commander of the Armed Forces and Army Chief of Staff could not postpone their retirement without permission from Suharto. Many officers left their military jobs upon reaching the retirement age in accordance with the retirement stipulation. The reason why compliance with the retirement stipulation could be ensured was none other than the fact that political and administrative posts were secured for officers after retirement. This fact—that post-retirement posts were guaranteed for officers—can also help explain the smooth generational transition of military officers.

Tables 2.2 and 2.3 provide an overview of the political and administrative posts given to the total of 575 high-level officers and 729 mid-level officers who were appointed to political or administrative posts between 1968 and 1989.

Based on these two tables, the following tendencies can be noted in regards to political or administrative posts offered to high- and mid-level officers.

General-class officers who served at the highest level of the military as Commander of the Armed Forces or Army Chief of Staff were offered key ministerial posts in the areas of politics, defense and security after retirement, including the positions of Coordinating Minister for Political and Security Affairs, Minister of Defense and Security and Minister of Home Affairs. Meanwhile, lieutenant general-class officers who served as Commander of Kostrad or Commander of Kopassus were provided with other ministerial posts, whereas major general and brigadier general-class officers who served as a commander or chief of staff of regional commands were given the position of governor of the same region or became high-ranking officials in the central government. Senior officers who were not allocated to these more important posts were assigned to positions such as ambassador or minister in diplomatic establishments abroad or became members of the DPR and MPR.

Meanwhile, positions offered to mid-level officers included: high-ranking officials of the central government, agents of state-run businesses, members of the DPR and MPR, regents and mayors as well as members of regencies and city representative councils (DPRD). Furthermore, although not mentioned in the above tables, lower-level officers and non-commissioned officers were also provided with posts such as agents in regency and city government offices as well as heads of subdistricts or administrative villages. Assumption of these political and administrative posts meant they could expect to take advantage of official power to gain economic benefits. Opportunities were extended to receive cash from private companies, as it was common for private firms to invite ex-Armed Forces personnel to assume executive posts. It was critical for private companies to bring in ex-military personnel and have the support of the military in the region if they wanted to run their businesses smoothly.

The military not only enjoyed the benefits of preferential allocation of political patronage in the form of political and administrative posts but economic

Table 2.2: Political and administrative posts allocated to high-ranking military officers (1968–1989)

	DPA MEMBER	MINISTER	HIGH-RANKING POST IN CENTRAL GOVERNMENT	MPR MEMBER	DPR MEMBER	PRESIDENT OF STATE-RUN BUSINESS	GOVERNOR OF PROVINCE	AMBASSADOR	OTHER	TOTAL
General	3	9	1	9	1	1	0	11	1	36
Lieutenant general	8	23	6	23	2	3	6	30	11	112
Major general	4	19	51	55	28	6	18	34	14	229
Brigadier general	1	3	40	66	33	5	18	11	21	198
Total	16	54	98	153	64	15	42	86	47	575

Source: Each issue of *Mimbar Kekaryaan ABRI*, Bachtiar (1988) and each year's edition of *Yearbook of Asian Affairs*.
Note: 'High-ranking post in central government' refers to posts equivalent to or above the level of director general of a ministry. Not all political or administrative posts given to high-ranking military officers are included here.

Table 2.3: Political and administrative posts allocated to middle-ranking military officers (1968–1989)

	HIGH-RANKING POST IN CENTRAL GOVERNMENT	POST IN CENTRAL GOVERNMENT	EXECUTIVE OF STATE-RUN BUSINESS	POST IN STATE-RUN BUSINESS	MPR MEMBER	DPR MEMBER	GOVERNOR OF PROVINCE	POST IN PROVINCIAL GOVERNMENT	REGENT OF REGENCY
Colonel	31	37	6	18	38	21	12	18	65
Lieutenant colonel	5	38	2	14	7	6	0	12	122
Major	3	26	0	14	1	3	0	10	13
Total	39	101	8	46	46	30	12	40	200

	POST IN REGENCY GOVERNMENT	MAYOR OF CITY	POST IN CITY GOVERNMENT	POST IN LOCAL BRANCH OF MINISTRY	MEMBER OF PROVINCIAL REPRESENTATIVE COUNCIL	MEMBER OF REGENCY REPRESENTATIVE COUNCIL	MEMBER OF CITY REPRESENTATIVE COUNCIL	ACADEMIC	OTHER	TOTAL
Colonel	4	16	5	6	6	0	0	11	20	314
Lieutenant colonel	14	16	7	7	1	9	2	0	9	271
Major	28	1	7	2	3	12	10	1	10	144
Total	46	33	19	15	10	21	12	12	39	729

Source: Each issue of *Mimbar Kekaryaan ABRI* and each year's edition of *Yearbook of Asian Affairs*.

Notes: 'Post in central government' refers to posts below the director general of a ministry. 'Executive of state-run business' refers to board members excluding the president and any other post equivalent to or above division manager. 'Post in state-run business' refers to posts below division managers. Not all political or administrative posts given to middle-ranking military officers are included here.

patronage was also a factor, in other words, off-budget funds were made available. Off-budget funds to compensate for the shortfall in the defense budget came from the following three sources. Firstly, funds were supplied directly by the President and secondly there were those afforded by the State Secretariat; these two were collectively called 'on-top budget' funds. The third kind was funds acquired from their own businesses (Widoyoko et al. 2003: 37–38).

Initially, at the beginning of the Suharto regime, funds from Bulog and Pertamina were diverted to the Armed Forces to compensate for the budget shortfall (Robison 1986: 229–242; Crouch 1988: 275–281), but these state-owned companies were criticized for having become hotbeds of corruption and misdemeanors. Then, with Pertamina's failure and the consequent dismissal of the President-Director of Pertamina Sutowo in the mid-1970s, the focus shifted to self-funding activities through military businesses. The instigation of military businesses was marked by the confiscation of western companies and plantations from the end of the 1950s to the beginning of the 1960s by the Suharto regime, which was left-leaning at that time. Management of many of the confiscated companies was then put in the hands of the military and military-affiliated companies. Under the Suharto regime, these companies started to develop businesses in partnership with Chinese-Indonesian companies and those of the Suharto family (Robison 1986: 250–254; Kingsbury 2003: 209–211).

The Armed Forces also established foundations and cooperatives and invested collected funds into businesses to earn profits; in the same manner the Suharto family used foundations to invest in businesses. Some generals justified such businesses citing budget deficiencies, explaining that those profits earned from businesses were being used for welfare programs for military personnel and to purchase equipment. Nevertheless, no information regarding the total amount of funds earned from military businesses or the breakdown of allocation of such funds to welfare programs and for the procurement of equipment has been made publically available.

A great number of foundations and cooperatives were formed on the basis of troops and units. In addition to those of utmost prominence such as Tri Usaha Bhakti, a corporate group founded by the Ministry of Defense and Security, and the Dharma Putra Foundation owned by Kostrad (Robison 1986: 261–263), a wide array of foundations and cooperatives were assembled one after another. A list of the thirteen foundations, eight cooperatives and 143 companies formed by different commands and units as of 1998 can be found in the work of Damien Kingsbury (2003: 214–220).

Many military officers, both active and retired, were involved in these kinds of military businesses that were virtually free from any restrictions, especially in conflict areas such as Aceh and East Timor. A state of military emergency was declared in these conflict zones and executive authority was temporarily transferred from local governments to the regional military commands. Under such circumstances, local military units abetted in illegal logging and the smuggling of narcotics, set up security checkpoints on roads to collect tolls and garnered a large sum of money from multinational corporations that were engaged in mining resources such as petroleum, natural gas and copper in the name of security charges (McCulloh 2003: 113–114; Kingsbury 2003: 194–198).

Divide and rule
The 'Dual Function' (*Dwi fungsi*) doctrine[5] of the Armed Forces advocated that the organization should stand above all political forces and play not only a defense and security function but also a socio-political function with the mission of stabilizing and revitalizing the nation. Under the Suharto regime, this doctrine played a role in justifying the military's vested interests. However, some military officers were disgruntled about the way the military was managed. Retired generals who used to hold top positions in the Army and Navy and gained popularity amongst the public such as retired Army General Abdul Haris Nasution, retired Army General Sumitro and retired Navy General Ali Sadikin heavily criticized the Armed Forces claiming it had become detached from the public and turned into merely an instrument to reinforce the authority of those in power, solely driven by their own business interests. Although their earnest attitude in calling for a tightening of discipline in the military was well received by the public, their demand failed to influence active military officers. It neither discouraged the assignment of military personnel on political and administrative posts nor stopped their involvement in businesses, and did nothing to mobilize active military officers to criticize President Suharto. This is because the majority of military personnel were beneficiaries of the patronage distribution system built by Suharto and their political and administrative posts, hence their status and livelihood, were guaranteed as long as they remained loyal to the President, even after retirement. Since the military itself largely depended on benefits from Suharto's patronage distribution, the call for the enforcement of discipline by retired generals had almost no impact within the military.

Gradually, Suharto began adopting a tough stance against officers critical of him. During the period from the end of the 1970s to the beginning of the 1980s, Nasution, Ali Sadikin, retired Army Major General Mochamad Jasin and retired Police General Hoegeng Imam Santoso jointly submitted with renowned Muslim politicians documents expressing criticisms against Suharto (Jenkins 1984: 162). Suharto was infuriated by the denigration and stripped those involved of every means of making a living and even banned them from leaving the country (Jenkins 1984: 183–187). Likewise, the Suharto government incarcerated and imposed a prison term on retired Army Lieutenant General Harsono Rekso Dharsono, who was also critical of the government, on the grounds that he was involved in the terrorist bombing of 1984. These events demonstrated that voicing criticism against Suharto entailed a substantial risk, even for military generals of high repute.

Suharto also took advantage of competition among officers to maintain his superiority. Suharto was surrounded by an endless series of competitions and conflicts over policies and concessions. Particularly, in the early 1970s, there was a serious rivalry between Ali Murtopo of the intelligence sector and the senior officers of the Armed Forces' mainstream faction led by Sumitro (Shiraishi 1997: 154). The Malari incident, or *peristiwa Malari*, which occurred in January 1974 involved a demonstration and riot in reaction to a visit by Japanese Prime Minister Kakuei Tanaka which fuelled student activists protesting against the expansion of Japanese businesses in Indonesia in collusion with military officers close to Suharto and Chinese-Indonesian conglomerates. However, it is believed that the power struggle between Murtopo and Sumitro may have been the real cause behind this incident. More specifically, Murtopo is said to have incited students to riot in order to push his rival Sumitro aside. In fact, Suharto dismissed Sumitro from the position of Commander of Kopkamtib as he was in charge of maintaining security. This incident happened to provide a convenient excuse for Suharto to remove Sumitro as well. Sumitro had too much influence within the military and was also popular among student activists.

The most prominent rivalry in the 1980s occurred between Commander of the Armed Forces Benny Murdani and Chief State Secretary Sudharmono. The former held the top post in the Armed Forces and was its most powerful officer throughout the Suharto regime. Having formed the 'Murdani clique' within the military, he tactically used two faces—one for the diplomatic front and another for undertaking political manipulation under Suharto's orders. On the other hand, Sudharmono was the most influential officer in administration and politics. He was entrusted with formulating all policies including budget preparation and held the position of Chief State Secretary of the State Secretariat, which was referred to as the 'cabinet of the cabinet' at that time. He also served as the Chairman of Golkar from 1983 to 1988. Sudharmono, who had been appointed Chief State Secretary by Suharto for his administrative competence, often worked in cooperation with technocrats as an executive of development policies and fiscal management. High-level officers of the Armed Forces were hostile toward him, resentful that he was responsible for the low defense budget. Suharto took full advantage of the rivalry between Murdani and Sudharmono who were competing for the number two spot below him. In regards to Murdani, who had expanded his influence within the Armed Forces, Suharto did not grant permission for the postponement of his retirement and disconnected him from the chain of command of the Armed Forces and later implemented the 'de-Benny-zation' (*de-Benny-sasi*) of the military by removing officers in the 'Murdani clique' from key positions one after another. Similarly, Sudharmono, who had tremendous influence in the State Secretariat and Golkar, was assigned by Suharto to the office of Vice President to draw him away from those two political bases and put him in a position where he could no longer be involved in policy planning.

Into the 1990s, Suharto's means of controlling the Armed Forces began to display changes. Suharto, having learned from his mistake in allowing the overexpansion of the Murdani clique in the 1980s, started to adjust personnel affairs in the 1990s so that a specific group could not accumulate too much power within the Armed Forces. Back then the military was divided into two groups: the mainstream faction called the 'red-white' wing which was descended from the Murdani clique and the devout Muslim 'green' wing led by devout Muslim officers. Suharto assigned a 'green' officer Feisal Tandjung to the post of Commander of the Armed Forces, replacing a 'red-white' officer Edi Sudradjat of the mainstream faction in 1993 and assigned a 'green' officer Hartono to the post of Army Chief of Staff in 1994. From this time on, the balance between 'red-white' and 'green' wings was always taken into consideration when making personnel decisions.

Violence and patronage distribution as a means of social control

Suppression and appeasement of opposition forces
Under the Suharto regime, groups that could potentially have become opposition forces such as student activists, Islamic forces, labor unions and the mass media were fragmented through suppression and appeasement by the government and could not organize effective protest campaigns against it.

Student movements
Even before independence, university students had a strong awareness that they were expected to act with leadership to direct the state and nation as next-generation elites. They played a leading role in the Youth Pledge (*Sumpah Pemuda*)[6] of 1928 as well as the declaration of independence of 1945 and also contributed to the establishment of the Suharto regime when the September 30th Affair erupted in 1965 by quickly raising anti-communist voices and taking strong initiatives in exterminating communist party organizations in cooperation with the Armed Forces. At the same time, driven by a sense of

responsibility for overseeing authorities and representing the public's voice, they often organized demonstrations to express their objections to the government during the Suharto regime.

Student movements had the strongest momentum between the late 1960s and the end of the 1970s. After the September 30th Affair, student activists from the University of Indonesia and the Bandung Institute of Technology organized the Indonesian Student's Action Front (KAMI), a student union formed across multiple universities, and carried out radical anti-communist and anti-Sukarno demonstrations, playing a major role in the ousting of President Sukarno. This group of students was dubbed the 'Generation of 66' (*Angkatan 66*) and this generation produced a large number of political elites inside and outside the regime. Student activists also engaged in student movements in response to the Malari incident of 1974. They condemned senior government officials and military officers who were earning a huge amount of profit through collusion with Japanese companies and staged a large-scale uprising setting Chinese- and Japanese-affiliated companies' stores and distributors on fire in Jakarta. Over the period from 1977 to 1978, they organized nation-wide demonstrations protesting against the reelection of President Suharto. The government generally took a lenient stance toward student activists, who were essentially elites. Nevertheless, whenever the government deemed their actions excessive, they suppressed the movement and arrested and detained those involved.

The government founded a youth organization called the National Committee of Indonesian Youth (KNPI) in 1973 in order to control student movements. The idea was to appease prominent representatives of student organizations by appointing them to the executive of the KNPI or offering them posts as members of the MPR to keep student movements to a manageable scale. However, government attempts to control these movements through the KNPI ended in failure because this organization was formed by merely throwing together a few student organizations and hence it lacked internal unity and was regarded as a government-controlled organization. The KNPI only started to show effect when the government's 'normalization of campus life' (NKK), which was implemented as a more heavy-handed student movement countermeasure in 1980, weakened student movements through forcing student councils to dissolve and freeze activities and banning student demonstrations and gatherings outside campuses. Since then, politically ambitious students began to join government-affiliated organizations such as the KNPI and the Indonesian Renewal Youth Organization (AMPI), which was established in 1978 as Golkar's youth organization. While student protests against the government decreased, student activists who took part in these regime-affiliated youth organizations grew to become regime elites as Golkar executives.

Islamic forces
The most powerful opposition forces to the Suharto regime were the Islamic forces. The most prominent Islamic organizations in Indonesia were Nahdlatul Ulama (NU), which is said to have had thirty million members and was led by traditional Islamic leaders such as the *ulama* and *kyai*[7], and Muhammadiyah led by Islamic reformists which was second to the NU in terms of membership. These Muslim organizations at first contributed to the purge of the Communist Party and ousting of President Sukarno after the September 30th Affair of 1965 in concert with the Armed Forces on the basis of anti-communist solidarity but later gradually diverted away from and took a clear stance against the government. Suharto could not extend patron-client relationships to the Islamic forces, as he did not have strong connections with devout Muslims and channels that led to powerful executives of the Islamic organizations due to the fact that he was a follower of Javanese mysticism (*Kebatinan*). Furthermore, over the period from the early 1970s to the mid-1980s, the government and the Islamic forces often disagreed, beginning with the issue of the formulation of the marriage law, the inclusion of Pancasila education in the mandatory curriculum and the application of Pancasila as the sole state principle. At the same time, the government conducted a series of sabotage operations against the United Development Party (PPP), an Islamic party regarded as a formidable rival of Golkar, to steer public support away from it.

The conflict between the two parties reached boiling point over the issue of the Suharto government's attempt to impose Pancasila. Pancasila was the five principles of Indonesian statehood first championed by Sukarno preceding independence on August 17, 1945. It comprised the following principles which were also incorporated into the preface of the constitution: 'belief in the one and only god', 'just and civilized humanity', 'the unity of Indonesia', 'democracy guided by the inner wisdom in the unanimity arising out of deliberations amongst representatives' and 'social justice for the whole of the people of Indonesia'. However, immediately after this, a heated discussion erupted over whether Pancasila or Islam should be the state principle. Major Islamic forces including the NU and Muhammadiyah wanted Islam to be the state principle, demanding Sharia, or Islamic law, be the national law. Conversely, nationalist and communist forces formed a united front with Christian forces and put forward a counterargument that Pancasila should form the state principle instead of Islam. This debate did not reach a conclusion in the era of President Sukarno.

Suharto began insisting on making Pancasila the state principle immediately after seizing political power but was countered by strong objections from the Islamic forces. The government tried to formulate the 'Guidance on Understanding and Implementing Pancasila' (P 4) program in 1978 and made it mandatory to teach the government's interpretation of Pancasila as the 'official interpretation' in schools and workplaces. This caused a backlash from the Islamic forces claiming that this constituted the imposition of Pancasila by the government. The PPP caused disruptions in the MPR by walking out in the middle of deliberations while other Islamic groups carried out a series of protests against the government. Despite strong opposition, the government enforced the P 4 program in the general session of the MPR. Moreover, in 1984, the government submitted five political laws to the DPR containing the law on mass organizations that mandated Pancasila be the sole principle for all political and mass-based social organizations. This created a strong sense of concern within the Islamic forces that they would be stripped of their identity by the government. These laws were enacted in 1985.

In an attempt to address such strong objections from the Islamic forces, the government tried to divide them by means of suppression and appeasement.

The primary means the government used to curb the Islamic forces was intervention in Islamic political parties through political manipulation. Nine Islamic parties were consolidated into a single party by the government and made a fresh start as the PPP in 1973. The integration of different political parties resulted in internal contests within the PPP. Taking advantage of this situation, the government fomented internal dissent to overthrow the central executive board of the party who did not conform to their wishes. The process, in more specific terms, was to firstly instigate those who disagreed with the central executive board to create a counter-executive board to compete against the existing one, then intervene in the personnel policy under the guise of mediation and finally direct them to create a brand new central executive board consisting of pro-government executives. Through this process, every time a conflict arose within the party, party executives were replaced with personnel more amenable to the government, increasingly disabling the PPP's ability to play a role as an opposition party.

The second means was to label leaders and politicians of the Islamic forces 'extremists' and arrest and detain them for 'having disrupted public order and security'. The period from the late 1940s to early 1960s saw an armed struggle called the *Darul Islam* movement in which Islamic forces fought for the establishment of an Islamic state within Indonesia in regions such as the province of West Java. In 1976, the security authorities claimed that the remnants of the movement were interfering with security and apprehended many devout Muslims including politicians who would run in the following year's election as candidates representing the PPP. Similarly, Islamic leaders who preached against the government on a daily basis at mosques were also arrested. Some were repeatedly transferred from one detention center to the next while others went through a cycle of arrest and release. In sum, those who presented a political challenge from the Islamic perspective were identified as 'extremists who planned to overthrow the state' and significant restrictions were imposed on their freedom of speech and mobility.

Thirdly, the end of 1970 saw the Suharto regime shifting away from policies based on suppression alone and slowly adopting appeasement approaches. In 1978, the government began listening to the growing list of demands that had been put forth by the Islamic forces since the 1960s, including but not limited to transferring *Kebatinan* from the Ministry of Religious Affairs to the Ministry of Education and Culture[8], banning the Jehovah's Witnesses and restricting the activities of Christian missionaries dispatched from overseas organizations. The government also started actively providing assistance to mosques and *pesantren* (Islamic boarding schools). Specifically, government officials led by the Minister of Religious Affairs frequently visited prestigious *pesantren* in Central and East Java and requested renowned *ulama* and *kyai* to consider approving Pancasila as Indonesia's sole principle, with the provision of a range of assistance measures for the Islamic facilities run by them (Parikesit and Sempurnadjaja 1995: 254–257).

The government's carrot and stick counter-Islamic measure paid off and Islamic groups were slowly but surely starting to agree with making Pancasila the sole principle. In 1985, the five political laws including a provision on the Pancasila as the sole principle were passed in the DPR and this marked a turning point for the relationship between the Suharto government and the Islamic forces. Since then, Suharto became less and less concerned about the Islamic forces and was even willing to co-opt them into the regime in the 1990s.

Labor movements and the mass media

The term 'Pancasila' began to connote special meanings under the Suharto regime. For example, 'Pancasila industrial relations' meant that labor and management were in a 'harmonious' relationship and 'Pancasila journalism' signified reporting 'with self-restraint' in such a way that would not harm the interests of the government.

Although labor movements gained momentum during the Guided Democracy era, with a communist-controlled labor union federation, SOBSI (All Indonesia Centre of Labor Organizations), playing the central role, this federation, along with the Communist Party, collapsed after the September 30th Affair[9]. Following the fall of the SOBSI, the Suharto government tried to implement strict control over labor movements in an attempt to eliminate their political involvement, which was the norm in the Sukarno era. The government consolidated twenty-one labor unions in 1973 to create a government-regulated labor union called the 'All Indonesian Labor Federation' (FBSI, renamed SPSI in 1985). The FBSI was supposedly the only channel through which the government and labor forces could communicate with each other; however, the reality was, it was used by the government as a means of controlling labor—that is, its only function was to serve orders from the government rather than to reflect labor's opinions in policies. The government propagated that it would protect labor rights while pursuing its development policy based on trilateral meetings involving the government, management and manual workers under the banner of 'Pancasila industrial relations'. However, the truth was that manual workers were forced to work for low wages with heavy restrictions on wage claims and strike action. In the 1990s, an independent labor union called the SBSI chaired by Mochtar Pakpahan was established in front of a backdrop of frequent eruptions of labor disputes. However, their demand for the improvement of working conditions including a minimum wage came to no avail and Pakpahan was arrested for 'inciting' labor movements (Kingsbury 2002: 183–184).

Similarly, control of the press was carried out under the name of 'Pancasila journalism'. The government asserted that news reportage should promote national development and the media should refrain from covering any news that may conflict with national interests (Kingsbury 2002: 126). Accordingly, the media was neither allowed to criticize state leaders and the government in any way nor raise issues on sensitive topics—referred to as SARA, the term coined as an acronym of the Indonesian words for ethnic group, religion, race and class—which could fuel controversies among the population.

The most effective media control measure was the implementation of publication permit systems such as SIT and SIUPP. If any article deemed 'not in line with Pancasila' by the government was published, the publication was suspended or forced to discontinue. Nevertheless, that deemed 'not in line with Pancasila' was left to the judgment of the authorities and the criteria involved were arbitrary and unpredictable. In addition, the authority's warnings though silent phone calls to media operators also exerted a substantial effect. As a result of these government controls, the media started to increasingly practice self-censorship of their news stories (Kingsbury 2002: 127–128).

Another way of regulating the media was the entrance of influential figures in the regime, especially members of the Suharto family, into the media business. Companies owned by government-backed heavyweights acquired high-profile newspapers and magazines that had been forced by the government to discontinue and republished their periodicals with a new design. Furthermore, with the onset of private television broadcasting in the late 1980s, Suharto's eldest daughter established her own television station and his second son followed suit (Kingsbury 2002: 129–130). Through these various means, the Suharto regime ensured most of the press was submissive to the government.

Changes in the use of violence

In the 1970s, although the government conducted political manipulations against opposition parties and apprehended and detained student activists and politicians, oppression through more cruel forms of violence—more specifically, murder—was hardly observed. This is because Suharto did not recognize that these opposition movements could possibly threaten his position. However, the spread of protest movements against the reelection of Suharto by students as well as the expression of strong objections against both the enforcement of Pancasila and Suharto's reelection by Islamic forces and retired military officers over the period from the end of the 1970s to the beginning of the 1980s forced Suharto to acknowledge that these movements could directly pose a threat to him and he began adopting a more stringent approach to suppress them.

Suharto delivered a speech in Pekanbaru, a central Sumatran town, and sent a forthright warning to the opposition forces. He declared that if there were 'any movement within the DPR to make changes to Pancasila and the 1945 Constitution', he would stop it even if he had to kidnap the members of the DPR who were involved (Jenkins 1984: 157–158). By 'any movement desiring to change Pancasila and the Constitution of 1945', he implicated the opposition against Suharto himself as a guardian of Pancasila and the Constitution of 1945. Having sacralized Pancasila, Suharto referred to his adversaries as 'forces trying to make changes to Pancasila and the Constitution of 1945' and declared that he would take a firm stance against such forces—even if that meant resorting to unlawful means.

This speech was the first time Suharto had issued a warning of this kind and came at a time when the government's social governance started to become more violent. This change in stance was clearly manifest in the mysterious shootings referred to as the *Petrus* incident of 1982–1983 and the *Tanjung Priok* incident of 1984.

The mysterious shootings was an incident in which a large number of petty criminals (*preman*) were murdered in a series of attacks by unidentified assailants in Jakarta and three provinces of Java from November 1982 through the first half of 1983. While the government announced the number of victims as over 300, foreign media reported it was actually somewhere between 3,000 and 4,000. It is now generally accepted that this incident was the work of the security agency the government employed to get rid of *preman* who were used by the government for political manipulation in the 1970s and the beginning of 1980 (*Tempo* Aug. 5, 2012: 44–45). It is also implied in Suharto's autobiography that was published in 1989 that he gave the order himself (Dwipayana and Ramadhan 1989: 389–390). Nonetheless, at that time, despite a vague awareness that state power was somehow involved, the whole nation was terrorized by the uncanny incident where the perpetrator and motive remained a mystery. Dead bodies were found lying in the streets when morning broke and such a scene, to many people, brought back memories of the massacre of communists following the September 30th Affair[9]. The incident itself lasted for only a short while but the terrorizing impact felt by the people was significant.

The *Tanjung Priok* incident was a massacre in which the Armed Forces opened fire in an area of Tanjung Priok near the Port of Jakarta in September 1984. While the bill for the five political laws including the designation of Pancasila as the sole state principle, which Islamic forces opposed at that time, was under deliberation in the DPR, four civilians were arrested and detained for protesting against the security officer who had taken down banners protesting against the bill nearby a local mosque. Amir Biki, who had been preaching against the arrest at the mosque, mobilized a mass demonstration in front of a local police station demanding the release of the four. In response, a security unit arrived and opened fire, killing numerous residents including Biki.

These two incidents that took place in the early 1980s signify the nature of the use of violence by the Suharto regime. One factor was the lack of respect for the rule of law. This was notably observable in Suharto himself. In regards to the mysterious shootings, Suharto wrote in his autobiography that 'those who were killed were *preman* and it was simply an execution of punishment for criminals. Those who got shot were those who resisted the authority' (Dwipayana and Ramadhan 1989: 389–390). However, even if the victims were criminals as Suharto argued, 'punishment' with no legal justification is merely the arbitrary use of violence by a man in power. Likewise, as for the *Tanjung Priok* incident, an investigation was only carried out for the sake of formality let alone implementation of disciplinary action against those security officers who were involved in the killings. Suharto went further than just conniving with killers and in fact actively employed violent means to repel the Islamic forces to facilitate the enactment of the bill of the five political laws.

Another point worth discussing is that both incidents were high-handed mass killings of non-elites, that is, ordinary people. In contrast to most dictators of personal rule who generally maintained strict control over political elites regardless of whether they were on the side of the regime or opposition, Suharto displayed a relatively benign attitude toward opposition elites such as opposition party politicians, retired military generals and Islamic leaders; violent means such as torture, execution and murder were rarely employed. Instead, ordinary people became the target of such relentless torment. The victims of the mysterious shootings were petty gang members. The victims in the *Tanjung Priok* incident were a *dai* (Islamic preacher) and his supporters. Amir Biki certainly did criticize the government, but he was neither especially radical nor influential enough to arouse public opinion across the wider Indonesian society. The only reason that he and his supporters were targeted in the massacre was to warn the opposition, to keep them at bay while the bill of the five political laws was being deliberated in the DPR.

This discrimination between elites and non-elites concerning the use of violence was particularly evident in the Marsinah incident of 1995 as well as the attack on the headquarters of the Indonesian Democratic Party (PDI) in 1996. In the former incident, Marsinah, who simply demanded a wage increase as one of the members of a labor union in a midsize firm in East Java, was brutally murdered. Her murder was committed by the Armed Forces as a warning to the labor movement, which had been escalating its activities since the early 1990s. By contrast, Mochtar Pakpahan, a leader of an independent labor union who was arrested for instigating the movement, received only a prison term.

The latter incident took place on July 27, 1996. The PDI supporters who backed Megawati Sukarnoputri, eldest daughter of President Sukarno, were holed up in the party headquarters, which was attacked by unidentified armed men. This bloodshed resulted in a considerable number of victims and missing persons. However, Megawati herself was only interrogated by the police and was not even taken into custody. These incidents provide a vivid portrayal of the way violence was used by the Suharto regime—extremely ruthless violence was meted out against ordinary people while elites were dealt with leniently.

Conciliation: presidential assistance and charitable foundations

The use of violence was not the only means Suharto employed to stabilize his rule. He believed that passing on gains from development and economic growth to the nation, along with the provision of political and economic patronage to elites loyal to him, would contribute to assuring the legitimacy of his regime. Suharto, upon seizing power, immediately replaced the national policy of 'revolution' championed by the former president Sukarno with 'development'. In addition to wide ranging development projects such as public works and industrial development programs funded domestically and internationally, goods and financial aid in a variety of forms were also distributed to the nation. Suharto was given the title 'Father of Development' (*Bapak Pembangunan*) by the parliament. His development projects and the pork-barrel goods and funds he distributed were often prefixed with the word 'presidential'. This prefix signified 'gifts' from the father of the country to the nation. Assistance provided to Golkar and opposition parties also played a role as a means to make them financially dependent on Suharto and keep them under control. The following sections will elaborate on the two forms of assistance employed by Suharto: presidential assistance known as *banpres* and assistance from Suharto's foundations known as *yayasan*.

Presidential assistance
'Presidential assistance' refers to funds and goods distributed to the nation under President Suharto's name. It started in the 1970s and was expanded in the 1980s. Although the precise figure cannot be determined as such assistance was highly nontransparent in nature, in 1988 it was reported that 187 trillion rupiah, equivalent to 110.9 billion US dollars at that time, was spent on 2,232 projects during the period of the Fourth Five-Year Plan (1983–1988)[10].

Funds for presidential assistance were sourced from granting exclusive rights to import cloves and logging permits to crony companies and having some of the profits generated from such concessions returned. Suharto allegedly gave exclusive rights to import cloves to his paternal half-brother Probosutedjo's company Mercubuana and Liem Sioe Lion's company Mega and received 246 billion rupiah in return (Dwipayana and Ramadhan 1989: 290). The capital collected in this way was managed and its allocation among projects was determined by the Secretary for Operational Control of Development (Setdalopbang), established under the State Secretariat. Although the Setdalopbang was placed within the State Secretariat in terms of its organizational structure, its director was able to contact the President directly, without mediation from the Chief State Secretary who was his immediate superior (Pangaribuan 1995: 31). This leads to the assumption that the President's opinions were largely reflected in project plans and fund allocation.

It appears that the beneficiaries and types of presidential assistance were extensive and that funds were allocated flexibly according to societal demand. Presidential assistance can be categorized into the following five principal areas: educational aid, religious aid, industrial development, aid for political and social groups and disaster recovery and public welfare assistance[11].

Educational aid included financial support for orphanages, scholarships to children of low-income families and subsidies for construction or repair costs for university laboratories, student centers and libraries.

Religious aid was predominantly granted to Islamic communities, such as for construction or repair costs for educational facilities including mosques, *pesantren* and Islamic schools known as *madrasa*, as well as Islamic orphanages and hospitals, in addition to alms-giving for the poor (*zakat*) and livestock for the Islamic festival of sacrifice (*Idul Adha*). Although small in proportion, non-Muslim religions such as Christians and Balinese Hindus also received some aid. The figure for the fiscal year 1986–1987 shows that Islamic-related aid amounted to 45,118,660,000 rupiah, accounting for ninety-six percent of the total amount of presidential assistance granted to religious purposes valued at 46,811,520,000 rupiah. The Christian- and Balinese Hindu-related spending totaled 1,310,310,000 rupiah and 382,550,000 rupiah respectively (Bantuan Pembangunan 1987?: 2).

Under presidential assistance allocated for industrial development, which mainly focused on agriculture and livestock businesses, cattle needed for farming, palm seeds, seedlings and water pumps were provided through regional governments such as those of the province and regency. These grants were often made in tandem with national policies such as transmigration and family planning programs. From the 1970s, the government actively encouraged migration from densely populated Java and Madura to sparsely populated Sumatra, Kalimantan and regions such as Irian Jaya and provided cows, palm seeds and seedlings to families that agreed to migrate under this transmigration program called *transmigrasi*. Couples who practiced the family planning program also received similar rewards for cooperating with government policies. For instance, 1,000 head of cattle, two small trucks and 2,000 seedlings were given to migrants to the Natuna Islands in 1984 (*Mimbar Kekaryaan ABRI* June 1984: 63). A total of one million seedlings were given to 37,000 couples in 1984 and 1,947,000 seedlings to 785,000 couples in 1986 (*Mimbar Kekaryaan ABRI* July 1984: 70; Nov. 1986: 61).

Disaster recovery and public welfare assistance included emergency aid in the form of food such as rice and organizing transportation means to carry injured people and relief supplies such as ambulances and trucks to areas affected by natural disasters including but not limited to earthquakes, floods and landslides.

Lastly, there was presidential assistance for political and social groups. In regards to political organizations and parties, the ruling party Golkar was not the only beneficiary of presidential assistance. The two opposition parties, the PPP and PDI, also received funding for activities and motor vehicles under the banner of presidential assistance. For example, in 1975, seventy-four sedans imported by a company called Indokarya were supplied to Golkar, the two opposition parties and other social groups (*Mimbar Kekaryaan ABRI* Jan. and Feb. 1975: 11). Likewise, in February 1987, 25 million rupiah was allocated to Golkar and the two opposition parties as presidential assistance to cover costs for the election that took place in April of that year (*Ajia Dōkō Nenpō* 1988: 438). In regards to social groups, the government-founded youth organization KNPI, agricultural organization HKTI, Golkar-controlled youth organization AMPI and Islamic organization Muhammadiyah were among those provided with cars and motorcycles under the name of presidential assistance.

Charitable foundations

Foundations were originally established by Suharto as a means of self-funding to compensate for budget deficits of the Central Java Regional Military Command of which he was in command at the time. After assuming the presidency, he leveraged foundations and augmented his family businesses with a massive amount of funds gathered from a wide range of Chinese-Indonesian conglomerates, public servants and state-run businesses. Nevertheless, the original purpose of these foundations was to provide welfare programs for the public and philanthropic programs for the poor and disaster-affected people, and some of the pooled funds were in fact used for such programs. However, similarly to presidential assistance, documentation that describes financial flow in his foundations such as income and expenditure statements and funds allocation reports has not been made publically available.

Senior government officials close to Suharto and his family members were responsible for managing the treasuries of the foundations. For example, the Deputy Director of the Dharmais Foundation was Bustanil Arifin, who also held the post of Chair of the Bulog (National Food Logistics Agency), and the executive officer of the Dakab Foundation was Zahid Husein, also the Director of the Setdalopbang under the State Secretariat (Murai et al. 1999: 60; Pangaribuan 1995: 32). Both were assigned to treasury management roles as they were highly trusted by Suharto. Zahid Husein was particularly trusted and was tasked with the management of funds for both presidential assistance and the Dakab Foundation. He was able to have direct consultations with Suharto about the management and allocation of funds without having his immediate superior, the Chief State Secretary Sudharmono, as an intermediary. Similarly, Suharto's first son Sigit and first daughter Tutut's husband Indra Lukmana acted as executive members of the Dharmais Foundation and Suharto's second son Bambang Trihatmodjo and third son Tommy served as executive members of the Dakab Foundation (Dwipayana and Ramadhan 1989: 293).

Of the thirteen foundations directed by Suharto, the six largest were the Supersemar Foundation, Dharmais Foundation, Amal Bakti Muslim Pancasila Foundation, Dakab Foundation, Gotong Royong Foundation and Damandiri Foundation.

The Supersemar Foundation was established in 1974 for the purpose of assisting the children of poor families with schooling needs, especially through the provision of scholarships for university students (Abdulgani-KNAPP 2007: 290–295). According to Suharto, the Supersemar Foundation's asset value was 62.9 billion rupiah (Dwipayana and Ramadhan 1989: 288), and it granted scholarships to high-achieving students of middle schools, high schools and universities who otherwise would not have been able to attend higher education as well as sports players who were considered to have potential. According to the records, 3,000 university students received scholarship from the Supersemar Foundation in 1975 and the number rose to 6,000 in 1985 (Dwipayana and Ramadhan 1989: 283–285; Abdulgani-KNAPP 2007: 293)[12]. The total amount of scholarship funding provided by the Supersemar Foundation in the fiscal year 1986–1987 was 4,074,400,000 rupiah (Bantuan Pembangunan 1987?: 2).

The Dharmais Foundation was established in 1975 with the objective of providing assistance for orphans and disabled people (Abdulgani-KNAPP 2007: 295–298). Its budget for the fiscal year 1985–1986 was five billion rupiah and its asset value for the same period was 60.8 billion rupiah (Dwipayana and Ramadhan 1989: 287). Over the period from 1967 to 2004, 474 billion rupiah was spent on assistance for the poor (Abdulgani-KNAPP 2007: 298).

The Amal Bakti Muslim Pancasila Foundation was created in 1982 with the objective of providing aid for Muslim communities in the form of mosque construction and repair and the payment of wages to *dai* (Islamic preachers) (Abdulgani-KNAPP 2007: 304). The creation of this foundation coincided with the intensive conflict between the government and the Islamic forces over the issue of whether Pancasila should be the sole state principle. Retired Army Lieutenant General Alamsjah Ratu Perwiranegara, who was the Minister of Religious Affairs at that time, requested the President establish this foundation (Parikesit and Sempurnadjaja 1995: 271–272). Suharto granted permission accordingly in order to appease the Islamic forces. He then proposed that public servants and military officers of the Armed Forces donate some of their income to the foundation based on the spirit of *zakat*, which is one of the religious obligations under Islam (Abdulgani-KNAPP 2007: 306). These donations amounted to 15,414,180,000 rupiah in the fiscal year 1986–1987 (Bantuan Pembangunan 1987?: 2), and the asset value of the foundation in the mid-1990s was 170 billion rupiah. In the first ten years of its establishment, 800 mosques were built and 4,000 *dai* received their wages with financial assistance granted by this foundation (Parikesit and Sempurnadjaja 1995: 273).

The Dakab Foundation was established in 1985 with the principle aim of providing financial assistance to Golkar. Its asset value in 1985 was forty-three billion rupiah and it supplied a total of 200 million rupiah to Golkar and its local branches every month (Dwipayana and Ramadhan 1989: 288–290). The source of funds was donations from individuals and companies (Abdulgani-KNAPP 2007: 310)[13].

The Gotong Royong Foundation was created in 1986 with the aim of providing support for victims of natural disasters, in response to a strong request made by Suharto's wife Tien. While a wide range of businesses made donations at the time of its establishment, President Suharto himself also contributed 17.5

billion rupiah. Over the period from its establishment to October 1998, 34 billion rupiah was spent on disaster recovery in 454 disasters in 714 locations (Abdulgani-KNAPP 2007: 312–315).

The Damandiri Foundation was created in 1996 with the objective of providing financial assistance to lower-income households in rural areas to help them start up their own businesses. Suharto issued a presidential decree mandating individuals and corporate bodies earning an annual net income of over 100 million rupiah donate two percent of their income to this foundation. Chairpersons of huge conglomerates such as Liem Sioe Lion also joined the list of directors of this foundation. By 2005, over 830 households were granted loans (Abdulgani-KNAPP 2007: 315–321).

This chapter illustrated how the Suharto regime, as an example of co-opting-type personal rule, ran the country based on political and economic patronage and violent oppression. In the 1970s, political patronage was preferentially distributed to the Armed Forces, which constituted Suharto's support base and at the same time acted as his partner in enforcing his authority. In regards to the distribution of economic patronage, Chinese-Indonesian entrepreneurs who had a close relationship with Suharto benefited from favorable treatment. However, this kind of bias in patronage distribution gave rise to widespread dissatisfaction in society, resulting in constant criticisms of the government as well as an outcry of objections. From the 1980s, Suharto adopted a policy to conciliate the public by extending the range of patronage distribution while oppressing the objections through a more blatant use of violence. Suharto needed a patronage distribution channel to successfully appease social elites who were critical of the government. This set the stage for Golkar to come to the fore and play an important role in and after the 1980s. However, Golkar neither had social underpinning nor was adequately integrated as an organization in the 1970s. The next chapter will provide a portrait of Golkar, particularly focusing on its establishment and stagnation in the 1970s.

3
Golkar in the 1970s: Fumbling Its Way

This chapter will discuss how Golkar was established and structured to become a ruling party under the Suharto regime. Golkar originated from a large number of organizations created by the Armed Forces during the Sukarno era. Suharto, upon assumption of the presidential office, amalgamated these organizations to form a single body called 'Golkar' to compete with existing political parties in the upcoming election. However, throughout the 1970s, Golkar lacked organizational unity and suffered from a talent shortage. This chapter will give an account of the creation of Golkar by the government and describe its period of stagnation, which lasted until the beginning of the 1980s.

The establishment of Golkar

The precursor of Golkar
The name 'Golkar' was coined from the first letters of the words '*golongan karya*', meaning 'functional groups'. 'Functional groups' was a concept developed by President Sukarno in the late 1950s, driven by the objective of establishing a more representational system of governance by sending representatives of functional groups such as farmers, labors, *ulama* and students into the parliaments to replace political parties, which had caused a great deal of political disruption under the parliamentary democracy (Reeve 1985: 116–118). This concept was in alignment with the stance of the Armed Forces, which was critical of the party system due to concerns about the growing hegemony of the Communist Party (PKI) (Reeve 1985: 120–121, 140). The Armed Forces planned to deter the expansion of the PKI by supporting Sukarno's concept of 'functional groups' (Reeve 1985: 143).

However, Sukarno gradually drifted away from the functional groups concept as he grew increasingly anxious about the burgeoning political influence of the Armed Forces and leaned more towards the PKI, which was rapidly enhancing its political power with significant mass mobilization capability. In the 1960s, Sukarno put forward the concept of 'NASAKOM', a term coined from the first letters of the Indonesian words *nasionalisme* (nationalism), *agama* (religion) and *kommunisme* (communism), and became dependent on support from political parties—namely the Indonesian National Party (PNI) which embodied nationalism,

Nahdlatul Ulama (NU) which embodied religion and the PKI which embodied communism. To the Armed Forces, this certainly did not mirror Sukarno's original goal of promoting more representational politics led by representatives of functional groups. Instead it was seen as a return to the party politics that Sukarno was supposed to be rejecting. The Armed Forces was given one of the core roles in Sukarno's 'Guided Democracy' system and thus generally supported him, but at the same time feared that he might deepen his connection with the PKI. Faced with the need to counter the PKI, the Armed Forces decided to implement Sukarno's functional groups concept themselves (Reeve 1985: 174).

The Armed Forces was entrusted with the operation of Western companies and agricultural land that Sukarno had confiscated under the banner of anti-neocolonialism and anti-imperialism during the period from the end of the 1950s to the early 1960s. The Armed Forces then created cooperatives and coordinating bodies on industrial relations for these companies, which they collectively called 'functional organizations' (*organisasi karya*) (Reeve 1985: 178). At the same time, they sent active military officers, as representatives of the Armed Forces group, into the Golongan Karya faction—appointed seats introduced for the first time in the Gotong-Rojong People's Representative Council (DPR-GR) summoned by President Sukarno in 1960. The Armed Forces attempted to justify the advance of active officers into the parliaments on the grounds that it reflected the President's functional groups concept. In other words, although Sukarno himself did not wish for an expansion of the military's political power per se, his functional groups concept led to such result.

On October 20, 1964, the Armed Forces established the Joint Secretariat of Functional Groups (hereinafter referred to as 'Sekber Golkar') by combining functional organizations with the ever-intensifying confrontation with the PKI in mind. Although the establishment of Sekber Golkar is conventionally regarded as the establishment of Golkar, Sekber Golkar at that time was merely a 'secretariat' located at the top of a large number of organizations, which were far from being united. Nevertheless, alarmed at the political movements of the Armed Forces, Sukarno tried to control Sekber Golkar by including left-leaning military officers and politicians close to him in the seven-member executive board of Sekber Golkar.

The Armed Forces seems to have been unclear as to what role Sekber Golkar would play or the way in which it would fight against the PKI at the time they created it. It was only after the Suharto regime seized power following the September 30th Affair that Sekber Golkar was finally given a clear role.

The 1971 election and the establishment of Golkar

The Suharto regime made Sekber Golkar run in and win an election and form a majority in the parliaments so that it could serve to underpin the regime, which lacked a support base outside the Armed Forces. However, reorganizing Sekber Golkar, which was no more than an assortment of diverse organizations at the time, into one body that would be capable of competing with other political parties posed a formidable challenge.

In November 1967, Sekber Golkar held the second national work conference (*mukernas*) and elected a new executive board. In this conference, Major General Sokowati of the Ministry of Defense and Security took over the position of chair of the board from pro-Sukarno Colonel Djuhartono, completely vanquishing all traces of Sukarno (Suryadinata 1989: 26). Nonetheless, the government was well aware that an organizational structure in which a small secretariat was placed at the head of over 200 organizations would definitely not lead to a successful election campaign against other parties (Suryadinata 1989: 27). Accordingly, a suggestion was made at the conference to consolidate these numerous organizations into several main organizational groups (KINOs), and the executive board was given authority to perform such restructuring. However, the leaders of the organizations resisted absorption by KINOs, fearing that their political bases would be lost, causing a pause in Golkar's restructuring process that lasted more than one year (Suryadinata 1989: 28).

Table 3.1 lists the members of the Central Executive Board (DPP) elected at the November 1967 conference. Active military officers occupied most of the core posts in the board, such as chair and vice-chairs as well as secretaries, and many were those who had held top positions in the functional organizations created by the Armed Forces during the Sukarno era.

The event of utmost importance for Sekber Golkar around that time was the reorganization of the DPR and MPR enforced by the government, which took place between February and March 1968. As a result of this reorganization, a great number of non-government-affiliated members who belonged to the Golongan Karya factions of the DPR and MPR were dismissed. The background for this is elaborated below.

Upon establishment of the DPR-GR in 1960, Sukarno created the Golongan Karya faction comprising appointed members representing functional groups and allowed military officers to hold seats. At the same time he arranged for party politicians to be included in the faction claiming that they were 'representing a functional group' so as to prevent the domination of the faction by the Armed Forces. For instance, some PNI members 'represented farmers' and other NU members 'represented *ulama*'. As a result, the Golongan Karya faction ended up including a host of party-affiliated members. In other words, the Golongan Karya faction was one for representatives of functional groups in name only. Ali Murtopo, who had been put in charge of political manipulation after Suharto's assumption of political power, tried to remove party-affiliated members as well

Table 3.1: Central Executive Board of Sekber Golkar (November 1967)

Chairman	Army Major General Sokowati (Ministry of Defense and Security)
Vice-Chair	Army Major General Djamin Gintings (GAKARI) Navy Brigadier General Soenardi Police Colonel Poerwoto Army Major General Mas Isman (KOSGORO) Army Colonel Mudjono (SOKSI) Air Force Major Suwarma Army Brigadier General R. H. Soegandhi (MKGR)
Secretary	Army Colonel Amino Gondohutomo (Organisasi Profesi)
Deputy Secretary	Sutomo Honggowongso
Accountant/Standing Committee Member	Mrs. Soedarsono (KORPRI)
Standing Committee Member/Committee Member	Radius Prawiro (Economic technocrat) Harjosudirdjo Army Brigadier General Soedharmono (Cabinet Secretariat) Harun Umar Mar'ie Muhammad (Economic technocrat) Marzuki Lubis
Committee Member	Tambunan Asrarudin Manuputty Rusli Junus Tasrin Mrs. Andres Sastrohusodo (GAKARI) Mrs. Maria Ulfah (GAKARI) Mrs. Soewito Husni Thamrin Naimun Aminuddin Damiri Nasution Mohammad Arifin Kuswondo (Ormas Hankam) Army Brigadier General Suradji Arikertawidjaja Kusumo Sujanto Muhammad Nuh Army Lieutenant Colonel Sutjipto (Ormas Hankam) Anwar Rasjid (Ormas Hankam) Iskandar Army Lieutenant Colonel Sampurno Dilapanga Sukijat Mrs. Tirtakusumah (GAKARI) Mrs. Rus Soh Sano

Source: Sekber Golkar (1968: 50) and Bangun (1994: 293).

as members critical of the government from the Golongan Karya faction as part of a scheme to transform it to one more inclined towards the government. In accordance with Murtopo's vision, the government henceforth dismissed a great number of members from the Golongan Karya faction and instead gave those who were members of the DPP of Sekber Golkar as listed in Table 3.1 parliamentary positions in the course of parliamentary restructuring between February and March 1968 (Masuhara 2004: 12–14, 21).

At that time, the 'Golongan Karya faction' (fraksi Golongan Karya) was renamed the 'Development Functional faction' (fraksi Karya Pembangunan, hereinafter referred to as the 'Golkar faction'). This parliamentary reorganization caused the DPP of Sekber Golkar and the Golkar faction of the DPR which had been existing as separate entities to become one. Meanwhile, a group of Armed Forces-affiliated members, who used to be part of the Golongan Karya faction, formed a new independent faction that became known as the 'Armed Forces faction' (fraksi ABRI). In other words, two pro-government factions, namely the Golkar and Armed Forces factions, resulted from the parliamentary reorganization. This gave rise to a situation where the number of members of the two pro-government factions became comparable to that of party factions in the DPR, ahead of the 1971 election[1].

Still, to ensure that the government factions would have a stable majority, Sekber Golkar's victory in the general election needed to be assured. This required unifying Sekber Golkar, which was no more than an incoherent amalgamation of a large number of organizations, into one integrated body.

The prolonged deliberations on the bill on a new electoral law was pushing back the election date, with persistent disagreement and continuous discussion between the party side advocating for the existing proportional representation system and the government side proposing the introduction of the single-seat constituency system. Eventually, both sides agreed on a compromise deal in which the government side would relinquish the single-seat constituency system in exchange for having appointed seats secured in the DPR, and the electoral law was finally passed in December 1969 (Notosusanto 1985: 42–62). In the meantime, the government was continuing its efforts to persuade the leaders of the organizations constituting Sekber Golkar to merge into KINOs. However, the gap between these organizations, which wished to field their own candidates, and the government, which wanted a consensus candidate representing Sekber Golkar, could not be bridged. In the end, Sekber Golkar's Chair Sokowati essentially had to force through the absorption into KINOs in July 1969, integrating about 200 organizations into seven KINOs; namely, KOSGORO[2], SOKSI[3], MKGR[4], GAKARI[5], Ormas Hankam[6], Karya Profesi[7] and Karya Pembangunan[8] (Suryadinata 1989: 29–30). Of these seven KINOs,

KOSGORO, SOKSI and MKGR were placed at the core and collectively called 'Trikarya'. Six of the seven KINO leaders were military officers.

Various projections were made in Sekber Golkar's internal meeting prior to the election, with some experts suggesting Golkar would win sixteen percent of the vote and others saying twenty-five or thirty-five percent (Sekber Golkar 1970). However, come election day, they managed to garner a staggering 62.8 percent of the vote, far surpassing the predictions. This was possible because of the following four actors which played major roles in leading Sekber Golkar to victory: Sekber Golkar's DPP consisting of representatives of the KINOs, the Ministry of Defense and Security, Ministry of Home Affairs and Sekber Golkar's General Election Controlling Body (BAPILU).

One organization that made a huge contribution to Golkar's win in the 1971 election was the Ministry of Home Affairs. Minister of Home Affairs Amirmachmud prohibited ministry employees from joining or becoming supporters of a political party, while fully utilizing the Corps of Officials of the Ministry of Home Affairs (Kokarmendagri) to ensure that a notice instructing employees to vote for Golkar was circulated to each and every person in the ministry. As a result, the PNI whose members included many public servants lost a great part of its supporters and thus votes in the election. Moreover, Amirmachmud issued the Regulation of the Ministry of Home Affairs No.12, (Permen 12), stipulating that all functional group representatives in the regional representative councils (DPRD) who belonged to a political party must leave the party and anyone who refused to do so must resign from the councils (Amirmachmud 1987: 340–342). This regulation forced many party-affiliated members who held their seats in the DPRD as a functional group representative to choose whether to secede from the party or relinquish their seats in the DPRD, causing many political parties to lose DPRD members. Furthermore, when it came to screening election candidates, Amirmachmud implemented a strict screening system abusing his authority as the Minister of Home Affairs—for example, he refused to authorize the candidacy of many politicians belonging to Islamic political parties based on vague criteria such as 'the candidate did not endorse Pancasila and the Constitution of 1945'.

As for the Ministry of Defense and Security, it not only utilized the Armed Forces network encompassing regional areas to establish Golkar's local branches but also played the role of a field operation unit monitoring and obstructing the election campaigns of other political parties.

Similarly, led by Ali Murtopo, BAPILU played a significant role in ensuring Sekber Golkar's victory in the election. Most BAPILU members were recruited through Murtopo's personal connections, including student movement leaders such as Jusuf Wanandi, Cosmas Batubara and David Napitupulu, and young intellectuals such as Murdopo, Jacob Tobing and Midian Sirait. The student movement leaders and young intellectuals who joined BAPILU were those who voiced anti-communist and anti-Sukarno sentiment in the wake of the September 30th Affair and strongly supported the Armed Force's purge of the PKI. Also, they distanced themselves from existing political parties and were seeking political reform to introduce the single-seat constituency system and reduce the number of parties. However, much to their disappointment, the government landed on a compromise deal with the political parties to maintain the current proportional representation system, abandoning their proposal to introduce the new system. As a result, student leaders and young intellectuals shifted their focus towards helping Sekber Golkar win the election to achieve political realignment and signed up for BAPILU under Ali Murtopo. They assisted Sekber Golkar in the areas of election campaigns and public relations and also demonstrated their capacity to gain support in universities (Ramadhan and Sriwibawa 1999: 177–180).

On one hand, the Ministry of Home Affairs, Ministry of Defense and Security, BAPILU and KINOs all contributed to Sekber Golkar's victory in the election, but on the other hand, each group tried to enter their own representative into the proportional representative list. Arrangements among the four groups in relation to the candidate lists of electoral districts did not always go smoothly and in some cases caused confrontation regarding who should be at the top of the list (Pradjamanggala 2000: 216–217). Among the four groups, the Ministry of Home Affairs had the edge in this competition. Of the 236 Sekber Golkar candidates elected in 1971, eighty-eight were public servants, accounting for almost forty percent (37.3 percent). Furthermore, seventy-five of the eighty-eight were regional public servants who had held the office of the head of a regional government such as a regent or governor (Masuhara 2005: 46–47). This implies that Minister of Home Affairs Amirmachmud had substantial influence over the candidate list creation process. On the contrary, there were relatively few military personnel among the successful candidates. One can assume that this was because the Armed Forces did not place much importance on having active military officers included in Sekber Golkar's candidate list, as seventy-five appointed seats were secured for the ABRI faction in the DPR anyway according to the law on general election of 1969.

After the general election of July 1971, Sekber Golkar made a fresh start under the new name 'Golkar'. Table 3.2 lists the members of the Central Executive Board assigned at that time. While Army Major General Sokowati remained as chairman, two personnel from the Ministry of Defense and Security including Army Major General Amir Murtono were newly assigned to the board as vice-chairs, whereas two personnel from the Ministry of Home Affairs also joined the

Table 3.2: Central Executive Board of Golkar at its establishment (July 1971–September 1973)

Chairman	Army Major General Sokowati (Ministry of Defense and Security)
Vice-Chair	Army Major General Amir Moertono (Ministry of Defense and Security)
Committee member	Army Colonel Moedjono (SOKSI) Malikus Suparto (Ministry of Home Affairs) Soemiskoem (Murtopo group) Cosmas Batubara (Murtopo group) David Napitupulu (Murtopo group)
Secretary-General	Army Major General Sapardjo (Murtopo group)
Deputy Secretary-General	Moerdopo (Murtopo group) Army Major General Rahardjo Prodjopradoto (Ministry of Home Affairs) Jusuf Wanandi (Murtopo group)

Source: Sekber Golkar (1968: 50) and Bangun (1994: 293).

board, increasing the influence of both ministries. Meanwhile, a great number of Murtopo's recruits joined the board from the BAPILU that was recognized for its achievement in leading Golkar to the election victory, enhancing the presence of the Murtopo group as well. As a consequence, the number of members of former KINOs such as KOSGORO, SOKSI and MKGR decreased.

Another change was that the Advisory Board (Dewan Pembina), was established as an advisory body to the DPP. Its members comprised ministers, military officers and representatives of the former KINOs (Suryadinata 1989: 167; *Ajia Dōkō Nenpō* 1970: 463).

A challenge to reinforce Golkar

Golkar as a tool to depoliticize the public

While the unexpected landslide victory over existing political parties gave Golkar a reputation as a vote-gathering machine, there was a leadership contest within Golkar between the four groups, namely the former KINO group, Ministry of Defense and Security group, Ministry of Home Affairs group and Murtopo group (former BAPILU group). The representatives of all of these groups were military personnel. There is no sign that indicates that President Suharto made any intervention in this conflict. Arguably, he may have preferred, as long as

Golkar could win elections, a certain degree of fragmentation preventing one particular group from gaining predominant power within Golkar.

Table 3.3 shows the structure of the Central Executive Board selected in the first Golkar national congress (Munas), held in September 1973. Army Major General Amir Moertono from the Ministry of Defense and Security group filled the chair position and the remaining posts were shared amongst the former KINO group, Ministry of Home Affairs group and Murtopo group. At this time, President Suharto assumed the position of chair of the Advisory Board in the central office for the first time, redefining the organizational structure in which the advisory boards were placed above and given a supervisory role over executive boards in the central office as well as local branches.

Of the four groups, the Murtopo group had the clearest vision of the direction Golkar should take as an organization. This group aimed to steer Golkar such that it would not be based on a specific ideology or religion but a comprehensive principle, Pancasila. Murtopo and the young intellectuals around him believed that it was important to bar the public from directly engaging in political and party activities while removing religious and ideological biases from politics in order to drive the public away from politics and make them focus on the development policy that the government was promoting. Behind this belief was their firm criticism of the ideology-driven politics of the Sukarno era. Sukarno's political approach, which mobilized the public toward politics with ideology and religion, ultimately gave rise to the confrontation between pro- and anti-communist forces. Murtopo made the following criticism in his 'Floating Mass' argument.

> Political parties formed a large number of affiliated organizations based on their ideology and tried to capture the power of the masses. These political and ideological interests of political parties victimized the public, especially farmers. As ideological confrontation between political parties interfered with the public, their everyday interests, that is, what they needed physically and mentally, were all sacrificed...this is precisely why political activities in rural areas must be restricted to the minimum. (Murtopo 1973: 95–96)

Murtopo's view gained support from the young civilian intellectuals around him. Midian Sirait, who was working within Golkar and was in the close circle around Murtopo in the early 1970s, was one of those who sympathized with Murtopo's view. He made the following argument on the 'Old Order' (*Orde Lama*) period, which refers to the time before Suharto's 'New Order' (*Orde Baru*).

> All labor unions, take a fishermen's union for example, were linked with political party activities at all levels from the central region to village communities and

Table 3.3: Central Executive Board of Golkar (1973–1978)

Chairman	Army Major General Amir Moertono (Ministry of Defense and Security)
Vice-Chair	Martono (KOSGORO)
First Deputy Vice-Chair	Mrs. Adam Malik (GAKARI)
Second Deputy Vice-Chair	Army Brigadier General A. E. Manihuruk (Ministry of Home Affairs)
Secretary-General	Army Major General Sapardjo (Murtopo group)
Accountant	Moerdopo (Murtopo group)
Secretary of General Affairs and Planning	Jusuf Wanandi (Murtopo group)
Secretary of Organization and Education	Cosmas Batubara (Murtopo group)
Secretary of Public Services	Army Major General Rahardjo Prodjopradoto (Ministry of Home Affairs)
Secretary of Labor	Sukijat
Secretary of Entrepreneurship	Oetojo Oesman (SOKSI)
Secretary of Cooperatives	Sulaeman Wirahadisurya
Secretary of Agriculture and Fishery	Rahman Tolleng (Murtopo group)
Secretary of Religion, Belief in the One and Only God and Social Culture	Pitut Soeharto (Murtopo group)
Secretary of Youth and Students	David Napitupulu (Murtopo group)
Secretary of Women	Mrs. Soedarsono (KORPRI)
Secretary of Intellectuals	Midian Sirait (Murtopo group)

Source: Bangun (1994: 295).

there was no independent labor union as such. Every social organization was controlled by a political party, whether it be a youth group, teachers' or farmers' association. The public was entirely affected by political tension generated through inter-party confrontations. As a consequence the public could not lead a normal, stable life but was constantly swayed by conflicts between parties. (Ramadhan and Sriwibawa 1999: 230)

As argued by Murtopo and Sirait, during the Sukarno era, an array of political parties were formed on the basis of various ideologies such as nationalism, communism and socialism as well as religions such as Islam, Catholicism and Protestantism and these parties clashed with one another on an everyday basis. Each political party was affiliated with associations such as those of youth, students, women, labor, farmers, fishermen and teachers. The public, regardless of whether they were living in urban or rural areas, was compelled to join or get involved in one way or another with one of the parties or affiliated organizations. Therefore, inter-party conflicts that erupted at the center of politics were propagated to even very rural areas through the networks of the parties and affiliated organizations. For example, an intensification of the conflict between the PKI and Islamic parties in the center would spark confrontation between people at the lowest levels of both parties—for example, erupting at university campuses and village offices. When a group of farmers backed by the PKI started to occupy land in villages, hostility between the parties in the center increased. The mass killing of PKI members and their sympathizers that occurred after the September 30th Affair was the result of not only the oppression of the Communist Party by the Armed Forces but also political confrontation involving the entire society.

Many Armed Forces officers and intellectuals who contributed to the oustering of President Sukarno after the September 30th Affair and advocated for political reform, particularly the limitation of political activities, believed that Sukarno's political approach that was based on competition between political parties and mass mobilization caused disunity in the nation and resulted in disaster. For this reason, they tried to introduce a political system whereby conflict and competition were kept to a minimum. In doing so, they adopted a high-handed approach based on the conviction that the Armed Forces, which was regarded as the only power not driven by ideology or religion, was the only force that could lead politics while containing party politics which had brought about ideological and religious confrontation and divided the nation. Furthermore, Pancasila, a comprehensive principle not driven by a specific ideology, was the perfect concept that the government could employ in its efforts to remove religious and ideological influences from politics.

Ali Murtopo, who put forward the idea of eliminating political parties' influence from politics as much as possible, possessed a great deal of political power in the early 1970s as the President's most influential personal assistant who undertook special missions including political manipulation. Under his strong influence, the government implemented a restriction regarding political activities. Although day-to-day political activities were allowed only in second-level regions and above, such as regencies and cities, Golkar and other political parties were banned from engaging in any political activities in lower-level regions such as villages. Having enforced this measure, the government also merged the nine political parties except Golkar into two parties, namely the United Development Party (PPP) and Indonesian Democratic Party (PDI) and prohibited the formation of other parties in 1973.

Murtopo saw Golkar as a potential tool to transform the party-centered political system and decided to tackle the issue of the organizational restructuring of Golkar now that the 1971 election was over. Golkar was able to win the 1971 election because of—and only because of—the full support it received from the Ministry of Home Affairs and Armed Forces. From an organizational point of view, Golkar was merely an assortment of diverse organizations. Murtopo, nonetheless, indicated that he believed Golkar could become an instrument to capture the political will of the public.

> The role of Golkar as part of Indonesia's political mechanism is to create and nurture occupational awareness among the nation through the establishment of occupational organizations, that is, organizations that have a function to directly engage in developmental issues. Golkar must gain an understanding of the will and interests of these occupational and functional groups at the national level. (Murtopo 1974: 84)

The organizations created by the Armed Forces over the period from the late 1950s to early 1960s as 'functional organizations' were not occupational or functional in a true sense, as exemplified by KOSGORO, a cooperative established for the purpose of providing welfare to military personnel, or SOKSI, an organization created to coordinate industrial relations in companies seized from the Netherlands and Britain. This drove Murtopo to establish a number of new occupational organizations more in line with his vision over the course of the period from 1973 to 1974. These included the following: the Indonesian Farmers' Harmony Association (HKTI), All-Indonesian Fishermen's Association (HNSI), All-Indonesian Labor Federation (FBSI, renamed SPSI in 1985) and the National Committee of Indonesian Youth (KNPI). These organizations became active support groups for Golkar and posts in their executive boards and advisory boards were given to Golkar executives.

Despite the establishment of the aforementioned occupational organizations, Golkar itself never transformed into a corporatist organization[9]. This is because the interests and demands of farmers and fishermen were hardly ever communicated successfully from these organizations to Golkar and in turn incorporated in government policies. At the same time, the various interests and demands raised by these farmers' and fishermen's associations were not coordinated in Golkar either. Golkar had neither an organizational base nor the human resources to carry out such function, not to mention the fact that they did not have a way to participate in the policy-making process despite being the ruling party. To summarize, although Golkar was born with the name 'functional group' and in fact owned a number of functional and occupational organizations under its umbrella, it never developed a corporatist nature.

Stagnant recruitment and internal conflict

Throughout the 1970s, Golkar continued to be largely backed by the Armed Forces and Ministry of Home Affairs. Throughout this period, Golkar lacked organizational integrity and had an inadequate pool of human resources to support it. Due to these factors, it recruited many of its executives and members of parliament from the Armed Forces and bureaucratic institutions and had to rely on support from the Armed Forces and Ministry of Home Affairs in elections.

For these reasons, in both central and local offices, the need for recruiting talent that could lead the organization, particularly young elites such as university students, was strongly voiced. For example, in Golkar's working meeting (*raker*), held in March 1972, the need for nurturing 'cadres' (*kadre*) of the younger generation—those in their twenties or thirties—was emphasized in the level A committee where the cultivation of Golkar's cadres was being discussed (DPP Golkar 1980). 'Cadres' referred to human resources that could take charge of Golkar and proactively initiate activities to secure support for the party in both central and regional areas. The importance of fostering cadres was again highlighted in the second Golkar national congress of 1978 (DPP Golkar 1978: 56–57). In spite of this, the cultivation of young talent that could lead the party organization made little progress during the 1970s. In and after the late 1960s, some university students and young intellectuals who helped found the Suharto regime gathered around Ali Murtopo and received positions as Golkar's executives, but few students and intellectuals were drawn into Golkar through their connections.

In the early 1970s, anti-Suharto student movements started to gain momentum and the government counteracted this by creating a youth organization called the KNPI (National Committee of Indonesian Youth). However, this organization fell short in its attempt to draw students to the regime side during the 1970s. The KNPI was established as a forum to facilitate dialogue and harmony between a few student and youth groups and succeeded in eliciting participation from the prominent student groups of the time such as the Islamic Students' Association (HMI), Protestant-led Indonesia Student Christian Movement (GMKI), Catholic-led Union of Catholic University Students (PMKRI) and the National Student

Movement of Indonesia (GMNI), closely linked to the PNI. The government assumed that participation from these student organizations in the KNPI would keep student movements at bay. However, at that time, HMI member students and non-HMI students were vying for leadership in the student councils of many universities, although the HMI often held dominant power in the councils. This conflict had created mutual distrust between student organizations and this distrust was carried into the KNPI. Abdul Gafur, who was one of the central executive board members at the time of the establishment of the KNPI, revealed that the KNPI was hardly operative for the first four years of its existence due to mutual distrust between the participating organizations (Gafur 1985: 135).

At the same time, students also strongly distrusted the government. The marriage law issue of 1973 and the Malari incident of 1974 further fuelled student-organized anti-government movements that came to a head in 1978 when students protested against Suharto's reelection. Under such circumstances where confrontation between the government and students was ongoing, it was virtually impossible for the KNPI to play the role of intermediary between the government and student organizations; it was therefore also unlikely that the KNPI would be able to recruit a large number of students to join Golkar, which was deemed a 'puppet' of the government.

The same situation was observed for other organizations. Documentation compiled by the Armed Forces at that time recorded how organizations formed under Golkar's umbrella were not functioning as expected. The HKTI, HNSI and FBSI were described as being too immature to nurture pro-government leaders from their membership of farmers, fishermen and laborers. It was also noted that an Islamic pro-government organization called the GUPPI (Islamic Education Reform Endeavour Movement), established by the government in the early 1970s, did not have adequate capability to recruit NU-affiliated Islamic leaders and politicians (Skarwil II 1974: 4–16).

The power struggle within Golkar was also intensifying. The former KINO group started to criticize the Ministry of Defense and Security group, which was expanding its influence within Golkar, regarding their attempts to curtail the former KINO group's power. In the national congress of 1978, an incident in which Suhardiman, a representative of SOKSI, which was part of the former KINO group, publicly denounced Golkar's Chairman Amir Murtono who belonged to the Ministry of Defense and Security group. The reason behind this was because Murtono had just established a youth organization called AMPI (Indonesian Young Generation for Renewal), an Islamic organization MDI (Council for Islamic Dakwah) and a women's organization HWK (Women's Functional Association) as Golkar's affiliated organizations without consulting them (Mochammad 1993: 177–179). Infuriated by this condemnation, Murtono

Table 3.4: Central Executive Board of Golkar (1978–1983)

Chairman	Army Major General Amir Moertono (Ministry of Defense and Security)
Vice-Chair	Army Brigadier General Soekardi (Ministry of Defense and Security/Veterans' Association)
First Deputy Vice-Chair	Army Major General R. H. Soegandhi (MKGR)
Second Deputy Vice-Chair	Army Brigadier General A. E. Manihuruk (Ministry of Home Affairs)
Third Deputy Vice-Chair	Mrs. Soedarsono (Ministry of Home Affairs)
Fourth Deputy Vice-Chair	K. H. Tarmoedji (Murtopo group/GUPPI)
Fifth Deputy Vice-Chair	Army Major General Sugiharto (Murtopo group)
Sixth Deputy Vice-Chair	David Napitupulu (Murtopo group)
Secretary-General	Soegianto
Deputy Secretary-General	Moerdopo (Murtopo group) Sukotriwarno S. U. Sidiki (MDI) Awan Karmawan Burhan (Student activist)
Accountant	Army Brigadier General Wahab Sjahrani (Ministry of Home Affairs/former Governor of East Kalimantan)
Deputy Accountant	Jusuf Wanandi (Murtopo group) Mrs. Darsojo (Ministry of Home Affairs)
Department of Research, Promotion and Cultivation of Cadre	Sudarmadji (PGRI) Istiwo
Department of Information and Mass Media	Harmoko (PWI) Mrs. Ida Ayu Utami Pidada (SOKSI/FBSI)
Department of Women's Roles	Kartini Tumbunan (Ministry of Education and Culture/ Perwani, or Indonesian Women's Union) Mrs. Legowo (Women's Army Association)
Department of Youth, Students and Intellectuals	Nugraha Besoes (Murtopo group/student activist) Hatta Mustafa (Murtopo group/University of Indonesia Student Council/BAKIN)
Department of Labor and Public Servants	Soekarno (FBSI) Sukijat
Department of Agriculture, Fishery and Craftwork	Soejoto Hardjosoetowo (KOSGORO) Wahju Djakaoethara
Department of Cooperatives, Entrepreneurship and Immigration	Imam Sudarwo (KOSGORO) Nurmadjid (SOKSI) Marconi Ismail (MKGR)
Department of Culture and Religion	Suparlan Surjopranoto R. O. Hudaya K. H. Qodratullah (Murtopo group/GUPPI)
Department of Facility Management	Sirman Widiatmo

Source: Bangun (1994: 296).

strenuously denied the former KINO group's view that the KINOs founded Golkar. This led to a decisive conflict between the Ministry of Defense and Security group and the former KINO group within Golkar.

With incessant internal conflict, the direction as to which group would take control of Golkar remained unclear. Table 3.4 shows the lineup of the Central Executive Board of Golkar selected in the second national congress of 1978. As with the previous board, the members mostly consisted of representatives of the Ministry of Defense and Security group, Ministry of Home Affairs group, former KINO group and Murtopo group, without any sign of a specific group holding a predominant position.

Nonetheless, Golkar's organizational structure became almost complete in this 1978 congress (refer to Figure 3.1). Both in the central and regional offices, an executive board to carry out the daily operations of the organization and an advisory board to supervise the executive board were established. President Suharto chaired the Advisory Board (Dewan Pembina) of the central office and the remaining members of the board were made up of senior officers of either the

Figure 3.1: Golkar's basic organizational structure

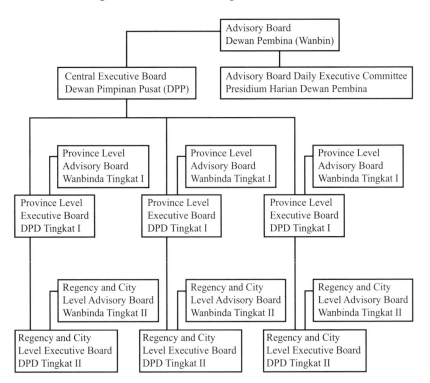

government or the military, such as ministers and the Commander of the Armed Forces. In this national congress of 1978, a new regulation, which gave the chair of the Advisory Board the authority to overturn decisions taken by the Central Executive Board and freeze any of its activities, was introduced. At the same time, the Daily Executive Committee (Presidium Harian) was newly established under the Advisory Board. It played a liaison role between the Advisory Board and the Central Executive Board and Suharto appointed its members from those of the Advisory Board. In short, Suharto enhanced the authority of the Advisory Board, which had been playing more of an advisory role, to allow them to have the power to control the Central Executive Board. Given the fact that the chair of the Advisory Board was Suharto, this move implied that Suharto, for the first time, indicated his intention to supervise the Central Executive Board himself. It has been pointed out that Suharto's decision to do so was motivated by his discontent over incoherence within the Central Executive Board (Ōgata 1995: 158–159).

Although Golkar won the election and acted as a vote-gathering machine, this did not lead to the stabilization of the Suharto regime. In fact, the latter half of the 1970s saw a further surge of anti-government movements led by students and Islamic forces. Besides, a growing number of retired military officers started to criticize Suharto's reelection at around the same time. The Islamic opposition party, the PPP staged walk-outs in the MPR session in protest against the 'Guidance on Understanding and Implementing Pancasila' (P 4) program in 1978 and strongly opposed the issue of the application of Pancasila as the sole state principle in the DPR in the early 1980s. The period from the latter half of the 1970s to the early 1980s was in fact when the Suharto regime experienced the most political instability since its establishment.

With the arrival of the 1980s, Suharto tried to change this political situation. He aimed to aggravate oppression against opposition forces while appeasing those who had been critical of or maintaining a distance from the government to co-opt them into the regime. To this end, he intended to transform Golkar into an instrument to accommodate new recruits. This marked the beginning of Golkar's transformation.

4
The Consolidation of Golkar and Recruitment of Social Elites

Under the Suharto regime, Golkar was recognized as no more than a vote-gathering machine whose only role was to ensure the government's victory in elections. As can be observed from Table 4.1, Golkar won over sixty percent of votes in all of the six elections held under the Suharto regime, from the first in 1971 through to the 1997 election, consistently securing a stable majority in the DPR. Golkar also supported Suharto's reelection as President in each MPR session held every five years.

Golkar received 62.8 percent of the votes in the 1971 election and its share of votes remained stable for the two subsequent elections, with 62.1 percent in 1977 and 64.3 percent in 1982. However, despite consistently receiving a decent number of votes, Golkar was a vulnerable organization lacking not only internal unity but also the social base required for a political party as discussed in the previous chapter.

In 1983, President Suharto installed State Secretary Sudharmono as the Chairman of Golkar and left the organizational consolidation of Golkar in his hands, as he was the person Suharto trusted the most and valued highly for his administrative capabilities. This appointment raises the question as to whether Suharto was discontented with the way Golkar was functioning solely as a vote-gathering machine and if so, what form of organizational transformation did he want to affect. This chapter will first describe the background of Sudharmono's assumption of the Golkar chair post, which became a catalyst for Golkar's transformation, and examine how Golkar underwent a series of major expansions through his organizational reform. It will then analyze the process of how a large number of social elites joined Golkar and were appointed to executive positions as a result of its expansion beginning in 1984.

Golkar's organizational reform under Sudharmono

The new Golkar Chairman Sudharmono
Sudharmono's assumption of the position of Chairman of Golkar in 1983 was by direct instruction from Suharto. At that time, Sudharmono was involved in

Table 4.1: Percentage of votes and number of seats won by Golkar in elections under the Suharto regime

YEAR OF ELECTION	1971	1977	1982	1987	1992	1997
Percentage of votes (%)	62.8	62.1	64.3	73.2	68.1	74.5
Number of seats	236 (360)	232 (360)	242 (360)	299 (400)	282 (400)	325 (425)

Note: The numbers in brackets represent the total number of seats reserved for elected members in the DPR.
Source: Lembaga Pemilihan Umum (1971, 1978, 1983, 1987, 1993, 1997b).

the planning of numerous laws and policies, from the formulation of drafts on Broad Guidelines of State Policy (GBHN) and the preparation of draft budgets to designing development projects as the head of the State Secretariat, which was dubbed the 'government within the government' on the back of Suharto's deep trust. He was one of the few who could access President Suharto's office without an appointment. His name remained largely unrecognized during his time as an Army legal officer. However, after he became the Secretary of the Cabinet Secretariat in 1966 and further rose to the position of Chief Cabinet Secretary in 1968, he unleashed his superior ability in drafting texts of various types of laws and orders as well as the President's speeches and also had a major hand in restructuring government ministries and agencies (Sudharmono 1997: 194–220). While he was serving as the Secretary of the Cabinet Secretariat, Sudharmono engineered the structure in which a secretary general as an assistant to the ministers, a directorate general as a policy implementation office and an inspector general as a supervisory office were placed immediately below ministers (Sudharmono 1997: 182–183). Having received high recognition from Suharto for the aforementioned work, Sudharmono was duly appointed as the State Secretary in 1972. For the following sixteen years until 1988, he was responsible for scrutinizing almost every single bill submitted by ministries and agencies to the President to gain approval to present the bill to the DPR (Sudharmono 1997: 220–294). He was a very capable official and his capability in administrative matters was the reason for Suharto's decision to install him as the Chairman of Golkar in 1983.

This raises the question as to why Suharto needed to make Sudharmono the Golkar Chairman.

In light of the political situation of the early 1980s, the key issue for the government was to pass the five political bills including the mass organization bill that had a provision specifying that Pancasila is to be the only principle of any political and social organization. Major Islamic organizations such as Nahdlatul Ulama (NU) and Muhammadiyah vehemently opposed this bill, which to them represented the forced imposition of Pancasila, and supported the opposition party, the United Development Party (PPP). Faced with the need to diminish the political momentum of the PPP, the government sought to split the Islamic forces that were backing the party. In other words, they needed to draw these supporters away from the PPP and turn them into Golkar supporters.

Another reason was that the retirement of ruling elites of the 'Generation of 45', who had been leading Indonesia in every aspect thus far, was approaching. In the Armed Forces, Benny Murdani was promoted to the post of Commander of the Armed Forces to facilitate the generational transition, and the so-called 'Bridging Generation' built around Murdani was already starting to carry on the leadership legacy of the 'Generation of 45'. Furthermore, this generational transition in the Armed Forces was expected to progress smoothly since the next generation—that is, the generation of officers who graduated from the military academy after 1945—had been solidly building their careers to take leadership positions in the Armed Forces in the generation to come. As for Golkar, on the contrary, the shortage of executive-level personnel was a serious problem. The current central leadership was not even adequately established let alone prepared for generational transition. The next-generation leader of Golkar needed to be someone who was worthy of becoming the national-level political leader. From this perspective, there was a recognized need for a system to recruit and nurture human resources who would take over and develop Golkar after the retirement of existing military officers within Golkar's executive boards.

From the 1970s to the beginning of the 1980s the Suharto regime drew its political support from the Armed Forces and bureaucracy while it was dependent on Chinese-Indonesian entrepreneurs in regards to economics. As for the social base, the regime was very weak, receiving very little support from society at large. Throughout this period, the government was constantly challenged by student protest activities and anti-Suharto demonstrations, the obstinate objection of opposition parties to a variety of bills in the DPR and protests against the imposition of Pancasila by Islamic forces. Despite having made desperate efforts to contain criticism and opposition, the government and the ruling party remained isolated from society and containment by force was not the answer.

Jacob Tobing, who was one of the original members of the Central Executive Board appointed at the time of Golkar's establishment, used the word 'bean sprout' (*taoge*) to portray Golkar before Sudharmono assumed the chairmanship.

> Golkar was compared to *taoge* among the Central Executive Board members. By this we meant it had a huge head but no roots. The members of the board wanted

Golkar to become an autonomous socio-political organization that could operate on its own and make policy decisions like the PPP and PDI; to become a society-based organization so that it could build bidirectional relationships with the people; and to be able to internalize and process the people's demands and communicate those to the government and convey the government's policies back to the people. (Tobing 1997: 394–396)

This sense of urgency was shared within the Central Executive Board. The appointment of Sudharmono to the post of chairman was undoubtedly a sign of the pressure Suharto himself was feeling. Suharto expected him to build a system to convene a wide spectrum of human resources while restructuring Golkar's organization with his capable hands and expanding public support for the government and its policies through Golkar. Suharto gave the following orders to Sudharmono when he made the appointment. The first was to reinforce Golkar as a powerful political body that could become the pillar of the Suharto regime. The second was to turn Golkar into an organization that could actively mobilize the nation in support of the development policy pursued by the government (Sudharmono 1997: 321).

Upon his inauguration as the new Golkar Chairman in the national congress in October 1983, Sudharmono announced the slogan 'Three Success Program' (*Tri Sukses*) consisting of the following: 'success in consolidation of the party', 'success in the Forth Five-Year Plan' and 'success in the 1987 general election and 1988 general session of the MPR' (Sudharmono 1997: 329–330). Akbar Tandjung, who joined the Central Executive Board for the first time under Chairman Sudharmono, looked back on that time and explained that in terms of the 'Three Success Program', the 'success in consolidation of the party' was especially important for accomplishing the remaining two goals. In other words, without the organizational consolidation of Golkar, there could neither be success in the development policy nor victory in elections—therefore, it was the 'absolute requirement' (*syarat mutlak*) for achieving success in elections and for the development policy (Tandjung 1997: 335).

In the same national congress in 1983, Suharto elaborated that this 'consolidation of the party' could be broken down into 'consolidation of ideals', 'consolidation of vision' and 'consolidation of the organization'. According to him, 'consolidation of ideals' meant further fostering unwavering loyalty to Pancasila and the 1945 Constitution, and 'consolidation of vision' signified that Golkar would pioneer the development of values, attitudes, behaviors and ways of thinking and working to realize state interests. He explained that 'consolidation of the organization' meant promoting the 'cultivation of cadres' (*kaderisasi*)[1]. As the largest political force in Indonesia, Golkar needed to nurture mature executives with a sense of responsibility who would be able to lead the nation. Suharto asserted that the issue of the cultivation of cadres would become increasingly important with the process of generational change and ordered the new Central Executive Board members to promote the cadre cultivation programs (DPP Golkar 1988a: 15–16).

We shall now examine how organizational consolidation and the preparation of the cadre cultivation system were carried out in practice.

Organizational consolidation of Golkar

Table 4.2 lists the members of the Central Executive Board selected in the third national congress held in October 1983.

Thirty-two out of forty-two members of the new board, including the Chairman, were newcomers. The lineup changed radically as Sudharmono was involved in a majority of the personnel selection processes and actively recruited young civilian politicians. Former student activist Sarwono Kusumaatmadja (a former member of KAMI's Bandung group[2]) was appointed to the Secretary-General position whereas Rachmat Witoelar, who was also a former member of the Bandung group, was appointed to the top position of the Department of Organization, Membership and Cultivation of Cadres. In addition, former student activists such as Akbar Tandjung from the Islamic Students' Association (HMI) and Tatto Pradjamanggala from Siliwangi Youth Force (AMS), as well as young *pribumi* entrepreneurs—non-Chinese, indigenous entrepreneurs—such as Siswono Yudohusodo and Eric Samola joined the Central Executive Board for the first time.

The organizational consolidation started from this Central Executive Board, now run by completely new faces. Sudharmono gave each of the eight vice-chairs the role of sectorial coordinators (*korbid*) for economy, politics, organization, religion, national security, welfare, law and social culture. He also assigned the role of regional coordinators (*korwil*) to them, so that each would be responsible for one of the eight regions, namely North Sumatra, South Sumatra, Jakarta/West Java/Central Java, East Java/Yogyakarta/Bali, Kalimantan, South Sulawesi/North Sulawesi/Central Sulawesi, Southeast Sulawesi/Maluku/Irian Jaya and Nusa Tenggara (Sudharmono 1997: 324).

Each of those in the eight senior positions, namely Secretary-General, Deputy Secretary-Generals, Accountant and Deputy Accountants, was assigned as an assistant to a vice-chair to assist with general operations. The thirteen departments conducted operations under the sectorial and regional coordinators in their respective sector and region (Sudharmono 1997: 325).

Sudharmono also defined the framework for meetings as regular fortnightly meetings (*rapat harian*, attended by eleven members consisting of the chair,

Table 4.2: Central Executive Board of Golkar (1983–1988)

Chairman	Sudharmono (Retired Army Lieutenant General, Chief State Secretary)
Vice-Chair	Soekardi (Retired Army Brigadier General, Veterans' Association)
	A. E. Manihuruk (Retired Army Brigadier General, Ministry of Home Affairs)
	K. H. Tarmudji (GUPPI)
	Mrs. Murpratomo (KOWANI)
	R. H. Soegandhi (Retired Army Major General, MKGR)
	Gatot Suwagio (Retired Army Major General)
	Imam Sudarwo (KOSGORO)
	Oetojo Oesman (SOKSI)
Secretary-General	Sarwono Kusumaatmadja (Former student activist/Bandung group)
Deputy Secretary-General	Akbar Tandjung (Former student activist/HMI)
	Oka Mahendra (FBSI)
	Sudarmadji (PGRI)
	David Napitupulu (Former student activist/Tanah Abang group)
Accountant	Zarlons Zaghlul (Ministry of Home Affairs)
Deputy Accountant	Mrs. Darsojo (HWK)
	Andi Mochtar
Department of Election Campaign Strategy	Daryono
	Tatto Pradjamanggala (AMS)
Department of Organization, Membership and Cultivation of Cadres	Rachmat Witoelar (Former student activist/Bandung group)
	Jacob Tobing (Former student activist/Tanah Abang group)
Department of Education	Basyuni Sriamihardja (PGRI)
	Ki Suratman (PGRI)
Department of Information, Publication and Mass Media	Zulharmans
	Anang Adenansi (Former student activist/PWI)
Department of Youth	Aulia Aman Rachman (Former student activist/University of Indonesia Student Council)
	Freddy Latumahina (Former student activist/University of Indonesia Student Council)
Department of Labor	Sukarno (FBSI)
	Effendi Jusuf (KOSGORO)
Department of Women	Mrs. Busyiri
	Sri Redjeki (HWK)
Department of Religion	K. H. Qodratullah (GUPPI)
	Z. U. Sidiki (MDI)
Department of Intellectuals	Ibrahim Hasan (Bulog/President of Syiah Kuala University)
	Albert Hasibuan (Former student activist/Lawyer)
Department of Culture and Art	Waskito (KORPRI)
	Moerdopo (Former student activist/Tanah Abang group)
Department of Cooperatives and Entrepreneurship	Siswono Yudohusodo (Entrepreneur)
	Eric Samola (Entrepreneur)
Department of Social Services	Hatta Mustafa (Former student activist/University of Indonesia Student Council)
	Noegraha Besoes (Former student activist)
Department of International Affairs	Jusuf Wanandi (Former student activist/Tanah Abang group)

Note: The 'Tanah Abang group' corresponds to the 'Murtopo group' in tables 3.2, 3.3 and 3.4.
Source: Bangun (1994: 297).

vice-chairs, secretary-general and accountant), a regular monthly general meeting (*rapat harian lengkap*, attended by seventeen members consisting of the aforementioned eleven plus the Deputy Secretary-General and Deputy Accountants) and bimonthly central executive board general meetings (*rapat pleno pengurus Golkar*, attended by all forty-two executive board members). He required the Advisory Board's Secretary to attend all of the meetings (Sudharmono 1997: 325). The Secretary's attendance was aimed at rapidly informing Suharto, the Chair of the Advisory Board, of the content of discussions in the Central Executive Board. Sudharmono initiated the organizational consolidation of Golkar from the Central Executive Board by assigning clearly defined roles and responsibilities to the members and holding meetings on a regular basis to unify the Central Executive Board into one coherent team to create an atmosphere in which everyone could voice their opinions (Sudharmono 1997: 331). Sudharmono explained that 'systems and rules were insufficient for the executive board to come together as a complete work team, but unity, mutual trust and a strong will to work together were required'. To this end, he strived to foster free and open communication and particularly promoted the open exchange of opinions and ideas in meetings. As a general rule, decisions needed to be made by unanimous consent and Sudharmono never made decisions at his own discretion (Sudharmono 1997: 331). Other members of the Central Executive Board made similar remarks regarding the atmosphere of the board. This kind of change had never been observed within Golkar.

In addition, Sudharmono took the initiative to travel to regional areas to carry out inspections with executive board members. A series of inspection tours called 'Safari' were conducted over weekends, from Friday nights to Sundays, as Sudharmono had duties as the State Secretary during the week, and were accompanied by young members of the executive boards and young executives of affiliated organizations. The party travelled almost every week and toured all over the country. They dropped in at villages, visited *pesantren* (Islamic boarding schools), attended anniversary ceremonies of schools and hospitals and held debate sessions with students at university campuses. It was the first time that Golkar's leader had embarked on inspection tours to regional areas with a large group of people at this frequency outside election campaign periods. Sudharmono appealed for participation in the government's development policy wherever he went and also made sure he prepared some kind of 'gift' such as promising the provision of funds to repair a mosque or donating copies of the Quran. Moreover, in 1984, a series of programs, such as social work month, was launched as part of Golkar's 20th anniversary commemoration event. Programs included but were not limited to blood donation campaigns, clean up campaigns, sports carnivals, visits to social facilities, meetings with farmers and fishermen and gift presentation ceremonies, to which members of executive boards in the central and regional branches as well as executives of affiliated organizations raced to participate. In addition, the foster parents program was established to provide assistance to foster parents who took in orphans (DPP Golkar 1984: 63–73).

According to Zarlons Zaghlul, who served as the Accountant in Sudharmono's Central Executive Board, around this time Golkar was beginning to gather an abundance of funds for the first time. The Dakab Foundation, a foundation designed to procure Golkar's working capital, was established in 1985, with Suharto as director. The motive behind the establishment of the foundation was that from 1984 to 1985, the 'individual membership system' and 'cadre cultivation program' introduced by Sudharmono upon his assumption of the chairmanship created the need for a substantial amount of capital. The creation of the Dakab Foundation enabled the Central Executive Board to routinely provide sufficient working capital and financial assistance to Golkar's local branches (province level as well as regency and city level) around the country. This was also the first time Golkar was able to do this. Sudharmono used this working capital as seed money for establishing more foundations for local branches and devised a mechanism by which local branches could also raise capital on their own, to add to the funds provided by the central office (Zaghlul 1997: 294–295).

After having completed the restructuring of the organization and operation of the Central Executive Board, Sudharmono embarked on the introduction of the individual membership system and cadre cultivation program. These two basically constituted the core of the restructuring of Golkar.

Although the individual membership system was already included in the law on political parties and Golkar of 1975, neither Golkar nor the opposition parties, the PPP and PDI, had implemented individual membership registration programs at that stage. In regards to Golkar, its members usually joined an affiliated organization, such as KOSGORO, SOKSI or MKGR, and individual membership did not increase even after the enforcement of the above-mentioned law in 1975. One of the possible reasons for this is that the former KINO organizations protested against the full-scale introduction of the individual membership system. They were concerned that their presence within Golkar would further weaken if individual members joined the organization (*Far Eastern Economic Review* Dec. 1, 1983: 40–41). Another reason is that a certain amount of capital and administrative capability was required to perform the membership registration process for individuals across the country and confer membership certificates with individual membership numbers. Golkar, of course, did not have such financial resources or administrative capability at that time. When Sudharmono took on this issue and consulted Suharto regarding the implementation of the individual membership system, Suharto not only gave approval but also provided funds to cover the costs associated with the membership registration process and printing membership certificates (Sudharmono 1997: 325). The introduction of the individual membership system in Golkar was only possible with financial support from Suharto coupled with Sudharmono's administrative skills.

The individual membership registration process, which was first rolled out in the second-level regional governments on January 1, 1984, drew participation from a large number of people and the number of Golkar members as of June 1988 is reported to have been 32,416,188 (DPP Golkar 1988a: 197–198)[3]. In the 1987 election in which the total number of voters was approximately 93,960,000, Golkar won around 68,780,000 votes—that is 73.2 percent of the total vote. Provided that this figure of 32,416,188 can be trusted, forty-seven percent of the votes for Golkar would have come from Golkar members. Golkar was aiming to win seventy percent of the vote (65,770,000 votes) in the 1987 election. This essentially meant that fifty percent of the target was already guaranteed and that made their prospects in elections significantly more promising. As can be observed from Table 4.1 above, the percentage of votes won increased by nine points, from 64.3 percent in the 1982 election to 73.2 percent in the 1987 election. It can thus be inferred that the introduction of the individual membership system contributed to the overwhelming victory of the ruling party. On another note, this individual membership system obliged members to pay 100 rupiah per month as a membership fee. This fee was expected to increase the financial independence of Golkar at the time, but the actual collection of the fee seems to have been problematic (*Media Karya* Jan.–Feb. 1989: 50). Nonetheless, even though revenue from membership fees did not greatly increase, donations from entrepreneur members appear to have jumped substantially around this time.

Cadre cultivation programs were launched in parallel with the individual membership system. The cadre cultivation program itself did exist from the 1970s but was not functioning as expected at that time (Ramadhan dan Sriwibawa 1999: 231). The new programs initiated from 1984 categorized the nurturing of cadres as follows: cadres would be based in villages called *karakterdes* and 'functional cadres' (*karaknal*), would act on behalf of their respective functional groups such as youth, women, teachers, *ulama* and laborers. In terms of the former, Golkar aimed to turn ten percent of the voters in every village (approximately eight million people nationwide) into 'village cadres'. Golkar wanted those 'village cadres'—villagers turned into Golkar supporters—to actively participate in the government's development policy and created education programs to nurture these village cadres. Under these education programs, village cadre candidates took courses of sessions on the 1945 Constitution and Pancasila, Golkar's party regulations and the rules and customs (*adat*) of respective regions, followed by training on speeches and debates (DPP Golkar 1984: 93).

In addition, 600,000 copies of the 'Golkar member pocket book' containing a guide on Pancasila and the 1945 Constitution as well as Golkar's regulations and rules were distributed to cadre cultivation instructors. Production of this pocket book became possible only because of financial assistance from Suharto (Sudharmono 1997: 338). Sudharmono reports that by 1987 eight million village cadres and one million functional cadres had taken part in the cadre education programs (Sudharmono 1997: 340).

The report as of June 1988 suggests that there were 8,280,728 village cadres, 911,027 functional cadres in regional areas consisting of 320,507 young men and women, 77,135 religious leaders, 181,745 women and 331,640 teachers, and 3,051 functional cadres in the central areas (DPP Golkar 1988a: 197–198). If we compare these figures to Golkar's records of 1978 in which the number of cadres at first-level regional governments is reported to have been 2,953 and that of second-level regional governments approximately 28,000 (DPP Golkar 1978: 29), Golkar's cadres can be said to have increased dramatically in the short span of a decade, in fact, in only five years from 1984 when the program was launched.

Changes in Golkar's personnel structure

What brought about more significant changes within Golkar than its substantial increase in membership were the qualitative changes in executive personnel. Many of the young politicians and entrepreneurs recruited during the Sudharmono era formed an important part of the Suharto regime and later became leading members of the 'Golkar Party' (*Partai Golkar*), after the fall of the Suharto regime. Some became parliament members, promoted to the Central Executive Board, or were even appointed as Cabinet members after joining Golkar in and after the 1980s. For them, joining Golkar was a huge step toward building their political careers. Golkar, which used to be an exclusive organization in the 1970s, transformed into a more open one during the Sudharmono era and became a channel to provide opportunities for political and economic success for the younger generations who did not have any special connection with influential elites.

This section will analyze young politicians and entrepreneurs who joined Golkar or started to gradually increase their presence as prominent leaders in and after the mid-1980s through the cadre recruitment and cultivation policy implemented under three categories: former student activists, *pribumi* entrepreneurs and Islamic group members. Their entry into the political sphere diminished the influence of the Armed Forces, which had been dominant in Golkar until then, and instead civilian elites increasingly began distinguishing themselves as Golkar's leaders. Firstly, I shall explain the process through which these young politicians were recruited into Golkar.

Former student activists
Former student activists had already begun to join Golkar by the early 1970s. Many of those who became members in the early days belonged to Christian groups or the Bandung group of the student organization KAMI, who joined Golkar on the back of support from Ali Murtopo.

Christian student activists such as Cosmas Batubara, Jusuf Wanandi, Jacob Tobing, Midian Sirait and David Napitupulu were conducting campaigns under Ali Murtopo, with Golkar's General Election Controlling Body (BAPILU) as well as the Centre for Strategic International Studies (CSIS) as the operational headquarters. They were also known as the 'Tanah Abang group', from the name of the district where the CSIS was located in Jakarta. Some held parliamentary seats as Golkar representatives and others served as Golkar's Central Executive Board members, holding a large presence in the early 1970s when Murtopo had strong political influence. However, their prominence began to fade in the early 1980s as Murtopo's power started to decline. Subsequently, the late 1980s saw a rapid reduction of their presence within Golkar.

The Bandung group consisted of student activists who played the central role in the Bandung branch of KAMI from the late 1960s to the early 1970s. The leading members included Sarwono Kusumaatmadja and Rachmat Witoelar. Similarly to the Christian group, they acquired seats in the DPR on the back of Murtopo's support in the early 1970s and later were even promoted to the position of Secretary-General of Golkar (Sarwono, 1983–1988; Rachmat, 1988–1993). The Bandung group possessed political power in the 1980s within Golkar, but their power gradually receded in the 1990s due to its limited political network[4].

Over the period from the mid- to late-1970s, several members of the University of Indonesia Student Council were recruited into Golkar. Those recruited were members of the so-called 'group of ten' (*Kelompok 10*), who comprised the student council at the time of the Malari incident (see Chapter Two), including Aulia Aman Rachman and Freddy Latumahina. Despite still being students at that time, they took orders from the State Intelligence Agency (BAKIN), and engaged in surveillance and control of student movements while serving as members of the council. With the strong ties with Murtopo built through such engagements, they became members of parliament as Golkar representatives and some were even added to the Central Executive Board. Similarly to the Bandung group, it was a relatively small group and their political network was limited.

Since the passing of Murtopo and Sudharmono's assumption of Golkar's chairmanship in 1984, HMI student activists rapidly started to increase their presence to replace the Tanah Abang group. The HMI had the largest force among student groups throughout the 1970s and HMI members filled important positions in the student councils of many universities. Meanwhile, the government's attempt to bring the HMI under control to counter its strong opposition against the government yielded very little results.

The key figure behind the influx of HMI student activists joining Golkar was Akbar Tandjung. He was a student activist from the HMI and one of the prominent individuals of the 'Generation of 66' which contributed to the establishment of the Suharto regime from 1966 to 1968. In 1972, he was selected as the Chair of HMI's central executive board and formed the 'Cipayung Group' (*Kelompok Cipayung*), along with other youth groups. Using this group as a support base, he managed to join the government-sponsored KNPI (National Committee of Indonesian Youth) in 1973, where he later progressed to the chair position of its central executive board in 1978. In the same year, he also participated in the AMPI (Indonesian Young Generation for Renewal), a Golkar-affiliated youth group, where he acted as Vice-Chair. In 1977, he was elected to the membership of the DPR as a Golkar representative and was later promoted to the position of Vice Secretary-General of Golkar under Chairman Sudharmono in 1983[5].

The surge in the number of former HMI activists joining Golkar since the late 1980s came with the expansion of Akbar Tandjung's power within Golkar. Many of those former HMI members who were close to him were, regardless of whether they were his seniors, juniors or contemporaries, elected as members of the DPR. Akbar Tandjung played a significant role in recruiting young civilian members to Golkar, in particular, young leaders of the HMI as well as senior members of Islamic student organizations and youth groups outside of the HMI (Effendy 2003: 334–335). One can suppose that the HMI's shift from its anti-government attitude in the 1970s toward a more pro-government stance in the mid-1980s was heavily influenced by him. In 1986, the HMI split into a pro-government group and one that maintained an anti-government stance. In response, the government took an appeasement policy in which they acknowledged pro-government groups as 'legitimate' HMI members, giving them positions in the MPR under appointed seats while oppressing anti-government groups. From this time on, a large number of former HMI members started to join the DPR as Golkar representatives.

From the 1980s to 1990s, two youth organizations called the KNPI and AMPI began playing major roles in Golkar's efforts at recruiting student activists. Both organizations started to function as recruitment channels for Golkar in the 1980s. In 1980, Minister of Education and Culture Daud Jusuf implemented

Table 4.3: Former student activists' membership history in the KNPI and AMPI

POLITICIAN (BY GROUP OF ORIGIN)	KNPI MEMBERSHIP	AMPI MEMBERSHIP
Tanah Abang group		
Cosmas Batubara	1973–1978 Central Executive Board Vice-Chair	—
Jusuf Wanandi	—	—
David Napitupulu	1973–1978 Central Executive Board Chair	1978–1979 Central Executive Board Chair
Bandung group		
Sarwono Kusumaatmadja	—	—
Rachmat Witoelar	—	—
University of Indonesia Student Council group		
Aulia Aman Rachman	1973–1978 Central Executive Board member	—
	1978–1981 Central Executive Board Vice-Chair	1981–1984 Central Executive Board Chair
Freddy Latumahina	1973–1978 Central Executive Board member	1978–1984 Central Executive Board Vice-Chair
	1978–1981 Central Executive Board Vice-Chair	
Hatta Mustafa	1974–1978 Central Executive Board Secretary-General	1979–1984 Central Executive Board Chair
	1978–1981 Central Executive Board member	
Potsdam Hutasoit	1981–1984 Central Executive Board member	1978–1984 Central Executive Board Vice-Chair
	1984–1987 Central Executive Board Vice-Chair	
HMI group		
Abdul Gafur	1973–1978 Central Executive Board Vice-Chair	—
Akbar Tandjung	1973–1978 Central Executive Board Vice-Chair	1978–1980 Central Executive Board Vice-Chair
	1978–1981 Central Executive Board Chair	

Name		
Abdullah Puteh	1978–1981 Central Executive Board member	1979 Central Executive Board member
	1981–1984 Central Executive Board Vice-Chair	
	1984–1987 Central Executive Board Chair	
Zamharir	1978–1984 Central Executive Board member	1981 Member
Abu Hasan Sazili	1981–1987 Central Executive Board member	1984–1989 Central Executive Board member
Mahadi Sinambela	1981–1984 Central Executive Board Vice-Chair	—
Syamsul Muarif	1981–1984 Central Executive Board member	1989–1994 Central Executive Board Vice-Chair
Rambe Kamarulzaman	1987–1990 Central Executive Board Vice-Chair	1989–1994 Central Executive Board Secretary-General
Mohammad Yamin Tawari	1990–1993 Central Executive Board Vice-Chair	1989–1994 Central Executive Board member
Herman Widyananda	1990–1993 Central Executive Board Vice-Chair	—
Ade Komaruddin	1993–1996 Central Executive Board member	1994–1999 Central Executive Board member
Ferry Mursyidan Baldan	—	1998–2003 Central Executive Board Secretary-General
Yahya Zaini	1996–1999 Central Executive Board Vice-Chair	—
Other		
Albert Hasibuan	1973–1974 Central Executive Board member	—
Marzuki Darusman	1974–1978 Central Executive Board Secretary-General	1977–1983 Central Executive Board Secretary-General
	1978–1981 Central Executive Board Vice-Chair	
Theo Sambuaga	1978–1981 Central Executive Board member	1984–1989 Central Executive Board Vice-Chair
	1981–1984 Central Executive Board Secretary-General	

Source: Prepared by the author.

the oppressive 'normalization of campus life' policy, which banned student demonstrations from being held outside university campuses. In addition, student councils were dissolved or pro-government student councils were newly established in many universities, making it extremely difficult for activists to organize drastic anti-government student movements. With the opposition party PPP also losing its political momentum, a large party of politically oriented students who had lost their way chose to join government-affiliated youth organizations such as the KNPI and AMPI to pursue their political careers. The KNPI and AMPI became channels to lead these young people to Golkar. As can be seen in Table 4.3, many student activist-turned Golkar politicians who emerged in the mid-1980s had served as executives in the KNPI or AMPI, or both, at some point during their careers. A great number of student activists who played leading roles in the KNPI and AMPI later joined Golkar and were appointed to executive posts in the central and regional offices.

Pribumi *entrepreneurs*
Table 4.4 shows a summary of the political and economic backgrounds of the major Golkar politicians of the Suharto era who began their career as entrepreneurs.

Many of them went on to achieve success as Golkar politicians even after the end of the Suharto era such as Jusuf Kalla (Vice-President, Chairman of Golkar Party, 2004–2009), Abrizal Bakrie (Coordinating Minister of Welfare, 2005–2009, Chairman of Golkar Party, 2009–) and Agung Laksono (Coordinating Minister of Public Welfare, 2009–, Vice-Chair of Golkar Party, 2004–). They were *pribumi* entrepreneurs who were initially at a disadvantage in the Indonesian business world, dominated as it was by Chinese-Indonesian and Suharto family corporate groups and major state-run companies. Apart from some exceptions, such as Jusuf Kalla who had joined Golkar at the time of establishment, an army of entrepreneurs started to join Golkar after the mid-1980s when Chairman Sudharmono actively recruited executive members. The 'Team for Presidential Decision 10' (*Tim Keppres 10*), a program to grant preferential support to *pribumi* entrepreneurs that was initiated in 1980 under the lead of the State Secretariat, acted as a catalyst for *pribumi* entrepreneurs to join Golkar. As described in Chapter Two, the government made very little effort to protect and support *pribumi* entrepreneurs throughout the 1970s since President Suharto favored Chinese-Indonesian entrepreneurs as business partners because of their financial clout and business skills. Needless to say, the government became the target of criticism by *pribumi* entrepreneurs, especially young businesspeople who did not have financial resources or connections with influential figures.

In 1972, these young *pribumi* entrepreneurs got together and formed the Young Indonesian Entrepreneurs' Association (HIPMI). In addition to the

Table 4.4: Business and political careers of entrepreneur Golkar politicians

NAME (PLACE AND YEAR OF BIRTH) NAME OF COMPANY/ CORPORATE GROUP	UNIVERSITY (YEAR OF GRADUATION) PARTICIPATION IN STUDENT MOVEMENTS (PERIOD)	BUSINESS CAREER MEMBERSHIP IN BUSINESS-RELATED ORGANIZATIONS	POLITICAL CAREER
A. A. Baramuli (South Sulawesi, 1930) Poleko Group	University of Indonesia (1955) Jakarta Student Movement (1954–1956)	After taking over a company from a family member in 1973, he led it to become the largest synthetic fiber maker by forming a joint venture with Toray. He exported timber produced in Halmahera to Japan through Marubeni and created a joint venture with Kaō to establish a chemical plant in Bekasi in 1977. He entered the hotel business in 1991. KADIN (Vice-Chair 1982–1993).	Public Prosecutor (1956–1960), Governor of North-Central Sulawesi Province (1960–1962), Advisor to the Ministry of Home Affairs, Monetary and Fiscal Team Leader (1963–1974), DPR member representing Golkar (1971–1992), Golkar Central Executive Board member (1988–1993)
Aburizal Bakrie (Jakarta, 1946) Bakrie & Brothers	Bandung Institute of Technology (1973) University student council	Bakrie & Brothers was established by his father Achmad Bakrie in Lampung in 1942 and expanded through peppercorn and coffee export during the Japanese military administration. It diversified its businesses into rubber, cacao and coconut plantations. Aburizal joined the company in 1972 and started production of iron tubes (for petroleum pipes) in 1981. The company formed a joint venture with Mitsubishi Kasei in 1986 and advanced into the financial sector. Aburizal owned a ten percent stake in Freeport. He assumed the chair post in 1988 and brought Tanri Abeng in as CEO. He split the group into several companies and separated ownership and management, delegating the general management to Tanri Abeng. The group expanded its business into a wide range of sectors including manufacturing, services, finance, agro-industry, mining, real estate, entertainment and trade. HIPMI (1972–1976, Chair 1977–1979), KADIN (Vice-Chair 1988–1993, Chair 1994–2004).	Enrollment into Golkar (1984), Golkar MPR member (1988–1998), ICMI Advisory Board member (1991–1995, 2000–2005), Golkar Party Central Executive Board member (2004–), Coordinating Minister for the Economy (2004–2005), Coordinating Minister for Welfare (2005–2009), Golkar Party Chairman (2009–)

Table 4.4: continued

NAME (PLACE AND YEAR OF BIRTH) NAME OF COMPANY/ CORPORATE GROUP	UNIVERSITY (YEAR OF GRADUATION) PARTICIPATION IN STUDENT MOVEMENTS (PERIOD)	BUSINESS CAREER MEMBERSHIP IN BUSINESS-RELATED ORGANIZATIONS	POLITICAL CAREER
Agung Laksono (Semarang, 1949) Hasmuda Group	Christian University of Indonesia (1972) KAPPI (1966–1968) University student council	He started his own cleaning business in 1972 and co-founded Hasmuda with Teuku Sjahrul and Anton Nangoi in 1977. In 1990 he co-founded AN-teve with Nirwan Bakrie and Aburizal Bakrie and entered the television broadcasting industry. Hasmuda grew to become a corporate group with seven subsidiaries in areas including electronics, carbon, taxis (Kosti Jaya) and agribusiness. It published the first issue of the tabloid newspaper *Target* in 1993 and started publication of business magazine *InfoBisnis* with Aburizal Bakrie, Fadel Muhammad and Ade Putra Tahir in 1994. HIPMI (1973, Chair 1983–1986). KADIN (Vice-Chief of Jakarta Branch 1981–1984, Vice-Chair 1985–1988).	AMPI Jakarta Branch Chief (1978–1980), AMPI Central Executive Board Chair (1984–1989), Golkar Jakarta Branch Chief (1984–1989), DPR member representing Golkar (1987–1998), DPR member representing Golkar Party (1998–2009), Golkar Central Executive Board member (1988–1998), KOSGORO (1990–1995), State Minister for Youth and Sports Affairs (1998–1999), Golkar Party Central Executive Board member (1998–2004), KOSGORO 1957 Chair (2002–), DPR Chair (2004–2009), Golkar Party Vice-Chair (2004–2014), Coordinating Minister for Public Welfare (2009–2014)
Edwin Kawilarang (Bandung, 1954) Bimantara Siti Wisesa (Bimantara Group), Abadi Guna Papan, Kripan Raya	Bandung Institute of Technology (1982)	He worked on construction projects such as Lebak Bulus Indah residence, Plaza Indonesia, Grand Hyatt Hotel, Palma Citra Apartment and Pulo Permatasari residence in Bekasi under Bimantara Siti Wisesa, as well as development of the Mega Kuningan district and Mega Rancasari residence of Bandung under Abadi Guna Papan. He also worked on Telaga Kahuripan residence in Parung under Kuripan Raya. REI (Secretary-General 1992–1995, Chair 1995–1998)	AMPI Central Executive Board member (1994–1997), MPR member representing Golkar (1987–2003), FKPPI Vice-Chair (1998–2003), Golkar Party Central Executive Board member (1998–2003), DPR member (2004–2014)

Name	Education/Early Affiliations	Business Background	Political Career
Fadel Muhammad (Ternate, 1952) Batara Group	Bandung Institute of Technology (1977) Mesjid Salman	He co-founded Bukaka Teknik Utama with Achmad Kalla in 1978 with a loan from Jusuf Kalla. The Keppres 10 project, which was launched in 1980, helped the company's growth. Its construction of asphalt mixing plants won recognition from the State Secretariat's Ginandjar and this helped them win the tender and they were subsequently awarded a loan from the World Bank. KADIN Vice-Chair (1999–2004)	MDI member, Golkar Central Executive Board member (1993–1998), ICMI Advisory Board member (1995–2000), Golkar Party Central Executive Board member (1998–), Governor of Gorontalo Province (2001–2009), Minister of Marine Affairs and Fisheries (2009–2014)
Fahmi Idris (Jakarta, 1943) Kodel Group	University of Indonesia (1973) HMI Jakarta branch Chief (1966–1969) Laskar Ampera ARH Chair (1966–1969) University student council (1967–1969)	He founded Kwarta Daya Pratama in 1969 and joined Krama Yudha in 1973 where he became president in 1976. He co-established Kodel (Kelompok Delapan) Group with Sugeng Suryadi and Said Umar Husin in 1978 and became the president. The group continuously expanded its business into wide-ranging sectors such as insurance, agribusiness, banking, real estate and hotels in the 1980s. The group owns the Regent Hotel. One of the founders and an honorary member of HIPMI. KADIN.	Enrollment into Golkar (1984), Golkar Central Executive Board member (1993–1998), Minister of Manpower (1998–1999), Golkar Party Central Executive Board member (1998–2009), Minister of Manpower and Transmigration (2004–2005), Minister of Industry (2005–2009), Golkar Party Advisory Board member (2009–)
Jusuf Kalla (South Sulawesi, 1942) Haji Kalla Group	Hasanuddin University (1967) HMI (1965–1966) KAMI (1965–1966)	He took over Haji Kalla Trading Company from his father in 1967. The company signed a Sulawesi distributorship agreement with the Astra Group to import and sell Toyota automobiles, pushing its market share to fifty percent in eastern Indonesia. After it entered the construction business, it was awarded most major projects in the Sulawesi region such as construction of Hasanuddin Airport. The company launched transportation services between the islands with used vessels purchased from Japan. It grew to become the second largest company in Sulawesi by 1989. KADINDA (1977, 1985–1998), KADIN.	Sekber Golkar South Sulawesi branch member (1964), DPRD member representing Golkar (1965), Golkar South Sulawesi branch's Advisory Board member, MPR member representing Golkar (1987), enrollment into ICMI (1991), Minister of Industry and Trade (1999–2000), Coordinating Minister for People's Welfare (2001–2004), Vice President (2004–2009), Golkar Party Chairman (2004–2009), Vice President (2014–)

Table 4.4: continued

NAME (PLACE AND YEAR OF BIRTH) NAME OF COMPANY/ CORPORATE GROUP	UNIVERSITY (YEAR OF GRADUATION) PARTICIPATION IN STUDENT MOVEMENTS (PERIOD)	BUSINESS CAREER MEMBERSHIP IN BUSINESS-RELATED ORGANIZATIONS	POLITICAL CAREER
Ponco Sutowo (Palembang, 1950) Nugra Santana Group	Bandung Institute of Technology (1972) Mesjid Salman	He took over a corporate group owned by his father Ibnu Sutowo, former Director of Pertamina in 1980. He served as presidents of Adiguna Shipyard and Indobuilco. He rebuilt Balai Sidang, a convention centre in Senayan and was a new owner of the Hilton Hotel and Hilton Residence (now the Sultan Hotel and Residence). HIPMI Chair. KADIN Vice-Chair (1999–2004).	DPR member representing Golkar (1982–1992), FKPPI Central Executive Board member, Golkar Central Executive Board member (1993–1998), Golkar Party Central Executive Board member (1998–)
Siswono Yudohusodo (East Kalimantan, 1943) Bangun Cipta Sarana Group	Bandung Institute of Technology (1968) Laskar Sukarno	He founded a construction company in 1969. The company built housing complexes in Kemang and Semanggi Apartment, as well as Cawang–Cikampek and Cengkareng–Kebon Jeruk highways. He also engaged in coconut farming in Kalimantan and Sumatra, agriculture in Sumbawa and cattle production in Semarang. HIPMI (Chair 1973–1977). REI (Chair 1983–1986). KADIN (Vice-Chair 1985–1988).	Golkar Central Executive Board member (1983–1988), State Minister for Public Housing (1988–1993), State Minister of Transmigration, Forestry and Settlement (1993–1998), HKTI Chair (1999–2004), MPR member representing Golkar Party (1999–2004), Golkar Party Central Executive Board member (2004–2009)

Name	Education	Career	Golkar-related positions
Surya Dharma Paloh (Banda Aceh, 1951) Media Indonesia Group	University of North Sumatra (1972) Islamic University of North Sumatra (1975) Pancasila Student Movement (1964) KAPPI (1966–1970)	He started his own delivery and catering business in Medan in 1968, while he was a student. After his first newspaper business in Medan failed, he obtained a publication license and issued a newspaper *Prioritas* in 1986 but this was banned a year later. He acquired *Media Indonesia* in 1992 and employed some journalists from two magazines *TEMPO* and *EDITOR* banned in 1994. He then published a tabloid newspaper *Detik* with Eros Djarot and Kristin Hakim. He launched Metro TV in 1999. HIPMI (North Sumatra Branch 1974–1977, Central Executive Board member 1977–1979, honorary member 1984–).	Golkar Medan branch member (1969–1972), one of the founders of FKPPI (1978), FKPPI Chair (1979–1983), FKPPI Advisory Board member (1984–1987), AMPI Vice-Chair (1984–1989), AMPI Advisory Board member (1989–), MPR member representing Golkar (1973–1988), Golkar Party Advisory Board member (2004–2011), founded the National Democratic Party (2011–)

Source: Masadiah (1993), *Majalah Tokoh Indonesia* (Vol. 10, 11), *Swasembada* (3/II-June 1986, 8/IV-January 1989, 5/V-August 1989).

promoter Abdul Latief, founding members included such entrepreneurs as Siswono Yudohusodo, Abrizal Bakrie and Ponco Sutowo, all of whom later emerged as leading Golkar politicians (Soesatyo 1995: 65–69). In the mid-1970s when they could not expect the government's support, they received projects from Ibnu Sutowo (the father of Ponco Sutowo), who was the president of Pertamina (state-run oil company) at that time (Robison 1986: 354–356). HIPMI members respected and relied upon Sutowo, who displayed a disapproving stance against the government, which placed higher importance on Chinese-Indonesians, and gave Pertamina's projects to *pribumi* entrepreneurs to nurture their business interests (Robison 1986: 354–356). However, they lost this important patron when Sutowo was dismissed from the presidency of Pertamina in 1976.

After the dismissal of Sutowo, the State Secretariat headed by Sudharmono became a supporter of young *pribumi* entrepreneurs. In 1980, Sudharmono was asked for advice on whether to use revenue surplus generated by a steep rise in the oil price for procuring goods required in ministries and agencies by Widjojo Nitisastro, one of the economic technocrats who was the Coordinating Minister for the Economy and Chairperson of the National Development Planning Board (Bappenas) at the time. Sudharmono gained Suharto's consent to create a team for 'Presidential Decision 10' (Keppres 10) and launched a policy to give higher priority to *pribumi*-owned businesses when selecting suppliers of goods and facilities. Into the 1980s, the oil price fell and state revenue followed suit but the government nonetheless decided to take advantage of this project to save costs by purchasing inexpensive domestic products while facilitating domestic industries at the same time. The government preferentially gave a range of projects valued at around two hundred million rupiah to domestic companies to promote *pribumi*-owned businesses. In cases where a foreign corporation won a bid, they then made the corporation either subcontract work to or form a joint venture with domestic companies (Sudharmono 1997: 295–315). The utmost responsibility for this project rested with State Secretary Sudharmono and Ginandjar Kartasasmita, who was working under Sudharmono in the State Secretariat, played the role of the main contact person for the 'team for Presidential Decision 10'. He was appointed as the State Minister for the Promotion of Domestic Products in the Fourth Development Cabinet announced in 1983 and met directly with young *pribumi* entrepreneurs to discuss projects, acting as a liaison between them and Sudharmono (Kartasasmita 1997: 179–185). Through these projects, Ginandjar built close relationships with the entrepreneurs who comprised the HIPMI as well as young *pribumi* entrepreneurs such as Jusuf Kalla, Fadel Muhammad, Arifin Panigoro and Iman Taufik, who came to be dubbed the 'Ginandjar boys'. These young entrepreneurs greatly expanded their businesses owing to the benefits they received from the project.

As described above, the pro-*pribumi* policy led by the State Secretariat drew a large number of *pribumi* entrepreneurs closer to the government. Abrizal Bakrie's Bakrie & Brothers, Siswono Yudohusodo's Bangun Cipta Sarana group, Jusuf Kalla's Haji Kalla group, Fadel Muhammad's Batara group, Fahmi Idris's Kodel group and Agung Laksono's Hasmuda group expanded their business operations significantly in the 1980s, managing to break into the business world dominated by Chinese-Indonesian and Suharto family corporate groups and growing to become mid-sized corporate entities[6].

The entrance of *pribumi* entrepreneurs into Golkar occurred at the same time as when they were seeking to participate in the State Secretariat's project to expand business operations. It need hardly be mentioned that they positively responded to the call to join Golkar in order to get as close as possible to Sudharmono, who was the State Secretary as well as the Chairman of Golkar. The Golkar side was also very eager to bring entrepreneurs into the organization as cadres around that time. The recruitment and cultivation of the executive personnel program formulated by Golkar's Central Executive Board's Department of Cooperatives and Entrepreneurship in May 1984 outlined the following in regards to the recruitment of entrepreneurs.

> It is ideal to place Golkar's executive members in the leading posts of central and regional executive offices of the Chamber of Commerce and Industry (KADIN) and other business organizations. Those in the leading posts need to ensure that the programs of their organizations are in line with Golkar's programs and that political demands of the members of the organizations are conveyed to the government through Golkar. For entrepreneurs who are Golkar-leaning, it is ideal to turn them from passive supporters into Golkar members, and into active executive members, through the entrepreneurs currently belonging to Golkar. It is also necessary to encourage entrepreneurs to participate in the educational activities for the village cadre cultivation program...make Golkar member entrepreneurs engage in the following activities with victory in the 1987 election in mind; support Golkar's local branches by providing operating funds and purchasing necessary equipment, cover operating costs for pro-Golkar mass-based social organizations such as the AMPI and KUKMI (Indonesian Association of Small and Medium Entrepreneurs), cover printing costs of textbooks used in the village cadre cultivation program, collect donations for the foster parents program implemented by Golkar, turn laborers into Golkar members by mobilizing laborers within their own companies, make their political demands to the government

through Golkar and encourage their laborers to participate in the village cadre cultivation program. (DPP Golkar 1988a: 105–107)

Unlike the case of former student activists, Golkar did not yet intend to foster entrepreneurs as next-generation Golkar leaders at that time. Golkar's intention was, instead, to have them provide funding for local branches and affiliated organizations by involving them in the cadre cultivation programs and preparation for general elections and have their company employees registered as Golkar members.

Entrepreneurs responded positively to the ardent call from Golkar, with seventy-four businesspersons from the KADIN[7], which was the overall coordinator of the Indonesian business world, joining Golkar in June 1984, including the Chair Sukamdani Sahid Gitosardjono (*Suara Karya* June 9, 1984). Of course, those who joined at that time included many of the young *pribumi* entrepreneurs, mainly those who belonged to the HIPMI, who had enjoyed benefits from the government's policy to favor *pribumi* entrepreneurs. Sukamdani held an exuberant Golkar joining ceremony at his Sahid Jaya Hotel, with Golkar Chairman Sudharmono as a guest (*Suara Karya* June 9, 1984). At that time, the KADIN was requesting that the government enact a bill that specified its position and role. Sudharmono, as one of the eleven-member team which was responsible for drafting the Broad Guidelines of State Policy (GBHN), included a phrase pertaining to the enactment of the KADIN law in draft form in the general session of the MPR in 1983 (Gitosardjono 1997: 536). This law was subsequently enacted in 1987. To return the favor, Sukamdani urged many entrepreneurs to join Golkar as the Chair of KADIN and held two induction ceremonies at his own hotel. Furthermore, Sukamdani suggested to Sudharmono that he should gather funds for political and election campaigns from the business world and gave an order to voluntarily support Golkar to the KADIN's regional branches ahead of the 1987 election. Entrepreneurs in regional areas who had become Golkar's cadres provided the transportation, accommodation and vessels required for election campaigns to Golkar's executives (Gitosardjono 1997: 536–538).

Entrepreneurs joined Golkar in the manner described above and those who were especially enthusiastic in promoting Golkar's campaigns were provided with executive posts in Golkar. Among those were some who took on a political career while continuing their business engagement such as Agung Laksono, who was elected to the parliamentary membership of the DPR in the 1987 general election and subsequently became a Central Executive Board member of Golkar in October 1988.

Table 4.5: Occupational backgrounds of DPR members elected from Golkar in the 1987, 1992 and 1997 elections

OCCUPATIONAL BACKGROUND	1987		1992		1997	
Official of central or local government, or governor, regent or mayor	91	(30.4)	78	(27.6)	102	(31.4)
Education	55	(18.4)	53	(18.8)	55	(16.9)
Entrepreneur or executive of private company	29	(9.7)	51	(18.1)	82	(25.3)
DPRD member	14	(4.7)	8	(2.8)	15	(4.6)
Military officer	63	(21.1)	53	(18.8)	36	(11.1)
Judicial post	10	(3.3)	10	(3.5)	5	(1.5)
Student	16	(5.4)	7	(2.5)	3	(0.9)
Housewife	10	(3.3)	7	(2.5)	6	(1.9)
Religious leader	—		—		3	(0.9)
Agriculture	—		—		1	(0.3)
Doctor	5	(1.7)	9	(3.2)	3	(0.9)
Media	5	(1.7)	5	(1.8)	6	(1.9)
Other	1	(0.3)	—		3	(0.9)
Unknown	—		1	(0.4)	5	(1.5)
Total	299		282		325	

Notes: Figures represent number of people. Figures in brackets represent percentage (%) of the total.
Source: Masuhara (2005: 47).

Table 4.5 indicates that the number of DPR members from Golkar who started as entrepreneurs increased significantly at every election after 1987. In fact, in the 1997 election, one in four elected Golkar representatives were entrepreneur-turned politicians.

Islamic group members

An influx of new members to Golkar from Islamic groups also became one of the important factors that brought changes to the nature of the organization.

The transformation of devout Muslims who had political influence into Golkar supporters was already an issue for Golkar in the 1970s. A variety of attempts had been made to tackle this problem, including the incorporation of existing Islamic organizations or creation of new Islamic organizations under Golkar's umbrella, such as the Islamic Education Reform Endeavour Movement

(GUPPI), Council for Islamic Dakwah (MDI), Al Hidayah and the Ulama Functional Union (Satkar Ulama). However, none of these organizations could impel a significant number of devout Muslims to join Golkar. From the early 1970s to the mid-1980s, the government and the Islamic forces such as Nahdlatul Ulama (NU) and Muhammadiyah were in a constant state of hostility as they disagreed on many issues including the issue of the marriage law, the issue of the legislation on the P 4 program to incorporate Pancasila education in school curriculums and public servant training programs and the issue of the enactment of the five political laws including the mass organization law which designated Pancasila as the sole principle for all social and political organizations. The PPP, an Islamic opposition party, was protesting against the government on the back of solid support from many Islamic forces. The government strove to bring PPP supporters over to their side while impairing the power of the PPP by manipulating intra-party dissent, but it was unlikely that they would be able to change the mindset of supporters of mainstream Islamic forces such as the NU and Muhammadiyah through the incorporation of existing Islamic organizations or the creation of its own Islamic organizations.

However, as Golkar became capable of raising sufficient funds under Sudharmono, the organization started to make generous donations to nationwide Islam-related facilities to gain support from devout Muslims. A report compiled by Golkar states that a total of 1,239,380,822 rupiah was provided by the Central Executive Board over the period from June 1984 to December 1987 for books, cassettes, cash contributions for the Festival of Fast-Breaking (Idul Fitri), charity donations, building construction expenses, funding to mosques for pilgrimages to Mecca (Haji), *pesantren* (Islamic boarding schools), orphanages, religion-related foundations and religious schools (DPP Golkar 1988b: 2363–2379). This kind of assistance to Islam-related facilities was in some cases provided via presidential assistance (*banpres*) or funds arranged through President Suharto's foundations. Even in these cases, aid and donations from the President were presented through Golkar Chairman Sudharmono when he visited rural areas for inspection as the State Secretary.

The fact that almost all of the key Islamic organizations accepted Pancasila as the sole principle in the period from 1984 to 1985 also had a major impact. During deliberations on the mass organization bill in the DPR, the NU decided to accept Pancasila at its national congress held in Situbondo, East Java in December 1984. The decision was implemented through changing the articles of the NU's platform in the form of 'NU accepts the principle of Pancasila and follows Islam' (*NU berasas Pancasila and beraqidah Islam*). Despite the fact that this represented a form of compromise between the government that required the acceptance of Pancasila as the sole principle and NU members who opposed it, the government not only accepted the NU's ambiguous decision, but also changed the preface of the mass organization bill to suit it—that is, the government included wording that acknowledged religious identity. Following the NU's lead, many Islamic organizations changed their platforms after the bill was passed. In the process of the deliberation of the bill, the relationship between Islamic forces such as the NU and Muhammadiyah and the Suharto government, especially the ruling party Golkar, was transformed from one of confrontation to one of relative harmony. Instead, the PPP was no longer the sole political party representing devout Muslims' interests in parliament. This markedly diminished the significance of the PPP as an Islamic opposition party.

The government sought to further appease the Islamic forces. They presented the religious court law, which the Islamic forces had been demanding for a long time, to the DPR in 1989 and Golkar approved this bill as the ruling party. In 1990, the Association of Islamic Intellectuals (ICMI) was established with the government's support. This association consisted of a wide spectrum of Islamic intellectuals outside the government as well as a large number of key government officials and Golkar politicians. In addition, President Suharto made a pilgrimage to Mecca (*Haji*) with his wife in 1991. This drew a lot of attention as the President had always been regarded as a follower of *Kebatinan*, the belief indigenous to Java (Kurasawa 2006: 129). By this time, the Suharto regime was no longer viewed as 'anti-Islamic'—in fact, the common perception was that the regime was in fact becoming Islamic and that the President was closing the distance with devout Muslims.

Vigorous recruitment of Islamic organization members into Golkar began at around this time. The first leader of an Islamic organization to be recruited to Golkar was Slamet Effendy Yusuf of the NU. He was well known as a representative figure of young NU leaders. Slamet, after having participated in student movements in the 1970s, served as the Chair of the Central Executive Board of the Ansor Youth Movement (GP Ansor), an NU affiliated youth group, for a decade from 1985 while working as a journalist and editor-in-chief of an Islamic daily newspaper (*Pelita*) and weekly magazine (*Forum Keadilan*). He strongly asserted that the NU should leave the PPP in the NU's national congress in 1984, where he also served as a secretary of the committee to discuss withdrawal from the PPP (*komisi khittoh*) and drafted a withdrawal proposal. In fact, the NU declared its disengagement from politics and did withdraw from the PPP under the slogan '*Khittah 1926*', signifying a return to the spirit of the year the NU was founded (*Majalah Tokoh Indonesia* vol.4,

2003: 8–9). For the government, Slamet was a prime target for recruitment as he had made a significant contribution in detaching the NU, the biggest support base, from the PPP.

Even though Slamet was not even a Golkar member, he attended Golkar's leaders' meeting in 1987 for the first time upon invitation by the Secretary-General of Golkar Sarwono Kusumaatmadja (*Majalah Tokoh Indonesia* vol.4 2003: 15) and joined the Central Executive Board headed by the new Chairman Wahono in the following year. It was utterly extraordinary that, aside from high-ranking military officers, a person who had never taken part in Golkar's activities until then would be recruited straight into the Central Executive Board—especially when taking into consideration the fact that he was the leader of an Islamic youth group. The position given to him—the head of the Department of Youth—can be taken as evidence that Golkar expected that this would help attract more young resources from the NU. Before the 1992 general election, Slamet made a prediction regarding the voting behavior of GP Ansor, an organization controlled by him, in which he estimated that ninety-five percent of the members in the West Java branch, seventy-five percent in the Central Java branch and sixty to seventy percent in the East Java branch would vote for Golkar (*Media Karya* Oct. 1990: 31–38). Furthermore, in the 1997 election, several Ansor-related candidates including the Chair of Ansor Muhammad Iqbal Assegaf were elected as members of the DPR as representatives of Golkar.

Muhammadiyah approached Golkar in a more voluntary way. In May 1988, the government presented the national education bill to the DPR and Muhammadiyah, welcoming this move, documented the points they wanted to correct pertaining to articles regarding religious education and submitted them to the government and each faction of the DPR. The proposals made by Muhammadiyah were reflected in the bill (Suny 2000: 141–144). Similarly, Muhammadiyah also expressed their welcome for the religious court bill presented in January 1989 and appealed to Golkar to support the bill (*Media Karya* June 1989: 58). In 1990, the central executives of the Muhammadiyah Youth (*Pemuda Muhammadiyah*), a youth group under Muhammadiyah's umbrella, visited Golkar and proposed to Chairman Wahono that Muhammadiyah Youth and Golkar form an alliance. On this occasion, the Muhammadiyah Youth side firstly expressed their gratitude for Golkar's endeavor in the passage of the national education bill as well as the religious court bill in the DPR and then shared Muhammadiyah's intentions in relation to a variety of issues such as the economic and social gap, reconciliation among religions and the 1992 election (*Media Karya* Aug. 1990: 48).

At that time, there was an ongoing power struggle between the Yogyakarta group led by Amien Rais and Syafii Ma'arif and the Jakarta group led by Lukman

Harun and Din Syamsuddin inside Muhammadiyah. It was the latter group that tried to approach Golkar. In 1990, Amien Rais was elected as the Chair of Muhammadiyah and the Yogyakarta group came to fill the organization's executive posts, but the Jakarta group continued to maintain its relationship with the government and Golkar. As a result, some Muhammadiyah executive members were elected to the DPR as Golkar politicians in the 1992 election. Subsequently, in 1993, Din Syamsuddin was added to Golkar's Central Executive Board—becoming the first Muhammadiyah executive member to join the Board. Given his background as the Chair of Muhammadiyah Youth from 1989 to 1992, Golkar hoped, just as they did for Slamet Effendy Yusuf, that Syamsuddin would attract more of the young, key members of Muhammadiyah to Golkar. In the 1997 election, Hajriyanto Thohari, who held the same chair position of the Muhammadiyah Youth, and several others were elected to the DPR from Golkar.

The 1990s saw an increase in the number of politicians belonging to the Association of Islamic Intellectuals (ICMI) within Golkar. Behind the establishment of the ICMI was the Islamization trend that was widespread in Indonesian society. Since the 1970s, more and more devout Muslims began receiving university education and those students who pursued deeper knowledge of Islam started to conduct voluntary study sessions in university campuses on a frequent basis (Miichi 2004: 68–77). On the backdrop of the worldwide Islamization since the 1979 Iranian revolution, middle-class Indonesians who emerged in the 1980s started to consciously believe in and practice Islam and the number of media covering Islam, which targeted this new middle class, also increased (Nakamura 1994: 279–280, 288). While Indonesian society was undergoing Islamization, university students and intellectuals initiated the call for the establishment of the ICMI. Their idea—to create an organization in which a broad range of Islamic intellectuals could come together—was welcomed by the Minister of Environment Emil Salim as well as the Head of the Agency for Assessment and Application of Technology Habibie, with the latter in particular strongly demanding that President Suharto grant permission for its establishment. Consequently, the ICMI was founded upon Suharto's approval in 1990 and this new forum offered a place for interaction between intellectuals outside the government and the government's high-ranking officials.

Despite being created as an association of intellectuals, this did not mean ICMI members were strictly Islamic scholars and *ulama*. While scholars and *ulama* comprised the Specialist Board (Dewan Pakar), the Advisory Board (Dewan Penasehat) consisted of senior government officials and former senior Armed Forces officers as well as Golkar politicians. No special qualification was required to join the ICMI; any Muslim with university-level education or anyone who engaged in some kind of Islamic activity was able to join, regardless of whether they were entrepreneurs, NGO employees or journalists. However, as a result of such openness and diversity in its membership, the role and purpose of the ICMI remained rather undefined. Nonetheless, the intention of the government, especially President Suharto himself, in encouraging the establishment of an organization that pulled together a broad range of Islamic intellectuals from outside the government who had been keeping their distance from or were critical of the government, was clear—they wanted to improve their image among devout Muslims. Furthermore, for the government, the organization offered a channel through which they could contact Islamic intellectuals with whom they did not have any prior form of connection. The existence of the ICMI enabled them to co-opt intellectuals who had been critical of the regime into the government or the ruling party and in some cases even control their activities[8].

In the 1992 and 1997 elections, sixteen ICMI executive members who were close to Habibie, who became the first Chair of ICMI, including Marwah Daud Ibrahim and Priyo Budi Santoso, became members of the DPR as Golkar faction representatives. They had not had any experience working for Golkar, but joined on the back of Habibie's political influence. Several of them including Marwah Daud were added to Golkar's Central Executive Board in 1993. Also, NGO-affiliated ICMI leaders such as Adi Sasono and Dawam Rahardjo, who were suitably close to Habibie, were appointed as members of the MPR as Golkar faction representatives in 1992.

Common characteristics of the recruited groups

In the 1980s, Golkar Chairman Sudharmono carried out restructuring of the personnel recruitment system, adding new elements to the personnel structure of Golkar. The addition of a diverse constellation of social elites was not only intended to expand Golkar as an organization but was also tightly linked with the Suharto regime's political and social controls—that is, the control of student movements and absorption of elite students, preferential treatment of *pribumi* in terms of economic policies, appeasement of the Islamic forces and dismantling of the PPP. The recruitment of former student activists, *pribumi* entrepreneurs and members of Islamic organizations into Golkar was indeed motivated by the fact that Golkar needed those elites to lead the organization in the future, but at the same time, also corresponded with the above government policies. The Suharto regime chose to incorporate social elements that had not previously been part of Golkar in its effort to overcome the issue of its weak social base and this eventually resulted in the stabilization of the Suharto regime in and after the mid-1980s. On the other hand, for those who were absorbed without particular connections with governing elites, joining Golkar meant that they gained an important channel to come closer to power. This section describes the common characteristics of and mutual relationships between the three social groups, namely former student activists, *pribumi* entrepreneurs and Islamic organization members.

High educational background and involvement in student movements

Most of those from the three groups who joined Golkar in and after the 1980s were highly educated. They were either university graduates or had studied at a tertiary level for a short period. Many were from prestigious national universities such as the University of Indonesia in Jakarta (Akbar Tandjung, Fahmi Idris, Theo Sambuaga), the Bandung Institute of Technology in Bandung (Siswono Yudohusodo, Abrizal Bakrie, Fadel Muhammad), the State Institute of Islamic Studies located all over Indonesia (Slamet Effendy Yusuf, Syamsul Muarif, Ade Komaruddin) or Hasanuddin University in South Sulawesi (Jusuf Kalla, Marwah Daud Ibrahim). They were highly respected as social elites and were considered as the leaders of the next generation since there were not many university graduates in Indonesian society at that time. Within Golkar too, elites who graduated from these reputable universities were considered as prospects for executive positions; moreover, educational background was given high importance when selecting candidates for membership in the DPR. As I have shown in my previous study on the educational background of Golkar members who were elected to the DPR, the proportion of university graduates to the total was consistently high with an increasing trend, with 58.5 percent (1971 election), 69.4 percent (1977 election), 65.3 percent (1982 election), 66.9 percent (1987 election), 71.3 percent (1992 election) and 85.5 percent (1997 election) (Masuhara 2005: 45–46).

These university-educated elites had, in many cases, engaged in student movements of some sort. The HMI, an Islamic student group formed across different universities, accommodated a large number of Islamic students who were interested in politics. Their sphere of activities was not limited to universities; they actively built networks outside universities. Leaders of regional branches interacted with and sometimes competed against HMI-member students from other universities in the same region where they sought to join the HMI central executive board through organizational elections. Joining the HMI's central board meant they were seconds away from making a political debut. This is because they gained opportunities to connect with their seniors who had now become former HMI politicians and high-ranking government officials.

There were many more student organizations and youth groups other than the HMI. Every religious or political community had their own student organization and youth group; traditional Islam-based NU established the Ansor Youth Movement (GP Ansor) and the Indonesian Islamic Student Movement (PMII), whereas reformist Islam-based Muhammadiyah created Muhammadiyah Youth under their wings. The GMKI was a Protestant student organization, the PMKRI was a Catholic student organization and the GMNI was a nationalist student organization previously under the Indonesian National Party (PNI). It was not only young people in their teens and twenties who belonged to these organizations, but those who were in their late-twenties to forties also made up a significant proportion and the higher the position in the organization, the older the members were. Most members comprising the central executive board were at an age that could no longer be referred to as 'youth' or 'student'.

Those elected to the membership of the central executive board of the youth or student organization gained multiple opportunities to interact and exchange opinions with other student organizations and youth groups. Under the Suharto regime, the KNPI and AMPI essentially offered a place for such cross-organizational engagement. For example, those who had entered the central executive board of the HMI would regularly visit the more inter-organizational KNPI and interact with leaders of other student organizations and youth groups. In other words, becoming an executive member of a student organization or youth group entailed interaction with key members of other religious or political communities.

Moreover, in addition to these horizontal relationships, vertical relationships that span generations also existed as conferences and social gatherings hosted within organizations offered a place for young members of the current generations to interact with their seniors who were alumni. The majority of organizations had central as well as regional executive boards, which would conduct the daily operation of the organization, and advisory boards whose role was to supervise the executive boards. While an executive board was made up of students and young people of the current generations, an advisory board typically consisted of alumni of the organization, often including influential officials of the government or politicians of the ruling party. In the HMI's case, an alumni association called KAHMI (Alumni of the Islamic Students' Association) whose executive board was composed of influential figures of the political and economic spheres, bureaucratic institutions and academic world sent their members to the advisory boards of the HMI and, in some cases, exerted influence on younger generation HMI members. The advisory boards of student organizations and youth groups could supervise and control the activities of the respective organizations by intervening in executive board elections. However, at the same time they acted as a bridge between younger generations and the government, parliaments, the ruling party and business circles, helping young elites to enter these worlds just as former HMI executive Akbar Tandjung recruited young HMI executive members to Golkar.

From the perspective of the alumni who had already been absorbed into the regime, networks of youth groups and student organizations offered them good opportunities to discover the trends in public opinion, especially students' views, through candid exchanges with younger generations and to inform students of the government policy. It was indeed a place for cross-generational interaction in this sense. The understanding and sympathy occasionally displayed by many Golkar politicians toward student movements can be accounted for not just because they had participated in student movements themselves but due to the fact that they had tangible connections with those of the current generation who were involved in the movements.

Those who belonged to a university and had participated in a student organization or youth group, especially key figures that led central activities, were provided with the opportunity to form an extensive, horizontal network with elites of the same generation as well as to participate in events where younger and senior elites could interact and exchange opinions across generations. Many social elites who joined Golkar had this experience in common.

Islam orientation and the focus on **pribumi**

The second characteristic is the tendency toward Islam orientation and the focus on *pribumi*. Many of those who joined Golkar in and after the 1980s were devout Muslims.

The primary reason that a large proportion of the newly recruited elites were devout Muslims was that many former student activists once belonged to the HMI. The HMI had '*membina Kadre Bangsa*', meaning 'development of national cadre', as its goal from the time of its establishment (Ranuwihardjo 1997: 12–13). However, during the 1970s, the HMI was sending its executive members to the PPP, the Islamic opposition party, rather than Golkar. It was only after Akbar Tandjung, who was the Chair of the HMI (1972–1974), became a member of the DPR from Golkar in 1977 and in 1978 joined the executive board of the AMPI, a youth group controlled by Golkar, that HMI began sending its members to Golkar. Since then, generations of HMI central executive board members as well as chairs of the HMI's regional branches were recruited into Golkar one after another. Eky Syafruddin (HMI central executive board member, 1966–1969), Abdullah Puteh (HMI central executive board member, 1971–1974), Abu Hasan Sazili (HMI central executive board member, 1971–1974), Mahadi Sinambela (HMI central executive board member, 1974–1976), Zamharir (HMI central executive board member, 1976–1979), Rambe Kamarulzaman (Chair of HMI Jakarta branch, 1977), Syamsul Muarif (Chair of HMI Kalimantan branch, 1977–1979), Mohammad Yamin Tawari (HMI central executive board member, 1983–1986), Herman Widyananda (Chair of HMI central executive board, 1988–1990), Ade Komaruddin (Vice-Chair of HMI central executive board,1989–1990), Ferry Mursyidan Baldan (Chair of HMI central executive board, 1990–1992) and Yahya Zaini (Chair of HMI central executive board, 1992–1994) were all recruited in this way.

Secondly, a large portion of the *pribumi* entrepreneurs who joined Golkar were devout Muslims who had their roots in heavily Islamic areas of Sumatra and Sulawesi. The 'roots' indicated here were not always place of birth, but sometimes that of their fathers or grandfathers. For example, Abdul Latief and Surya Paloh were from Aceh, Abrizal Bakrie and Ponco Sutowo from South Sumatra, Fahmi Idris from West Sumatra and A. A. Baramuli and Jusuf Kalla from South Sulawesi. While their core activities, both business and political, were inevitably based in Jakarta, many of the entrepreneurs were devout Muslims who came from heavily Islamic regions. They created foundations for philanthropic purposes to support Islamic education and provide assistance to the poor and aspired to be leaders themselves for the social empowerment of devout Muslims. They often emphasized the need for the government to protect *pribumi*-owned businesses, if the position of *pribumi* entrepreneurs was to be improved in the economic world dominated by Chinese-Indonesian corporate groups. A large number of organizations, including the HIPMI, KUKMI and HIPPI (Association of Pribumi Entrepreneurs), were established by *pribumi* entrepreneurs in the 1970s to put forward such demands.

In and after the 1970s, devout Muslim elites with university degrees increased in number across society and advanced into not only Golkar but also a wide variety of fields including bureaucracy, politics and economics. However, they felt this was insufficient and had a strong awareness that they must further expand the presence of devout Muslims. In addition to those who joined Golkar from Islamic organizations, devout Muslim student activists and entrepreneurs shared this awareness and those who participated in the ICMI in the early 1990s echoed similar views. The ICMI clearly expressed that its goal was to redress the proportion of devout Muslims in the political and economic spheres as well as bureaucratic agencies so that it would rightly reflect that in society (Hefner 2000: 140–141).

Nevertheless, the fact that they were devout Muslims did not make their argument radical in any way. They did not seek to have Islamic law (Sharia) incorporated into the constitution or turn Indonesia into an Islamic state. They placed the highest priority on the unification of Indonesia and Pancasila as reflective of the national consensus. They were indeed quite amenable from the government's perspective, which is precisely why they became the target of recruitment into the government and Golkar.

Social connections and personal networks outside the government
As a result of the absorption of various social elites into the organization, in the 1990s, a degree of social connectivity developed within Golkar, which could not possibly have emerged in the 1970s when the leadership consisted of Armed Forces officers and bureaucrats. For example, Slamet Effendy Yusuf, who joined Golkar from GP Ansor, acted as a liaison to link the NU community with Golkar and the government, and Din Syamsuddin, who came from the Muhammadiyah Youth, became a channel to connect Muhammadiyah with Golkar and the government. Similarly, entrepreneurs who became Golkar members joined the ruling party as representatives of *pribumi* entrepreneurs on the back of support from a range of entrepreneurs' groups and business associations such as the HIPMI and KADIN.

In the case of the HMI and ICMI, the nature of their networks played a role in determining the way they connected people within the regime, that is, members of Golkar and the government, with those outside the regime. While the HMI sent many of its members to bureaucratic institutions and Golkar[9], it also produced human resources for a variety of other organizations and fields. The opposition party, the PPP included a great number of former HMI activists such as Chairperson Ismail Hasan Metareum (1993–1998), whereas Islamic intellectuals such as Nurcholish Madjid and Djohan Effendy as well as Adi Sasono and Dawam Rahardjo, who campaigned on behalf of an NGO organization, were also from the HMI. Those who started their career in the HMI played an active role in arranging a place where government and non-government actors could engage in dialogue.

Nurcholish Madjid, one of the most prominent Islamic intellectuals from the HMI, asserted that Islamic political parties were not necessarily the only instruments that could realize the interests of Muslims. He argued that it was possible to promote their interests through non-Islamic political institutions, even when state systems or political institutions were not based on Islam (Effendy 2003: 326–327). This view was proffered to put an end to the dispute that had been ongoing since the independence of Indonesia between the group of devout Muslims, who argued that the state and constitution should be based on Islam, and the group opposing this idea. Akbar Tandjung was the one who sought to implement this thought in the political arena. He led many of HMI's young members to Golkar based on Nurcholish's perspective (Effendy 2003: 332–334). Nurcholish's view became an ideological foundation for former

HMI activists. In this sense, the HMI community in the Suharto era can be considered as having formed a web of networks based on a common ideological base—spanning within and outside the regime.

The ICMI had participation from an even broader spectrum of people than the HMI. The top layer of the organization consisted of the executive board, advisory council and specialist council. While the executive board included high-ranking government officials such as Habibie and Haryanto Danutirto as well as non-government intellectuals such as Imaduddin Abdul Rahim and Adi Sasono, the advisory council comprised mainly Golkar politicians, high-ranking government officials and entrepreneurs whereas the specialist council was composed of non-government academics and intellectuals such as Amien Rais (Chair of Muhammadiyah). One of the defining characteristics of the ICMI was that it not only brought together Islamic intellectuals of high repute in society who had distanced themselves from the government, but also secured the participation of those who were rather critical of the Suharto regime, such as Amien Rais and Adi Sasono. The first Chair of the ICMI, Habibie, who was known as Suharto's crony, did not remove them for being critical of the government but instead gave them important posts. Despite the fact that the ICMI was often criticized for its lack of organizational integrity and restrictions imposed on members' actions due to its close proximity to the government, its inclusivity—accommodating senior government officials as well as those critical of the government—provided a vital place for government and non-government social elites to interact and exchange opinions. For those in the ruling party and the government, the ICMI was a place that enabled them to come into contact with non-government social elites. As for non-government social elites as well, it became a key channel through which they could communicate with government personnel.

After the mid-1980s, by virtue of the appeasement of anti-government forces and co-optation into Golkar, overt opposition toward the Suharto regime gradually disappeared and the political situation began to stabilize. The incorporation of a broad range of social elites into the organization enabled Golkar to have groups with social support bases as its components for the first time. These social elites did not sever ties with their original bases and organizations but maintained these relationships and this had a significant impact on the political change of 1998.

5
Dilemmas of the Giant Ruling Party: The Struggle for Independence and Its Failure

The organizational reform carried out under Chairman Sudharmono transformed Golkar into a giant organization with as many as thirty million members. In addition, the restructuring of the personnel recruitment system added a diverse array of social elites to Golkar, some of who were elected to join the DPR or promoted to the party's executive posts in and after the 1980s. Golkar was reborn anew distinct from its image of the 1970s—a government-founded body with its executive posts dominated by military officers.

In the 1987 election, Golkar won over seventy percent of the vote without overt support from the Armed Forces for the first time. By that time, there was almost no group that could be called an opposition force left in Indonesia. Criticism and demonstrations against the Suharto regime had disappeared and both the ruling party and the opposition parties now supported every government policy in the DPR. The period from the late 1980s to the early 1990s was indeed the time when the Suharto regime enjoyed the greatest degree of stability. This deepened Suharto's confidence in the durability of the regime and caused him to allow 'openness' (*keterbukaan*). Relaxed regulations on speech and media raised high expectations for political liberalization in Indonesia.

Under such circumstances a series of shifts emerged that aimed to improve Golkar's role as a political party from within. These motions were collectively aimed at 'independence'. Golkar attempted to become independent from the government through the enhancement of the DPR's functions of lawmaking and supervising the government, as well as from the Armed Forces, which regarded itself as the 'founder' of Golkar, but both were destined to fail. This chapter gives an account of the way Golkar's pursuit of independence began, developed and eventually failed and at the same time reveals the dilemmas faced by Golkar, which became a giant ruling party.

Dilemmas as the ruling party: Suharto and Golkar

The issue of Golkar's independence
Golkar's sweeping victory in the 1987 general election resulted in the common view that Golkar's organizational consolidation, undertaken by Chairman Sudharmono, was a success. In the 1987 election, the Armed Forces is said to have acted in a neutral manner, in contrast to previous elections in which their regional military commands had always provided full support for Golkar's election campaigns. The fact that Golkar won the election was recognized as the first victory it accomplished without depending on the Armed Forces. Having gained a boost in confidence from this victory, some Golkar executive members began to see their organization as an independent political power. The direct catalyst for this shift occurred in Golkar's leadership meeting (*rapim Golkar*) held in November 1987 when the Chair of the Advisory Board's Daily Executive Committee (*Ketua Presidium Harian Dewan Pembina*) Maraden Panggabean indicated that Golkar was starting to develop the capacity to achieve 'independence' (*kemandirian*) (*Media Karya* Nov. 1987: 46). Considering that Panggabean was a former Armed Forces Commander highly trusted by Suharto, this statement from him, as a representative of the Advisory Board, was understood to have been made on the back of permission from Advisory Board Chair Suharto. After this event, Golkar's executives began to be highly aware of the issue of independence.

Golkar's independence issues can be analyzed from two aspects. One was the relationship between Golkar and the Armed Forces. Regarding itself as the 'founder' of Golkar, the Armed Forces guided the organization in the 1970s and provided extensive support during elections. However, after Sudharmono's assumption of Golkar's chairman position in 1983, a distance began to grow between the Armed Forces and Golkar. From the Armed Forces' perspective, the issue over Golkar's independence that surfaced in 1987 was quite simply an attempt to assert its independence from the Armed Forces. This relationship shift will be discussed in the second section of the chapter.

The second aspect of Golkar's independence is that its executives started to pursue the improvement of its role as a ruling party. This signified the executive members' ambitions to fill the state's key positions—the posts they believed were appropriate for the executives of the ruling party—as well as their motivation to perform decent work as DPR members elected with public support and serve due functions expected of a political party, that is, to reflect public opinion in policies and laws. To achieve this, Golkar politicians in the DPR could no longer act as the government's puppets. The view that they needed to supervise the government, criticize it if necessary and advocate their own opinions more vigorously in the DPR as representatives of the nation became prevalent.

Furthermore, the entry of three young executive members who had been promoted to Golkar's Central Executive Board under Chairman Sudharmono, namely Sarwono Kusumaatmadja, Akbar Tandjung and Siswono Yudohusodo, into the Fifth Development Cabinet formed in March 1988 raised the incentive to foster national leaders in Golkar even further (*Media Karya* Apr. 1988: 9). In order to enlist human resources with the potential to become national leaders, a bottom-up system was employed, and as part of this initiative, Golkar's congress system was revised in 1988 to the new format in which regional congresses would be held prior to the central national congress, as opposed to the previous three congresses (1973, 1978, 1983), all of which began with the national congress (*Media Karya* Apr. 1988: 45).

Congresses were held in 298 local branches corresponding to second-level regional governments (regencies and cities) between June and July 1988, and in twenty-seven branches corresponding to first-level regional governments (provinces) between August and September of the same year. The branch head and executive board members were named in each regional congress and subsequently Golkar's chairman and Central Executive Board members were selected in the national congress held in October.

At both regional and central levels, the following six criteria needed to be satisfied for one to be chosen as an executive board member: the candidate must (1) have a good reputation, be dedicated and have no shortcomings; (2) be able to cooperate in a group to improve Golkar's roles; (3) have the ability to gain social support and trust; (4) be able to appoint senior and junior executives in a good balance; (5) have played an active role in Golkar in the last five years; and (6) be able to easily make time to carry out their role as an executive board member. In a congress, a formation team (*tim formatur*) consisting of seven people chosen from representatives of various groups decided on the formation of the executive board, taking into consideration the above-listed criteria (*Media Karya* May 1988: 39–40). In addition, operational programs were determined in local branch congresses and used as material for discussions on operational programs in higher-level branch congresses (*Media Karya* May 1988: 44). Granting the authority to decide on the formation of the executive boards and operational programs autonomously to the local level was also interpreted as a sign of Golkar's move toward independence (*Media Karya* May 1988: 44).

Retired Army Major General Wahono was the new Golkar chairman who came to be elected through this process. Behind the election of Wahono, who used to serve as the Governor of East Java Province, to the chairman position was a feud between the Armed Forces and Golkar over the vice presidential election. More specifically, high-ranking officers of the Armed Forces who were displeased with the election of Golkar Chairman Sudharmono to the vice presidential post in the general session of the MPR in March 1988, took full advantage of the bottom-up system to prevent Sudharmono's reelection as Golkar's chair. The Armed Forces achieved this by installing retired military officers to the top positions of many local branches by manipulating the election process. These military personnel-turned branch heads then implicitly indicated their disapproval of the reelection of Sudharmono by nominating military officers other than Sudharmono as candidates for the next chairman for the upcoming national congress, ultimately causing Sudharmono to renounce his reelection bid (Sudharmono 1997: 387). The bottom-up system, which was introduced with the expectation that it would promote democracy within the party, resulted in an ironic outcome—the Armed Forces took advantage of the system in opposing the incumbent Chairman Sudharmono's reelection. Wahono, who became Sudharmono's successor, was chosen by Suharto from a shortlist of several candidates proposed by the formation team in the national congress. Thus, his chairmanship was the product of a compromise between Suharto and the Armed Forces.

Table 5.1 shows the members of Golkar's Central Executive Board elected in the national congress held in October 1988.

Rachmat Witoelar from the Bandung group, a former student activist as was his predecessor Sarwono Kusumaatmadja, was selected to the Secretary-General post. Besides older executive members such as Manihuruk, K. H. Tarmudji, Oetojo Oesman, Imam Sudarwo and Jacob Tobing, young generation leaders including Mohammad Hatta from the MDI, Didiet Haryadi from the FKPPI and Slamet Effendi Yusuf from the GP Ansor entered the Board. Also from the business circle, Ponco Sutowo, Gunaryah Kartasasmita, A. A. Baramuli, Iman Taufik and Agung Laksono joined the Executive Board for the first time. In the sense that representatives of the groups that were given key roles during the Sudharmono era were again elected to the Central Executive Board in 1988, the new board kept much of the foundations he established.

In the 1988 national congress, a few changes were made to the organizational structure of the Advisory Board. The chair position was removed from the Daily Executive Committee Advisory Board, which was responsible for managing the day-to-day activities of the Advisory Board, and instead the coordinator role was established to conduct the same operations (*Tempo* Jan. 21, 1989: 14).

Under the new Central Executive Board, the issue of Golkar's independence developed into a discussion on the improvement of the Golkar faction's function in the DPR. Chairman Wahono triggered this by giving the following statement at a work conference that took place in February 1989.

Table 5.1: Central Executive Board of Golkar (1988–1993)

Chairman	Wahono (Retired Army Major General, former Governor of East Java Province)
Vice-Chair	A. E. Manihuruk (Retired Army Brigadier General, Ministry of Home Affairs)
	K. H. Tarmudji (GUPPI)
	Oetojo Oesman (SOKSI)
	Imam Sudarwo (KOSGORO/SPSI)
	Mrs. Aminah Sugandhi (MKGR)
	Retired Army Major General Sugeng Widjaja (DPR's Armed Forces faction)
	Jacob Tobing (Former student activist/Tanah Abang group)
Secretary-General	Rachmat Witoelar (Former student activist/Bandung group)
Deputy Secretary-General	Usman Hasan (HKTI)
	Andi Mochtar
	Suhadi (Retired Army Brigadier General)
	Freddy Latumahina (Former student activist/University of Indonesia Student Council)
Accountant	Eric Samola (Entrepreneur)
	Mrs. Darsoyo (HWK)
	Ponco Sutowo (Entrepreneur/HIPMI/FKPPI)
Department of Election Campaign Strategy	Anang Adenansi (PWI)
	H. T. Barir
Department of Membership, Cultivation of Cadre and Consolidation of Organization	Anton Priyatno
	Mohammad Hatta (MDI)
Department of Education	Basyuni Sriamihardja (PGRI)
	Thomas Suyatno
Department of Information, Publication and Mass Media	Zulharmans Said
	Agus Tagor
Department of Youth	Didiet Haryadi (FKPPI)
	Slamet Effendi Yusuf (GP Ansor)
Department of Agriculture and Fishery	Widjanarko Puspojo (Former student activist)
	Suyoto Hardosutowo
Department of Labor	Marzuki Achmad (FBSI)
	Potsdam Hutasoit (Former student activist/University of Indonesia Student Council)
Department of Women	Sri Redjeki (HWK)
	Gunaryah Kartasasmita (Entrepreneur/HIPMI)
Department of Religion	Umar Mansur (Islamic religious leader)
	Kafrawi Ridwan (Islamic religious leader)
Department of Intellectuals and International Relations	Aulia Aman Rachman (Former student activist/University of Indonesia Student Council)
	Djoko Sudjatmiko (Former student activist/Bandung group)
Department of Culture and Art	Irsyad Sudiro (MKGR)
	Erwan Sukardja (FKPPI)
Department of Cooperatives and Entrepreneurship	A. A. Baramuli (Entrepreneur/KADIN)
	Iman Taufik (Entrepreneur)
Department of Social Services	Mrs. Tati Sumiarno
	Agung Laksono (Entrepreneur/HIPMI)
Department of Research, Development, Energy, Environment and Natural Resources	Haryanto Danutirto (Agency for Assessment and Application of Technology)
	Alfian (Political scientist)

Source: Bangun (1994: 298).

Golkar's cadres have an obligation to understand the public will, explain the government's policies to the public and implement these policies, and play the role of a mediator between the public and the government. The legislature's cadres should actively work to improve expertise in every activity in the DPR. They should stand up for what they think is right and what they think is wrong, without being timid. The Central Executive Board will not dismiss members who try to speak up. So long as the Golkar faction members of the DPR firmly uphold decisions made in the national congress, the Executive Board will never dismiss a member from the DPR. (*Media Karya* Mar. 1989: 41)

The new Secretary-General, Rachmat Witoelar, also made a similar statement as follows.

Golkar members in the DPR took a passive stance more often than an active one. Therefore, these members were not able to respond to changes happening in society. DPR members must have the courage to say what they want to say. They must boldly speak about a variety of issues. Golkar faction members will not be dismissed because they have voiced their opinion with courage. I seek to create an environment where the members do not have to be afraid of being dismissed, in order to enhance the 'openness' and boldness of the members. (*Media Karya* Jan./Feb. 1989: 47)

Since the beginning of the Suharto regime, DPR members had been removed from their positions and replaced by the factional leadership. This was because the law recognized the authority of a party's executive board to dismiss DPR members belonging to their faction. This law specified that election-participating organizations (Golkar and the two opposition parties, the PPP and PDI) could switch parliamentary members within their own faction during their term provided that they consult with the DPR or MPR leadership and gain approval from the president (Tambunan 1986: 218–236, 367–382)[1]. This provision was applied when Rahman Tolleng, who was a member of Golkar's Central Executive Board, was dismissed in 1974 for his involvement in the Malari incident and on another occasion six DPR members from the PDI were dismissed as the result of an intra-party conflict (*Forum Keadilan* Mar. 2, 1995: 18–39).

Although the DPR had legal rights to submit bills, investigate government affairs and demand an explanation from the president[2], these rights were never executed, not even once, under the Suharto regime. One of the reasons that led to the dysfunction of the legislative branch under the Suharto regime was that members of parliament only made statements that were in line with the government's policies for fear of dismissal. If DPR members' comments raised the government's concern, they could be seen as being too 'vocal' and dismissed. Regardless of whether one was a member of the ruling party or an opposition party, their position as a member of parliament was never fully guaranteed. The pledges made by the new Chairman Wahono and Secretary-General Rachmat Witoelar, promising they would not dismiss any DPR members, were thus aimed at improving the situation of the parliament as much as possible, where fear of dismissal was hindering members' performance of their originally intended roles. They believed that if DPR members were able to speak out on various issues during deliberations without hesitation, free from fear of dismissal, that would be the first step toward Golkar's independence.

The discussion concerning 'openness' in the DPR

Prior to the introduction of the 'openness' initiative in June 1989, which raised high hopes among the public for the possibility of political liberalization (*Tempo* July 8, 1989: 23; Uhlin 1997: 160), there were voices coming from within Golkar actively promoting 'openness'. When the government announced a decision to increase the electricity price in March 1989, Secretary-General Rachmat Witoelar (also the secretary of the Golkar faction in the DPR) criticized the price rise and insisted that they should streamline the operation of the State Electricity Company (PLN) before deciding to increase the price (*Tempo* July 15, 1989: 24). Similarly in June, Rachmat demanded that the government review the recently introduced state-controlled lottery (SDSB and TSSB) (*Tempo* July 15, 1989: 24).

This series of events led to the discussion on the level of 'openness' in the DPR. In June 1989, in the Second Committee of the DPR, the Armed Forces faction's members invited retired Army General Sumitro and Alfian, a political scientist, and solicited advice on how to promote 'openness'. The Golkar faction's member Marzuki Darusman (former student activist) welcomed this move and pledged that the Golkar faction would cooperate in every possible way (*Tempo* July 15, 1989: 23). With additional support from media and many organizations such as student groups, the discussion of the 'openness' in the DPR delivered high hopes for liberalization in Indonesian society. Over the course of the period from 1989 to 1992, the mass media started to enjoy more freedom in news reporting and students began raising their voices demanding the freedom to hold street demonstrations (*Tempo* Apr. 22, 1989: 22–33). At around the same time, laborers started demanding wage increases and the number of NGOs that engaged in social activities skyrocketed.

The above-described shifts in the DPR and society at large were tolerated as long as Suharto deemed them harmless. In 1985, the five political laws including the application of Pancasila as the sole principle, which Suharto had long been seeking to achieve, were finally passed. Moreover, in 1987, Golkar won a landslide victory gaining over seventy percent of the vote in the general election for the first time. Accordingly, there was no longer anyone who would publicly disapprove of Suharto's rule. The Suharto regime was enjoying stability and Suharto's position and authority had become completely established. Therefore, it came as no surprise that he allowed some degree of liberalization. Of course, Suharto did not give a green light to full-scale liberalization. At Golkar' twenty-sixth anniversary commemoration event held in October 1990, Suharto reminded everyone that the divergence of opinions generated through the 'openness' must not divide the nation and caution must be taken to prevent such situation (*Media Karya* Oct. 1990: 10–12).

Nevertheless, both in regards to the issues of the electricity price rise and the state-controlled lottery, demands for revision from the ruling party did not result in a change in government policies. Also, when Javanese and Balinese tenant farmers visited the DPR and insisted that the government return the land they had confiscated from them, all the DPR members—including those in the Golkar faction—could do was to listen to their petition, and the issue of land expropriation was barely discussed in the DPR (*Tempo* Apr. 16, 1990: 15; *Tempo* Mar. 16, 1991: 14–17). Golkar, despite being the ruling party, did not have a say in the government's policy-making process. Although some Golkar leaders had been appointed as ministers, there was no mechanism by which the ruling party's policies could be reflected in government policies through these ministers. The ministers were merely the 'servants' of the President and thus their role was to mirror the President's views and orders in policies. Although they could certainly express their opinions to the President, it was up to Suharto to be the judge of those views. Moreover, for ministers, belonging to the ruling party did not necessarily mean that their opinions and ideas should be based on the party's policy.

The fact that the ruling party's policies were not reflected in the government's policy was also evident in the 1992 election campaign in which Golkar avoided making a manifesto. Anang Adenansi, who headed the Department of Election Campaign Strategy in Golkar's Central Executive Board, instructed local branches that they did not need to talk about Golkar's public commitments as part of the campaign, since the Central Executive Board did not intend to make a manifesto (*Media Karya* Apr. 1991: 35). This is because even if Golkar won the election with a manifesto, it would not necessarily be reflected in government policy. 'If requested to dig some wells in a village, Golkar is capable of immediately taking action; however, Golkar is not a government office, therefore, cannot intervene in the work of government offices'[3]. Instead of formulating a manifesto, Adenansi gave local branches the order to appeal to Golkar that it would try to reflect public will in government policy as much as possible (*Media Karya* Apr. 1991: 36).

Golkar was certainly a ruling party in the sense that it held a majority in the parliament and supported the government. However, in fact, it was no different to the opposition parties in that Golkar members could not participate in the decision-making process of the government. It was only natural that some Golkar members felt the positioning of the 'ruling party' was contradictory and started to feel frustrated. Adenansi described this frustration in the following words.

> Golkar is often referred to as the 'government' but if Golkar really was a ruling party then the government should implement all of the ruling party's policies. However, the reality is, we cannot get government consent on many of our policies. One good example is the government-managed lottery. The DPR's Golkar faction appealed to the government that this lottery should be abolished but the government did not approve it. The same goes for the issue of the electricity price increase. If Golkar was the ruling party, then Golkar's policies must be implemented by the government. This is irrefutable. It is not acceptable for the government to deviate from the decisions of the party. (*Media Karya* May 1991: 34)

Similarly, Golkar's DPR member Marzuki Darusman stated as follows.

> The fact that the government contains a large number of Golkar's executives does not automatically mean Golkar is the ruling party. In fact, Golkar members in the DPR have different opinions from the government on many issues. (*Media Karya* May 1991: 25)

Marzuki Darusman and Anang Adenansi were amongst the few who could express this contradiction which many Golkar DPR members and executives were feeling. Golkar was the ruling party in name only and its position was not much different from that of the opposition parties in the sense that even its role to modify laws submitted by the government was not particularly recognized. Those DPR members of Golkar who attempted to address and change such reality were alienated from Suharto and lost their positions.

Friction with Suharto (1): compiling election candidate lists
Suharto's intervention in Golkar had already begun as the candidate lists were being drawn up for the 1992 general election.

In Golkar, the process of making the proportional representation candidate lists was reviewed during Chairman Sudharmono's era and almost the same procedure was followed under Chairman Wahono. Firstly, the Central Executive Board prepared a list of 4,000 candidates, a tenfold of the 400 elected seats available in the DPR. There were twenty-seven province-based electoral districts and the number of seats was allocated according to the number of voters within the district. Local branches then narrowed the list down to 2,000. They could either simply choose half of the 4,000 candidates from the given list or propose other candidates not named on the list. After that, the local coordinators of the Central Executive Board further reduced the list from 2,000 to 1,200[4], and lastly, the Central Executive Board finalized a shortlist of 800, a twofold of the total number of seats (*Tempo* Sept. 14, 1991: 26–27).

During this last step of the selection process, a discussion among the Golkar Chairman, Commander of the Armed Forces and Minister of Home Affairs took place. The trilateral coordination was required to arrange the order of candidates as the Armed Forces and bureaucratic institutions would have nominated their own candidates such as retired military officers and high-ranking government officials. The completed list was submitted to the General Election Bureau (LPU) and upon the consent of Suharto, Chair of Golkar's Advisory Board, underwent screening by the information agency and was finalized as the proportional representation list ready for the election (*Tempo* Sept. 14, 1991: 26–27).

The formulation of candidate lists for three elections in 1971, 1977 and 1982 was relatively simple. The trilateral coordination by the Golkar Chairman, Commander of the Armed Forces and Minister of Home Affairs sufficed as the absolute number of candidates was not that large and there were not many groups trying to stand candidates (*Tempo* Sept. 14, 1991: 26). However, during the Sudharmono era, a new selection method, in which parliamentary candidates were chosen from a pool of 4,000 contenders, was introduced. This lengthened the selection process, causing the formulation of the candidate list to begin as early as over a year before the election. While the list making process became more democratic than before as Chairman Sudharmono allowed local branches to be involved in the process, it also became more complex, requiring time and effort for communication between the central and regional offices. Furthermore, the complexity of the candidate list making process was further heightened as a great number of newly emerging Golkar-affiliated organizations such as the AMPI began frenetic lobbying to put as many of their representatives as possible on the list, and at electable positions.

Suharto particularly wanted Sudharmono to take the chairmanship. He was highly trusted by Suharto and was in a position to be able to contact the President at any point as he also served as the State Secretary; therefore, there was never a time when he and Suharto had conflicting views on Golkar's election strategy and candidate list. However, this was not the case with the relationship between Chairman Wahono and his Executive Board and Suharto. Firstly, Suharto did not particularly want Wahono to be the chairman and there was a distance between the two from the outset. In addition, Wahono, unlike Sudharmono, did not seek

Suharto's approval before making statements in regards to the issue of Golkar's independence as well as the improvement of the Golkar faction's role in the DPR. Wahono and Secretary-General Rachmat Witoelar repeatedly urged the Golkar faction to actively voice their opinions in the DPR. Moreover, Rachmat made a critical comment about the government's policy and some DPR members including Anang Adenansi and Marzuki Darusman not only criticized the policy but went even further, pointing out the contradiction inherent in the political system in which the ruling party Golkar, the largest faction in the DPR, could not participate in the policy-making process. Suharto increasingly displayed displeasure with Golkar's executives' and DPR members' motions for independence.

In addition, Wahono eschewed nominating Suharto as a presidential candidate in 1993. In Indonesia during the Suharto era, there had been a custom of 'unanimous decision' (*kebulatan tekad*) regarding the reelection of Suharto orchestrated by high-ranking officials close to him since the 1970s. Wahono and his Executive Board saw this practice as outdated and shunned it. In May 1990, former Minister of Religious Affairs Alamsjah collected signatures to support Suharto's reelection from eminent Islamic leaders. He gathered signatures from a total of 120 religious leaders including the Chair Hasan Basri and K. H. Ibrahim Hosen of the Council of Indonesian Ulama (MUI), the NU's prestigious *ulama* Kyai Asad Syamsul Arifin, K. H. Masjkur and K. H. Ali Yafie, former Chair of the PSII Harsono Tjokroaminoto, Lukman Harun from Muhammadiyah, K. H. Thohir Widjaja from the MDI and the Vice-Chair of Golkar's Central Executive Board and PERTI member Ismael Hasan. They all stressed that they signed their names as individuals, rather than as representatives of the organization to which they belonged. Nonetheless, it was the first time that so many prominent Islamic leaders had expressed their support for Suharto's reelection and therefore was seen as one of the important events that signified the ever-increasing proximity between the Suharto regime and the Islamic forces (*Tempo* May 26, 1990: 22–29). However, when questioned about Golkar's Central Executive Board's stance regarding Suharto's reelection when this signature-gathering process was covered in the news, Chairman Wahono responded that he only needed to indicate Golkar's position in the general session of the MPR in 1993, and that it was not necessary to announce Golkar's support at this point in 1990.

The formulation of election candidate lists gave rise to yet another disagreement in the relationship between Wahono's Executive Board and President Suharto. Secretary-General Rachmat Witoelar and the head of the Department of Election Campaign Strategy Anang Adenansi were opposing the tactic that had been taken in the previous elections, in which 'vote getters' who were more capable of gathering votes due to their high profile, such as active ministers, were placed at the top of the list. Article 38 of Law No.2 of 1985 prohibited members of parliament from holding office as high-ranking government officials such as minister. In spite of this, active ministers who were often featured in the mass media were named toward the top of the proportional representation list of the electoral district. Below the active ministers, Armed Forces' senior officers and their wives were listed, followed by Central Executive Board members. This was designed so that the ministers whose victory was certain would decline due to their position as Cabinet member, allowing the next candidates on the list to move up to fill the seats. The opposition parties consistently criticized Golkar's 'vote getters' tactic as deceiving voters (*Tempo* Aug. 10, 1991: 27). Thus, Golkar's Central Executive Board appealed to Suharto that they wished to change this tactic. Though the Executive Board compromised with Suharto, who objected to their opinion, and agreed to have a number of ministers included on the list, they determined they would not place them at the top of the list (*Media Karya* Sept. 1991: 45) and eventually managed to gain Suharto's approval[5].

However, Suharto's frustration with the Central Executive Board was manifested in the form of corrections made to the candidate lists. At the final stage of the list making process, Suharto instructed the Central Executive Board to alter the order of several candidates. As a result, Marzuki Darusman, who was an active promoter of 'openness' and had made critical remarks against the government, was moved from nineteenth down to forty-fourth in the West Java electorate, and similarly, head of the Department of Election Campaign Strategy Anang Adenansi, who had expressed his objection to the vote-gathering tactic which placed ministers at the top of the lists, was moved from first to tenth position in the South Kalimantan electorate. Since in the 1987 election the number of candidates elected in the West Java electorate were forty-four and seven for the South Kalimantan electorate, these two could not be elected unless Golkar gained more seats than the 1987 election in each electorate (*Tempo* Sept. 14, 1991: 25). In the same manner, one of the Central Executive Board members Djoko Sudjatmiko, who was close to Secretary-General Rachmat Witoelar, was demoted from third to tenth—an unelectable (*mustahil*) position—in the list of the West Kalimantan electorate (*Tempo* Sept. 21, 1991: 36–37). Changes in the order of the list like those described above could only have been made via very specific instructions from Suharto. Chairman Wahono tried to save at least Executive Board members from being moved down. However, he had no choice other than to yield to Suharto's instructions and the absolute authority he held as the Chair of Golkar's Advisory Board.

Golkar members were not the only candidates who were made unelectable as a result of alterations to the lists. Some members of the Armed Forces faction, who were on Golkar's candidate list because they planned to move to the Golkar faction in the 1992 election, were removed as they were vocal in the

DPR. Examples of such candidates include retired Army Major General Saiful Sulun and retired Police Colonel Lukmini Kusumo Astuti, who initiated the 'openness' discussion in the Second Committee of the DPR in June 1989 (*Tempo* Sept. 14, 1991: 31–33).

At the end of September 1991, shortly after altering the election candidate lists, Suharto addressed a group of former student activists of the 'Generation of 66'[6] about his views on the relationship between the parliament and the government as follows.

> We should not think of rendering the DPR more bold and daring. That is to claim that the DPR does not qualify as a legislature if it does not have the courage to disagree with the government. The relationship between the government and the DPR must not be an 'exchange of punches' [*antem-anteman*]. If we are to implement the Constitution of 1945, then what is required is the division of roles. In a unified, familist state, roles are divided. Each of the executive, legislative and judicial branches is given different authorities. If they were all given the same authority, then they would have to compete against each other and inevitably clash. This would be contradicting the Constitution of 1945. (*Tempo* Oct. 5, 1991: 22)

This speech was a sign that indicated that Suharto was displeased with the move of the Golkar and Armed Forces factions, which were trying to enhance the role of the DPR by encouraging members of parliament to raise their voices against the government in an atmosphere of heightened hope for political 'openness'. Suharto moved the DPR members who were engaged in such activities down toward the end of the candidate lists to prevent them from winning seats. No matter how high one's status was within the ruling party, they could not escape expulsion once they acted against Suharto's will. Even Central Executive Board members who were at the top of a political organization with thirty million members were no exception.

Friction with Suharto (2): aftermath of the 'defeat' in the 1992 election

The election results further deteriorated the relationship between Suharto and Wahono's Executive Board. In the general election held in June 1992, Golkar's share of the vote fell by five points from the previous election in 1987 (from 73.2 percent to 68.1 percent) and the number of seats also decreased by seventeen seats, from 299 to 282. Of course, the decline in the share of votes did not result in Golkar's election defeat, as the party was able to maintain a stable majority in the DPR. Nonetheless, Suharto felt a deep sense of frustration, attributing the decrease to the change to the election tactic made against his will, and wasted no time outlining his discontent with the personnel policy.

In October of the same year, an announcement was made in regards to the appointed seats for the general session of the MPR, which was scheduled for March 1993. Customarily, most candidates who could not be elected to the DPR were appointed to join the MPR. However, this time, Marzuki Darusman and Anang Adenansi, who lost seats in the DPR, were not appointed to the MPR (*Tempo* Oct. 3, 1992: 29). Of particular significance was the exclusion of Central Executive Board member Adenansi from the list, which provoked unrest within the Executive Board. As a well-known student activist of the 'Generation of 66' from Kalimantan, Adenansi kicked off his career in the world of journalism and had been in the DPR as a Golkar member since 1979. He also took a critical stance against the Press Publication Enterprise Permit (SIUPP), which restricted the freedom of the press and publication (*Media Karya* Nov. 1992: 39–40). He was held accountable for the 'defeat' in the election in the form of removal from his seat, as he was the head of the Department of Election Campaign Strategy[7].

Furthermore, the Sixth Development Cabinet announced by the President in March 1993 did not include members from Golkar's Central Executive Board who were close to Wahono. This was in stark contrast to the 1987 election in which some members of Sudharmono's Executive Board, which brought about the landslide victory, were promoted to important posts, with Sudharmono being appointed as Vice President and Secretary-General Sarwono and several other members from Sudharmono's Executive Board being assigned as ministers in the Fifth Development Cabinet in 1988. Wahono was appointed to the Chair of the DPR as well as the MPR, whereas Secretary-General Rachmat Witoelar was appointed as the Ambassador to Russia. The appointment of Witoelar as the Ambassador took place as early as two months prior to October 1993, when his term as Golkar Central Executive Board's Secretary-General would end, and he was immediately sent to Moscow. It was already unusual that Golkar's Secretary-General was assigned to an ambassadorship—especially to Russia. For Indonesians who live in the tropics, transfer to a cold country is seen as a harsh duty. Moreover, Russia at that time was in the ongoing political turmoil following the collapse of the Soviet Union. This meant that the appointment of Witoelar as the Ambassador to Russia was a 'punishment' for incurring the wrath of Suharto (*Tempo* July 17, 1991: 38; *Forum Keadilan* Sept. 2, 1993: 31–34).

At Golkar's national congress held in October 1993, the Advisory Board's Daily Executive Committee's Coordinator Habibie presented a report as a representative of the Advisory Board in front of 3,000 participants. Habibie used this occasion to criticize the Central Executive Board for having lost some share of the vote in the 1992 election on behalf of Suharto (*Media Karya* Nov. 1991: 18; *Tempo* Oct. 30, 1991: 32–33). In response to the denunciation from the Advisory Board, Chair Wahono rebutted that laying the onus upon the Executive Board alone was wrong because the Executive Board continuously consulted with the Advisory Board when developing election tactics. This refutation further fuelled Suharto's anger. Consequently, only eight of Wahono's Executive Board members were retained in the forty-five Central Executive Board members newly selected in this national congress, and none of those eight was close to either Wahono or Rachmat. Ismael Hasan, one of the members reappointed to the Central Executive Board, had participated in the signature-gathering effort to support the reelection of President Suharto by Islamic leaders mobilized by Alamsjah in 1990 and was thus at odds with Wahono who took a critical stance against the excessive mobilization of support.

Those who helped lead the mobilization of support for Suharto maintained their posts, while those who criticized the government to promote the enhancement of the DPR's role lost their seats or posts in the Executive Board. Executive Board members who made changes to the election tactic against Suharto's intention were also ousted for being responsible for having lost some share of the vote. Regardless of how eager Golkar's executives were to improve the autonomy of the organization, the veto power of Suharto as the Chair of the Advisory Board did not allow Golkar to have the capacity to act with autonomy.

Kwik Kian Gie, who was a senior politician of the opposition party, PDI, and also a well-known political economist, made a remark that summarized the difficult situation in which Golkar's executives were placed.

> The largest political organization, Golkar, is facing a major dilemma. Despite being the ruling party with a substantial number of seats in the DPR, it does not have the authority that a ruling party should have, to organize the cabinet or participate in the policy-making process. Even if there is a gap between the will of the public and government policy, Golkar cannot do anything but simply speak the public's will on their behalf. Golkar says that they adopted a bottom-up system but I do not think so. How can they possibly have a bottom-up system when they are still following all the instructions and orders from the leader? Golkar's independence is almost impossible. They may be able to achieve independence if they stopped thinking that they were a ruling party and realize that they no longer need to be a supporter of the government... Golkar's key figures are, albeit not being able to exercise influence in the government's policies and decisions, close to authority. Being close to authority means that they are in a place where they can enjoy benefits, and the bottom line is that they share material interests with people in power. There is no way they can reflect the public's will if they profit from each other. Corruption and monopoly are problems closely intertwined with the government's policies and Golkar has been overly hesitant to resolve these issues. Every one of those who raised their voices eventually ended up getting 'fired'. (*Media Karya* Oct.1993: 27)

Golkar's executives who aspired to independence tried to express the party's autonomy through the role of the DPR and election tactics, but this created friction with Suharto. Besides, they provoked outrage from Suharto for having lost a proportion of the vote and were eventually obliged to bow to his will. Despite holding a majority in the DPR, Golkar's title as the 'ruling party' was in name only. In fact, Golkar had an extremely powerless existence, both in terms of exerting influence on the government and performing the role that the DPR should have been performing.

Competition over political posts: The Armed Forces and Golkar

Vice president and Golkar chairman posts in 1988

As mentioned at the beginning of the first section, the proposition of Golkar's independence in its leadership meeting held in October 1987 spurred speculation that Golkar was intending to assert its independence from the Armed Forces that was regarded as its founder. In spite of Golkar's executives' efforts to dispel the concerns of the Armed Forces by repeatedly claiming that this was not the case, Golkar's independence from the Armed Forces was increasingly recognized as an unavoidable trend.

As described in Chapter Three, the Armed Forces indeed established the organizations that constituted Golkar. The Armed Forces worked together with the Ministry of Home Affairs to provide full support for and contribute to the victory of Golkar in three elections conducted in 1971, 1977 and 1982. The Ministry of Home Affairs and Ministry of Defense and Security maintained influence in Golkar by sending their key members to Golkar's Central Executive Board and local branches. Besides, the Golkar and Armed Forces factions were constantly taking the same stance and acting in a united manner as the 'government faction' in the DPR. This involvement of the Armed Forces and Ministry of Home Affairs in Golkar was justified by the concept known as the 'Great Golkar Family' (*Keluarga Besar Golkar*). The 'Great Golkar Family' was made up of three components, A, B and G, representing the Armed Forces (ABRI), bureaucracy (Birokrasi) and Golkar respectively, which were supposed to work together in cooperation to help foster Golkar[8]. The representatives of the Armed Forces, bureaucracy and Golkar were the Commander of the Armed Forces, Minister of Home Affairs and Golkar Chairman, and a trilateral discussion among them was held before consultation with Suharto, in some cases on Suharto's instruction, before every important decision was made. The Commander of the Armed Forces, the Minister of Home Affairs and the Golkar Chairman from 1973 to 1983 were high-ranking Army field officers. Therefore, major conflict rarely arose among the three parties and the 'Great Golkar Family' kept its harmony.

However, this trilateral relationship started to undergo change when State Secretary Sudharmono assumed the Golkar Chairmanship in 1983. Although Sudharmono was a former high-ranking Army officer, he did not have influence in the Armed Forces Command and Army General Staff, as he used to be a legal officer rather than a field officer. Due to the lack of influence in the Armed Forces, his appointment to the State Secretary by the President and his involvement in controlling the defense budget caused a sense of aversion among the Armed Forces. Since Sudharmono became Golkar Chairman, the Armed Forces gradually distanced themselves from Golkar. Sudharmono succeeded in expanding Golkar by introducing the membership system and recruiting young civilian elites into the organization. However, this gave rise to a concern within the Armed Forces that Sudharmono was trying to establish his power base in Golkar to compete against Commander of the Armed Forces Benny Murdani for the number-two position under Suharto.

On the occasion of the 1987 election, the Armed Forces declared they would no longer give their full commitment to support Golkar as they had been doing thus far. The explanation provided was that they no longer needed to take a pro-Golkar stance since Pancasila was now the sole principle of every political and social organization and thus the conflict over ideology no longer existed in Indonesia. However, Golkar achieved an emphatic victory in this election without full support from the Armed Forces, providing a foothold for its independence. In an attempt to dispel the concerns of the Armed Forces, Golkar's Central Executive Board stated 'Golkar's independence does not mean estrangement from the Armed Forces'; however, the gap between Golkar and the Armed Forces further widened in the following year in the course of the vice presidential candidate selection process which took place in March 1988.

Suharto created an informal 'Team of Nine' ahead of the upcoming presidential/vice presidential election in the general session of the MPR in 1988 and requested that every member of the team present their individual opinion on who was suitable for the state's highest-ranking posts such as President, Vice President, Chair of the DPR and Chair of the MPR (Sudharmono 1997: 391–402). This was a circuitous procedure typical of Suharto's attempts to have political elites unanimously nominate him along the lines of 'no one but Suharto could make a presidential candidate'. At the same time, in terms of the selection of vice presidential candidates, this Team of Nine played a role in having Sudharmono, whom Suharto had in mind, nominated. This is clear if we look at the composition of the team. At that time, Suharto was not going to allow Benny Murdani, who had just handed over the Commander of the Armed Forces post to Try Sutrisno in February 1988, assume the vice presidential office since Suharto was alarmed about his enormous influence within the Armed Forces. Therefore, the Team of Nine consisted of three members from the Armed Forces, namely, Commander of the Armed Forces Try Sutrisno, Armed Forces Command Staff for Sociopolitical Affairs Sugiharto and Army Chief of Staff Edi Sudradjat; three from the State Secretariat, namely, Chief Cabinet Secretary Murdiono, Sukarton and Ginandjar Kartasasmita; and three from Golkar, namely, Vice-Chair R. H. Sugandhi, Secretary-General Sarwono Kusumaatmadja and Deputy Secretary-General Akbar Tandjung (Sudharmono 1997: 391–395). This meant that only three of the team were from the Armed Forces and the remaining six were chosen from Sudharmono's immediate subordinates from the State Secretariat and Golkar's Central Executive Board. The three selected from the State Secretariat were all former Armed Forces officers, but Murdiono and Ginandjar had not served as field officers and were assigned to key posts in the State Secretariat for their administrative competence, as was the case for Sudharmono. Similarly, Golkar's R. H. Sugandhi was also a former Army officer, but he served as the head of the MKGR, one of the former KINOs that constituted Golkar, for a long time and had been away from the Armed Forces for over twenty years.

Secretary-General Sarwono Kusumaatmadja and Deputy Secretary-General Akbar Tandjung, former student activists who rose to power in Sudharmono's Executive Board, vigorously conducted a lobbying effort to elect Sudharmono as vice president. They not only recommended Sudharmono to Suharto but also worked to lay the groundwork for the unanimous nomination of Sudharmono as vice president by the Golkar faction in the DPR/MPR. These two affirmed to Sudharmono that Golkar intended to push Sudharmono as the vice presidential candidate even if the Armed Forces faction fielded their own candidate (Sudharmono 1997: 392–393).

Ultimately, their lobbying proved successful. The Armed Forces faction gave up fielding their own candidate and nominated Sudharmono as the vice presidential candidate in conformity with other factions. Notwithstanding this, the selection of the vice president in the general session of the MPR did not necessarily proceed smoothly. An incident occurred in which a member of the Armed Forces faction raised an objection to the procedures for the selection of the vice presidential candidate and stopped the proceedings of the session[9]. Eventually, Sudharmono was selected as Vice President but the Armed Forces took action to block the reelection of Sudharmono in the election for Golkar Chairman held in the same year. The method the Armed Forces adopted was, as described in the previous section, to firstly have active military officers elected as heads of local branches in regional Golkar congresses, then make them nominate new candidates for the chair position other than Sudharmono. Having become keenly aware of the Armed Forces' disapproval, Sudharmono confirmed Suharto's intention—the President himself did not agree with the reelection of Sudharmono—then gave up his candidacy for the position of Golkar Chairman (Sudharmono 1997: 387). It became clearer than ever before that the relationship between the Armed Forces and Golkar was growing increasingly competitive over political posts through the elections for vice president and Golkar chairman.

Regional political posts from 1992 to 1994

The competition between the Armed Forces and Golkar over political posts extended beyond the central level and played out on the regional level as well. The central authorities often had difficulty controlling these competitions and were in a situation where they were left with no choice but to intervene and reconcile the parties involved. These kinds of competitions were observed mainly in the selection processes for the positions of chairs of the Regional Representative Councils (DPRD, provincial, regency and city representative councils) and heads of regional governments (governor of province, regent of regency and city mayor). Table 5.2 summarizes the competitions and conflicts that took place between the Armed Forces and Golkar over the DPRD chair posts in 1992[10].

The DPRDs formed on the basis of first-level (province level) and second-level regions (regency and city levels) were designed to operate as part of the regional administration, together with the head of the regional government. However, the role of the DPRDs was significantly limited, as the law did not impose responsibility on the heads of regional governments for the DPRDs and policy-making was thus largely controlled by the regional governments. Therefore, the DPRDs had no means of reflecting the will of local residents in politics (Fukao 1995: 108–109). Law No.5 concerning regional administrations that passed in 1974 specified that heads of regional governments were responsible to the Minister of Home Affairs and ultimately the President, but not to the DPRD. The head of a regional government was obliged to provide an explanation for the policies they had implemented on at least a monthly basis, but that was about the extent of the obligations imposed on them regarding the DPRD (Fukao 1995: 108). Local regulations were supposed to be determined jointly by the DPRDs and the regional heads, and the DPRD was given rights to prior deliberation as well as revision rights; however, these rights were hardly executed due to the complexity of the operational process coupled with the inadequacy in regulation formulating capability (Fukao 1995: 110–111). The DPRDs also had budgetary rights, but their scope of involvement in regards to budgetary matters was highly limited as local bodies had to rely on the financial resources held by the central government, without the availability of many independent revenue sources (Fukao 1995: 111).

Table 5.2: Competition and conflict between the Armed Forces and Golkar over Regional Representative Councils' chair posts in 1992

Time	Region	Post	Details of disagreement/confrontation
1 July 1992	North Sumatra	Chair of Provincial Representative Council	The Armed Forces and Golkar factions nominated different candidates for the chair position.
2 July 1992	Central Java	Chair of Provincial Representative Council	The comment made by the Commander of the Central Java Military Command that he would run for the chair post provoked fierce opposition from the Golkar faction. Golkar faction members indicated that they would resign if their nominee, the head of Golkar's local branch, did not become the chair.
3 July 1992	Bali	Chair of Provincial Representative Council	When the Armed Forces faction fielded an active brigadier general as a candidate for the chair position, four candidates from the Golkar faction including the head of Golkar's local branch (retired brigadier general) withdrew their candidacy.
4 August 1992	Southeast Sulawesi	Chair of Provincial Representative Council	The Armed Forces faction fielded an Army brigadier general who was a former deputy governor, whereas the Golkar faction fielded a retired brigadier general who was the head of Golkar's local branch.
5 August 1992	Surakarta (Central Java)	Chair of City Representative Council	The Armed Forces faction's candidate (Army lieutenant colonel) won the vote but later resigned due to an alleged problem with the selection process. Golkar's candidate (civilian) was elected as a result.
6 August 1992	East Nusa Tenggara	Chair of Provincial Representative Council	The fielding of a candidate by the Armed Forces faction as instructed by the military command of the same region provoked opposition from the Golkar faction which then fielded the civilian head of Golkar's local branch as a candidate for the chair.
7 August 1992	North Tapanuli (North Sumatra)	Chair of Regency Representative Council	The Golkar faction fielded their own civilian candidate, whereas the Armed Forces faction fielded an Army lieutenant colonel. Golkar's candidate won the vote.

Source: Items 1–3, 4–5 and 6–7 are based on *Tempo* (Aug. 1, 1992: 33–34), *Tempo* (Aug. 29, 1992: 14) and *Forum Keadilan* (Sept. 17, 1992: 79–85) respectively. Fukao (1999: 101–115) was also used as a reference.

Similarly to the DPR, many members of DPRDs were elected from Golkar and the two opposition parties, that is the PPP and PDI, in elections held every five years. However, members of the Armed Forces faction were appointed, with the local military command's commander exercising substantial influence over these appointments. Considering that the chair posts of the DPRDs were supposed to be decided either by ballot or through deliberation among the factions within the council, the natural consequence would have been that many of the chairs would come from Golkar, which was the largest faction within the council. However, in fact, there was an informal rule that prescribed that the chair would be someone from the Armed Forces faction if the number of Golkar's seats was less than half of the total number of seats, as otherwise 'opposition parties may gain control in deliberations and voting'. However, the Armed Forces faction often tried to establish their member in the chair post even when Golkar did hold over half the number of seats (*Tempo* Aug. 1, 1992: 33). This is because, at the regional level, the commander of the regional military command exercised powerful leadership along with the provincial governor (often an active or retired military officer) and the Armed Forces faction of the DPRD was acting under the commander of the regional military command, governor or Chief of Staff for Sociopolitical Affairs of the Armed Forces Command, who on many occasions ordered them to secure the chair post to gain control of the DPRD (*Tempo* Aug. 1, 1992: 33).

However, the Golkar faction in the DPRDs started to raise objections to this practice. It is only natural that they began protesting as to why the chair should come from the Armed Forces faction instead of the Golkar faction—the largest faction in the council—and especially when the latter held the majority of the seats. When the Armed Forces began taking a more neutral stance in elections and the awareness began to spread within Golkar that they won the election in their own right, this view that the chair must now be someone from the Golkar faction began to be expressed widely (*Tempo* Aug. 1, 1992: 33; *Forum Keadilan* Sept. 17, 1992: 79–81).

In many cases, retired military officers served as the heads of Golkar's local branches. The Golkar faction would nominate them as a candidate for the chair of the DPRD, often against the candidate put up by the Armed Forces faction. Political scientist Nazaruddin Syamsuddin pointed out that the reason for this was that retired officers within Golkar were starting to develop more civilian personalities (*Forum Keadilan* Sept. 17, 1992: 81). While many of the members of the Armed Forces faction acted according to the order of central or regional military commands of the Armed Forces, retired officers who joined Golkar received orders from Golkar's Central Executive Board and acted in concert with other members of the regional Golkar branch. Even if the head of the branch was a retired military officer, most of the branch members were civilians. 'Many young, talented civilian leaders have come to the fore in local branches' (*Forum Keadilan* Sept. 17, 1992: 81), and if the head was ineffectual towards the Armed Forces faction, he would lose support from these young civilian leaders. For them it was of course 'objectionable if the head of the branch supported a candidate nominated by another faction' (*Forum Keadilan* Sept. 17, 1992: 81), and even if the head of the branch wanted to avoid friction with the regional Armed Forces Command, it was difficult to suppress demands from within the local branch.

The above-described change in the relationship between Golkar and the Armed Forces at the regional level became even more apparent in the elections for the regional governments' top positions—provincial governors. Unlike the DPRDs, heads of regional governments, especially provincial governors, were granted the authority to determine regulations as well as the regional budget. Therefore, conflicts over the election of governors were even more complicated, involving a much wider range of stakeholders both at the central and regional level.

In the 1970s, President Suharto selected governors in consultation with Minister of Home Affairs Amirmachmud (Fukao 1999: 99), and high-ranking Army officers filled most posts. The percentage of governors from the Armed Forces in the early 1970s was ninety-two percent (twenty-four out of twenty-six provinces) and that of regents was fifty-nine percent (*Forum Keadilan* May 14, 1992: 13). However, after Sudharmono became Chairman of Golkar in 1983, a new selection procedure—that is, trilateral consultation between the Minister of Home Affairs, Commander of the Armed Forces and Golkar Chairman—was established (Sudharmono 1997: 350–351). These senior officials would pick three candidates for the post of provincial governor, including one 'real candidate' (*calon jadi*) and two 'accompanying candidates' (*calon pendamping*) upon obtaining Suharto's agreement, and arrange matters so that the real candidate would be elected at the provincial council (*Tempo* Sept. 26, 1992: 22–33). Firstly, the Armed Forces, Ministry of Home Affairs and Golkar would hold discussions at the central and regional level, then consult with the President to make a quadripartite decision as to who should be the real candidate and accompanying candidates and finally notify the province of their decision. The steps described above were informal processes and after the decision had been passed to the province, the formal procedure would take place. Each faction would field a candidate in the DPRD so there would be three candidates and the real candidate of the three would win the election. The President would appoint a governor based on this election result (Sudharmono 1997: 350–351; *Tempo* Sept. 26, 1992: 22–33). At a glance, the provincial governors appeared as though they had been democratically elected within the regional councils but, as a matter of fact, the

Table 5.3: Competition and conflict between the Armed Forces and Golkar over provincial governor and regent posts from 1992 to 1994

	TIME	REGION	POST	DETAILS OF DISAGREEMENT/CONFRONTATION
1	September 1992	Jakarta	Provincial Governor	The Armed Forces faction and the Golkar faction fielded an active Army major general and a retired Army major general respectively. Golkar's candidate ended up withdrawing.
2	September 1992	Southeast Sulawesi	Provincial Governor	A civilian candidate close to the current governor received endorsement from the Golkar faction. The groups opposing the current governor requested that the Armed Forces faction field their own candidate.
3	September 1992	Maluku	Provincial Governor	The Golkar and other factions together fielded five civilian candidates. The Armed Forces faction tried to field its own candidate. The central Armed Forces Command accepted civilian candidates but declared that the Armed Forces would field its own candidate if they deemed a civilian governor insufficiently competent to perform the role adequately.
4	May 1993	Aceh	Provincial Governor	The candidate pushed by Golkar's Central Executive Board lost to the candidate pushed by the Golkar faction and Armed Forces faction in the region by vote.
5	May 1993	North Sumatra	Provincial Governor	The candidate pushed by Golkar's Central Executive Board and the central Armed Forces Command lost to the incumbent governor. All votes from the Armed Forces faction went to the former, but Golkar's vote was split and many went to the latter.
6	August 1993	East Java	Provincial Governor	The Golkar faction fielded a retired Army brigadier general whereas the Armed Forces faction fielded an active Army major general.

Table 5.3: continued

TIME	REGION	POST	DETAILS OF DISAGREEMENT/CONFRONTATION
7 August 1993	Central Java	Provincial Governor	The Golkar faction and the Armed Forces faction each fielded different Army major generals.
8 August 1993	East Nusa Tenggara	Provincial Governor	The fielding of an Army major general by the Armed Forces faction provoked a conflict with the Golkar faction, which was supporting the incumbent governor. The commander of the regional military command intervened and designated the former as the first and the latter as the second candidate.
9 March 1994	Central Kalimantan	Provincial Governor	Twenty-one Golkar faction members rejected the candidate elected by vote and warned that they would resign if this candidate took office.
10 March 1994	Deli Serdang (North Sumatra)	Regent of Regency	The Golkar faction warned that they would resign if the Minister of Home Affairs removed Golkar's nominated candidate. The candidate endorsed by the Ministry of Home Affairs who was an Army lieutenant colonel, was elected as the regent and consequently six of the Golkar faction members were dismissed.
11 March 1994	Kutai (East Kalimantan)	Regent of Regency	Seventeen Golkar faction members protested against the Minister of Home Affairs for removing the candidate they nominated and boycotted the regent election. A rerun election was held.

Source: Items 1–3, 4–5, 6–8 and 9–11 are based on *Tempo* (Sept. 26, 1992: 21–30), *Tempo* (May 22, 1993: 39–40), *Tempo* (Aug. 8, 1993: 28–29) and *Forum Keadilan* (Mar. 31, 1994: 16–17) respectively. Fukao (1999: 101–115) was also used as a reference.

process was intentionally designed so that the real candidate designated by the central authority would almost definitely win[11].

However, Rudini, who assumed the office of Minister of Home Affairs during the time of 'openness' at the end of the 1980s, criticized the above-described selection procedure and adopted a different one in which an election would be conducted without accompanying candidates, which meant the candidate with the most votes among the three 'real candidates' would be selected as governor (*Tempo* Sept. 26, 1992: 22–33). From Rudini's perspective, this may have been an effort to make the governor selection process as democratic as possible, but this led to the repeated occurrence of chaotic situations in gubernatorial elections conducted over the course of the period from 1992 to 1994 around the country, as mentioned in Table 5.3. Elections without a 'real candidate' clearly specified by the central authority often caused confusion. The fact that the Minister of Home Affairs Rudini and his successor Yogi Suwardi Memet removed some candidates fielded by factions of the DPRDs without their consent also became a source of conflict (Fukao 1999: 103; *Forum Keadilan* Mar. 31, 1994: 16).

In gubernatorial elections, each of the groups rushed to field their own candidate and conducted heavy lobbying campaigns. Different groups entangled in a web of interests started competing with each other, at both regional and central levels, and three candidates were fielded without adequate coordination of those interests. As a result, it was often the case that ongoing conflicts spanning the central and regional levels existed behind election campaigns, or in some cases, regional stakeholders refused to accept the view of the central authority (Fukao 1999: 101–115). By then, the Armed Forces and Golkar factions rarely agreed to back the same gubernatorial candidate, meaning two factions, despite both being pro-government, were fighting for the gubernatorial post. Though puzzled by this situation, the opposition party faction supported Golkar's candidate in some cases and the Armed Forces' candidate in others.

The political 'openness' and Golkar's push for independence at the central level inspired Golkar's regional leaders to also take action to have their views reflected in politics by fielding their own candidates in elections for the chair of the DPRD and provincial governor. To Golkar, the expansion of Golkar's local branches' power was a natural move considering that Golkar was the ruling party with the most number of seats. On the other hand, for the Armed Forces, it meant that a new actor joined local politics, which had been dominated by the regional military command (commander) and provincial government (governor) of province) until then. The addition of an actor—particularly a civilian—would increase the complexity of the decision-making process. Furthermore, it would be even more difficult to have their way if the Ministry of Home Affairs and Golkar's Central Executive Board started to intervene in the process for reconciliation on a frequent basis. Above all, it gave rise to a situation in which the Armed Forces now had to compete with Golkar for key political posts, which had been filled by military officers until then. Golkar was not an enemy of the Armed Forces, but at the same time was no longer a friend. Faced with such circumstances, the Armed Forces sought to strengthen their political power at the central level in order to gain an advantage in the battle over political posts.

Vice president and Golkar chairman posts in 1993
Two major changes took place at the center of authority prior to the vice presidential election and the Golkar chairmanship election in March and October 1993 respectively.

One of them was a change in the relationship between President Suharto and the Armed Forces. Concerned about the formation of a powerful group consisting of the officers close to former Commander of the Armed Forces Benny Murdani in the 1980s, Suharto carried out a major personnel shuffle as well as organizational restructuring within the Armed Forces in an attempt to eradicate the influence of Murdani. Especially, the shooting incident that took place in Dili in East Timor in November 1991[12] became a perfect excuse for eliminating the 'Murdani clique' within the Armed Forces. The commander and other officers of the Nusa Tenggara Regional Military Command in a close circle around Murdani were held responsible and replaced. Meanwhile, Suharto was also increasingly inclining toward the Agency for Assessment and Application of Technology's Head Habibie and approved the establishment of the ICMI upon Habibie's request, undeterred by the disagreement over this issue with the Armed Forces. The Armed Forces was taking a critical stance against the foundation of the ICMI on the grounds that it would allow a certain group of people to form an exclusive force, creating a rift in national unity. However, Suharto ignored such criticism and imposed the foundation of the ICMI to form a closer relationship with and gain support from the Islamic forces.

The other change occurred in the relationship between President Suharto and Golkar. As discussed in the first section, Suharto maintained a high level of distrust and discontent with the Wahono-led Executive Board, which was building strong aspirations toward independence and making changes to election tactics. For this reason, the President agreed to replace the existing executives close to Chairman Wahono and Secretary-General Rachmat Witoelar with those close to Habibie in the MPR's member list. As a result, over forty senior officials from Habibie's home territory, the Agency for Assessment and Application of Technology and the ICMI joined the MPR (*Forum Keadilan* Mar. 4, 1993: 14). In the Working Committee (*Badan Pekerja*) of the MPR responsible for preparing drafts for MPR resolutions such as the GBHN (Broad Guidelines of State Policy), half of the forty-five committee member positions from the Golkar faction were filled with people close to Habibie (*Forum Keadilan* Mar. 4, 1993: 14). In addition, Suharto appointed Habibie to the position of Coordinator of Golkar's Advisory Board's Daily Executive Committee in January 1993. Officials from the Agency for Assessment and Application of Technology, members of the ICMI and Golkar's Executive Board members close to Habibie such as Harmoko and Akbar Tandjung occupied the key posts in the Golkar faction of the MPR and rewrote the draft of the GBHN created by Executive Board members close to Wahono (*Forum Keadilan* Mar. 4, 1993: 14).

However, the expansion of the influence of Habibie's group within Golkar would naturally widen the distance with the Armed Forces, which took a dim view of Habibie. This growing rift between the two parties reduced the Armed Forces' influence in Golkar, and as the competition with Golkar over political posts intensified at the same time, the Armed Forces began making even more exhaustive efforts to display its political influence. Commander of the Armed Forces Try Sutrisno declared that he was aiming to further improve the Armed Forces' political and social capabilities in the Armed Forces leadership meeting held in October 1992 to demonstrate the presence of the Armed Forces as a political force (*Forum Keadilan* Oct. 15, 1992: 71–72). He asserted that 'the Armed Forces must pay closer attention to political and social issues and play a role in determining political and social policies' in light of Law No.2 of 1988 which legally legitimated the doctrine of the 'Dual function of the Armed Forces' (*Dwi fungsi ABRI*), stating that 'the Indonesian Armed Forces claimed the right to play not only a defense and security function but also a socio-political function'[13] (*Forum Keadilan* Oct. 15, 1992: 72).

At the time of the vice presidential election of March 1993, the Armed Forces, determined not to repeat the failure of the 1988 vice presidential election, listed a set of criteria for suitable vice presidential candidates at an early stage. By doing so, they indicated that they intended to push Commander of the Armed Forces Try Sutrisno for the position of vice president, though they did not particularly mention his name. Golkar Chairman Wahono, who was a former military officer, also stressed implicitly that Try Sutrisno was the ideal vice presidential candidate in the same manner as the Armed Forces, without specifically naming him, as if to keep in line with the Armed Forces (*Forum Keadilan* Mar. 4, 1993: 11). However, the Golkar faction of the MPR, which included a large number of politicians close to Habibie, expressed their intention to nominate Habibie as a vice presidential candidate rather than Try Sutrisno (*Forum Keadilan* Mar. 4, 1993: 14). On the one hand, the Armed Forces made an organization-wide effort to push Try Sutrisno as a vice presidential candidate, but on the other hand, Golkar was split in two, with Wahono's group pushing Try and Habibie's group seeking to nominate Habibie.

Under such circumstances, Suharto formed a 'Team of Eleven' ahead of the general session of the MPR in 1993. The members were Golkar Chairman Wahono, State Secretary Murdiono, Minister of Tourism, Post and Telecommunications Susilo Sudarman, Minister of Home Affairs Rudini, Chair of the Agency for Assessment and Application of Technology Habibie, Minister of Information Harmoko, Army Chief of Staff Edi Sudradjat, Commander of the Armed Forces Try Sutrisno, Governor of West Java Province Yogi Suwardi Memet, Governor of Aceh Province Ibrahim Hasan and Governor of Southeast Sulawesi Province Alala (*Tiras* Jan. 12, 1998: 90). It is believed that Suharto solicited opinions on vice presidential candidates from the members of the Team of Eleven. Although Suharto himself had Try Sutrisno in mind (Sudharmono 1997: 18), he had not yet given 'official endorsement' to him in advance of the general session of the MPR.

As the Armed Forces faction was perturbed by the lack of 'official endorsement' by the President, they raised Try Sutrisno's name and announced that they would officially back him as a vice presidential candidate in the general session of the MPR. However, mentioning Try's name before consulting the President had the effect of incurring the strong displeasure of Suharto toward the Armed Forces faction (Sudharmono 1997: 18; Hisyam 1999: 494). While Try Sutrisno did get elected to the vice president post, the Chair of the Armed Forces faction Harsudiono Hartas—he was Chief of Staff for Sociopolitical Affairs of the Armed Forces Command—who raised Try's name in the general session of the MPR lost his position and was not reassigned in the personnel reshuffle within the Armed Forces which occurred immediately after the close of the general session. In addition, in May 1993, Minister of Defense and Security/Commander of the Armed Forces Edi Sudradjat, who was following in the footsteps of Armed Forces' mainstream leaders such as Murdani and Try Sutrisno, lost the Commander of the Armed Forces post after only three months in the role and was left with just the Minister of Defense and Security post, as the postponement of his retirement from the military was not approved. To replace Edi Sudradjat, Feisal Tandjung became Commander of the Armed Forces. Unlike Edi Sudradjat, he was a non-Murdani affiliated devout Muslim officer and had close relationships with civilian politicians such as Habibie as well as personal connections with Islamic leaders.

Both Edi Sudradjat and Harsudiono Hartas had commented that a candidate from the Armed Forces must become Golkar's Chairman for the next term in light of the Golkar chairmanship election anticipated in October of the same year to inhibit Habibie's group from gaining power within Golkar. However, after Edi Sudradjat was replaced by Feisal Tandjung and Harsudiono Hartas by Hariyoto, the way high-ranking Armed Forces officers spoke about the Golkar chairmanship election changed significantly. This was because Feisal received an instruction directly from Suharto to 'restore order within the Armed Forces' when he assumed the Commander post. Suharto gave the instruction to Feisal Tandjung and Edi Sudradjat to ensure that the 'blunder' of the vice presidential election was never repeated, referring to the way Harsudiono Hartas 'tried to impose his own preference going ahead of the nation's representatives' (Hisyam 1999: 494).

Upon assumption of the Commander post, Feisal proclaimed that a civilian should be elected as the Golkar Chairman in the national congress scheduled for October 1993. He asserted that the Armed Forces did not need to field a candidate for the position of Golkar Chairman and instead needed to 'support from behind' (*tut wuri handayani*) (*Forum Keadilan* Oct. 28, 1993: 94). Before Golkar's national congress, Harmoko was rumored to be the candidate Suharto had in mind. In spite of the fact that there was strong resistance within the Armed Forces against handing over the Golkar Chairman post to a civilian, as it had always been occupied by a military officer since the establishment of Golkar, Feisal decided to back Harmoko's bid for the chairmanship after confirming Suharto's intention (Hisyam 1999: 560).

In the regional congresses held ahead of the national congress, military personnel came to assume the positions of branch heads of many local branches, including 230 out of 301 branches at the regency and city levels (*Forum Keadilan* Sept. 30, 1993: 88) and twenty-one out of twenty-seven branches at the provincial level, with civilians elected in only six branches (*Tempo* Oct. 23, 1993: 30). However, this did not affect the upcoming national congress in the same manner as the previous 1988 congress when the reelection of Sudharmono was hindered. This is because the selection of Harmoko as Chairman was in accordance with Suharto's intention. In the national congress, a seven-member formation team was created to select the new Chairman and members of the Central Executive Board. The formation team consisted of one representative from the Advisory Board, two from the Central Executive Board and four from local branches. Although the seven members selected the new Chairman and the Central Executive Board members through discussion, all the final decisions were made only after consultation with President Suharto, who was the Chair of the Advisory Board. This procedure ensured that Harmoko was elected to the Chairman post in accordance with Suharto's will.

As the restructuring of Golkar, which began in 1984, ushered a great number of young social elites into the organization, a competition emerged between the Armed Forces, which had entrenched vested interests, and Golkar over a variety of political posts given preferentially to military officers until then at both central and regional levels. At the central level, the Armed Forces began taking an assertive stance over the vice presidential and Golkar chairman posts in stark contrast to their previous attitude. At the regional level too, the interests of Golkar and the Armed Forces gradually started to clash. Golkar began asserting its position as the ruling party and demanding posts that military officers had customarily been occupying such as the chair of the DPRD, provincial governor, regent of regency and city mayor. The intensification of competition over political posts led the Armed Forces to take advantage of its position as a member of the 'Great Golkar Family' by taking control of the leadership in regional and central Golkar—in other words, occupying the posts of heads of local branches as well as the chairman of central Golkar—in order to gain a competitive edge over Golkar. In short, the emergence of civilian politicians in Golkar ultimately resulted in the promotion of the politicization of the Armed Forces. The Armed Forces was able to secure the top positions of most Golkar local branches with almost no difficulty. Therefore, it was highly probable that the candidate they wanted to win would be elected as chairman, just as was the case in 1988.

However Harmoko, a civilian politician, was elected as the Golkar chairman. This must have been possible only because it was the intention of Suharto. Without Suharto's intervention, Harmoko would not have been elected. Concerned about the Armed Forces' influence over Golkar, Suharto replaced the Commander of the Armed Forces with someone who had a conciliatory relationship with Habibie and Harmoko and then gave this new Commander direct orders to smooth the way for Harmoko to win the Golkar chairman post. This means, in other words, civilian groups within Golkar had no other choice but to rely on Suharto if they wanted to compete for political posts against the Armed Forces.

This reliance on Suharto, however, further restricted Golkar's independence movement. Suharto displayed concerns about the competition and confrontation caused by active campaigns of Golkar members in the DPR as well as DPRD and issued an instruction to restore 'organizational discipline' to Golkar's Central Executive Board (*Tempo* Feb. 12, 1994: 36–37). In accordance with this instruction, Harmoko gathered representatives of local branches and ordered them to improve the relationship with the Armed Forces and the regional government in their region and at the same time, gave an instruction that banned the heads of local branches from running for the position of head of regional government in their region to avoid conflicts with the Armed Forces (*Forum Keadilan* Nov. 10, 1994: 14). Moreover, he forced the resignation of or directly dismissed several Golkar members in a regency representative council who were in a state of confrontation with the regent due to having violated 'organizational discipline' (*Forum Keadilan* Nov. 10, 1994: 14).

Furthermore, Harmoko dismissed and replaced Golkar's DPR member Bambang Warih Kusuma, who was severely critical of several ministers in the DPR's deliberations (*Forum Keadilan* Mar. 2, 1995: 18). He also removed the chair of the Golkar faction in the DPR Usman Hasan from the chair post and then further dismissed him from the DPR (*Forum Keadilan* Mar. 30, 1995: 15). Bambang Warih Kusuma was not only questioning the Ministry of Manpower over the issue that their staff were collecting unjust fees from laborers going abroad to work but also severely criticized the Minister of Industry, Minister of Public Works and Minister of Finance on other issues. The official reasons provided for his dismissal were something along the lines of 'his arguments deviated from the policy of Golkar' and 'he lacked discipline' (*Forum Keadilan* Mar. 2, 1995: 18). As for the removal of Usman Hasan, his effort to investigate the company Kanindo's bad debt problems in the Seventh Committee of the DPR with Bambang Warih Kusuma is believed to have been the reason (*Forum Keadilan* Mar. 30, 1995: 15). It has been suggested that this was a result of the new Chairman Harmoko's effort to wipe out those within Wahono's network from the DPR, since those two were close to the former Chairman (*Forum Keadilan* Mar. 2, 1995: 18–20). Nevertheless, regardless of the motivation, the fact remains that those who raised questions and tried to rigorously investigate important issues in the DPR were targeted for dismissal.

The more Golkar tried to become independent from the Armed Forces, the more heavily they had to depend on Suharto and this reliance in turn led to the decline of the autonomy of Golkar. As a consequence, Golkar's independence was slipping further away, both in terms of enhancing the role of the DPR and improving its autonomy as a political party. Amid such circumstances, new forces were about to gain substantial prominence within Golkar, namely, Suharto's family members and the Armed Forces Son's and Daughter's Communication Forum (FKPPI) group. With these two groups coming to the forefront at the same time, both with the strong backing of the President, Suharto's involvement in Golkar underwent a qualitative change. While it marked the end of the era of 'openness' and triggered ever-increasing political oppression, Suharto's children appeared on the political scene, creating a huge rift in Golkar.

6
The Rise of the Suharto Family and a Rift in Golkar

During his rule, Suharto tactically controlled political posts to balance the competition among elites and maintain his supremacy. From the 1970s to the early 1980s, posts were preferentially allocated to the Armed Forces, which constituted the core of the regime. The domination of key posts by Armed Forces officers at both the central and regional level ensured the establishment of social control and helped solidify Suharto's status as a distributor of patronage. However, the monopolization of political power and patronage by a specific group provoked strong antagonism in Indonesian society. This was expressed in the form of criticism against the 'Dual function' of the Armed Forces and objections to the reelection of President Suharto, and this had an unsettling effect on the Suharto regime.

In order to overcome this situation, Suharto tried to appease opposition forces by extending the range of patronage distribution from the mid-1980s. The instrument that acted as a channel for patronage distribution as well as the entry point for opposition forces to join the regime side was Golkar. Golkar enabled social elites who comprised the opposition forces to gain political posts by attracting a large number of young social elites and preparing a path for them to attain such positions. As a result, in and after the latter half of the 1980s, anti-government voices diminished and the Suharto regime entered a period of stability.

However, the absorption of social elites fuelled the competition over patronage distribution among elites within the regime. The Armed Forces officers who had been given priority in the distribution of political posts protested against the influx of new competitors and became increasingly politicized to protect their entrenched interests. On the other hand, faced with increased competition against the Armed Forces, Golkar was put into a situation in which it had no choice but to rely on Suharto.

Into the 1990s, even more intense competition over political posts unfolded within Golkar, triggered by the rapid emergence of the FKPPI and the rise in power of the President's children. Suharto began considering making his eldest daughter his successor and accordingly started to skew the distribution of political posts to his children and the groups close to them. This chapter examines the way in which the escalation of competition over political posts within Golkar and the gradual concentration of patronage distribution on the inner circle of the Suharto family created a rift in the Suharto regime.

Emergence of the FKPPI

Becoming the leading youth group

The FKPPI, the Armed Forces Son's and Daughter's Communication Forum, was founded in 1978. The original purpose of the establishment of the organization was not political. Rather, it was formed as a 'forum' to develop relationships between the sons and daughters of military personnel. At the time, the children of military personnel tended to form groups on the basis of the military accommodation in which they grew up and fighting among these groups as well as between these groups and delinquents often received attention as a social issue. The FKPPI was created to alleviate this kind of discord and restore the social reputation of military families. Initially, it lacked organizational unity and was positioned as a sub-organization controlled by the Veterans' Association within the 'Great Armed Forces Family' (KBA[1]).

The FKPPI became politically oriented in the mid-1980s when Djoko Mursito Humardani (the son of retired Army Lieutenant General Sudjono Humardani) became the organization's Chair. As a result of his strong lobbying to the government to establish its independence as an organization, the FKPPI managed to leave the umbrella of the Veterans' Association and gain the status of an independent youth group within the KBA. Subsequently, the FKPPI declared that it was going to express its political intentions through Golkar and its members started campaigning as Golkar members or executives.

The attainment of the independent youth group status had a significant implication for the FKPPI. This is because belonging to an independent youth organization made its members eligible to participate in the competition over DPR and DPRD posts in Golkar, meaning they no longer needed to go through the Veterans' Association. Indeed, in the 1987 election, with the help of an aggressive lobbying campaign to the Central Executive Board (DPP) of Golkar, they succeeded in entering some of the organization's members on the candidate lists and managed to produce twelve DPR members for Golkar.

The 1987 election further elevated the political ambitions of the FKPPI and motivated it to field more members for political posts. A quick way to achieve this was to gain executive posts in youth groups that were sending many of their leaders to Golkar such as the KNPI and AMPI. As shown in Chapter Four, the mid-to-late 1980s saw the establishment of the recruitment system for young

Table 6.1: Golkar legislators with past membership in the KNPI and AMPI

Year of election	1977	1982	1987	1992	1997
Both KNPI and AMPI	—	26	47	69	55
KNPI only	16	10	20	27	46
AMPI only	—	8	21	16	29
Total	16	44	88	112	130
Percentage to the total number of Golkar legislators	6.9	18.2	29.4	39.7	40.0

Source: LPU (1978, 1983, 1987, 1993, 1997a).

elites within Golkar, and from that time, Golkar's seats in the DPR and MPR were increasingly being given to KNPI and AMPI executives. As can be observed in Table 6.1, approximately thirty percent of the successful candidates in the 1987 election and around forty percent in the 1992 and 1997 elections had at some point in their career belonged to the KNPI or AMPI or both.

In order for the FKPPI to send their own representatives to the DPR and DPP Golkar through the KNPI and AMPI, they needed to occupy important posts in the executive boards of these organizations such as chair and vice-chair. However, members of other student and youth groups comprising the KNPI and AMPI did not necessarily welcome the inroads made by FKPPI members. Within the KNPI, the 'Cipayung Group' (*Kelompok Cipayung*[2]), which consisted of the members who joined the organization at its establishment in 1973, held great influence. Of particular prominence was the HMI, which had been consistently producing KNPI chairs and vice-chairs until that point. As for the AMPI, its members also included entrepreneurs' organizations such as the HIPMI in addition to the Cipayung Group, and this business community held a certain degree of influence.

The reason why the FKPPI was not appreciated by other organizations can be attributed to several factors. One of them was that unlike other social organizations and youth groups, one needed to meet the condition of having a parent in the Armed Forces to join. In other words, the acceptance or rejection of one's admission was determined by one's parent's occupation. This created a more closed and exclusive impression compared to other associations with relatively open admission policies (*Media Karya* Sept. 1992: 28–29).

Another was that many FKPPI executives were the sons of high-profile military figures. For example, Indra Bambang Utoyo was the son of retired Army Mayor General Bambang Oetojo who served as the Army Chief of Staff in the 1950s, Ponco Sutowo was the son of retired Army Lieutenant General Ibnu Sutowo who served as the President of Pertamina and Bambang Riyadi Sugomo was the son of retired Army General Yoga Sugama who served in the top position of an intelligence apparatus, the BAKIN, for almost twenty years. They had an advantage in that they received political as well as economic patronage due to their parent's power. A large percentage of children of major military figures, including the children of President Suharto, chose to pursue business careers taking advantage of their parent's powerful connections, instead of following their parent's footsteps in the military.

The magazine *Info Bisnis* ranked the top fifty *pribumi* (non-Chinese) entrepreneurs based on asset value. All of Suharto's children's businesses placed high on this list; the Bimantara Group owned by Suharto's second son Bambang Trihatmodjo was number one, his eldest daughter Tutut's Citra Lamtoro Group came third, his eldest son Sigit's Hanurata Group came fifth and his third son Tommy's Humpus Group placed eleventh. In addition to Suharto's children, Ponco Sutowo's Nugra Santana Group and his younger brother Adiguna Sutowo's empire were ranked forty-fifth and forty-seventh respectively (*Info Bisnis* Jan. 14, 1997: 37b–39b). Many entrepreneurs who achieved success on the back of their military parent's influence became members of the FKPPI.

It is surely no surprise that other groups became jealous and hostile due to the fact that these already successful FKPPI executives were seeking to enter the political sphere and seize key political posts. Besides, not only did they have the support of their parents, they were also in a position to receive aegis from the Armed Forces for being members of the KBA. The FKPPI was an unwelcome rival for other social groups that were sending their young elites into Golkar as its members were in a favorable position to begin with, being the children of high-profile military figures, and what's more, they also had the Armed Forces as a powerful patron.

The vigorous attempt by the FKPPI to join the competition for executive posts in the KNPI and AMPI fuelled internal competition and confrontations in both organizations. This was observable in the chairmanship elections of the KNPI and AMPI conducted over the period from the end of the 1980s to the early 1990s. In the chairmanship election of the KNPI national congress held in October 1987, the Cipayung Group fielded HMI's Chair Saleh Chalid while the FKPPI backed Didiet Haryadi and Harris Ali Murfi (son of retired Army Lieutenant General Ali Murtopo). This was the KNPI's first democratic election—the first chair to be elected not based on the government's order. Thirty-one youth groups participating in the KNPI, twenty-seven regional branches and the central executive board and advisory council (*dewan pertimbangan*) had one vote each and the criteria for running for the position of chair was to win at least five votes. Each of the candidates who had succeeded in gaining five or more votes ran campaigns and the formation team of seven electors who were chosen from the congress made the final decision on the chair position (*Tempo* Nov. 7, 1987: 22). Despite the endorsement of Saleh Chalid by former HMI member and State Minister for Youth and Sports Affairs Abdul Gafur, Didiet Haryadi from the FKPPI was elected as the chair (*Tempo* Nov. 7, 1987: 22). The newly elected KNPI Chair Didiet Haryadi joined the Central Executive Board of Golkar with Ponco Sutowo and several others in October 1988 to become the first FKPPI executives to attain such achievement.

Indra Bambang Utoyo was elected as Chair of the FKPPI in November 1987, and this ambitious leader called for the further expansion of the organization, instructing its members to take leadership over other youth groups at both central and regional levels (*Tempo* Nov. 21, 1987: 25). Indra himself was aiming to grab the position of chair of the central executive board of a Golkar-affiliated youth group, the AMPI. He was already serving as the Vice-Chair of the KNPI's central executive board as well as the Chair of the AMPI's South Sumatra branch. For him, the assumption of the chair post of the AMPI was a promissory note to ensure his entry into the Central Executive Board of Golkar. However, he encountered unexpected resistance in the chairmanship election of the AMPI's national congress held in December 1989. Indra won a large number of votes in the ballot carried out in the congress by mobilizing regional branches of the FKPPI. In spite of this, the formation team of five electors who had the authority to make the final decision on the selection of the chair instead chose Indra's rival candidate Widjanarko Puspojo. This was because one of the team of electors, former AMPI Chair Agung Laksono (an HIPMI-member entrepreneur) strongly opposed Indra's election. After a series of acrimonious debates between Widjanarko supporters and Indra supporters, the Indra side finally submitted to the decision of the formation team (*Tempo* Dec. 23, 1989: 21; *Media Karya* Dec. 1989: 33–36).

The chairmanship election of the KNPI's congress held in November 1990 saw much of the same confusion and disarray. While FKPPI candidate Harris Ali Murfi gained many votes from regional branches and youth groups, the formation team of seven electors designated Tjahjo Kumolo, who obtained only half the number of votes of Harris, as the chair. On this occasion too, the FKPPI members who supported Harris vehemently protested to the formation team, causing a great deal of chaos. Eventually, State Minister for Youth and Sport Affairs Akbar Tandjung, who had the responsibility of supervising the chairmanship election and reporting to the President, sought direction from Suharto, and consequently, in agreement with the formation team's decision, Tjahjo was designated as the chair (*Tempo* Nov. 10, 1990: 22).

Political breakthrough

The membership of the FKPPI grew from 200,000 in 1987 to 500,000 by 1991 (*Media Karya* Aug. 1991: 41), more than doubling in the short span of four years. The FKPPI launched an offensive to wrest the top positions of the KNPI and AMPI, which were closely associated with Golkar, to access political power, but met with resistance from other student and youth groups—predominantly Islamic ones—that reacted against the emergence of the FKPPI. This situation finally began to change and the FKPPI started to see a way forward at around the time of the 1992 election. On that occasion, the FKPPI ensured it was among the first to announce its support for Golkar and actively mobilized its members for Golkar's election campaign. As a result, FKPPI Chair Indra Bambang Utoyo received recognition for his leadership and the FKPPI successfully demonstrated its superior mobilization capability.

In contrast to the FKPPI, other student and youth groups such as the HMI, NU-affiliated GP Ansor and Muhammadiyah-affiliated Muhammadiyah Youth were all limited in their capability to mobilize support in elections. The reason for this was that even if some executive members supported Golkar, they were unable to force other members to vote for Golkar. Although the HMI sent many alumni into the regime as cabinet members, government officials or legislators, their relationship with the government was merely at the individual level. Within the HMI were supporters of the opposition party the PPP, not to mention quite a significant number of anti-government members. The connection with influential figures in the government enabled the HMI to receive funding for the running of the organization and made it possible for its executives to be nominated as members of the DPR and MPR. However, the close relationship between some HMI executives and government and ruling party heavyweights including their senior, former HMI activist Akbar Tandjung—who was a member of the Central Advisory Board of Golkar as well as a cabinet member (State Minister for Youth and Sports Affairs)—became the target of criticism of the anti-government group within the HMI. HMI executives close to the government were criticized for no longer taking a moral stance that guided their student movement activities in the past. In particular, Chair Ferry Mursyidan Baldan (1990–1992), who was very close to Akbar, drew severe criticism from fellow HMI members for having issued a statement as HMI Chair agreeing with Golkar's announcement endorsing Suharto's reelection and was ousted from the chair post as a result (*Tempo* Dec. 12, 1992: 24–25). Within the HMI were some members who tried to obtain political posts by supporting the government and using their personal connections, while others sought to maintain the organization's independence from the government, and these groups competed with each other at times resulting in confrontation. This sort of inter-organizational competition was not a problem specific to the HMI, but is commonly seen in many other social organizations and student and youth groups[3].

The strength of the FKPPI was that they avoided this kind of dilemma. They provided total support for Golkar and this made a significant contribution during elections and drew Suharto's attention. As their loyalty to the government and Golkar and strong solidarity became increasingly recognized, the FKPPI gradually began expanding its influence within Golkar. The 1992 election saw a dramatic increase in the number of FKPPI members who joined the DPR as Golkar representatives, from twelve in 1987 to thirty-five. Meanwhile, as for the number of HMI members, while it increased markedly from fifteen to twenty-nine over the period from 1982 to 1987, there was only a minor increase between the 1987 and 1992 elections, from twenty-nine to thirty-two. This signifies that the FKPPI gained a greater voice in Golkar's Central Executive Board over the candidate list creation process for the 1992 election.

In the new cabinet formed in March 1993, Hayono Isman (son of retired Army Major General Mas Isman, one of the founders of Golkar) was named State Minister for Youth and Sports Affairs, becoming the first cabinet member to come from the FKPPI. Until then, this post had been filled by former HMI members, namely Abdul Gafur and Akbar Tandjung since 1983. Now that this cabinet post, which was responsible for supervising student and youth groups and organizations and conveying the government's policies to these organizations, had fallen into the hands of the FKPPI from former HMI members, the FKPPI was in a significantly advantageous position. From that time onward, members of the FKPPI dominated the chair posts of the central executive boards of both the KNPI and AMPI. The FKPPI's candidates emerged victorious in the following central executive board chair elections: the KNPI's national congress in 1993[4] and 1996[5] and the AMPI's national congress in 1994[6]. Meanwhile, through these chairmanship elections, Islamic student and youth groups such as the HMI, GP Ansor, PMII and Muhammadiyah Youth and FKPPI-affiliated youth groups such as the FKPPI, Pancasila Youth (*Pemuda Pancasila*)[7] and Panca Marga Youth (*Pemuda Panca Marga*) started to take a clear stance against each other within the KNPI and AMPI, and the strong predominance of the latter became increasingly marked as they came to occupy every chair position in the KNPI and AMPI central executive board.

The competition and confrontations that were occurring within the KNPI and AMPI were carried into Golkar in and after the mid-1990s.

Table 6.2 shows the members of Golkar's Central Executive Board formed in October 1993.

Table 6.2: Central Executive Board of Golkar (1993–1998)

Chairman	Harmoko (Minister of Information/PWI)
Vice-Chair	Abdul Gafur (Former student activist/HMI) Ismael Hasan (PERTI) Waskito Reksosudirdjo (KORPRI) Mochtar (Retired military officer) Agung Laksono (Entrepreneur/HIPMI) Siti Hardiyanti Lukmana (Eldest daughter of the President/Entrepreneur/FKPPI) Warno Hardjo (SOKSI) Pinantun Hutasoit (MKGR/HNSI)
Secretary-General	Ary Mardjono (Retired Army Lieutenant General)
Deputy Secretary-General	Achmad Mustahid Astari (BAKIN) Aulia Aman Rachman (Former student activist/ University of Indonesia Student Council) Irsyad Sudiro (MKGR/ICMI) Theo Sambuaga (Former student activist)
Accountant	Bambang Trihatmodjo (Second son of the President/ Entrepreneur/FKPPI)
Deputy Accountant	Ponco Sutowo (Son of retired Army Lieutenant General Ibnu Sutowo/Entrepreneur/HIPMI/FKPPI) Gunaryah Kartasasmita (Entrepreneur/HIPMI)
Department of Election Campaign Strategy	Bambang Riyadi Sugomo (Son of retired Army General Yoga Sugama/Entrepreneur/HIPMI/FKPPI) Rully Chairul Azwar (Son of retired Army Major General Azwar Anas/Entrepreneur/FKPPI)
Department of Organization, Membership and Cultivation of Cadre	Mulyono Gendon Bambang Wahyudi
Department of Education	Bawadiman (KOSGORO) Aloysius Aloy (Former student activist)
Department of Information, Publication and Mass Media	Sofyan Lubis (PWI) Abdullah Fahmi Alatas (Entrepreneur)
Department of Youth	Indra Bambang Utoyo (Son of retired Army Major General Bambang Oetojo/Entrepreneur/FKPPI) Rambe Kamarulzaman (Former student activist/HMI/ KOSGORO)
Department of Agriculture and Fishery	Irawadi Jamaran (Agency for Assessment and Application of Technology) Ida Bagus Putra
Department of Labor	Erwan Sukardja (FKPPI) Marzuki Ahmad (SPSI)

Table 6.2: continued

Department of Women	Sri Redjeki (HWK) Didiek Hadidjah Hasan (ICMI)
Department of Religion	Kafrawi Ridwan (GUPPI/DMI) Nelly Hassan (Islamic Women's Education Association/ICMI)
Department of Intellectuals, Technology and International Relations	Burhan Magenda (Former student activist/HMI/Political analyst) Marwah Daud Ibrahim (Former student activist/HMI/Agency for Assessment and Application of Technology/ICMI)
Department of Culture and Art	Bobby Suhardiman (Son of retired Army Major General Suhardiman/SOKSI/FKPPI) Ais Anantama Said (Son of retired Army Major Ali Said/FKPPI/GAKARI)
Department of Cooperatives and Entrepreneurship	Fahmi Idris (Former student activist/HMI/Entrepreneur/HIPMI) Fadel Muhammad (Entrepreneur/KADIN/ICMI)
Department of Social Services	Tantyo Sudharmono (Son of retired Army Lieutenant General Sudharmono/Entrepreneur/FKPPI) Herry Alamsyah (Son of retired Army Lieutenant General Alamsyah/Entrepreneur/FKPPI/Mathlaul Anwar)
Department of Research and Development	Sutadji Djajakusumo (Aide to National Development Planning Agency) Din Syamsuddin (Muhammadiyah Youth/ICMI)

Source: *Media Karya* (Nov. 1993: 34–36).

Around that time, the group close to State Minister of Research and Technology Habibie was expanding its influence within Golkar. At the national congress held in October 1993, this group, especially Akbar Tandjung who was selected to chair the congress, carried out vigorous lobbying efforts to have Harmoko elected as Chairman of Golkar. They also played a part in the selection of new Central Executive Board members. As a result, Habibie's immediate subordinates in the Agency for Assessment and Application of Technology (the agency Habibie was in charge of) such as Irawadi Jamaran and Sutadji Djajakusumo and the leading members of the ICMI (an organization chaired by Habibie) such as Nelly Hassan, Marwah Daud Ibrahim and Din Syamsuddin entered the Central Executive Board. Former student activists, journalist association members and entrepreneurs close to Harmoko, Abdul Gafur and Akbar Tandjung such as Theo Sambuaga, Rambe Kamarulzaman, Sofyan Lubis, Fahmi Idris and Fadel Muhammad were also added to the Executive Board.

However, Suharto's opinions were strongly reflected in the selection of the new Executive Board in 1993. We can consider the emergence of Suharto's eldest daughter Siti Hardiyanti Rukmana (commonly known as Tutut) and second son Bambang Trihatmodjo in the Executive Board as evidence of the change in Suharto's view on Golkar. Until then, Suharto thought of Golkar as a vote-gathering machine during elections. Now, he began to recognize Golkar as the political base for his children. In that regard, a large number of FKPPI members were also added to the Executive Board, along with a group close to the Suharto family including Ismael Hasan, Ary Mardjono, Achmad Mustahid Astari and Fahmi Alatas. Needless to say, Tutut and Bambang were members of the FKPPI as their father Suharto was a retired Army General, and Suharto added an army of FKPPI executives to the Executive Board of Golkar with the expectation that they would serve as supporters for his children. On the other hand, the FKPPI began to take advantage of its strongest asset—its close proximity to the children of the President—to 'promote' it from a youth organization to a social organization, thus achieving a higher-level status.

The reason behind the FKPPI's conversion into a social organization in 1995 was the problem of the 'aging' of its executive members. For every organization registered as a youth organization, be that the HMI, GP Ansor, AMPI or KNPI, the age limit was set at forty. Therefore, once a member exceeded the age of forty, they had to leave the organization. Nevertheless, one could maintain their organizational identity and personal network by joining their respective organization's parent social organization, such as the NU for members of the GP Ansor or PMII, Muhammadiyah for members of Muhammadiyah Youth or the KAHMI (HMI's alumni group) for HMI members. However, such an organization did not exist for the FKPPI. Members of the FKPPI could not join the Veterans' Association since they themselves did not have a military background. In 1995, FKPPI Chair Indra Bambang Utoyo who was born in 1954 was already at the age of forty and other executives were soon to turn forty as well. The executives of the FKPPI, who were emerging as powerful political actors at that time, were looking to achieve further political promotion, remaining in the FKPPI past the age of forty by making use of the proximity to the children of the President.

The strategy adopted by the FKPPI to achieve this was to install the President's second son Bambang Trihatmodjo as the Chair of the FKPPI, then have Bambang negotiate with Suharto in person about its conversion from a youth organization with an age limit into a social organization without one (*Tiras* Sept. 28, 1995: 18, 20–22). The FKPPI's executive board had made repeated requests regarding this change but had always been declined by the Commander of the Armed Forces who chaired the advisory board of the FKPPI. Given such situation, they resorted to the strategy of bringing the President's second son forward and obtaining approval directly from Suharto.

Upon Suharto's agreement with the FKPPI's request, two organizations were established in September 1995, namely the FKPPI as a social organization and its sub-organization the FKPPI Youth (GM-FKPPI). Bambang Trihatmodjo was installed as the Chair of the reorganized FKPPI, Indra Bambang Utoyo became the central executive board's secretary-general and Yapto Suryosumarno, the leader of Pancasila Youth as well as Ponco Sutowo and Bambang Riyadi Sugomo filled the vice-chair positions (*Tiras* Sept. 28, 1995: 21).

While Suharto's second son took office as the FKPPI Chair, Suharto himself assumed the position of the Chair of the FKPPI's advisory board (*Tiras* Sept. 28, 1995: 18). Until then, the Commander of the Armed Forces had always served in this position whose role was to supervise the organization. Having such post replaced by the President meant that the FKPPI would now act under direct orders from the President rather than the Armed Forces. It also meant that the President would protect the organization. The only other organization whose advisory board was chaired by the President himself was Golkar, and the FKPPI was thus now seen as having been 'promoted in rank' (*naik pangkat*) (*Tiras* Sept. 28, 1995: 18; *Forum Keadilan* Oct. 9, 1995: 26).

From Suharto's perspective, the FKPPI's conversion into a social organization signified building an organizational foundation that could support his children's political careers, while from the Armed Forces' perspective, it resulted in the reinforcement of the political base of the 'Great Armed Forces Family' (KBA) (*Tiras* Sept. 28, 1995: 22, 27). According to a former Golkar legislator Marzuki Darusman, the Armed Forces no longer needed to send its officers to Golkar. All they had to do now to have the opinions of the KBA echoed in Golkar was to work on the FKPPI (*Forum Keadilan* July 17, 1995: 103).

Now, the question is what did this mean for Golkar? According to political scientist Arbi Sani, on the one hand, it signified Golkar had gained a powerful support group that would put it in a favorable position in the forthcoming 1997 election, greatly enhancing Golkar's electoral prospects in terms of vote gathering (*Tiras* Sept. 28, 1995: 27). On the other hand, however, for the non-Armed Forces groups within Golkar, this meant the emergence of a formidable rival inside the party. Some political scientists made the pessimistic projection that a large number of non-Armed Forces affiliated executives would fall from power in the wake of the 1997 election (*Forum Keadilan* Oct. 9, 1995: 26).

Rise of the Suharto family

Emergence of Suharto's eldest daughter Tutut

The new Central Executive Board of Golkar set its goal as reclaiming the votes it lost in the 1992 election, and Chairman Harmoko and executive members lost no time in embarking on a campaign to gather support. The member who became the focal point in the campaign was Suharto's eldest daughter Tutut, who joined the Central Executive Board for the first time in the national congress held in October 1993. She was an entrepreneur who led a giant corporate group called the Citra Lamotoro Group. Dubbed the 'Queen of the toll road' (*Ratu jalan tol*), Tutut's reputation as a businessperson was nevertheless not of the best kind—for example, she was infamous for having passed the loss she incurred from the construction of an expressway in Malaysia onto another company and was given expediency in the tender process for a toll road in Jakarta. However, there was another side of her that was actively engaged in social services to help the poor. She had had almost no history of working for Golkar but began engaging in vigorous political activities when she was named one of the vice-chairs of Golkar.

Aside from the Chairman, each of the executive board members was allocated with a region for which they would be responsible and carried out campaigns to raise support within this area. Tutut was allocated three regions, Central Java, Yogyakarta and East Java. These regions were the most densely populated in Indonesia along with West Java. Furthermore, these regions contained many supporters of the opposition parties, namely the PPP and PDI, and Golkar had lost seats in these areas in the 1992 election. Entrusted with raising support in these strategically important regions, Tutut eagerly visited *pesantren* (Islamic boarding schools) in Central and East Java where she received a warm welcome from *ulama* and *kyai* (*Forum Keadilan* June 23, 1994: 20). Islamic leaders such as *ulama* and *kyai* who run *pesantren* were highly regarded in rural areas and winning their support was believed to be a key to drawing many votes. Tutut is said to have promised financial aid to *ulama* every time she paid a visit to *pesantren*. The statement issued by a large number of *ulama* in East Java in June 1995 that declared their support for the reelection of President Suharto was reported in the mass media as being attributable to this financial aid (*Gatra* June 17, 1995: 22).

Moreover, Tutut visited the grave of the first President Sukarno located in Blitar, East Java in December 1993 with the Chiarman of Golkar Harmoko and praised the former president's achievements addressing him as the 'Father of the nation (*Bapak bangsa*) (*Forum Keadilan* June 23, 1994: 21). Even though it was a publicity campaign aimed at engaging the supporters of the PDI who worshipped Sukarno, her actions as a politician started to increasingly attract attention from the public.

Hartono, who came to the position of Army Chief of Staff in June 1995, further enhanced Tutut's political influence. Like Commander of the Armed Forces Feisal Tandjung, he was a devout Muslim. However, as opposed to Feisal who had close relationships with Golkar members such as Habibie and Harmoko, Hartono was very close to the President's eldest daughter. Since the 1980s when Sudharmono became the Golkar Chairman, the Armed Forces had distanced themselves from Golkar and withheld their full support for the party in the 1987 and 1992 elections. Under such circumstances, Suharto tried to reconcile the ever-worsening relationship between the Armed Forces and Golkar by giving Feisal Tandjung and Hartono the top posts in the Armed Forces and Army respectively over the period from 1993 to 1995. Suharto's aim was to motivate the Armed Forces to actively support Golkar in the upcoming 1997 election to recover from the loss of votes it suffered in the 1992 election.

Army Chief of Staff Hartono participated in Golkar's campaigns led by Tutut in Central and East Java, accompanied by Staff for the Sociopolitical Affairs of the Armed Forces Command Syarwan Hamid, Army General Staff Assistant for Territorial Affairs Suparman and Commander of the Central Java Regional Military Command Subagyo, wearing a yellow jacket—Golkar's color—and declared that the Armed Forces would provide full support for the party. Furthermore, he appealed that the officers of the Armed Forces were essentially the cadres of Golkar, therefore they must support the party, and claimed 'it is my duty, as a cadre of Golkar, to be loyal to Vice-Chair of DPP Golkar Tutut's advice and instructions' (*Forum Keadilan* Apr. 8, 1996: 100).

This statement made by Hartono as the Army Chief of Staff, implying that the Armed Forces had changed its attitude regarding keeping a distance toward Golkar, caused much controversy. This was because, although Golkar and the Armed Forces were once likened to a parent and child, the view that 'the Armed Forces should stand above all political forces and should not be committed to a particular political force' had become dominant among the Armed Forces' mainstream faction as Golkar grew increasingly independent from the Armed Forces. Hartono's statement was considered as a declaration to reverse the stance of the Armed Forces, which had been denying its special relationship with Golkar. Retired military officers who believed that the Armed Forces should distance itself from Golkar criticized Hartono's comment, asserting that 'the Armed Forces must remain politically neutral', while the opposition party also voiced misgivings about the possibility of the Armed Forces providing full support for Golkar in the election (*Forum Keadilan* Apr. 8, 1996: 100–102).

In response to these criticisms, Hartono explained that the Armed Forces as an organization designed to support the nation's defense and security must take a neutral stance; however, he went on to say that there is nothing wrong with an individual military officer supporting Golkar since every individual military officer was essentially a cadre of Golkar (*Gatra* Mar. 23, 1996: 34). In addition, Syarwan Hamid stated that 'President Suharto stressed in his speech at Pekanbaru in 1980 that the Armed Forces as a social force must choose a reliable partner. The words of Chief of Staff Hartono were nothing else but a restatement of that' (*Gatra* Mar. 23, 1996: 34). Nevertheless, as a matter of course, Hartono's 'support' for Golkar was merely an expression of his loyalty to the President as well as the President's eldest daughter and his loyalty was never directed toward Chairman Harmoko.

The increased political power of the President's family members within Golkar led to the emergence of three groups within the Armed Forces based on their relationship with Golkar. The first was Commander of the Armed Forces Feisal Tandjung's group, which was closely associated with Golkar's Habibie and Harmoko; the second was Vice President Try Sutrisno and Minister of Defense and Security Edi Sudradjat's group, which was closely linked to the President's second son Bambang and FKPPI members; and lastly there was Army Chief of Staff Hartono's group, which had a close relationship with the President's eldest daughter Tutut. The rift among these groups with different positions became more and more apparent as it grew to span Golkar and the Armed Forces.

Competition over legislative seats in the 1997 election

Chairman Harmoko was not only tasked with the mission of winning back votes and legislative seats for Golkar, but also faced another issue pertaining to the 1997 election—the generational change of DPR members. In 1995, the number of appointed seats for the Armed Forces in the DPR was reduced from 100 to seventy-five seats, and twenty-five seats were added to the elected seats in the 1997 election, increasing the number of elected seats from the previous 400 to 425. While this increase improved the chance for Golkar to garner more seats, the party struggled to handle the pressure from its affiliated organizations as many youth groups waged intensive lobbying campaigns to the Central Executive Board to have as many of their own executive members as possible registered on candidate lists. The groups that engaged in aggressive, organization-wide campaigns to make their executive members Golkar candidates included the AMPI, FKPPI, KOSGORO Youth, MKGR Student Association, GAKARI Youth, KOSGORO Student Association, Pancasila Youth and Panca Marga Youth. In addition, executive members of the HMI, GP Ansor and Muhammadiyah Youth were also engaging in lobbying efforts as individuals.

In November 1995, the Central Executive Board decided on a policy to have first-term legislators fill sixty percent or more of the total legislative members in Golkar by restricting candidates for the 1997 election based on age and term in office. More specifically, they set guidelines that barred anyone from running for candidacy who was at or over the age of sixty-five as of 1997 or had served four terms in the DPR as a Golkar representative (*Tiras* Dec. 28, 1995: 66–67; *Gatra* Dec. 23, 1995: 21–32). Additionally, the policy also included a guideline to have young persons under the age of forty fill twenty-five percent of Golkar's DPR membership (*Gatra* Dec. 23, 1995: 24). These were guidelines only and designed to be applied flexibly in reality, but even so, having freshmen fill over sixty percent of the DPR was a considerably bold policy. Nevertheless, this did not provoke significant resistance from within Golkar. This was because there was a certain degree of consensus within the party concerning opinions such as 'Golkar needs a generational change and the renovation of its membership and this has already become part of the cadre cultivation programs', as stated by Vice-Chair Ismael Hasan (*Tiras* Dec. 28, 1995: 66–67), as well as 'amid increasing numbers of young cadres, [it is necessary to] provide a place, more specifically, legislative seats, for talented cadres to showcase their talent', as outlined by Chairman Harmoko (*Gatra* Dec. 23, 1995: 26). Even the senior DPR members who faced retirement following this set of guidelines hardly raised an objection. They showed their understanding of the Executive Board's decision, as exemplified by Imam Sudarwo's comment, 'there are too many cadres of Golkar and they need a platform' (*Gatra* Dec. 23, 1995: 30–31). The lobbying campaigns conducted by young Golkar leaders in pursuit of DPR member posts were more aggressive than those seen in the 1992 election, and Golkar needed to respond to their demands partly to get Golkar-affiliated youth groups to mobilize support in electoral campaigns in return.

Indeed, these efforts came to fruition in the election held in May 1997 in which nearly seventy percent of DPR members were first-termers (refer to Table 6.3).

Despite the implementation of further rigorous measures to increase the number of new legislative members more than ever before, the process of

Table 6.3: New and re-elected Golkar legislators under the Suharto regime

ELECTION	1971	1977	1982	1987	1992	1997
First-termer	221 (93.6)	118 (50.9)	135 (55.8)	140 (46.8)	141 (50)	223 (68.6)
Second-termer	15 (6.4)	114 (49.1)	56 (23.1)	96 (32.1)	79 (28)	71 (21.9)
Third-termer	—	—	51 (21.1)	35 (11.7)	35 (12.4)	29 (8.9)
Fourth-termer	—	—	—	28 (9.4)	17 (6)	2 (0.6)
Fifth-termer	—	—	—	—	10 (3.6)	—

Notes: Figures in brackets represent the percentage to the total number of Golkar legislators.
Source: LPU (1978, 1983, 1987, 1993, 1997a).

forming candidate lists turned out to be rather chaotic. As part of the process, the provisional list (*daftar calon legislatif sementara*) and the final list (*daftar calon legislatif tetap*) were released five and two months before the elections in January 1997 and April 1997 respectively. Following the release, in Golkar's local branches across Indonesia, those who were not on the lists or were listed but toward the bottom of the lists as well as those whose order on the final list was lower than that on the provisional list staged protests along with their supporters against the local branch or Central Executive Board, whichever it was that determined the candidates. Table 6.4 shows the incidents of confrontation and disorder that occurred within Golkar over the selection of candidates.

The competition over legislative posts within Golkar that had been taking place since the 1990s became even more intense around the 1997 election, at both the central and regional level. At the central level, the Executive Board of Golkar now had to choose among candidates nominated by local branches and the central office, while also coordinating among the three parties, the Armed Forces, Ministry of Home Affairs and Golkar.

The ranking on the legislative candidate lists for the 1997 election to some extent illustrates the power relationship among each group within Golkar. The particularly notable trend was that FKPPI members were generally placed toward the top of the lists, especially in the electoral districts of Jakarta, West Java, Central Java, Yogyakarta and East Java. In the 1997 election, the very top of the lists of each electoral district was filled mostly by members of the Central Executive Board, followed by other influential candidates such as retired generals, former vice governors or bureaucrats nominated by the Armed Forces and Ministry of Home Affairs. Members of the FKPPI were placed next and candidates close to Habibie, Harmoko and Akbar Tandjung generally tended to be positioned below FKPPI members.

For example, if we look more closely at the electoral district of West Java, Chairman of Golkar Harmoko was placed in the number one spot, with other members of the Executive Board in the fourth, seventh and tenth positions. Retired generals were placed in the second, fifth, eighth, eleventh and twelfth positions with former bureaucrats in the third, sixth and ninth spots. Following these were members of the FKPPI who were placed in the fifteenth, eighteenth, twenty-first, twenty-fourth, twenty-ninth, thirty-second, thirty-fourth, forty-forth and forty-ninth positions and candidates from the HMI and GP Ansor as well as the ICMI were ranked in the sixteenth, twentieth, thirty-fifth, fortieth, forty-first, forty-third, forty-fifth and forty-sixth positions on the list. The difference in the ranking of FKPPI and Islamic candidates was more notable in the Central Java electoral district, where the former were placed in the first, eighth, ninth, tenth, twenty-seventh and thirtieth and the latter in the fourth, twentieth,

Table 6.4: Incidents over the selection of Golkar's legislative candidates for the 1997 election

REGION	DETAILS
North Sumatra	The governor of the province tried to register a retired lieutenant general who was his childhood friend on the list and the regional command's commander raised an objection.
Riau	The head of Pancasila Youth's Riau branch protested that his order on the list was too low. Members of the same youth group caused a riot in Golkar's branch.
Palembang	Approximately 5,000 AMPI members staged a demonstration in protest that the head of the AMPI's local branch was placed low on the list and warned that they would leave Golkar.
Jakarta	AMPI's Jakarta branch protested against the inclusion of a large number of people who had barely engaged in activities under Golkar (such as celebrities) on the list. They warned that they would withdraw their executive members from Golkar when their demand to Golkar's Jakarta branch to revise the list was rejected.
Central Java	Some staged a protest arguing that one of the candidates named on the list was not compliant with the guideline of 'retirement after four terms or at the age of sixty-five or older'.
South Sulawesi	The head of the AMPI's Pare-Pare branch protested over his low position on the list and made a direct plea to Chairman Harmoko to increase his rank. The action caused much controversy in Golkar's Pare-Pare branch.
South Sulawesi	A protest erupted over a controversy where a person who allegedly provided a false statement regarding his academic career secured a place on the list where he had a good chance of being elected.
Irian Jaya	DPRD members protested that the list included only a few representatives who were local to the region.
Irian Jaya	The head of the KNPI's local branch whose name was removed from the final list despite being on the provisional list made a protest.

Source: *Gatra* (Jan. 4, 1997: 73; Mar. 1, 1997: 40; Apr. 5, 1997: 41) and *Forum Keadilan* (Mar. 10, 1997: 25–27; Apr. 7, 1997: 27).

twenty-first, thirty-first, thirty-seventh and thirty-ninth places (Lembaga Pemilihan Umum 1997b: 91–117). Thereupon, sixty-five members of the FKPPI were elected—an increase of thirty from the previous election (*Tiras* July 7, 1997: 92). This can be interpreted as a result of the increased influence of FKPPI members being reflected in the list making process that allowed their names to be placed in promising positions on the proportional representative lists.

In this election, Golkar put people with diverse backgrounds such as celebrities and Islamic leaders in addition to ministers and the President's family members on the candidate lists, and was also able to gain support from high-ranking Armed Forces officers. This contributed to Golkar's landslide victory with 325 out of 425 seats, which marked a leap from 68.1 percent in the 1992 election to 74.5 percent in 1997. Meanwhile, the PDI had their popular leader Megawati ousted from the top position and faced an attack on its headquarters that resulted in a large number of casualties. Subsequently, unpopular Suryadi took over the leadership and led the election campaign, but that ended in a crushing defeat, with the share of vote decreasing from 14.9 percent in the 1992 election to just 3.1 percent in the 1997 election and a dramatic decrease in the number of seats from fifty-six to ten. The PDI's votes flowed not only to Golkar but also to the PPP. The PPP who had 17.9 percent of the votes with sixty-two seats in the 1992 election won 22.6 percent of the votes with ninety seats in the 1997 election, regaining about the same number of seats it had won in the 1982 election (ninety-four seats).

Golkar's huge win in the 1997 election produced an unexpected by-product. That is, the Islamic candidates who were placed low on the lists in each electoral district ended up being elected. As described earlier, Islamic candidates tended to be ranked lower than FKPPI ones except for certain influential figures, and this tendency was especially strong in the electoral districts in Java. However, Golkar gained a significant amount of votes in Java and that resulted in the election of a large number of Islamic candidates who were on the borderline between winning and losing.

The Islamic candidates unexpectedly elected included: in the electoral district of West Java, Ferry Mursyidan Baldan (thirty-fifth), Eky Syafruddin (fortieth) and Ade Komaruddin (forty-first) from the HMI, Endang Saefullah (forty-fifth) from the ICMI and Mohammad Hatta (forty-sixth) from the MDI; in the electoral district of Central Java, Muhammad Iqbal Assegaf (thirty-seventh) from the GP Ansor and Yusuf Hidayat (thirty-ninth) from the HMI; in the electoral district of East Java, Aisyah Hamid Baidlowi (thirty-eighth) and K. H. Muhammad As'ad Umar (fortieth) from the NU; and in the electoral district of Jakarta, Ery Chajaridipura (twelfth) from the HMI (Lembaga Pemilihan Umum 1997b: 99–103).

The same can be observed for electoral districts outside Java. Syarfi Hutauruk (seventeenth) from the HMI in North Sumatra, Basri Bermanda (twelfth) from the MDI in West Sumatra, Muhammad Awal (fifth) from the PMII in Jambi, Syaffiuddin Ali Rachman (fourth) from Muhammadiyah and the ICMI in Bengkulu, Chairunissa (fifth) from the ICMI in Central Kalimantan, Yasril Ananta Baharuddin (twentieth) from the ICMI and Ibrahim Ambong (twenty-first) from the HMI in South Sulawesi, Muhammad Sofian Mile (fourth) from the HMI in Central Sulawesi and Hasanuddin Mochdar (third) from the

Muhammadiyah Youth in Maluku were all Islamic candidates who were elected despite being on the borderline between winning and losing (Lembaga Pemilihan Umum 1997b: 92, 93, 95, 97, 105, 112, 116).

The result of the election of many Islamic candidates who were ranked low on the lists was that the Golkar faction within the DPR was now composed of about 100 from the group consisting of members of the Veterans' Association, Indonesian Women Armed Forces Corps and FKPPI, another 100 from the Islamic and former student activist group consisting of members of the HMI, GP Ansor and ICMI with the remaining seats being filled by legislators not belonging to either group, such as bureaucrat-turned politicians. That is to say, the group closely affiliated with the President's eldest daughter and second son and that closely linked to Chairman Harmoko and Habibie came to hold equal power in the Golkar faction within the DPR. This had a huge impact on the political change that took place in May 1998.

Rift in Golkar

The issue of the succession of Suharto

The expanded influence of the President's eldest daughter, which had become increasingly notable during the making of DPR candidate lists, exacerbated the rift within Golkar involving the issue of the succession of President Suharto in the post-election political process.

The issue of Suharto's succession did not suddenly surface in 1997. Since Golkar's national congress held in October 1993, when Suharto's eldest daughter and second son were added to the Central Executive Board for the first time, speculation surrounding Suharto's intention to have his eldest daughter Tutut build a political career to ultimately succeed his throne had been rife. Then, in 1996, it became a common opinion that Tutut was going to become the Chairman of Golkar after Harmoko. Golkar's victory in the 1997 election was a defining event that proved her success in rallying support for the party and made everyone believe that her assumption of the post of the Chairman of Golkar in the next term was indisputable. After the election, in August 1997, President Suharto himself awarded the Bintang Mahaputra—one of Indonesia's most distinguished awards—to her, and former Army Chief of Staff Hartono, a sworn friend of Tutut, also offered her lavish praise, stating that she had reached a stage where she was not only suitable to be the future leader of Golkar but also of the country (*Gatra* Aug. 23, 1997: 48).

Later, Akbar Tandjung, who at that time was the State Minister for Public Housing and one of the members of Golkar's advisory board, claimed that it was obvious that the President was planning to transfer his power to Tutut, stating 'back then, Tutut was considered to be a powerful candidate for the successor to Chairman Harmoko and it was certain that she would become a front runner to take over the presidency if she indeed become the Chairman of Golkar' (Hisyam 1999: 628). It appeared that the power transfer scenario Suharto envisioned—to have Tutut occupy the top position of the ruling party Golkar and then let her take over the presidential office with the support of the Armed Forces—was moving toward realization.

Suharto's intention was also reflected in the fact that Army Chief of Staff Hartono was promoted to Minister of Information upon his age-based retirement from the military (*Gatra* June 14, 1997: 34–41). As Hartono was installed in this post in June 1997, Golkar Chairman Harmoko, who had been serving as the Minister of Information for the previous three terms, was dismissed from the office mid-term and 'relegated' to the position of State Minister without Portfolio. Since Harmoko was elected as the Chair of the DPR and MPR in October 1997, four months after that, the 'relegation' was a temporary measure. Nevertheless, from Harmoko's perspective, this made no difference to the fact that Suharto gave higher priority to allocating posts to his eldest daughter's political partner, despite the fact that Harmoko had been extremely loyal to the President and had led Golkar to a landslide victory in the 1997 election.

In addition to the 'relegation' of Harmoko, none of the ICMI executives close to him and Habibie were appointed as MPR members and this was regarded as evidence of their declining political power within Golkar. In particular, even the ICMI's executive members who were in Habibie's 'inner circle' such as Adi Sasono, Dawam Rahardjo and Watik Pratikrya, whose appointment as members of the MPR to be convened in October 1997 was believed to be certain, were not included in the MPR member list (*Tiras* Aug. 18, 1997: 16–17). Adi Sasono and Dawam Rahardjo were NGO activists (both former student activists) and belonged to the group that criticized the dual function of the Armed Forces and the Suharto family's businesses along with the Chair of Muhammadiyah Amien Rais in the ICMI. The failure of these men who were close to Harmoko and Habibie to obtain seats in the MPR was taken to be, in the words of Amien Rais, 'related to conflicts within Golkar' (*Tiras* Aug. 25, 1997: 92–93). That is to say, the Habibie and Harmoko group was at a disadvantage within Golkar and at the same time the ICMI's political influence was also on a downward trend. Behind the shift in Suharto's distribution of posts in Golkar from the group close to Habibie and Harmoko to those that supported the President's eldest daughter was the fact that Suharto's succession was becoming more and more imminent. Although Suharto's election as president for a seventh term in the MPR general session scheduled in March 1998 was guaranteed, many political elites believed that it was going to be his last term as he was turning seventy-seven that year. However, when Suharto asked everyone to 'think again if he as an aged man was really suitable to be the president' (*Tiras* Oct. 27, 1997: 88–89), no one in Golkar took this seriously nor suggested that they should reconsider the reelection of Suharto. This was a rhetorical comment that Suharto always made during the presidential election process—indeed a very typical one—and no one received it as if President Suharto was seriously thinking of leaving the presidential post.

In July 1997, when the rupiah fell for a prolonged period of time due to the currency crisis, and in December of the same year when Suharto's health became the subject of speculation and rumor as he suffered from a mild heart attack, Golkar and the Armed Forces' support for the election of Suharto for a seventh term remained unwavering. This was because they were anticipating the allocation of some of the most critical political posts to take place in the near future, including the appointment of MPR members in October 1997, substantial personnel changes of high-ranking Armed Forces officers in February 1998 and the election of the president and vice president as well as the formation of a cabinet in March 1998. Although rumors of Suharto's retirement due to the economic crisis and his health concerns were starting to circulate in towns, such talk never came from within the regime because the political elites were making every effort to refrain from any behavior that could have their loyalty to the President questioned, with the allocation of key posts around the corner.

The 1998 vice-presidential election

However, it was also true that every political actor also recognized that the vice presidential post had become more important than ever due to the aging of Suharto. The constitution stipulated that the vice president would take over on behalf of the president, should the president be unable to serve their duties. There was no guarantee that the elderly President would not come to be in such a state.

Golkar was divided over the nomination of vice presidential candidates as follows: the FKPPI group which strongly backed incumbent Vice President Try Sutrisno (former Armed Forces Commander); the group led by the President's eldest daughter which supported Minister of Information Hartono; the ICMI group which supported State Minister of Research and Technology Habibie; the group consisting of *pribumi* entrepreneurs which wanted to nominate State Minister of National Development Planning and Head of the National Development Planning Board Ginandjar Kartasasmita; and finally the group headed by Chairman Harmoko which supported Harmoko (*Gatra* Dec. 20, 1997: 25–29).

Suharto ordered Golkar to decide on two people to nominate as vice presidential candidates. Until then, to select vice presidential candidates, Suharto had elected a team of nine or eleven composed of representatives of the Armed

Forces, bureaucrats and Golkar members and he himself had made the final decision on the candidates after having consulted their opinions. This time, he did not create such team but ordered Golkar's Central Executive Board to hold an internal consultation and instructed the Chairman of Golkar, Armed Forces Commander and Minister of Home Affairs—the representatives of the three elements of the Great Golkar Family—to have a trilateral deliberation and then select two candidates (*Gatra* Jan. 31, 1998: 34–35). By doing so, Suharto tried to avoid the situation in which the Armed Forces faction would nominate a candidate they were backing, as was the case in the MPR general session in 1993. Hence, he clearly displayed his intention that it was going to be Golkar that would name the vice presidential candidates, not the Armed Forces. The introduction of this procedure can be accounted for by Suharto's plan to transfer his power to Tutut. It is not unreasonable that Suharto would have thought he needed to establish the 'precedent' of a Golkar-nominated candidate becoming the vice president in order to stop the Armed Forces from producing powerful rival candidates in the future.

Golkar's Central Executive Board held a general meeting on February 11, 1998, to decide on the two candidates but the discussion became heated (*Tiras* Feb. 23, 1998: 16–17; *Gatra* Feb. 21, 1998: 36–37; *Gatra* Feb. 28, 1998: 36). Harmoko was chosen as the first candidate as he was recognized for leading Golkar to electoral victory as chairman. However, two groups—the FKPPI group that was vigorously calling for other Board members to choose Try Sutrisno and ICMI members who strongly backed Habibie—argued strenuously over the selection of the second candidate (*Gatra* Feb. 28, 1998: 36). Eventually, Habibie, who was seen to be more in line with Suharto's intention, was chosen as the second candidate. Akbar Tandjung, one of the attendees of this meeting, alleges that Suharto intervened to support Habibie (Hisyam 1999: 637).

In any case, Golkar proposed two vice presidential candidates, Harmoko and Habibie, to the President, from whom Suharto chose Habibie. Following this, Habibie was elected as the vice president by unanimous consent in the MPR general session in March 1998. Suharto's selection of Habibie can be explained as follows. For Suharto, the vice president to be chosen on this occasion was not going to be his successor, but merely a 'filler' who would occupy the office until he was ready to transfer power to Tutut. In this situation, it would be more suitable to choose a civilian with no support from the Armed Forces rather than an influential military officer who might be deemed suitable to take over the presidency. Furthermore, when compared with Harmoko, Habibie was more proficient in foreign languages and had extensive experience in negotiating with Western countries. Given his waning strength, Suharto wanted to have Habibie cover some of his presidential duties. This was evident in the way the vice president was given a new responsibility; as part of their duties, the vice president was to assist the president at international conferences hosted by the United Nations, the Conference of the Non-Aligned Countries and ASEAN (*Forum Keadilan* Apr. 6, 1998: 17).

Regardless of the reason, the fact that the vice presidential post had now gone to Habibie drove Tutut's group and the FKPPI group to embark on an effort to recover lost ground in the cabinet reshuffle that immediately followed the close of the MPR general session. This reshuffle was a crucial event that solidified the rift within Golkar.

The selection of cabinet members announced by Suharto in mid-March 1998 is said to have been heavily influenced by the President's eldest daughter Tutut (*Forum Keadilan* Apr. 6, 1998: 10–13). This was because the list of cabinet members included a large number of Tutut's supporters and only a few who were close to Habibie. Tutut herself became the State Minister for Social Affairs while former Minister of Information Hartono assumed the position of the Minister of Home Affairs. Meanwhile, Golkar's Secretary-General Ary Mardjono entered the cabinet as the State Minister of Agrarian Affairs, Fuad Bawazir as the Minister of Finance and Bob Hasan, who was a long-term business partner of the Suharto family, became the Minister of Industry and Trade. Especially, the addition of Tutut and Bob Hasan to the cabinet became the target of much criticism in that it revealed the extent of Suharto's nepotism even more blatantly than before.

A large section of the Golkar executives who were presumably nominated by Habibie and Harmoko were not given cabinet positions. According to Central Executive Board member Din Syamsuddin, the list of nominees Harmoko submitted to the President included himself, along with Fahmi Idris, Sri Redjeki, Agung Laksono and Theo Sambuaga (Prasetyo 1999: 36). From this list, Suharto chose only two, Agung Laksono and Theo Sambuaga, who he thought capable of cooperating with Tutut. Habibie is also said to have nominated Adi Sasono, Marwah Daud Ibrahim, Jimly Assidiqie and Haryanto Danutirto, who were the core members of the ICMI, for cabinet positions, but only Haryanto Danutirto became a cabinet member (Prasetyo 1999: 36).

The implications of all of this was that Suharto's distribution of political posts was now increasingly skewed toward the groups surrounding Tutut. He made a decision to give preferential treatment to his family members and prioritize the groups close to them in allocating posts at a time when what he really needed to do was to draw broad support from the elites within the regime as the serious economic crisis was substantially damaging the government's credibility. This not only further turned the public away but also triggered the defection of elites within the regime, even including those who were close to Suharto.

The defection of elites started from the ICMI, whose members were excluded from the MPR and the cabinet. At the end of March 1998, the ICMI selected an acting chair upon Chairman Habibie's assumption of the office of vice president. The acting chair elected at that time was Achmad Tirtosudiro, who was critical of the government (*Forum Keadilan* Apr. 6, 1998: 22). Tirtosudiro was a retired Army Lieutenant General and had at one point served as the Chair of Bulog at the beginning of the Suharto regime, but was later ousted due to the misappropriation of funds at the agency. After that, he formed a connection with Habibie during his time as the Ambassador to West Germany and provided support for the establishment of the ICMI in 1990. Meanwhile, his comments consistently maintained some distance from the government. The election of Tirtosudiro as acting chair of the ICMI was ensured through a careful process, by which the anti-government group within the ICMI led by Adi Sasono and Amien Rais had gathered signatures to show support for Tirtosudiro in the lead up to the election because there was widespread speculation that Suharto wanted retired Army Major General Azwar Anas to be elected to this post (*Forum Keadilan* Apr. 6, 1998: 22).

New Acting Chair Tirtosudiro, soon after taking office, urged members that the ICMI must achieve greater independence from the government. Indicating the ICMI's dissatisfaction with only gaining a few cabinet posts, he declared that the organization would not hesitate to openly criticize the government. He claimed that the 'ICMI is certainly positioned close to the government but we do not cling to the government. The ICMI should raise its voice against the injustice the nation is facing. We will speak out and criticize the cabinet freely from now on' (*Forum Keadilan* Apr. 6, 1998: 22). Thereafter, the ICMI began acting in exactly the manner he described as the reformist movement amplified.

DPR reform from within

Over the course of the period from 1997 to 1998, while Suharto's distribution of political patronage gradually skewed toward his family members and those around them, a new development was starting to emerge in the DPR—the movement to enhance the function of the DPR as a legislative body. The previous chapter described how the discussion over Golkar's independence arose within the ruling party, and part of this involved the movement to extend the role of the DPR involving various factions that surfaced in the period from the end of the 1980s to the early 1990s. Although this did not result in concrete changes in either the process or system of the preparation of bills at that time, the drive to improve the representative function of the DPR, even in the slightest degree, maintained its vigor and emerged as a specific series of changes in the legislative process in 1997. One of them involved amendments to bills presented by the government and the other concerned DPR member-initiated legislation.

Of the former, the most prominent example was the changes to the labor bill. This bill, submitted by the government in December 1996, was passed at the end of the DPR session in September 1997 after eight months of debate[8]. During the debate, as much as almost seventy percent of the text of the bill was rewritten and the number of articles increased substantially from 159 to 199 (*Tiras* Sept. 22, 1997: 15–18). In regards to the content of the law, opinion was divided among both specialists and the media; some viewed that it improved labor rights to a certain degree while others pointed out its insufficiency (*Tiras* Sept. 22, 1997: 24–25; *Forum Keadilan* Oct. 6, 1997: 104). For example, such articles as those that stipulated that any non-employee must not intervene in the establishment of labor unions, employers must pay wages to employees involved in strike actions and companies that failed to pay the minimum wage must be penalized were highly valued, while those that made it necessary to register with the government when forming a labor union and established the obligation to notify the employing company in advance when carrying out strike action drew criticism (*Tiras* Sept. 22, 1997: 17–18, 21–22).

In any case, the amendments to the labor bill signified a change in the deliberation process that had thus far been controlled by the government. Previously, both significantly amending a bill and adding articles to one had been unacceptable. In the words of Golkar legislator Iskandar Mandji, who was a member of the special committee on the labor law, 'there has never been a case where the addition of articles was accepted and therefore it was truly revolutionary that as many as forty new articles were added' (*Tiras* Sept. 22, 1997: 17). Another important point here was that, throughout the debate, the DPR side actively initiated the amendments and addition of the articles, and the government side (the Ministry of Manpower) then accepted their demands. This was not enough to completely overturn the undesirable, powerless image of the DPR but it gave confidence to DPR members in the sense that the government was now taking their opinions into consideration and allowing changes to be made to bills. A senior Golkar legislator, Oka Mahendra, made a positive remark regarding the amendments to the labor bill in that it was empowering the DPR's function to make laws and formulate budgets in conjunction with the government (*Forum Keadilan* Oct. 6, 1997: 103).

The DPR member-initiated legislation—passing bills introduced by the DPR rather than the government—had not yet been attempted under the Suharto regime. However, around that time, there was a growing awareness that the rules concerning the DPR needed to change to allow DPR members and factions to create drafts themselves or take the initiative in introducing bills. The movement began in 1997 in the form of a challenge to modify the standing orders of the DPR (*Tata Tertib DPR*) (*Tiras* June 23, 1997: 22–24). According to the standing orders of the DPR[9] established in 1983, the DPR and its members were granted the right to interpolate the president (*Hak Interpelasi*), the right to investigate government affairs (*Hak Angket*), the right to make amendments to bills (*Hak Amandemen*), the right to express opinions (*Hak Mengajukan Pernyataan Pendapat*), the right to make recommendations (*Hak Menganjurkan Seseorang*) and the right to submit bills (*Hak Inisiatif Pembentukan RUU*). Nevertheless, these rights were accompanied by conditions, such as 'the submission must be made by at least twenty members from at least two factions' regarding the right to submit bills and 'the demand must be made by several members from at least two factions' for the right to investigate government affairs. Although appeals to relax these conditions associated with the standing orders had been made since the beginning of the 1990s, the fractious relationships between the factions impeded this from being realized (*Tiras* June 23, 1997: 22–23).

The situation changed in March 1997 when the PPP faction made a proposal regarding the revision of the standing orders of the DPR that was seconded by the Golkar faction. Subsequently, in June of the same year, the four factions in the DPR formed a consensus and established the Special Committee on the Revision of the Standing Orders of the DPR (*Tiras* June 23, 1997: 22–24). At the center of the disagreement in the debate on the revision was the wording 'from at least two factions' included in the articles on the right to submit bills and the right to investigate government affairs. The PPP insisted that this wording be removed, but the Golkar faction rejected their demand on the grounds that, as DPR member Umbu Mehang Kunda put it, 'removing this would allow one faction to submit a bill on its own without support from any other faction and may give rise to dictatorship by the majority, or autarchy by the minority' (*Gatra* Sept. 27, 1997: 41). The real motive behind this comment was probably that the Golkar faction did not think favorably of the initiative to allow the submission of bills by the opposition parties. As a compromise solution, Golkar proposed to retain the wording 'from at least two factions' but replace the phrase 'at least twenty members' with 'at least ten members'. They ultimately settled for this expression, finally making the revision of the standing orders of the DPR a reality (*Gatra* Sept. 27, 1997: 41).

Golkar also decided to assign two to five field experts for each of eight committees—a total of twenty-five—to support its faction members, and the PPP faction decided to place at least one expert in each committee (*Tiras* 7 July 1997: 96; *Gatra* Sept. 27, 1997: 41).

This institutional change was brought about as a result of the mutual agreement on the enhancement of the DPR's function by all four factions, including that of the Armed Forces. This suggests that the DPR, including the ruling party, was aware that its role as a national legislature must improve. Chairman of Golkar Harmoko who assumed the office of the chair of the DPR and MPR in October 1997 stated as follows.

> ... now that the Seventh Five-Year Development Plan has been launched, the DPR's function and role must be further enhanced. Enhancing the DPR's function and role means enabling it to serve the function as set forth in the Constitution of 1945. The constitution stipulates that the legislative and executive branches are of equal power. The DPR has the mandate to make laws. The DPR must also hold discussions on the revision of outdated laws such as those created in the colonial era as required...The people want the DPR to become stronger, grow in importance and hold more power. What the DPR must do in the next session is to successfully fulfill the fundamental role prescribed for the DPR, particularly its role in the legislative process—to enact laws. (*Gatra* Sept. 27, 1997: 42–43)

It is, of course, possible to regard the above as merely empty rhetoric offered by Harmoko as the Chair of the DPR. In fact, during deliberations on the MPR resolutions and the general national policy framework, the GBHN, which were conducted over the period from October 1997 to March 1998, the MPR's Golkar faction agreed to develop a resolution to grant the president the emergency prerogative—special authorities (*wewenang khusus*) to quell social riots should they occur—as requested by Suharto[10]. Concerned about the possibility of demonstrations and the deterioration of public order due to the economic crisis, Suharto demanded that this be adopted in the MPR general session and the MPR's Golkar faction accepted this mandate without resistance. Golkar was still unable to escape from being referred to as the President's puppet for having accepted such demands.

However, the aforementioned words of Chair of the DPR Harmoko gradually became a reality over the course of the reformist movement that was to gain full momentum in March 1998. More specifically, a group of DPR members from Golkar who were willing to respond to the calls of the reformist groups came to the fore and started making moves to fulfill their demands. At the MPR general session in March 1998, the PPP appealed that the five political laws that were restricting political participation must be revised in order to achieve political reform. As a matter of fact, the voices that sought to revise the five political laws, which was considered akin to taboo at the time, were even raised in the Golkar faction's internal meetings (*Forum Keadilan* Mar. 23, 1998: 12). Behind this was the slow but steady work of the DPR members who recognized the need to reform the legislature, as has been discussed above. There were, however, more than a few members within the Golkar faction who opposed the revision of the five political laws, and therefore, as of the beginning of March 1998, a compromise deal to 'implement reform in stages' was arranged as a tentative solution. Nonetheless, the very fact that such a proposal was raised can be seen as a sign of change within Golkar. Soon after this, this harbinger of a shift within Golkar would evolve into dramatic political reform, driven by the rapid development of the political situation. It was not a mere coincidence that the alliance of the reformist groups with groups within the regime occurred in the parliament.

7
The Reformist Movement and the Fall of the Suharto Regime

What distinguishes the Indonesian political change that occurred in May 1998 from others is that it took only a short period of time for consensus to be achieved between reformist forces and the regime, and that this consensus prompted the resignation of President Suharto. There are three reasons that can be attributed to how the resignation of Suharto was brought about in the short timeframe of three months from the beginning of the reformist movement.

Firstly, there was a rift within the ruling party Golkar stemming from before the beginning of the reformist movement. As discussed in the previous chapter, this rift was the result of Suharto's skewed patronage distribution. With the succession of his eldest daughter Tutut in mind, Suharto favored influential military officers and FKPPI members who were close to his family in the distribution of posts, causing the marginalization of groups consisting of former student activists and Islamic group members. Once the internal rift was created, it kept growing alongside the ever-worsening economic crisis until it became one of the factors that led to the collapse of the regime from within.

Secondly, the group consisting of former student activists and Islamic group members within Golkar and the reformist forces had a relationship that enabled them to engage in dialogue and negotiation. As a result of the extension of the range of patronage distribution to social elites to recruit them into the ruling party, people who shared the same ideological basis and awareness of the crisis were now existing on a continuum both within and outside of the regime. Since many of those who were absorbed into the regime came from the same groups and organizations as the students and intellectuals at the forefront of the reformist movement, the wall between those within and outside the regime was no obstacle, and thus they had ample opportunities to engage in dialogue and negotiation.

Thirdly, there were almost no radicals completely opposed to engaging with the government with the sole aim of overthrowing the government. Under co-opting type personal rule, where many social elites and a large proportion of the public is absorbed into the patronage distribution scheme of the ruler and the use of violence is relatively mild, strong hatred and fear toward the ruler is less likely to emerge. Further, its conciliatory distribution policy prevents the formation of any radical anti-government group large enough to be considered a real force. Therefore, transition under co-opting-type personal rule is highly likely to be a three-player game among 'moderate anti-government groups', 'soft-liners within the regime' and 'hard-liners within the regime'. Due to the absence of radicals who would otherwise call for the complete elimination of the old regime, there is one less factor that prevents negotiation and consensus building between 'moderate anti-government groups' and 'soft-liners within the regime'. At the same time, this absence of radicals means that the 'hard-liners within the regime' can more easily come to a compromise with the consensus formed between the other two.

With these points in mind, this chapter describes the process in which an alliance and consensus was established between the reformist forces, that is the 'moderate anti-government groups' and those within Golkar, the 'soft-liners within the regime'. The catalyst for the reformist movement was nationwide confusion over the economic crisis. The reformist forces and the regime's soft-liners held numerous rounds of negotiation and gradually strengthened ties while the economic crisis snowballed into a political crisis. The consensus regarding the resignation of Suharto was built during that process and led the whole affair to end in 'pacted transition'. The aim of this chapter is to elucidate the abovementioned processes that took place during Indonesia's political transition in more detail.

From currency crisis to social unrest

Spread of the currency crisis

The currency crisis that spread from Thailand in July 1997 caused substantial damage to the Indonesian economy, provoking an economic crisis that destabilized Suharto's rule. This crisis exposed the problems of the decision-making processes in the Suharto government, and consequently the technocrats who had been making the economic decisions for Indonesia until then were largely discredited. Subsequently, Suharto began to directly intervene into economic policy himself. However, his intervention only added to the economic confusion.

Prior to the spread of the currency crisis, the exchange rate was 2,400 rupiah per US dollar. Indonesia operated a managing float and devalued the rupiah little by little every year. Everyday transactions were performed within the exchange rate band set by the Bank of Indonesia (BI), Indonesia's central bank. On July 11, 1997, the BI increased the exchange rate band from four to six percent when the rupiah came under pressure as a result of the spillover effect from the collapse of the Thai baht (Aramaki 2002: 6). Subsequently, on August 14, amid intensifying selling pressure, Minister of Finance Mar'ie Muhammad announced a shift to a free-floating exchange rate system and simultaneously the BI increased the domestic interest rate to stymie selling of the rupiah. From late August to September, monetary policy was tightened, and an announcement was made that some of the major infrastructure projects would be reviewed. Those that became the subject of review included projects managed by business groups owned by the President's family members (McLeod 1999: 210–211; Kenward 2002: 26–35).

As described above, the financial authorities' response was prompt. However, the policy the government adopted was somewhat ambiguous and had a problem in terms of inconsistency. It was unclear as to whether these major projects were to be postponed or cancelled because State Minister for Research and Technology Habibie claimed in the DPR that the projects for strategic industries would not be delayed, as if to deny the Minister of Finance's statement. Similarly, Head of the National Development Planning Agency (Bappenas) Ginandjar also made a comment noting that there were sufficient funds for the projects to be completed (Kenward 2002: 36). The market responded negatively to the government's inconsistency in the handling of the matter.

Behind this disagreement within the government was a problem intrinsic to the economic policy-making process under the Suharto regime. Although the Coordinating Minister for the Economy and Finance called regular weekly meetings with all economic cabinet members and the finance committee concerning macroeconomics met on a frequent basis, Suharto did not appreciate the idea that economic policy was discussed in these meetings. Accordingly, key economic proposals were not decided upon during the discussion in these meetings. Instead, in most cases, a person responsible for the policy would visit with and present the proposal to the President in person and the decision would be made upon the President's approval or instruction.

Under this decision-making process in which important decisions were made during personal talks with Suharto, the views of those who had more contact with the President naturally had a stronger influence on the President's decisions and therefore were more often reflected in policy. Economic policies were never a product of comprehensive discussions within the government, and only those proposals that were given the President's personal permission were drafted. As such, in many cases industrial development was carried out with no consistency between macroeconomic and microeconomic policies. This policy-making system did not pose a major problem while the economy was in good shape. However, once the economic situation took a turn for the worse, it became a huge issue. The Indonesian government lost its international credibility due to the fact that the inconsistency between macroeconomic policy makers including Minister of Finance Mar'ie Muhammad and Governor of the BI Soedradjad

Djiwandono and microeconomic policy makers such as State Minister for Research and Technology Habibie and the Head of Bappenas Ginandjar was exposed through their respective responses to the currency crisis in 1997.

Suharto had given key posts to technocrats who promoted libertarian economic policy, such as Widjojo Nitisastro and Ali Wardhana, since the very beginning of the New Order and always followed their decisions on every occasion of economic crisis. They proved worthy of his trust every time and succeeded in delivering economic growth. Some of their legacies include the salvation of the Indonesian economy that was on the verge of bankruptcy in the late 1960s, success in weathering the crisis of state-run oil company Pertamina in the mid-1970s and the implementation of structural adjustments to steer Indonesian economic policy from import-substituting industrialization toward export-oriented industrialization in the mid-1980s. However, the power of the technocrats began to decline with the arrival of the 1990s (Komatsu 2002: 67). This was because technocrats like Widjojo who had been guiding the economic policy from the beginning of the Suharto regime were now in their old age and had left the decision-making center stage, despite remaining in politics as economic advisors to Suharto. Unlike Widjojo, Suharto did not particularly trust the younger generation of technocrats such as Minister of Finance Mar'ie and Governor of the BI Soedradjad and their influence on the President was limited.

Under such circumstances, the economy entered a boom period in the 1990s. A huge amount of foreign funds flowed into Indonesia as a result of the relaxation of regulations as well as banking liberalization, encouraging ambitious industrial policy and large-scale infrastructure projects. Consequently, bureaucrats who were specialists in the field of technology, called technologists, such as Habibie who was leading the development of strategic industries including the aviation industry came to the fore and were given key posts by Suharto. Habibie and other microeconomic policy makers who were eager to have the growth of strategic industries prioritized started to make proposals to Suharto regarding a variety of projects and began to impact on his decisions. Emil Salim, who had been involved in the economic policy-making process under the Suharto regime for many years as a technocrat, made the following comment in criticism of this situation.

...the resulting decisions were ad hoc in nature and the connection between macro- and micro-economy was ignored as priority was given to microeconomic decisions. Industrial policies were drawn up in such an uncoordinated fashion and economic and financial meetings no longer served a coordinating function but were undermined by the spread of egoism to have industrial policies on their own area of responsibility prioritized over others, and policies that resulted from such circumstances were almost like a mixture of Habibie-nomics and Widjojo-nomics shoved together. (Salim 2000: 99)

Furthermore, the 1990s saw the increased presence of Suharto's children who were trying to push through large-scale projects in pursuit of the expansion of their own businesses (Komatsu 2002: 67). Foreign funds that flowed into Indonesia on the one hand provided a boost to the development of strategic industries and implementation of large-scale projects, but on the other hand also made a significant contribution to the growth of businesses owned by Suharto's children. Technocrats had only a limited say in the President's family members' businesses and that allowed Suharto's children's businesses to grow 'unchecked'. Although the problems with these projects in terms of efficiency and profitability, let alone nepotism, were often pointed out, these were largely left unaddressed. A large number of private banks were established one after another to finance large-scale projects, but many started to gradually accumulate bad loans as some loans became irrecoverable. The BI, which was aware of this unfavorable situation before the onslaught of the currency crisis, requested the President's permission to take a resolution measure for banks with bad loans, but the President's order was to leave it for the time being (Djiwandono 2005: 128). This is a good example of microeconomics being given higher priority, leaving the technocrats' corrective measures concerning macroeconomics to be dealt with later.

Suharto's intervention into economic policy

On October 8, 1997, given the depreciation of the rupiah that was showing no signs of slowing down, the government requested emergency assistance from the IMF. Upon receipt of this request consultations began at the IMF and an agreement was formed with the Indonesian government in less than a month, leading to the announcement of a Letter of Intent (LOI) concerning support for Indonesia on October 31. However, from the announcement of the IMF's first assistance package onward, technocrats were gradually forced away from the policy-making process.

The central members of the team who engaged in the negotiations over this first package included technocrats such as Minister of Finance Mar'ie and Governor of the BI Soedradjad[1]. Against Indonesia's request to the IMF that the assistance be made under the precautionary program, the IMF announced to the Indonesian government that a condition of the loan was that it would be made under the stand-by program, which imposes overall structural economic reform. The IMF side was not willing to make concessions regarding this condition and the Indonesian negotiation team had no other choice but to accede to the offer (Djiwandono 2005: 67–73). Consequently, contracting the fiscal stance by postponing major infrastructure projects, tightening the monetary stance by reducing the money supply and implementing a dear-money policy, reforming the financial sector by closing sixteen banks saddled with bad loans and structural reform based on deregulation and the promotion of competition including the abolishment of the national car project and termination of the monopoly over agricultural imports were incorporated into the first assistance package agreed between the two parties (Aramaki 2002: 16–18).

This package caused major chaos in Indonesian society. Indonesia saw a surge in company failures as the tight financial and monetary policy was implemented without addressing the issue of company debt repayment, making it even more difficult for many companies that were suffering from a lack of funds. In addition, the closure of sixteen banks without a full deposit guarantee in place triggered a bank run, causing a stampede of depositors rushing to private banks to withdraw their funds. Those who had significant funds in private banks tried to withdraw and transfer to a safer state-run or foreign bank. Furthermore, the situation around the fact that among the closed banks were those in which the President's second son Bambang and paternal half-brother Probosutedjo owned shares escalated into a fracas that resulted in legal action against the Minister of Finance and Governor of the BI. Bambang eventually accepted the closure of the banks but acquired a smaller bank and moved some of the funds from the closed banks to it instead. Such social disorder and the behavior of the President's family members, which was inconsistent with the agreement with the IMF, elicited a negative response from the market, putting the rupiah back on a declining path, despite a temporary recovery that followed the announcement of the package.

In the period from November to December 1997, when critical policy decisions were due, the Minister of Finance and Governor of the BI, who were holding negotiations with the IMF, did not have any opportunity to meet with the President (Djiwandono 2005: 146–147). The primary reason for this, among others such as the President's overseas trips and health issues, was possibly that Suharto was gradually losing trust in the IMF and the technocrats. Suharto believed that the crisis Indonesia was facing was essentially a result of monetary and financial problems, and its root cause was market speculation. If it was just a monetary problem, then the depreciation of the rupiah should have slowed down in a matter of a few weeks. However, the rupiah's fall showed no sign of ending. What's more, the closure of banks as prescribed under the IMF's assistance program provoked social panic. Suharto began to think that there were problems with the measures implemented by the Minister of Finance and Governor Soedradjad—the heads of the currency and monetary authorities—under the direction of the IMF and gradually started to intervene directly in economic policy, disregarding the two parties (McLeod 1999: 223; Djiwandono 2005: 190–191).

In spite of the IMF's instruction to maintain high interest rates, the President ordered the BI to reduce the lending rate to bail out small and medium-sized enterprises. With no power to formulate policy independently, the central bank was caught between conflicting demands from the IMF and the President (Djiwandono 2005: 112). Suharto also ordered major state-run banks to provide loans at low interest rates to small and medium-sized enterprises, and this instruction further contradicted the agreement with the IMF. Neither the Minister of Finance nor Governor of the BI was called to the meeting to deliberate on this issue (Djiwandono 2005: 148), and important economic policy was now discussed and determined without their knowledge. Moreover, the President replaced four directors of the BI on December 19, without any consultation with Governor Soedradjad.

On January 6, 1998, the government presented a draft budget to the DPR, but the market reacted negatively due to the following reasons: it was prepared based on the rate of 4,000 rupiah to one US dollar, the economic growth target of four percent was too optimistic and it did not include the goal of a budget surplus equal to one percent of GDP as agreed with the IMF (Aramaki 2002: 8). As a result, the rupiah took a sharp plunge to more than 10,000 rupiah per dollar. Though the subsequent announcement of the second IMF package temporarily halted the decline, it later plummeted again, this time to more than 12,000 rupiah per dollar due to the rising prediction that Habibie's election as vice president was a certainty. Under such circumstances, the President formed a new committee to deal with the economic crisis on January 21 and assumed the chairmanship of the committee himself[2]. At the same time, he requested that the IMF newly appoint a liaison official to liaise between him and the IMF (Djiwandono 2005: 160). That is to say, the President set out to deal with the economic crisis himself, ignoring the Minister of Finance and Governor of the BI who had been negotiating with the IMF thus far.

Over the period from the end of January to the beginning of February, the press reported that the President was considering the introduction of the currency board system (CBS[3]) in order to stabilize the rupiah. The market showed a significant response to this and the rupiah hit 14,000 to the dollar. Following this, a CBS specialist, Steve Hanke from the Johns Hopkins University, was invited to the new economic committee as an advisor by Fuad Bawazir who was the committee's vice secretary-general, through a business entrepreneur close to the Suharto family[4]. Although the introduction of the CBS was later dropped as the result of international pressure, including a series of visits by the IMF as well as G7 heads of state or government (Kenward 2002: 75–77), this issue clearly demonstrated to the international community how lost the Suharto government was. On February 17, Suharto sacked Governor of the BI Soedradjad, who was strongly opposing the introduction of the CBS, and replaced him with Syahrir Sabirin. This was an exceedingly unusual replacement as it took place just three weeks before the formation of a new cabinet. The replacement of the governor was followed by the successive dismissal of three directors. This was an extraordinary situation indeed, with a total of eight top executives of the central bank including the governor and seven directors being replaced within a short period of about two months in the midst of the economic crisis.

The mess over the introduction of the CBS and associated major reshuffle of the executives of the central bank as well as the tight political schedule with the presidential and vice presidential elections and the formation of a new cabinet just around the corner all contributed to the delay in negotiations on the third package between the government and the IMF. In the meantime, the issue of company debt repayment was left unaddressed. As a consequence, declining corporate performance and bankruptcy led to increased layoffs and unemployment and at the same time commodity prices skyrocketed with necessities leading the trend. Poverty triggered riots across Indonesia deteriorating public security, with the people's frustration directed at Chinese-Indonesians. Behind this was the circulation of various malicious false rumors intended to divert the fury of the people towards Chinese-Indonesians. One such rumor was that Chinese-Indonesians were transferring their assets overseas. Shops owned by Chinese-Indonesians were set on fire and a Chinese-Indonesian entrepreneur, Sofyan Wanandi, was placed under police investigation for allegedly 'planning a terrorist bombing to overthrow the government'.

Amid such circumstances, the President announced a new cabinet on March 14, 1998. The economic ministers in the new cabinet were noticeably different from before. The public presence of the technocrats who had been dealing with the economic crisis in conjunction with international institutions such as the IMF vanished, as exemplified by Minister of Finance Mar'ie being replaced by Fuad Bawazir who was critical of the IMF. He was one of those who agreed with Suharto's idea of introducing the CBS and also had a very close relationship with the Suharto family. In the same manner, bureaucrats and economists who were oriented toward nationalistic economic policy were appointed to other posts, as evident in the assignment of Ginandjar Kartasasmita as the Coordinating Minister for Economy, Finance and Industry as well as the Head of the Bappenas, the promotion of Kuntro Mangkusubroto to the position of Minister of Mines and Energy and the reappointment of Syahrir Sabirin, who was installed as the Governor of the BI three weeks previously, to the same position (*Forum Keadilan* Apr. 6, 1998: 14). The addition of Suharto's long-term business partner

Bob Hasan to the cabinet as the Minister of Industry and Trade as well as the inclusion of the President's eldest daughter Tutut attracted fierce criticism in that it was seen as the ultimate act of cronyism.

The reformist movement and dialogue

Movements on campus

Student movements calling for reform slowly began around January 1998 and started spreading all over the country following the MPR general session held at the beginning of March. Student demonstrations, which erupted at several university campuses, sought the MPR's understanding as to the current condition of people who had been impoverished by the economic crisis and called for the resolution of the national crisis. The demonstration held at the University of Indonesia in Jakarta on March 2 demanded the early resolution of the crisis, the formation of an uncorrupt government and a reduction in the price of life's necessities (*Kompas* Mar. 3, 1998). Student demonstrations of this sort quickly expanded to campuses all over Indonesia, turning prestigious universities into a hub for the mobilization of several hundred to several thousand students on each campus.

When the new cabinet lineup driven by nepotism caused great disappointment among the public, students calling for reform started to feel the need to expand the movement. Initially, student demonstrations were organized by the student senate (*Senat Mahasiswa*) of each university or mobilized by student or youth groups such as the HMI, but new mobilization networks across different universities began to appear in the latter half of March. The biggest among them was the Indonesian Muslim Student's Action Front (KAMMI). Founded on March 29 by a group of student representatives from sixty universities across Indonesia (*Gatra* Apr. 18, 1998: 64), this organization closely resembled the Indonesian Student's Action Front (KAMI), a cross-university student union formed to condemn the PKI and President Sukarno after the September 30th Affair of 1965[5]. A variety of student groups and university networks such as the KAMMI slowly brought students together who then began participating in demonstrations and gatherings on a frequent basis.

Students adopted the simple slogan '*Reformasi*', meaning 'Reform', to plea for the improvement of the economic situation including the reduction of commodity prices and the elimination of corruption, collusion and nepotism (KKN). Academics and intellectuals from universities joined the students in leading the reformist movement. Academics participated in student demonstrations from an early stage. The gatherings held on February 5 and 11 at Gadjah

Mada University in Yogyakarta were attended by renowned academics from the university such as Amien Rais, Riswanda Imawan and Affan Gafar (*Kompas* Apr. 4, 1998). Amien Rais especially, who took a critical stance against the Suharto regime and was also widely known as the Chair of Muhammadiyah and an executive of the ICMI, frequently made appearances in demonstrations and gatherings held at universities in Jakarta as well as other regions of the country and appealed for the government to solve the economic crisis and eradicate corruption.

Nurcholish Madjid, who was one of the most prominent Islamic intellectuals in Indonesia, was one of the key figures leading the reformist movement. Nurcholish expressed strong dismay and declared his sympathy for the reformist movement (*Kompas* Mar. 23, 1998) when the newly appointed Minister of Home Affairs Hartono (a political partner of Tutut and previously the Army Chief of Staff and Minister of Information) condemned the student reformist movement as 'incompatible with Indonesian culture' (*Kompas* Mar. 19, 1998). This direct opposition from an intellectual who had been showing willingness to compromise with the Suharto regime surprised political elites as well as the public.

Along with Amien Rais and Nurcholish Madjid, Professor Emil Salim from the University of Indonesia became a key figure in the reformist movement. He had supported the Suharto regime as an economic technocrat for many years until the mid-1990s, when he gradually shifted his stance to adopt the anti-regime view and came to be regarded as one of the moderate democratic leaders.

The political standing of academics and intellectuals from universities who came to play a role in the reformist movement along with students was complicated. First of all, many were academics from state universities, in other words, public servants. They were often required, insofar as they were public servants, to take a pro-government position by the Ministry of Education and Culture. Nevertheless, unlike regular public servants and bureaucrats, quite a few were critical of the Suharto regime, and their work environment that involved frequent contact with students made them more likely to sympathize with the student reformist movement.

Secondly, they had diverse political stances. For instance, Emil Salim had played a core role in the Suharto regime as a technocrat for a long period of time, although he was starting to adopt an anti-government position. On the other hand, Nurcholish was neither particularly anti- nor pro-government but took a more neutral position. As for Amien Rais, he did not necessarily lead the anti-government movement, but consistently indicated a critical attitude toward the government. As described above, the political position varied among scholars and intellectuals. This meant that these academics were not recognized as a unified force advocating a particular political view.

Lastly, they belonged, or had belonged in the past, to multiple social organizations and engaged in activities as part of those organizations and their networks, as was the case for other political elites. Nurcholish Madjid belonged to the 'Generation of 66' which played a major role in the political change that took place over the period from 1965 to 1966 and led the student movement as the chair of the central executive board of the HMI. He also had many friends of similar age from the HMI in Golkar, including Abdul Gafur, Akbar Tandjung and Fahmi Idris. Similarly, Chair of Muhammadiyah Amien Rais had some of his fellow Muhammadiyah executive members working for Golkar, such as Din Syamsuddin and Lukman Harun. In addition, he was friends with several high-ranking government officials such as Vice President Habibie and Minister of Religion Malik Fadjar.

Amien Rais, Nurcholish Madjid and Emil Salim all belonged to the ICMI. As discussed in Chapter Four, the ICMI was an organization that drew a wide spectrum of intellectuals from within and outside of the Suharto regime, spanning top officials at the center of the regime and opposition party members. This placed the large number of Islamic intellectuals outside the government that came together in the ICMI into a grey zone that was neither a clear regime force nor a straightforward opposition force. However, as examined in the previous chapter, Suharto began distributing significantly less patronage to the ICMI in the late 1990s and this gradually drove it to adopt a more critical stance against the government. The secession of a large number of the academics and intellectuals who had been placed in the grey zone or half co-opted into the regime or their participation in the student reformist movement while staying in the grey zone had an extremely important implication for the dialogue and alliance between them and the politicians within the regime who shared an ideological base with them.

Into April, student demonstrators started to clash with the security unit frequently. The catalyst for this was Coordinating Minister for Political and Security Affairs Feisal Tandjung's comment in response to the students' demand to have a direct dialogue with the President, in which he remarked that students should express their intention and opinions through the DPR and DPRD (*Kompas* Mar. 27, 1998). Minister of Home Affairs Hartono also asserted that the demand for reform should be made through the DPR rather than demonstrations (*Kompas* Mar. 25, 1998). Despite the fact that both ministers' statements were intended to curb 'extreme' actions, they had the opposite effect of encouraging students to take the demonstrations and gatherings that were held on university campuses to the street, marching toward the DPR and DPRD to express their demands for reform. This resulted in a skirmish between student demonstrators and the security unit that tried to prevent students from leaving the campus that left some students injured (*Kompas* Apr. 3, 1998).

Minister of Education and Culture Wiranto Arismunandar gathered the rectors and vice rectors of universities and ordered them to regulate student demonstrations. However, many rectors who sympathized with student demonstrations offered rebuttals to the Minister's order, claiming that the students' actions did not meet the requirements for regulation on the grounds that they constituted a moral movement rather than political activities. They demanded that if the Minister wanted to label students' actions as political activities then the Minister should first describe the criteria for determining what constitutes a political activity, otherwise they could not regulate the students' activities (*Kompas* Apr. 9, 1998). Faced with unexpectedly strong opposition, the Minister of Education and Culture had no other choice but to give up on regulating student movements through university authorities.

Initiating dialogue

The reformist group led by students and intellectuals began hosting debate sessions, seminars, symposiums and forums on reform at universities and other locations. They generally had an open attitude toward and responded to dialogue with anyone from the regime including government officials, cabinet members, senior Armed Forces officers and members of parliament. From the very beginning of the movement, academics and intellectuals in particular were seeking cooperation from groups within the regime, as they did not have a radical reform agenda to pursue the overthrow of the Suharto regime; their goal was first and foremost to embody and realize the political and economic reforms sought by students. The reformist movement was moderate in nature in this sense.

One of the groups eager to engage in dialogue with students and intellectuals from an early stage was the Armed Forces. In the middle of March, Commander of the Armed Forces and Minister of Defense and Security Wiranto expressed that he was prepared to hold talks with students while reaffirming the Armed Forces' intention not to support radical reform (*Kompas* Mar. 13, 1998). He gave Armed Forces Command Staff for Sociopolitical Affairs Susilo Bambang Yudhoyono an order to hold a forum with students at the earliest date possible (*Kompas* Mar. 21, 1998). Meanwhile, Army Chief of Staff Subagyo also issued an order for regional commands of the Army to actively create opportunities for dialogue with students (*Kompas* Mar. 18, 1998). This signified that the top leadership of the Armed Forces was aware that the government and the Armed

Forces needed to show that they were willing to support and implement reform to quell the student demonstrations that were sweeping across the country.

However, the students' side was hesitant to respond to their call as they had a deep-seated distrust of the Armed Forces which some believed were involved in the disappearances of student activists that had been causing much controversy since January. The Armed Forces planned a forum with students on April 4, but students from the University of Indonesia and Gadjah Mada University flatly refused this invitation, stating that 'a ritualistic, pro forma dialogue was worthless' (*Forum Keadilan* Special Edition 1998: 14). Meanwhile, at a forum hosted on April 11 by State Minister for Youth and Sports Affairs Agung Laksono inviting the Armed Forces and thirty-two youth and student groups, a youth group representative stepped towards the Commander of the Armed Forces and accused him saying, 'this dialogue is set up to tame us' (*Kompas* Apr. 12, 1998). This indicates the difficulty of building a trusting relationship between the Armed Forces and students.

The Armed Forces vigorously sought to hold exchanges of opinion with not just students but also academics and intellectuals, and most intellectuals viewed their attitude toward dialogue in a positive light. On March 27 and 30, a forum between Armed Forces leaders and university academics including Amien Rais was held in Yogyakarta and Jakarta respectively. However, at the meeting in Yogyakarta on March 27, a comment made by the Head of the Armed Forces Intelligence Agency Zacky Anwar Makarim concerning the economic crisis—'George Soros was behind the currency crisis and it was a foreign conspiracy to attack Indonesia'—drew fierce denunciations from the thirty university academics in attendance. Similarly, as for the meeting held in Jakarta on March 30 which had fifty participants including a broad spectrum of NGO activists, *ulama* and intellectuals, the reformist side expressed severe criticism on a wide range of topics including personnel selection for the new cabinet, allegations of high-ranking government officials unjustly amassing wealth and the practice of oligopoly and monopoly in the economy, to which the Armed Forces side only responded with generalities in defense of its position (*Forum Keadilan* Apr. 20, 1998: 16–17).

From the perspective of the reformist forces, the Armed Forces leaders were at least responding to dialogue, and should have been easier to deal with than the President's eldest daughter who refused to engage stating 'there is no need for any further dialogue' (*Forum Keadilan* Apr. 20, 1998: 18). Despite this, those who had been consistent critics of the Armed Forces such as Adi Sasono from the ICMI were skeptical about dialogue with them from the beginning. This was because even if the demand for reform was raised in dialogues with the Armed

Forces, they would not be able to reflect it in policy as a concrete reform agenda or implement the proposed changes (*Suara Karya* Mar. 25, 1998).

In addition to the Armed Forces, the government and ministers also maintained an open channel for dialogue. When President Suharto received the students' demand for direct talks, he firstly ordered his ministers to hold dialogues with the students, and they showed a readiness to participate in forums as per the President's order (Laksono 2004: 45–46). Nonetheless, there was no way that Minister of Home Affairs Hartono, who repeatedly made negative comments regarding the reforms, or Minister of Education and Culture Wiranto Arismunandar, who condemned student demonstrations as unacceptable, could facilitate dialogue with students considering their unpopularity among them. Given such circumstances, forums with students were mostly organized by State Minister for Youth and Sports Affairs Agung Laksono. He hosted a large forum on April 18 in Jakarta, drawing participation from seventeen ministers including the Commander of the Armed Forces, twenty-five notable public figures, twenty-four rectors and vice rectors of universities, representatives of thirty-nine youth groups and representatives of thirty-nine universities. Notwithstanding the scale, by the end of the forum each party was able to have its say and 'not much of a conclusion was drawn from this meeting' (Laksono 2004: 46–47).

The impasse between cabinet members and students was also evident in a series of student walkouts. At a forum held at Pancasila University in Jakarta on April 22, an incident occurred in which several dozen among the 150 student participants left the room together in protest of State Minister for Youth and Sports Affairs Agung Laksono's announcement of the government's 'official view' as follows: the 'government has been carrying out reform so far and plans to continue further reform efforts in all areas now and in future' (*Kompas* Apr. 22, 1998). A similar incident also occurred at a large forum held in Jakarta on April 25 hosted by the HMI with participation from the Minister of Home Affairs, Minister of Justice, Minister of Finance and Minister of Education and Culture as well as Vice President Habibie and 170 representatives from fifty universities, where an assertion made by Minister of Home Affairs Hartono that there was no need for political reform provoked intense booing and protests, causing several dozen students to walk out and leave the forum (*Gatra* May 2, 1998: 38). Furthermore, a debate session scheduled for two days after this incident was cancelled due to a walkout by students who were indignant that the planned participation from Minister of Education and Culture Wiranto Arismunandar was cancelled on the day with two senior officials from the Ministry of Education and Culture sent as replacements (*Gatra* May 2, 1998: 38).

All these cases imply that dialogue between cabinet members and students was limited. It is true that some cabinet members were showing a relatively responsive attitude toward the reformist movement, such as State Minister for Youth and Sports Affairs Agung Laksono, but the closer they were to the President, the more negative an attitude they were likely to show toward the reformist movement, as was the case with Minister of Home Affairs Hartono who was a known hard-liner. This kind of stance provoked negative responses from students, giving the impression to the reformist forces that it was worthless to engage in dialogue with cabinet members.

While the reformist forces' efforts in dialogue with Armed Forces leaders and cabinet members struggled to make progress, DPR members, on the other hand, were more responsive toward their demands for reform. Behind this was a change in the reform agenda sought by the reformist forces.

Reform agenda: empowerment of the legislature
In parallel with the Armed Forces and cabinet members, all factions in the DPR were appealing to the students' side that they were prepared to engage in dialogue. The four factions in the DPR—the government-affiliated ones, namely the Golkar and Armed Forces factions, as well as the opposition factions, namely the PPP and PDI factions—were all in agreement from the beginning in regards to pressing ahead with the dialogue with the reformist forces. With respect to the Golkar faction, on March 13 Chair of the DPR Harmoko and the Chair of the Golkar faction Theo Sambuaga invited students to engage in dialogue (*Suara Karya* Mar. 14, 1998). Secretary of the Golkar faction Slamet Effendy Yusuf addressed students from the University of Indonesia who came to the DPR upon receipt of the invitation, claiming that the DPR was intending to implement economic reform (*Suara Karya* Mar. 20, 1998). Moreover, on March 27 Chair Harmoko appealed to the public that Golkar's Central Executive Board would ensure that DPR members of Golkar who criticized the government's policy would no longer be dismissed and that they would like the public to step forward and inform the Golkar faction of their various opinions and views (*Kompas* Mar. 18, 1998).

Such a call from the DPR and the ruling party propelled the reformist movement to establish a concrete agenda for political reform, and university academics and intellectuals became the leaders in establishing the reform agenda. They started to highlight problems with the current political system and raise specific proposals focusing on political reform in debate sessions, seminars and symposiums that were now organized on a more frequent basis. At a seminar held at the University of Indonesia on March 21, they reported that administrative efficiency and decentralization must be pursued as part of democratization (*Kompas* Mar. 23, 1998). Similarly, at a debate session held at the Tujuh Belas Agustus University on March 24, they identified the existence of appointed seats in the DPR and MPR as an obstruction to political reform (*Kompas* Mar. 25, 1998).

The reason the focus of the reform agenda gradually shifted from economic to political reform was because people started to feel that the cause of the near-collapse of Indonesia hit by the unprecedented economic crisis lay in the political system after all. The continued depreciation of the rupiah and seemingly unending decline of the Indonesian economy was caused by a loss of international credibility, and in order to restore that lost trust in the government, the creation of an uncorrupt government was of utmost importance. On the contrary, the cabinet lineup was far from adequate to restore the international community's trust in Indonesia, as the President's formation of the cabinet was based on cronyism. As the judicial and legislative branches that should have been supervising the government were under the strong influence of the administrative branch— especially the President—they were hardly able to serve such function. In regards to the judicial branch, the President appointed the Supreme Court justices as well as the Attorney General. Furthermore, the judicial branch was corrupt to the extent that judicial decisions were dictated by political connections and money. As for the legislative branch, there were seventy-five appointed seats in the DPR, and five hundred—that is, half of the total seats—in the MPR. Most appointed members were senior Armed Forces officers, cabinet members, heads of regional governments or high-ranking government officials and their spouses, since the President's intention was largely reflected in the appointments. Further, elected members of the DPR could easily be dismissed if the President put pressure on the respective party's central executive board.

Under such circumstances, it was impossible for the legislative branch to supervise its administrative counterpart, thus it was also impossible to create the efficient and uncorrupt government that was a requirement for economic recovery. Therefore, Nurcholish Madjid had every reason to state that 'the first agenda for reform is to revise the five political laws' (*Kompas* Mar. 23, 1998). The awareness that political reform could not be realized without revising these five laws, a set of laws passed in 1985 which majorly restricted political participation and the power of the legislative branch, was widely shared especially amongst intellectuals. Since these laws were the cornerstone of the Suharto regime's political system as such, proposing to revise them had been seen as a taboo. However, once Nurcholish had broken the taboo, voices calling for a review of the laws began to pour in from reformists as if a floodgate had been opened.

A symposium was held at the University of Indonesia on March 30 and April 1 on the theme of the 'empowerment of the parliament'. At this symposium,

Miriam Budiardjo from Diponegoro University claimed that 'the issues that Indonesia is now facing are caused by the long-term lack of adequate supervision and control over the government. Had the DPR and MPR been fulfilling their respective duties and responsibilities appropriately, neither the severe loss of international credibility nor the financial crisis would have occurred', and proposed to abolish the appointed system in the MPR and press the DPR to take initiatives in the preparation of bills as a first step forward (*Suara Karya* Apr. 1, 1998). Since representatives from the Armed Forces faction, PPP faction and PDI faction of the DPR attended this symposium, it became an opportunity for them to recognize the importance of the DPR taking the initiative (*Kompas* Apr. 1, 1998). Furthermore, at another symposium held at the University of Indonesia on April 9, Emil Salim took the rostrum, arguing 'economic reform can only begin after political reform has been achieved. The focus of the political reform is democratization, in other words, division of power, and we must change the current selection system of MPR members if we want to make the MPR true representatives of the nation' (*Kompas* Apr. 11, 1998).

Students led the reformist movement that had gathered momentum since March 1998, but it was in fact largely shaped by intellectuals. Despite its nationwide surge, the student movement lacked concreteness in terms of the logistics of reform. University academics and intellectuals, who had been a constituent in the Suharto regime until then, arrived on the scene amid such circumstances to set a specific reform agenda. As summarized by Emil Salim, 'students called for reform and academics and intellectuals complemented this by giving it a concept' (*Gatra* May 16, 1998: 40). In response to the reformist forces' strong demand, all factions in the DPR, especially the largest faction Golkar, embarked on efforts to enhance the DPR's control over the government by allowing the legislators to take initiatives supported by the reformist forces.

The birth of the alliance

Dialogue through networks

There were three groups within the Golkar faction that tried to cooperate with the reformist forces. The first group consisted of Chair Harmoko and Vice-Chair Abdul Gafur of the DPR leadership. The DPR leadership, known as *Pimpinan DPR*, was composed of five members with one chair and four vice-chairs representing each faction. Its chair was Golkar Chairman Harmoko and the vice-chairs were Vice-Chair of Golkar Abdul Gafur (Golkar faction), Army Lieutenant General Syarwan Hamid (Armed Forces faction), Chair of the PPP Ismail Hasan

Metareum (PPP faction) and Chair of the PDI Fatimah Achmad (PDI faction). In the process of the political change, Golkar's Harmoko and Abdul Gafur acted under the DPR leadership in conjunction with the other factions and played an active role in the formation of an alliance with the reformist forces.

The second group was the Golkar faction leadership (*Pimpinan FKP*). This group consisted of a total of twenty-two members, but not everyone involved sympathized with the reformist movement. Among those who were eager to cooperate and engage in dialogue with the reformist forces were Chair of the Golkar faction leadership Irsyad Sudiro (member of the ICMI), Vice-Chair Slamet Effendy Yusuf (former Chair of the GP Ansor, member of the ICMI), Vice-Chair Andi Mattalatta (former HMI member) and Secretary Syamsul Muarif (former HMI member).

The last group was rank and file members of the Golkar faction. In particular, former HMI members such as Eky Syachrudin, Ade Komaruddin, Ferry Mursyidan Baldan and Abu Hasan Sazili, Muhammadiyah members such as Lukman Harun and Hajriyanto Thohari, former Chair of the GP Ansor Muhammad Iqbal Assegaf and ICMI member Priyo Budi Santoso especially played significant roles in the dialogue and cooperation between DPR members and the reformist forces.

These three groups within the Golkar faction actively engaged in dialogue with the reformist forces where they discussed the reform agenda and developed cooperative relationships. In this sense, they could be referred to as 'regime soft-liners'. In regards to the negotiation and cooperation efforts with the reformist forces undertaken by regime soft-liners, the following three points can be highlighted. Firstly, they directly participated in negotiation over the creation of a concrete reform plan by attending forums and debate sessions on reform and even hosted such events themselves. Secondly, they tried to implement ideas proposed during the process of the negotiations as part of the reform agenda by bringing them to the DPR for debate. Finally, they stuck to the alliance and agreement with the reformist forces without yielding to resistance from the hard-liners within Golkar and the regime and managed to preserve the political initiative in progressing the reformist movement. Below is an account of how the negotiation and cooperation process progressed between the reformist forces and soft-liners within Golkar centered on these three points.

Of the groups within Golkar mentioned above, the keenest participant in the dialogue with the reformist forces was the third group. Most were freshman DPR legislators from Golkar who were former members of Islamic student groups or youth associations such as the HMI, GP Ansor and Muhammadiyah Youth. They positioned themselves as the 'second class citizens' (*warga kelas dua*) of Golkar[6] as the groups close to the President's family were gradually expanding their influence within the party. However, at the same time, they were closest to the reformist forces within Golkar. They were seniors to the student and youth reformists who belonged to student groups or Islamic organizations as well as peers with whom students could exchange opinions in regular study groups and debate sessions. These legislators, students and youths developed a shared awareness of the need for political reform through meetings held on a continuous basis from even before the beginning of the reformist movement, which provided them with opportunities to discuss various political issues[7].

As the reformist movement got under way in earnest, legislators began to be frequently invited to seminars hosted by student groups, student senates of various universities and NGOs and engaged in lively exchanges of views[8]. Despite the frequent criticism that they were essentially members of Golkar working to uphold the regime, these legislators as individuals, on the other hand, were regarded as being on the reformist side and were afforded a certain degree of trust by the students[9]. Some even attended forums between the reformist forces and the government as representatives of the former. For instance, HMI members-turned Golkar legislators such as Ferry Mursyidan Baldan and Mohammad Yamin Tawari (both freshman legislators elected for the first time in the 1997 election) attended a major forum conducted by the Armed Forces and students in Jakarta on April 11 on the reformist side as representatives of youth groups (*Kompas* Apr. 12, 1998). In sum, they had an extremely high affinity for the students who were leading the reformist movement, despite coming from within the regime.

While young legislators exchanged opinions with students, those belonging to the 'Generation of 66' such as Eky Syachrudin and Abu Hasan Sazili actively sought to engage in dialogue and debate with intellectuals of their generation (those who were aged in their early- to mid-fifties). Particularly, Eky Syachrudin was one of Golkar's legislators who strongly criticized the inability of the DPR to function in its role as a representative of the nation, specifically, that it could not even fulfill its role in the midst of the economic crisis (Syachrudin 2006: 34–35, 40)[10]. He was a member of the 'Wednesday Meeting' (*Majelis Reboan*)[11], which was an informal meeting of intellectuals that started around January 1998, and began spending a lot of time debating with Nurcholish Madjid (Islamic intellectual), Malik Fadjar (executive of Muhammadiyah and senior official of the Ministry of Religious Affairs) and Djohan Effendy (Islamic intellectual) on a regular basis through this gathering (Hudijono and Thayib 2006: 143–144). Although members of the Wednesday Meeting came together essentially through the HMI network, it started to draw participation from a wider range of intellectuals from outside the HMI arena including Amien Rais (Chair of Muhammadiyah), Syafii Ma'arif (Vice-Chair of Muhammadiyah),

Abdurrahman Wahid (Chair of NU), Jacob Oetama (President of the Gramedia Group, the publisher of the daily newspaper *Kompas*) and Harry Tjan Silalahi (Centre for Strategic and International Studies (CSIS)) (Hudijono and Thayib 2006: 144).

The members met at Malik Fadjar's residence located in the central area of Jakarta. The expansion of the reformist movement spurred discussion on a concrete reform plan at the Wednesday Meeting, also leading to a gradual increase in the number of participants. Those who joined included Achmad Tirtosudiro (ICMI's Acting Chair), Abdul Latief (former Minister of Manpower and entrepreneur), Sugeng Suryadi (entrepreneur), Fahmi Idris (member of Golkar's Central Executive Board and entrepreneur), Adnan Buyun Nasution (lawyer), Kemal Idris (retired Army Lieutenant General), Ali Sadikin (former Governor of Jakarta Province and retired Marines General) and Akbar Tandjung (State Minister for Public Housing and member of Golkar's Advisory Board) (Hudijono and Thayib 2006: 153). From this lineup it is evident that the Wednesday Meeting provided a discussion forum not only for intellectuals but also religious leaders, entrepreneurs, active cabinet members, lawyers and retired military officers, crossing the boundary between groups within and outside the regime. The Wednesday Meeting came to be seen as one of the 'headquarters for reform' (*markas reformasi*) (Hudijono and Thayib 2006: 153), and a concrete reform plan raised later by Nurcholish and others was based on the discussions held in this meeting.

Eky Syachrudin served as moderator in numerous debate sessions and symposiums held to discuss the reform plan while acting as an intermediary between the reformist forces and groups within the regime, leveraging the personal connections of the 'Generation of 66' (*Kompas* Apr. 19, 1998; *Forum Keadilan* June 15, 1998). Meanwhile, with the opening of the DPR session, the Golkar legislators who were seeking to work with leaders of the reformist forces took their appeals for reform to the DPR to express their position on reform in front of the nation.

Reform through the empowerment of the DPR

At forums on reform, students and intellectuals sternly criticized the DPR and its members for never having tried to fulfill their roles. However, in a sense this kind of criticism benefitted the parliament side. More specifically, the reformist forces' demand to improve the functions of the legislative branch in turn became a chance for the DPR to transform administrative branch-controlled politics. Members of the Golkar faction leadership such as Andi Mattalatta, Slamet Effendy Yusuf and Syamsul Muarif as well as Chair of the Golkar faction Irsyad Sudiro welcomed students' criticisms of the DPR, appealing:

Students must participate in the empowerment of the DPR. If you think that the DPR's functions and roles are insufficient, then let's make it better with them. The more students who communicate their views to the DPR, the stronger the position of the DPR becomes. Students cannot convene an MPR special session, but we DPR members can. (*Suara Karya* Apr. 11, 1998)

While the revision of the five political laws was increasingly becoming the focal point of the reform agenda, DPR members began coordinating so that discussion on the revision could be held in the upcoming DPR debate to be convened on May 4. Vice-Chair of the DPR leadership Syarwan Hamid stated on April 13 that all factions in the DPR agreed to review the five political laws (*Suara Karya* Apr. 14, 1998) and moreover, on the following day, Chair of the Golkar faction Irsyad Sudiro announced that the Golkar faction was planning to start preparing for the revision (*Suara Karya* Apr. 16, 1998).

Gradually, DPR members started to raise their voices more vigorously, expressing their views even against policies of the central and regional governments. On April 20, at the DPR's Eighth Committee, all factions collectively asserted that necessary national projects did not need to be reviewed, in criticism of the government's reversal of the hydroelectric power station construction project in Bengkulu Province due to the economic crisis (*Suara Karya* Apr. 21, 1998). Furthermore, in the case of the sticker tax proposed by the provincial government of Jakarta[12], DPR members Slamet Effendy Yusuf from the Golkar faction and Lukman Hakiem from the PPP faction jointly expressed their opposition and demanded the provincial administration abandon the tax. Although this tax was already approved by presidential decree, the two argued that this decree itself could be in violation of traffic laws (*Suara Karya* Apr. 23, 1998). The Golkar faction again demanded the postponement of the implementation of the sticker tax on April 24 (*Suara Karya* Apr. 25, 1998), and managed to elicit a statement from the Governor of Jakarta Province saying that there was no need to force the tax through (*Suara Karya* Apr. 30, 1998).

Moreover, DPR members changed their attitude toward the Armed Forces. At the HMI's discussion held on April 25, a guest speaker, Armed Forces Command Staff for Sociopolitical Affairs Susilo Bambang Yudhoyono, read out a statement on behalf of Commander of the Armed Forces Wiranto which declared that the Armed Forces would take decisive measures if any of the following five elements were to be threatened in any way: (1) Pancasila, (2) the 1945 Constitution, (3) integration of the nation, (4) continuation of development or (5) stabilization of the state (*Suara Karya* Apr. 29, 1998). In response to this statement, DPR member Abu Hasan Sazili from the Golkar faction defended the students' side, arguing that students' demands for reform were within an expected range and not at a particularly dangerous level (*Suara Karya* Apr. 29, 1998).

While a series of forums attended by senior Armed Forces officers and cabinet members faced an impasse, the reformist forces found that DPR members were more responsive to their calls and sought to facilitate a cooperative relationship with the DPR, especially its largest faction Golkar. On April 23, fifty members from the HMI's Ciputat branch in South Jakarta visited Golkar's Central Executive Board to request that it take the initiative in revising the five political laws. Din Syamsuddin, the Executive Board member of Golkar who met with the students on that occasion, explained that Golkar was currently in the process of considering changes to the electoral and political party systems as well as the liberalization of political activities in rural areas and asked the students to offer their opinions (*Suara Karya* Apr. 24, 1998).

Furthermore, at a symposium of Golkar's Central Executive Board on April 24, participating Board members including Abdul Gafur, Din Syamsuddin and Rambe Kamarulzaman asked the rector of the Institute of Government Studies (IIP) Ryaas Rasyid and Bahtiar Effendy from the State Institute of Islamic Studies (IAIN, now State Islamic University, UIN) Syarif Hidayatullah Jakarta for their views on concrete plans for the reform of the parliamentary and party system (*Suara Karya* Apr. 25, 1998). On April 27, another symposium was held at the IAIN Jakarta, with Chair of the Golkar faction of the DPR Irsyad Sudiro included on the guest list. Emil Salim, who took the rostrum at this symposium, asserted that 'the most pressing need for reform is to empower the DPR. To achieve this, the system that allows for the dismissal of legislative members must be abolished and the legislative function of the DPR must be improved. This would enable the parliament to enhance its function to supervise the government' (*Kompas* Apr. 29, 1998). On April 29, Loebby Lukman from the Faculty of Law of the University of Indonesia followed suit and expressed that the empowerment of the DPR was crucial for political and legal reform (*Suara Karya* Apr. 30, 1998). Similarly, at a symposium held in Semarang, social scientist Lukman Strisno also argued that the demand for reform resulted from the failure of the DPR and political parties to perform expected duties (*Suara Karya* May 3, 1998). As can be seen, the reform plan—to pursue the improvement of the DPR's functions through revision of the five political laws—set out by the reformist forces and DPR members including Golkar was becoming aligned.

Meanwhile, on May 1, immediately before the opening of the DPR session, President Suharto invited a total of fifty-four guests including the DPR leadership, leaderships of each faction and party executives along with cabinet members to the Presidential Palace for a meeting. It was the first time since the beginning of the Suharto regime that the President had officially invited DPR members and party executives to the Presidential Palace for such purpose. In that meeting, the President explained his theory on the reform. According to Minister of Home Affairs Hartono and Minister of Information Alwi Dahlan who were in attendance, Suharto said that 'the government does not stand against the reform but is making its own efforts to carry out reform. In fact, reform had begun even before Indonesia's proclamation of independence' (*Suara Karya* May 2, 1998). Having said that, the President agreed with the revision of the five political laws and indicated that he would not mind if DPR members initiated the preparation of bills necessary for reform anyway (*Suara Karya* May 2, 1998). While the DPR leadership was partly relieved, for they were given permission from the President in regards to the revision of the five political laws and DPR member-initiated legislation, they became acutely aware that there was a wide divergence of the meaning of 'reform' in Suharto's view and that discussed among the reformist forces.

The first difference rested in the reform agenda. In Suharto's view, since the election of the president and vice president, adoption of the Broad Guidelines of State Policy (GBHN) and formation of the new cabinet were all completed in the MPR general session in the previous March, these should remain unchanged for the next five years until 2003; therefore, a new national policy framework that would include a reform plan, a cabinet reshuffle and the election of a new president and vice president should only take place after 2003. Nonetheless, he noted that reform in the form of the revision of laws could be implemented before that, and suggested that the first step toward reform could be the preparation for the revision of the electoral law towards the 2002 election (*Gatra* May 9, 1998: 34). However, this was too late for the reformist forces, who were aiming to launch reforms as soon as possible.

The second difference was the content of the amendments each party wanted to make to the five political laws, including the electoral law. Although the President expressed that he did not mind changing from the current proportional representation system to the constituency system, he showed reluctance to have electoral districts divided into regency and city levels, which would then be further narrowed down depending on the size of the population from the current provincial level (*Gatra* May 9, 1998: 34). As for the number of appointed seats and number of parties in the DPR and MPR, he advocated the maintenance of the status quo. Suharto indicated his intention to prevent changes to the appointed seats system unless the continued presence of the Armed Forces in the parliaments was secured, arguing that if all the seats in the DPR and MPR were to become elected seats, then the system should be revised to enable the Armed Forces to have their officers elected into the parliaments in some way. Similarly, in regards to the number of political parties, he stated that the configuration of Golkar and the two opposition parties had become a consensus and there was no need to change it (*Gatra* May 9, 1998: 34), essentially denying any change to the number of political parties and liberalization in terms of the formation of new parties. In other words, the political reform envisioned by Suharto was merely a shift from the proportional representation system to the constituency system without any changes to the party or parliamentary systems—neither the liberalization of the political system nor the expansion of political participation was on his mind.

Lastly, there was a variance between the two parties as to the interpretation of the reformist movement. The President is said to have made the following comment regarding the reformist movement:

> There is a group that has been working to undermine the trust people have in the government since before the MPR general session, and this group has wormed their way into university campuses and started backing the demand for reform after the general session. This is destructive behavior that undermines stability. (*Gatra* May 9, 1998: 34)

Suharto had repeatedly pointed out the 'existence of a group plotting the destruction of trust in the government' since the onset of the economic crisis (Djiwandono 2005: 190). To put it simply, for Suharto, the reformist movement was simply part of 'the plot'. As long as Suharto maintained this interpretation, it was impossible for him and the reformist forces to find common ground.

Nevertheless, Suharto's agreement on the reforms to be effected by the DPR gave its members a sense of confidence that, in the words of the Chair of the Golkar faction leadership of the DPR Irsyad Sudiro, 'the ball of reform is now in the hands of the legislature' (*Suara Karya* May 4, 1998). In regards to the revision of the five political laws that was now approved by the President, Chair of the DPR leadership Harmoko expressed his willingness to complete it by the 2002 election (*Kompas* May 5, 1998). The DPR began pursuing the enhancement of the legislative function, albeit cautiously so as not to disturb the President.

Following the opening of the DPR session, on May 5, the DPR leadership and leaderships of each faction held a meeting and formed an agreement on the course of action to be taken—specifically, that they would carry out reform in the political, economic and judicial spheres through the revision of laws and enactment of new laws. DPR Chair Harmoko explained in a press conference that in the political sphere, the electoral law, law on political parties and Golkar and law on the composition of the MPR, DPR and DPRD were the primary targets of the revision whereas the anti-monopoly law, consumer protection law and banking law in the economic sphere and the anti-subversion law and anti-corruption law in the judicial sphere were being looked into as subjects of the revision and in terms of legislating new laws (*Suara Karya* May 6, 1998). Further, all factions agreed in this meeting that they would deepen the discussion on the legislative revision and enactment of new laws by engaging in dialogue with a variety of social groups and leverage the outcome of these dialogues and exchanges as a springboard for further discussion among the factions, which would then ultimately be drafted into a bill (*Suara Karya* May 6, 1998). Golkar and the PPP expressed their positive attitude toward the implementation of the constituency system, whereas Harmoko showed his approval for increasing the number of political parties (*Kompas* May 5, 1998). Meanwhile, the DPR leadership and leaderships of each faction declared that they were planning to improve not only the legislature's function to create laws but also its function to monitor the government to create an uncorrupt, efficient administration (*Suara Karya* May 6, 1998). Then, an ideal opportunity for the DPR to demonstrate its function to oversee the government in practice arose in the form of the DPR's opposition to the government's decision to increase the price of petroleum and electricity.

A set of the presidential decisions announced on May 4 included the reduction of government subsidies on a few types of petroleum, resulting in an increase in the prices of heavy and light oil in the range of twenty-five to 71.43 percent, an incremental twenty percent rise in the electricity price and an increase in the cost of using public transport such as buses and trains. This was based on the agreement with the IMF and was in fact the deciding factor behind the IMF's loan to Indonesia (*Kompas* May 4, 1998). Therefore, from the government's perspective, it was an unavoidable measure. Nonetheless, it imposed even heavier burdens on those who were already under severe economic pressure. In response, the Eighth Committee's Eky Syachrudin and Paskah Suzetta (both from the Golkar faction) and the Fifth Committee's Chair Marzuki Achmad (Golkar faction) and Saleh Chalid (PPP faction) made the criticism that important decisions that would have a substantial impact on people's lives were being made without any consultation whatsoever with the DPR, ignoring the role of the legislature (*Suara Karya* May 5, 1998). They further expressed their intention of calling the Minister of Mines and Energy to the committee deliberation to have him explain this price hike (*Suara Karya* May 6, 1998) before the full-scale kickoff of committee deliberations in the DPR.

The deliberations in the Fifth Committee that took place on May 8 with the presence of the Minister of Mines and Energy Kuntro Mangkusubroto lasted for fourteen hours including breaks, and the discussion was broadcast outside the committee room for the scoop of journalists. Conscious of the mass media, all legislators, regardless of whether they were from the ruling party or an opposition party, protested against the two presidential decisions that specified the price increases for petroleum and electricity and pressed the minister to abolish or at least postpone the enforcement (*Suara Karya* May 9, 1998). Not a single committee member made a comment in support of the price increase. Actually, it was decided in the Golkar faction briefing that was held in advance of the committee deliberation that they would 'neither accept nor deny' the government's decision on the price increase. However, this instruction was ignored by Golkar faction members such as Priyo Budi Santoso, who objected most strenuously to the increase. He pressured the minister on the necessity of rectifying the inefficient supply of petroleum before increasing the price, pointing out that crude oil from Middle Eastern countries was often imported by Pertamina at an inflated price (*Suara Karya* May 9, 1998). After this committee deliberation, the Golkar faction leadership gave retroactive approval to members for their actions in the Fifth Committee and decided that the faction leadership would also support its members' opposition to the government (*Forum Keadilan* June 1, 1998: 85).

At the deliberation on May 8, the Minister of Mines and Energy apologized that the decision on the price increase made before discussing the matter with the DPR was a procedural mistake, but at the same time rejected the possibility of changes to the decision as it had already been finalized (*Kompas* May 9, 1998). Unsatisfied with this response, the DPR side organized a joint deliberation between the Fifth and Eighth Committee one week later on May 15, inviting Minister of Mines and Energy Kuntro and Minister of Finance Fuad Bawazir, and once again presented their argument against the price increase. The DPR members argued that it did not make sense to reduce petroleum and electricity subsidies to assist the poor, which only amounted to a paltry sum, while pouring a large amount of capital into major banks owned by the President's family members. They demonstrated that the 27 trillion rupiah subsidy cut was only about a quarter of the 103 trillion rupiah that had been injected into the banks that were suffering from excessive liabilities. Prior to the deliberation, the Minister of Mines and Energy had gained permission from President Suharto regarding his intention to make a compromise with the DPR side. Accordingly, the government and the DPR side reached a consensus at the joint committee deliberation to slightly bring down the price of petroleum (*Kompas* May 16, 1998). Although it was not a full retraction of the price increase demanded by many DPR members, it was seen by the DPR side as a success, to an extent, in terms of extracting a post-decision concession from the government.

The DPR's Fifth and Eighth Committee's opposition to the petroleum and electricity price rise was aimed at demonstrating that DPR members were willing to and capable of accepting and implementing the people's demands for reform. From this experience, they started to expect that the more they showed their willingness to confront the government, the more support they would receive from the people. At the same time, the reformist forces began to feel that legislative reform was slowly coming closer to becoming a reality.

Limiting presidential power

Students had been calling for the dismissal of President Suharto since the beginning of the reformist movement, but this appeal started to receive substantial attention in the latter half of April in the form of calls for the 'convening and holding of an MPR special session'. An MPR special session differed from a general session that was regularly held once every five years, and only held when specially convened by the DPR. The first ever special session was held in March 1967, when Indonesia's first president Sukarno was ousted[13]. In other words, convening a special session implied the legislature's intention to exercise the authority to dismiss the president. However, there were conditions for convening an MPR special session, and it was not possible to convene one unless it could be deemed that the president was clearly in violation of the 1945 Constitution or the GBHN, as determined by the MPR[14]. Since it was very unlikely that they could justify that the President had clearly violated the GBHN that was just recently adopted in the MPR general session of March 1998, jurists on the reformist side at first suggested that it was unrealistic to dismiss the President by convening a special session (*Suara Karya* Apr. 24, 1998; *Suara Karya* Apr. 25, 1998; *Kompas* Apr. 25, 1998).

Despite this, the call for an MPR special session was raised in the panel discussion held at the University of Indonesia on April 23. This occurred because the MPR special session was a symbolic representation of the restoration of power to the legislative branch over the administrative branch—especially the President. At this panel discussion, it was made clear that an 'MPR special session is the ultimate means to control the government'. Subsequently, the month of May saw the gradual spread of the call for a special session. On May 5, a demonstration organized by the HMI demanded the holding of an MPR special session, and on May 6, the ICMI's Acting Chair Achmad Tirtosudiro and Adi Sasono made a public statement urging that 'the possibility of a cabinet reshuffle and the holding of an MPR special session must not be dismissed in order to resolve the crisis' (*Suara Karya* May 7, 1998). While the reformist forces welcomed this statement, Vice President Habibie was surprised by the fact that the representatives of the ICMI made such an 'aggressive' political comment and responded by announcing that this statement was not the opinion of the ICMI but the representative's personal view (*Suara Karya* May 12, 1998).

However, Acting Chair Tirtosudiro countered that while Habibie was certainly the Chair of the ICMI, the organization was already being run under the office of the Acting Chair (*Kompas* May 16, 1998), in an attempt to create the impression that the ICMI was no longer under the government's control.

In step with the demand for an MPR special session, in-depth discussions and suggestions concerning the limits of presidential power were going on between Golkar and the reformist forces. For instance, at the debate session jointly hosted by the HMI's alumni group (KAHMI) and the National University (*Universitas Nasional*) on May 2, Lukman Strisno from Gadjah Mada University made a proposal that suggested the need for a legal measure to limit the presidential term (*Kompas* May 4, 1998). In concert with this, on May 8, Chairman of Golkar Harmoko, having prefaced that it was his own personal view, indicated that he wanted to make a proposal to impose a two-term limit to the office of president at the upcoming MPR general session in 2003 (*Kompas* May 9, 1998). This proposal was immediately welcomed by the reformist forces and was highly praised at GP Ansor's forum held on May 10 in Jakarta, for this proposition came from none other than the ruling party Golkar (*Suara Karya* May 12, 1998).

Moreover, at this forum, Emil Salim strongly insisted that Suharto's 'right to veto' (*hak veto*) Central Executive Board decisions as the Chair of the Advisory Board of Golkar—the right to nullify a decision made by the Central Executive Board and freeze its activity—must be abolished (*Kompas* May 12, 1998). As long as Suharto maintained this right, Golkar would never be free from him. Conversely, if Golkar could achieve freedom from Suharto, it would be able to act with stronger initiative as the largest faction in the DPR and MPR and help make significant progress in empowering the legislature. Therefore, the forum arrived at the conclusion that, in order to improve the functions of the parliament, the wide range of powers that were concentrated in Suharto must be curbed. On May 12, Emil Salim visited the DPR accompanied by a group of sixty academics from the University of Indonesia and tendered 250 signatures from the university's teaching staff in support of the student movement calling for reform. Together with this, they also submitted a letter mentioning items that they believed were necessary for the empowerment of the DPR in detail, underscoring once again the importance of the legislative branch having equal status with the administrative branch (*Suara Karya* May 13, 1998).

Building consensus for Suharto's resignation
In addition to the shared awareness of the need to limit presidential power, the deterioration of the political crisis also facilitated the rapid spread of students' calls for the removal of Suharto among intellectuals and DPR members.

Amid ever-intensifying student demonstrations, an incident occurred in which four student demonstrators were shot dead by security forces. This fatal incident that took place at Tri Sakti University in Jakarta on May 12 substantially incited the situation. With this incident as the catalyst, a series of major riots erupted in Jakarta over the period from May 13 to 15. Shopping malls and shops were looted, destroyed and set on fire by a large crowd that turned violent and a vast number of assaults and murders took place over 100 locations across a broad area from Jakarta to neighboring cities such as Tangerang and Depok, throwing the capital city into chaos (Simanjorang 2008: 103–108). A large number of people who entered shopping malls to loot amidst the turmoil died in fires. In the northern district of Jakarta where a Chinese-Indonesian population was concentrated, many women and children were raped and murdered. According to the Jakarta provincial government's announcement that followed immediately after the riots, the death toll was 288 (*Kompas* May 18, 1998); however, a later study by the Fact-Finding Combined Team (TGPF) reported that 1217 people died, ninety-one were wounded and thirty-one went missing (Simanjorang 2008: 132–134).

The value of the rupiah suffered a dramatic fall due to this series of riots, from 8,700 rupiah to one US dollar on May 8 to 11,700 rupiah per dollar on May 14. President Suharto happened to be on a diplomatic trip overseas at the time, while the Armed Forces who were responsible for maintaining national security and order received much criticism for the shooting at Tri Sakti University and failing to quell the riot. They were requested to provide a full account of the Tri Sakti incident and were even held responsible for being unable to suppress the riots at an early stage. Actually, quite a number of aspects of this riot have been labeled mysterious, including the existence of the provocateur (*provokator*) that incited the looting and vandalism and the delayed reaction of the security unit to the riots (Zon 2004: 106–114, 117–118; Simanjorang 2008: 200–202, 256–257). Some view the power struggle within the Armed Forces as somehow involved in the incident[15].

There are many aspects that are not yet clearly understood in regards to this affair. Nevertheless, above all, what can definitely be said is that at the time Indonesian society was in a state in which once a fire was started, it would spread at lightning speed regardless of who lit it. People's patience was being overstretched amid the economic crisis and political confusion to the point that anything could have happened if not handled correctly. The awareness that the political crisis must be brought to an end as soon as possible rapidly proliferated across political elites within and outside the regime, adding significant momentum to the movement to demand the immediate resignation of Suharto. One of the leaders of the reformist forces, Amien Rais, launched the People's

Mandate Council (MAR) with prominent members of the reformist forces and demanded the resignation of the President.

Upon receiving news of the massive riots in Jakarta, Suharto, who was in Cairo to attend the G-15 meeting from May 9 at the time, flew back to Indonesia in the early hours of May 15 ahead of his planned return. Before he left for his homeland, the President said 'if the nation no longer has trust in me, then that's it. I do not intend to go so far as to use armed power in order to hold on to the position' (*Kompas* May 16, 1998). *Kompas* newspaper dated May 14 reported that the President indicated that he was 'prepared to resign' (*Kompas* May 14, 1998). In reaction to this report, fourteen retired military officers and NU executives released a statement welcoming the President's announcement of his resignation (*Kompas* May 15, 1998). However, the President denied the media report claiming that he had not stated that he was 'prepared to resign' upon his return (*Kompas* May 16, 1998). Some even suspect that *Kompas* 'purposely reported misinformation', taking advantage of the ambiguity of the expression the President used.

In either case, the claim that the President did 'not intend to go so far as to use armed power in order to hold on to the position' turned out to be false. In fact, on the following day, May 16, Suharto summoned Commander of the Armed Forces Wiranto, Army Chief of Staff Subagyo and Chief State Secretary Saadillah Mursjid to notify them of his decision to create a new security apparatus and instructed Wiranto to start preparing for the establishment of its command. Suharto himself made the decision to set up this unit to restore security and order in Jakarta, which was in a state of disorder from the extensive riots. At first, Suharto called this new unit the 'Operational Command for the Restoration of Security and Order' (Kopkamtib), but it was renamed 'Operational Command for National Alertness and Safety' (KOPKKN), after having taken into consideration the opinion of Coordinating Minister for Economy and Finance Ginandjar that the original name may give an undesirable impression to foreign investors, especially at times like this when Indonesia was suffering from an economic crisis (Sukmawati 2004: 172–173).

As the original name suggests, Suharto regarded KOPKKN as an institution equivalent to the Kopkamtib that he created to purge the Communist Party (PKI) shortly after the September 30th Affair in 1965. The Kopkamtib was an informal apparatus of violence with no legal foundation that played a role in the means of oppression adopted by the Suharto regime, even after the annihilation of the PKI. It might be more plausible to suppose that the reason Ginandjar suggested the name change was in an attempt to alleviate the terrorizing impact that the name 'Kopkamtib' could have on the people, even if only slightly, rather than that he was concerned about the reaction of the international community.

Unlike the Kopkamtib, the establishment of the KOPKKN could be legally justified thanks to the adoption of the resolution to grant the President the emergency prerogative that allowed him to set up agencies of this sort in the MPR general session of March 1998. Those who learned of the plan to create a new security apparatus were horrified, fearful of the potential scale of victims, in the knowledge that the students and citizens who participated in demonstrations would become targets of the crackdown. However, there were not many who could directly challenge Suharto.

The DPR leadership met with President Suharto on May 16. At that meeting, Chair of the DPR Harmoko explained to the President the contents of the discussions that had taken place between DPR members and its factions and the people in a series of debate sessions and forums as well as the contents of the letter submitted by universities regarding reform, and ultimately presented the people's will summarised in the following three points: total reform (*reformasi total*), the President's resignation and the holding of an MPR special session (Sekretariat Jenderal DPR-RI 1998: 19–20). In response to the DPR leadership, Suharto again denied the announcement of his resignation as reported by *Kompas*, but then stated 'if all the factions in the DPR think that the resignation of the president is necessary, then it might be time for me to quit. I leave it up to the DPR factions' (Sekretariat Jenderal DPR-RI 1998: 19–20)[16]. However, the President then went on to describe his plan of promoting reform and reshuffling the cabinet as well as establishing the KOPKKN as 'a necessary measure for protecting the people and the wealth, unification and integration of the nation, as well as Pancasila and the 1945 Constitution' (Gafur 2000: 78–79). At the time, one of the vice-chairs of the DPR leadership, namely Chair of the PPP Ismail Hasan Metareum, raised an objection to the establishment of the KOPKKN, but the President paid him no heed (Sekretariat Jenderal DPR-RI 1998: 20–21; Yusuf 1999: 88).

After the meeting, the DPR leadership held a press conference and announced that the President had promised to bring about reform and reshuffle the cabinet, preaching that he would 'exercise the authorities given to myself to protect the people and their wealth as well as Pancasila and the 1945 Constitution'. The DPR leadership did not mention the President's plan to establish the KOPKKN in this press conference. Neither did they mention the fact that the DPR leadership had informed the President of the people's demands including his resignation and the holding of an MPR special session. The reason behind this was that the DPR leadership had not gone through the procedure of forming a consensus involving all factions and thus wanted to avoid making an important political announcement until they were ready (Gafur 2000: 80).

In the meantime, the pressure from the reformist forces on the DPR and Golkar was increasing. At the DPR's First Committee hearing held on May 15, members of lawyers' associations and human rights activists were called on to give testimony about the shooting by the Armed Forces at Tri Sakti University and the cases of missing activists. Together they demanded that the holding of an MPR special session was imperative if they were to solve the crisis at the hearing (*Suara Karya* May 16, 1998). On May 16, a meeting at the University of Indonesia was organized among retired military officers, NU leaders and the university's academics and the establishment of the 'Indonesian National Committee for Reform' (*KNI-Reformasi*) was proclaimed. The representatives of this organization visited the DPR on May 18 and presented the 'Salemba Declaration', which demanded that 'the national leader be replaced in the shortest time possible'. Dimyati Hartono concluded the meeting saying 'we request that the DPR hold an MPR special session as soon as possible' (*Kompas* May 18, 1998). On the same day, academics from the Bandung Institute of Technology (ITB) made a declaration stating 'our trust in the national leader is now lost' and called for cabinet members who were graduates of the ITB to resign (*Kompas* May 18, 1998). Likewise, Rector of the Bogor Agricultural University (IPB) Soleh Solahuddin declared the restoration of its student council (*Dewan Mahasiswa*) in front of several thousand students and academics, pronounced his full support for the reformist movement and demanded that Golkar become the engine to drive the reform effort proclaiming that academics of the IPB would leave Golkar if they refused. The delegation from the IPB visited the DPR on May 18 to present a reform proposal, while other universities such as Tanjungpura University in West Kalimantan and Abulyatama University in Banda Aceh also submitted letters demanding the holding of an MPR special session to the chair of the provincial council of their respective provinces (*Kompas* May 18, 1998; *Suara Karya* May 16, 1998).

The focus of the discussion among intellectuals who attended the Wednesday Meeting such as Nurcholish Madjid shifted to how to settle the situation without creating more victims and causing added confusion to the political scene. Since pursuing the dismissal of the President through an MPR special session could cause Suharto to take a harsher stance, they sought the means to remedy the situation while avoiding humiliation for the President. Accordingly, they summarized the results of the discussions into the following six proposals: (1) the President shall apologize to the people for the economic crisis; (2) the President shall acknowledge his past political failures; (3) the President shall return wealth to the nation; (4) the five political laws shall undergo full-scale revision; (5) an election shall be held on January 10, 2000, under the new political laws, immediately followed by an MPR general session; and (6) Suharto shall not nominate himself to run for President. Nurcholish advised Armed Forces Command Staff for Sociopolitical Affairs Susilo Bambang

Yudhoyono of these six proposals on May 14 (Hudijono and Thayib 2006: 154–156).

Moreover, Nurcholish described the six proposals to participants at a meeting held at the Regent Hotel in Jakarta on May 16. Among those who attended were Golkar's executive members close to Nurcholish, namely Fahmi Idris (Golkar Central Executive Board member and entrepreneur who was also the owner of the hotel), Fadel Muhammad (Golkar Central Executive Board member and entrepreneur), Akbar Tandjung (State Minister for Public Housing and Golkar Advisory Board member), Tanri Abeng (Minister for State-Owned Enterprises and entrepreneur) and Abdul Latief (Minister of Tourism and Arts and entrepreneur) (Hudijono and Thayib 2006: 157), indicating that a certain segment of Golkar's executive membership including active cabinet members were committed to the movement to demand the resignation of the President.

On May 17, a meeting to discuss the proposals raised by Nurcholish on the previous day was held at the Wisata Hotel attended by intellectuals affiliated with the HMI, ICMI and Muhammadiyah, entrepreneurs and Golkar legislators. Namely, participants included intellectuals Nurcholish Madjid, Emha Ainun Nadjib, A. M. Fatwa and Djimly Assidiqie, entrepreneurs Fahmi Idris, Fadel Muhammad and Sugeng Suryadi and the DPR's Golkar legislators Eky Syachrudin, Ferry Mursyidan Baldan and Laode Kamaluddin. Anas Urbaningrum, Chair of the HMI, also joined the event representing the younger generations (*Kompas* May 18, 1998). During the discussion, Nurcholish shared his vision of electing a new president and vice president in March 2003 (Hudijono and Thayib 2006: 157–161), but the participants of the meeting argued that it would be too late. Having made that remark, the participants demanded that the three Golkar legislators work toward the holding of an MPR special session (*Kompas* May 18, 1998). In other words, the Golkar legislators were requested to pave the way for the resignation of Suharto in the DPR.

Upon receipt of this request, legislator Eky Syachrudin drafted a declaration demanding the immediate resignation of Suharto together with Ade Komaruddin who was also a former-HMI young Golkar legislator[17]. This declaration included the demand to hold an MPR special session to dismiss the President should he refuse to respond to the calls for his resignation. On the following day, that is, May 18, Eky Syachrudin and Ade Komaruddin collected signatures from a total of twenty legislators including Ferry Mursyidan Baldan and Laode Kamaluddin, the fellow Golkar legislators who had attended the meeting with them on the previous day, as well as other Golkar legislators who conformed to their view, and submitted them to Chair of the DPR Harmoko and Vice-Chair Abdul Gafur[18]. A large number of the signatories belonged to the ICMI or had experience in serving as executive members in organizations such as the HMI,

Muhammadiyah Youth or GP Ansor. Dubbed the 'Group of Twenty' (Kelompok 20), they became the most vocal group within the Golkar faction in the DPR advocating for the immediate resignation of Suharto.

Eky Syachrudin, who was the central member of this 'Group of Twenty', had been the first to welcome the alleged statement of resignation from the President in Cairo when the news broke out. He stated:

> Many people are waiting for the resignation of President Suharto. Even if the President's word was lip service (*basa-basi*), we will not respond with lip service. If the President did say he would resign if he loses trust from the people, the DPR shall not pay lip service but let him literally resign. (*Suara Karya* May 15, 1998)

Yanto, another member of the 'Group of Twenty' also made a similar claim stating:

> If the DPR was too slow to take necessary action including convening a special session, then another group not from the legislative branch may take over the initiative. If that happens, a large number of people will become victims of illegal actions, for which the DPR will have to bear a great deal of blame. (*Suara Karya* May 19, 1998)

He indirectly suggested the possibility of a coup by the Armed Forces with the wording 'illegal actions' and emphasized the DPR's obligation to carry out a constitutional transfer of power.

On the morning of May 18, crowds of students demanding the resignation of President Suharto started to gather in the DPR, resulting in the occupation of the DPR by several thousand students who rallied from universities in Jakarta and neighboring regions. Student groups such as the PMII and HMI as well as cross-university student networks such as the KAMMI, FKSMJ (Communication Forum of Student Senates throughout Jakarta), FKPMJ (Press Communication Forum of Students of Jakarta) and FKMIJ (Communication Forum of Muslim Students of Jakarta) assembled in the DPR. Several tens of thousands of students are reported to have been at the scene during its peak (Cokro 2008: 88, 92). One of the students who took part in the occupation of the DPR explained their reason as follows:

> The reason why we had to occupy the DPR was because it is the 'house of the people' (*rumah rakyat*). Change must start from the parliament. We did not think the parliament represented the people until now. This was because it was always made light of by the government. However, this is exactly why we came to think

that we must empower the parliament. We chose the DPR as the place to make the change happen. (Tim Penyusun IRSED 1999: 139)

They continued to occupy the DPR from May 18 to 23, demanding the removal of President Suharto. During the round-the-clock occupation, NGOs and citizens provided water and food for the students. Not only students but also high-profile retired military officers and intellectuals such as former Governor of Jakarta Province and retired Navy General Ali Sadikin, former Governor of West Jakarta Province and retired Army Lieutenant General Solihin G. P., the poet Rendra, academic Dimyati Hartono and economic analyst Razal Ramli as well as a delegation from the Jakarta campus of the Indonesian University of Education and a delegation of 200 members from Bogor Agricultural University led by Rector Soleh Solahuddin arrived at the DPR in succession. They met with representatives of each faction of the DPR and expressed their demand to have the national leader replaced. When representatives of the reformist forces including Amien Rais and A. M. Fatwa were called in to give testimony at a morning hearing of the DPR Second Committee, Amien Rais took the opportunity to stress the need for a new president (*Kompas* May 19, 1998).

The DPR leadership's recommendation for the President's resignation was a product of lobbying by the reformist forces and allied DPR members. While students and social representatives visited the DPR one after another and demanded the replacement or dismissal of the President, the DPR leadership arranged locations for dialogues with the leaders of the four factions and notified them of their intention of recommending that the President resign. Abdul Gafur, one of the members of the DPR leadership, claims that on this occasion the chairs of the leaderships of all factions generally indicated an affirmative stance toward the opinion of the DPR leadership (Gafur 2000: 86–87; Syam 2008: 173). However, according to parliamentary procedure, the Golkar and opposition party factions needed to discuss the matter with, and gain approval from, their respective party executives, and the Armed Forces faction needed to do the same with the Armed Forces Command. Therefore, the DPR leadership held a press conference before these procedures were finished, making an announcement calling for the President's resignation as the 'opinion of the DPR leadership' rather than the 'general will of all factions of the DPR' (Gafur 2000: 88).

> At today's meeting, the DPR leadership considered carefully and took seriously the people's demands for reform including the holding of an MPR special session and the resignation of the President and the domestic state of affairs that is evolving at an extremely fast pace… In such context, the DPR leadership recommends the President step down, to maintain unification and integration of the nation. The DPR

leadership calls for the people to help restore security and order by keeping calm and disciplined and adhering to the unification and integration to let all things be solved through laws. (Gafur 2000: 89)

The recommendation regarding the President's resignation by the DPR leadership received a rapturous welcome from the reformist forces, especially students. However, the statement issued by Commander of the Armed Forces Wiranto four hours later threw cold water on the hope that was brought about by this recommendation. In this statement, Wiranto asserted that the DPR leadership's recommendation for the President's resignation did not have legal grounds because it was merely the individual opinion of the DPR leadership and not based on a consensus formed by all factions of the DPR (*Kompas* May 19, 1998).

Power transition

The previous section described the process in which an alliance between the reformist forces led by students and intellectuals and the DPR, particularly its largest faction the Golkar faction, was formed at the parliament and how the focus of the demand for reform voiced by these groups gradually converged to become the 'empowerment of the DPR' and 'immediate resignation of Suharto'. This section reveals the transition of power that took place while the pro-reform groups within the ruling party gained power and the consensus on Suharto's resignation became widely shared, in the context of the cooperation with the reformist forces. Before digging deeper into this topic, it is important to explain a development that was taking place at the top of the Armed Forces, one of the key political actors in the political change behind the consensus building process and power transition.

Armed Forces: between the reformist forces and Suharto

The reformist forces could not afford to make an enemy of the Armed Forces. However, at the same time, they could not become a completely trusted friend. The reason why the reformist forces remained relatively self-restrained, keeping their activities within campuses despite their capability to mobilize several hundred or thousand students from across universities, was because the students themselves wanted to avoid the catastrophe that could have resulted from a clash with the Armed Forces' security units. The intellectuals who participated in the reformist movement also denied transition by 'people power' as occurred in the Philippines, and repeatedly expressed that their reformist movement followed a peaceful and moderate path.

The Armed Forces side was relatively responsive when compared to President Suharto and Minister of Home Affairs Hartono, who took a negative attitude toward the reformist movement. The Armed Forces repeatedly emphasized the importance of dialogue with the reformist forces and displayed their readiness to respond to the call to organize forums. However, at the same time, they were suspected of having been involved in the series of cases of missing activists that happened in January concerning the disappearance of a total of about thirty student and human rights activists. Furthermore, as discussed in the first section of this chapter, the Armed Force was not an organization that could bring about political reform through legislation and policy formulation. From April to May, as the reform agenda gradually converged toward the revision of the five political laws and resignation of the President, the Armed Forces was becoming less and less a major partner for negotiation and cooperation with the reformist forces. In order to realize political reform and Suharto's resignation through a legal measure, the reformist movement needed to involve the parliaments. The more they tried to highlight the legality of their movement, the clearer it became that the negotiating partner should be the legislature rather than the Armed Forces.

Nevertheless, the Armed Forces continued to indicate their willingness to talk regardless, as they feared that the demonstrations and gatherings held across the country might lead to a large-scale mass mobilization. In fact, as mentioned above, the Armed Forces failed to suppress the massive riots that broke out in Jakarta from May 13 to 15 at an early stage. It is questionable as to whether the Armed Forces, which could not prevent riots from occurring or suppress them at an early stage even in relatively heavily guarded Jakarta, would have been able to swiftly bring a nationwide uprising under control. Even if they could, drawing criticism from within and outside the country for the oppression of the reformist forces would have been inevitable. The Armed Forces Command showed tolerance for student demonstrations to a certain extent and appealed for resolution through dialogue because they wanted to end the political crisis peacefully while maintaining security. In May, some groups within the Armed Forces initiated preparation of their own reform plans upon hearing the reformist forces' proposal. Nurcholish Madjid visited the Armed Forces Command accompanied by intellectuals such as Indria Samego and Salim Said on May 14 and presented their reform plan to Armed Forces Command Staff for Sociopolitical Affairs Susilo Bambang Yudhoyono (Hudijono and Thayib 2006: 156). However, the situation changed faster than the Armed Forces' top officers anticipated.

President Suharto had been maintaining his superiority by tactically taking advantage of rivalry and antagonism between military officers within the Armed Forces. Especially since the 1990s, he had been paying close attention to the task of preventing a specific person or group from having concentrated power. In contrast, he allowed Prabowo Subianto, the husband of his second daughter, to achieve extraordinarily fast career promotion and to appoint his right-hand men to key posts within the Armed Forces. There were more than a few high-ranking officers within the Armed Forces who took a dim view of Prabowo because of the special treatment he received due to his family ties with the President. Above all, the relationship between Wiranto, who assumed the position of Commander of the Armed Forces and Minister of Defense and Security in February 1998, and Prabowo, who was installed as Commander of Kostrad in the following March, had been strained before the reformist movement progressed[19]. In spite of the constant public emphasis on the unity of the Armed Forces, the fact that the relationship between Wiranto and Prabowo was deteriorating under political crisis was becoming clear to all.

Prabowo and his close associates Commander of Kopassus Muchdi and Commander of Jakarta Regional Military Command Sjafrie Sjamsoeddin, were the subjects of rife speculation that they were involved in the shooting incident at Tri Sakti University on May 12 as well as the riots in Jakarta, particularly the violence against Chinese-Indonesian women and children that took place in northern Jakarta. Moreover, Prabowo met with political elites who were at the center of political power such as Vice President Habibie on May 14 and had personal contact with representatives of the reformist forces such as Amien Rais (Simanjorang 2008: 202–210, 234), causing Wiranto to grow increasingly alarmed about his political actions (Azhari 2003: 79–80).

On May 15, the Armed Forces Command was preparing a press release regarding the NU's statement that they welcomed the announcement of resignation by Suharto. Although it was Commander of the Armed Forces Wiranto himself who gave the order to prepare this press release, he was preoccupied with other matters such as the establishment of a new security apparatus, with no time to check the contents of the press release that was being created at the Armed Forces Command (Azhari 2003: 81). Later, the press release was cancelled and the material that was distributed to the press beforehand was recalled because Suharto himself denied his announcement of resignation, and thus the press release announcing the Armed Forces' support for the NU's statement was no longer appropriate (Butarbutar 2003: 185). Nevertheless, Prabowo got hold of this material and showed it to Suharto on May 16 (Zon 2004: 140–141), suggesting that he should replace the Commander of the Armed Forces, recommending Army Chief of Staff Subagyo as his successor (Sukmawati 2004: 166–167).

This dispute occurred immediately after the President had made the decision to establish the KOPKKN and ordered Commander of the Armed Forces Wiranto to prepare for it. When the President told Wiranto about the KOPKKN, he indicated that he did not intend that the Commander take on another role as KOPKKN Commander due to the substantial amount of work that the head of the Armed Forces already had. However, in reaction to this, Wiranto asked the President to reconsider, arguing that having different individuals occupy the post of Commander of the Armed Forces and the post of KOPKKN Commander could lead to the disruption of military command (Simanjorang 2008: 239). It is not difficult to imagine that Wiranto was wary about the possibility that the post that would have tremendous powers regarding security matters may be given to Prabowo.

The issue of the press release regarding the NU's statement happened to take place in such a setting, and Prabowo reported it to the President as if it was a 'betrayal' on the part of Wiranto. On the following day, May 17, Wiranto provided an explanation of the press release issue to Suharto and declared he did not intend in any way to 'betray' him (Azhari 2003: 81). After that, Wiranto informed Suharto that Prabowo had been in contact with political elites including prominent members of the reformist forces over the course of several days, implying that it was in fact Prabowo who was plotting the removal of the President (Simanjorang 2008: 236–237). It is not certain how Suharto viewed each of the accounts given by Prabowo and Wiranto.

On the same day, May 17, Suharto invited Army Chief of Staff Subagyo to his residence and sounded him out about taking command of the KOPKKN (Sukmawati 2004: 174). Although Subagyo was close to Prabowo, this was probably not the reason behind Suharto's selection; it is rather believed that Suharto simply trusted his professionalism and loyalty. However, Subagyo turned down the President's offer. In doing so, he gave the following explanation. Firstly, he claimed that the Commander of the Armed Forces was the right person to take command of the KOPKKN and the Army Chief of Staff who did not have commanding authority should not play this role since it had the potential to disrupt military command. Secondly, he stated that the establishment of the KOPKKN would not be well received domestically and internationally. Finally, he suggested that it was untimely to establish a security apparatus on May 18, when the public security situation was on the way to recovery, and it would be better, in terms of timing, to launch it on May 20, when the reformist forces were planning a major demonstration (Sukmawati 2004: 174–175).

Suharto listened to Subagyo's points. As such, he decided to appoint Commander of the Armed Forces Wiranto to the post of KOPKKN Commander and Army Chief of Staff Subagyo to the post of KOPKKN Vice Commander. However, Suharto waited until the night of May 20 to actually hand the presidential decree concerning the establishment of the KOPKKN Command to

Wiranto and Subagyo (Sukmawati 2004: 176–177)[20]. It could be argued that he did so in accordance with Subagyo's advice, but it is highly possible that Suharto used the post of KOPKKN Commander as 'insurance' in the fluid situation fraught with uncertainty. His intention was to keep the Armed Forces—at least the Commander of the Armed Forces—under his control. The possibility that the post of KOPKKN Commander could be given to his rival would stop Wiranto from taking any action against Suharto's intentions. If Suharto postponed the grant of the presidential decree until May 20 with such strategy in mind, it would be successful in terms of having Wiranto under control. Wiranto not only vowed not to support the DPR when they recommended that the President resign, but also issued a firm warning to cancel a major long march the reformist forces had planned for May 20. In the end, this march was called off. Wiranto was not able to engage in any behavior that could have had the President suspect his loyalty. He was faced with the challenge of vying for power against his formidable rival Prabowo behind the scenes, retaining the President's trust and avoiding the organizational schism of the Armed Forces, all at the same time. Eventually, he won the power struggle against Prabowo and managed to regain leadership of the military[21], but in exchange lost an opportunity to take the lead in the political process that was occurring outside the Armed Forces.

Golkar: victory of a pro-reformist coalition

Golkar was the actor that met with the greatest impact in terms of the intra-organizational power redistribution that came about through the political change. In specific terms, some groups within Golkar that were responsive to the demands of the reformist movement and were able to establish an alliance with the reformist forces came to power during the process of Suharto's fall and succeeded in seizing control of the party.

As discussed in the previous section, cooperation between the reformist forces and Golkar began with the groups that were most amicable to the reformist forces. Following this the DPR leadership and Golkar faction leadership were later absorbed into the alliance one after another. On that account, the demand for the President's resignation by the DPR leadership was not an arbitrary decision by any means. However, Chair of the DPR Harmoko (Golkar Chairman) and Vice-Chair of the DPR Abdul Gafur (Vice-Chair of Golkar) met with strong criticism from the pro-President members within Golkar's Central Executive Board. Unlike the Golkar faction in the DPR, the pro-President members dominated the Executive Board as they included Suharto's eldest daughter and second son as well as Secretary-General Ary Mardjono who were highly loyal to the President as well as the FKPPI's Indra Bambang Utoyo, who was close to the

President's second son. On the night of May 18, when the DPR leadership made a request to the President to step down, the Central Executive Board of Golkar held a general meeting attended by all members except Suharto's eldest daughter and second son[22]. At that meeting, Harmoko and Gafur were accused of taking selfish action without taking into consideration their positions as Chairman and Vice-Chairman of Golkar by pro-President members such as Ary Mardjono and Indra Bambang Utoyo (Gafur 2000: 94). Especially, Indra Bambang Utoyo delivered blistering attacks on the basis that requesting resignation without consulting the supreme authority of Golkar, that is Advisory Board Chair of Golkar Suharto, was contrary to Golkar's decision-making process, labeling the two as traitors who were ungrateful for all that the President had done for them (Gafur 2000: 95).

Fahmi Idris, an Executive Board member, defended Harmoko and Gafur at this midnight meeting. Being a former-HMI hardcore student activist who belonged to the 'Generation of 66', he had a close relationship with Nurcholish Madjid and Eky Syachrudin and also frequently participated in debates on reform organized by the Wednesday Meeting. He was also one of the entrepreneurs who publicly supported the reformist movement along with Siswono Yudohusodo, Sugeng Suryadi and Jusuf Kalla[23]. He had argued that 'for a long time the business community has been feeling that there are too many distortions. We need comprehensive reform and a clean, efficient government. The political and economic reform the business community seeks includes replacement of the President' (*Warta Ekonomi* May 25, 1998: 18–23; *Kompas* May 19, 1998). Further, he had been offering rooms in the Regent Hotel, which he owned, as the meeting place for the reformist forces.

At the meeting of the Central Executive Board held on May 18, Fahmi Idris defended Harmoko and Gafur stating that the DPR leadership's request for the President's resignation was the right action to take (Gafur 2000: 94–95), and clearly expressed his intention to fight against the pro-President members within the Executive Board of Golkar. With the support of Fahmi Idris, the Harmoko and Gafur side refused to withdraw the demand for resignation and the Executive Board closed the meeting in the early hours of May 19 without reaching a conclusion on the issue. At the end of the meeting, the participants agreed on the following two points: the members of the Golkar faction in the DPR would hold a meeting during the same day to decide on its stance as a faction, and then Chair of the faction Irsyad Sudiro would hold a deliberation with other factions (Gafur 2000: 97).

Unlike the Central Executive Board meeting dominated by pro-President members, pro-reform groups dictated the Golkar faction meeting held on May 19. In particular, members of the 'Group of Twenty' who were calling for the holding of an MPR special session played a leading role in a heated discussion with the FKPPI group.

The Golkar faction was divided into roughly three groups. The first group consisted of supporters of the President such as FKPPI members and retired military officers, who, generally speaking, wanted to carry out reform under President Suharto. They insisted that if the President were to resign immediately, then Vice President Habibie should resign with him. If Habibie advanced to the presidency, then his close associates who were essentially their rivals would seize political power and that would threaten their position. Therefore, the fundamental principle for this group was to support Suharto, but it was also important to remove Habibie if Suharto was to resign, to start the game of politics over again.

The second group consisted of Habibie supporters who were from the ICMI or South Sulawesi, where Habibie was born. They sought the immediate resignation of the President and advancement of Vice President Habibie to the presidency and argued that the reform should be carried out under President Habibie.

The third group was composed of reform advocates mainly consisting of former HMI members who were not necessarily particular supporters of Habibie. Their utmost priority was the immediate resignation of Suharto. Although the advancement of Habibie to the presidency was not something they strongly hoped for, they supported it regardless based on the view that it would enhance their position within Golkar against Suharto's family members and FKPPI members.

The 'Group of Twenty' that collected signatures petitioning for the holding of an MPR special session consisted of the second and third group. As they formed a coalition on the common goal of the immediate resignation of the President, they became the majority force. Since the meeting was convened at very short notice, out of 325 DPR members from Golkar, only 160 were able to attend, and of those who attended, the majority belonged to the second or third group. The pro-reform groups that formed the majority at this meeting put the matter to a vote and won with approximately 120 votes, confirming that the Golkar faction's stance supported the DPR leadership's demand for the President's resignation (Prasetyo 1999: 72). Despite vehement objections to the outcome of the vote by members including Indra Bambang Utoyo, the Golkar faction leadership supported the result of the vote as Chair and Vice-Chair Irsyad Sudiro and Slamet Effendy Yusuf belonged to the reform advocate group (Prasetyo 1999: 72–73). After that, the DPR leadership deliberated with the leadership of each faction in the DPR and all factions unanimously agreed on the DPR's direction, to carry out total reform in political, economic and legal spheres and demand the resignation of the President (Sekretariat Jenderal DPR-RI 1998: 28–29).

Suharto's resignation

The pro-Suharto group was slow to react to the seizure of political power by the pro-reform group within the ruling party and the subsequent unanimous request for the President's resignation from the DPR leadership and all factions in it. FKPPI members who could not stop the Golkar faction's announcement of support for the request for resignation not only threatened the pro-reform DPR members and their families[24], but also planned to mobilize 300 members of Pancasila Youth and Panca Marga Youth to launch an attack on the DPR that was occupied by students on May 20. They entered the DPR building from the back door brandishing banners that read 'bring down Harmoko', 'our leader is Suharto' and 'say no to the MPR special session', creating a volatile situation with the students who were occupying the DPR. However, it did not develop into chaos thanks to the mediation by military officers who were guarding the parliament as well as its members (*Kompas* May 20, 1998).

Among retired and active military men who held key posts in the government and parliament, there were some such as Minister of Home Affairs Hartono that tried to stop the resignation of the President by various means, but their efforts were on an individual basis and lacked coordination with others. Coordinating Minister for Political and Security Affairs Feisal Tandjung remained a silent observer, whereas Vice-Chair of the DPR leadership Syarwan Hamid who represented the Armed Forces faction and Chair of the Armed Forces faction Hari Sabarno acted in concert with the DPR leadership and other factions as part of the alliance with the reformist forces, despite the fact that they were expected to act under the orders of the Commander of the Armed Forces[25]. Put simply, military personnel who held political posts acted on the basis of their own political position and interpretation and never took unified action to stop the dismissal of Suharto. This contrasts with how the reformist forces and pro-reform group within the DPR took concerted action to realize the goal of the removal of Suharto. The elites who constituted the 'hard-liners' did not share a mutual interest that made it necessary to keep Suharto in the presidency at any cost, for the fear of 'punishment' accompanied with the transfer of power was almost non-existent in Indonesia's reformist movement. Most of the prominent members of the reformist forces were moderate in nature, besides, it was commonly expected that there was not going to be substantial change to the lineup of the governing elites if Habibie took over power, at least for some time.

While an increasing number of groups within the regime switched sides to the reformist movement, Suharto tried once more to concentrate power in his hands. He delivered a televised speech on May 19 and announced the following seven items: (1) the President will lead the reform himself; (2) he will create a 'Reform Committee' (Komite Reformasi) comprised of specialists, intellectuals and socially renowned figures and promptly establish laws including a general election law, political party law, MPR, DPR and DPRD law, anti-monopoly law and anti-corruption law; (3) he will hold an election at the earliest possible date based on the new general election law; (4) he will hold an MPR general session after the election to decide on the national policy framework and elect a president and vice president; (5) he will not run for the presidency; (6) he will reshuffle the cabinet to form a 'reform cabinet'; and (7) the Armed Forces will continue to concentrate on the maintenance of public security and order (Sekretariat Jenderal DPR-RI 1998: 26–28).

However, the reformist forces and DPR members had already agreed that revision of the five political laws such as the general election law and political party law and the new laws required for reform were going to be enacted in the parliament and the President was supposed to have already accepted this. The idea that the President raised—creating an informal organization called the 'Reform Committee' to revise and enact the laws and leading the reform himself as the head of this committee—disregarded the role of the DPR. At the same time, this could be seen as a replay of what Suharto had enacted at the beginning of his regime when he established informal policy-making teams such as the ASPRI, SPRI or OPSUS while depriving the parliament of the legislative function.

On the same day, before the televised speech, Suharto met with nine Islamic leaders and intellectuals and suggested the creation of this organization. At that time he planned to call it the 'Reform Council' (Dewan Reformasi). He changed its name to 'Reform Committee' (Komite Reformasi) because Nurcholish Madjid, one of the nine, disagreed with the name 'Dewan Reformasi' in that it may be perceived as competing with the DPR (Dewan Perwakilan Rakyat) (*Kompas* May 21, 1998). There is no doubt, however, that Suharto envisioned that this body would be involved in the legislative process[26].

Everyone must have questioned the necessity of establishing the 'Reform Committee' to revise the five political laws and formulate new laws that were supposed to be the responsibilities of the DPR, and suspected that after all Suharto was trying to set up an extralegal organization aside from the DPR that was no longer under his control, ignoring the consensus between the DPR and the reformist forces. Emha Ainun Nadjib, one of the Islamic intellectuals who attended the meeting with the President, accurately criticized Suharto's idea claiming 'the President's proposal may make the DPR dysfunctional. The legitimacy of the organization would be questionable if that's the case' (*Kompas* May 21, 1998). The President did not understand that the reformist forces were striving to implement reform through the legislature, and attempted to carry out 'reform' through a counter institution. This is precisely why no one expressed the intention of joining the 'Reform Committee'. It became clear to everyone's eyes that, as Ali Yafie, a well-known *kyai* from the NU who attended the aforementioned meeting, said to Suharto in person, 'reform means the resignation of the President' (*Forum Keadilan* June 15, 1998: 80).

Given the President's persistent refusal to understand their consensus, the reformist forces reinforced the idea that the only means to remove the President was to hold an MPR special session. Legal scholars Ateng Syafrudin and Dimyati Hartono claimed that the President's announcement to bring the election forward was in violation of the GBHN[27] and therefore would provide the legal basis for the DPR to convene an MPR special session, and encouraged the DPR to convene one as soon as possible (*Kompas* May 21, 1998).

In response to this claim, the Golkar faction of the DPR arranged a factional general meeting on May 20 and adopted a resolution to demand the early holding of an MPR special session—in one month's time at the latest. For this factional general meeting, the Golkar faction leadership prepared the following five options: (1) to carry out reform in accordance with the reform plan proposed by the President on May 19; (2) the President resigns upon which Vice President Habibie advances to the presidency and stays in the office of president until the end of the term; (3) both the President and Vice President resign upon which the Minister of Home Affairs, Minister of Foreign Affairs and Minister of Defense and Security hold an MPR special session as the government's representatives and elect a new president and vice president; (4) the President, the DPR leadership and factions in the DPR jointly hold an MPR special session wherein the President will not be held accountable for his rule but instead resign and return the mandate delegated by the MPR; or (5) the President, the DPR leadership and factions in the DPR jointly hold an MPR special session wherein the President will not be held accountable for his rule but both the President and Vice President resign and return the mandate delegated by the MPR. In this meeting, attended by 198 Golkar legislators, the majority chose option (4) or (5) (*Kompas* May 21, 1998), making the supporters of the President's reform plan who endorsed option (1) the minority. Many legislators who had been quietly watching the development of the situation were carried along by their fellows who formed an alliance with the reformist forces and came to believe that the resignation of the President was inevitable.

The DPR leadership held a discussion with thirty-two chairs of student senates of respective universities among the students who were occupying the DPR (*Kompas* May 21, 1998). The students' side demanded that a timeframe be set for the resignation of the President. Chair of the DPR Harmoko listened to this opinion and proposed that if the President did not respond to talks with the DPR by May 22, then they would convene the MPR's factions to discuss the holding of an MPR special session. The students' side agreed with this proposal (Sekretariat Jenderal DPR-RI 1998: 31–32).

While the DPR and the reformist forces began detailed discussions on the process of the resignation of the President, Coordinating Minister for Economy and Finance and Head of the Bappenas Ginandjar Kartasasmita held a meeting with economic ministers on the evening of May 20[28]. Ginandjar explained that the economy was in a very dangerous situation and several ministers also reported that the economy was facing paralysis[29]. Ginandjar asserted that overcoming such situation required reform in all areas, claiming that a cabinet reshuffle would not solve the problem. Having made that statement, he declared that he would not join the new cabinet that Suharto was going to reorganize and asked for the other cabinet members' approval[30]. In response, the economic ministers at this meeting, except for State Minister of Agrarian Affairs Ary Mardjono who voiced strong opposition to this statement and Governor of the BI Syahril Sabirin, agreed with Ginandjar (Kartasasmita 2013: 192). State Minister for Public Housing Akbar Tandjung wrote a letter of resignation[31] with the signatures of the fourteen cabinet members at the time and it was sent to the President's residence. Three more coordinating ministers—Coordinating Minister for Political and Security Affairs Feisal Tandjung, Coordinating Minister for Development Supervision and Administrative Reform Hartarto and Coordinating Minister for People's Welfare and Poverty Alleviation Haryono Suyono—responded to Ginandjar's call, joining the meeting halfway through and viewing the contents of the letter. They are said to have raised no objections to the decision by the cabinet members (Hisyam 1999: 689; Kartasasmita 2013: 195).

Ginandjar, who encouraged the cabinet members' resignation, had not only been pressured to leave office by technocrats such as Emil Salim, Ali Wardhana and Widjojo Nitisastro but had also been urged to make a 'political decision' by Arifin Panigoro, an entrepreneur who was siding with the reformist forces (Makka 2008: 126). As for Akbar Tandjung, who wrote the resignation letter, he had participated in meetings organized by the reformist forces, even taking part in discussions regarding the President's resignation. In the meantime, he had been urged to side with the reformist forces by the ICMI's Acting Chair Achmad Tirtosudiro and Golkar legislator Ade Komaruddin who was his junior in the HMI[32]. The cabinet members' acceptance of the consensus on the immediate resignation of Suharto formed between the reformist forces and DPR members came about as a product of the considerable pressure they received from numerous directions.

Suharto decided on his resignation on the night of May 20 when he received the economic ministers' letter of resignation. Suharto's words in his announcement of resignation delivered the following morning were as follows.

...Considering the situation, I reached the conclusion that it would be very difficult for me to implement duties in governing the state and in progressing development. Therefore, in line with article 8 of the 1945 Constitution and after earnestly taking into consideration the views of the leadership of the DPR and the leadership of the factions in it, I have decided to declare that I have ceased to be the president of the Republic of Indonesia as of the time I read this on this day, Thursday, May 21, 1998. (Gafur 2000: 157)

The resignation of the President took the form of accepting the recommendation of the DPR. In the end, the President himself approved the consensus between the reformist forces and the parliament.

Conclusion: The End of Personal Rule and Regime Change in Indonesia

What led to the end of personal rule?

Indonesia's Suharto regime ended as a result of consensus building, in other words, it concluded in a 'pacted transition'. The reformist forces led by students and intellectuals started the reformist movement in pursuit of the reform of the political system to overcome the economic crisis. The reformist forces fleshed out their reform agenda through a series of negotiations with elites within the regime, especially legislators from the ruling party Golkar, and as a result, they began seeking the improvement of the functions of the legislature. As the focus of the reform agenda was fixed on the empowerment of the legislature, the reformist forces' and DPR members' interests coincided. Moreover, since the reformist forces and these elites within the regime had come from or belonged to the same organizations, they had the kind of relationship that allowed them to share a sense of solidarity in times of economic and political crises through day-to-day communication that took place regardless of their position in relation to the regime. This coincidence of interests and sense of solidarity enabled the cooperation between the two parties. The groups within the ruling party that collaborated with the reformist forces played the role of 'soft-liners' who called for the restructuring of the political system from within the regime.

With the worsening of the political crisis, the goal of the reformist movement further developed into the immediate resignation of the President. Even when faced with the rising tension brought about by the Jakarta riots, Suharto tried to maintain his political power by planning to establish an informal legislative organization of which he would take charge, essentially disregarding the parliament. Many political elites came to think that genuine reform could not be achieved while Suharto reigned supreme as President, and if they were not able to achieve reform, then Indonesia was destined to go down with Suharto. Consequently, consensus regarding the immediate resignation of the President was achieved. Suharto finally accepted that he must resign immediately as he judged that it would be difficult to challenge the consensus on this issue, as it was such a broad consensus formed across the political spectrum and included elites within and outside the regime. Until then, he had been concerning himself with securing support through patronage distribution. He continued to rely on this approach to mobilize support until the end. However, once the support mobilization system had collapsed, he came to the realization that it was no longer possible to maintain his rule, even with a new security apparatus or reform committee.

There are limits to the number of political posts and economic concessions able to be distributed as patronage. Especially in the co-opting type of personal rule, in which the ruler distributes patronage comprehensively, as more elites are co-opted into the regime through the distribution of political posts, fewer posts are available for distribution. This fuels competition within the regime over posts, making it difficult for the ruler to coordinate and resolve the rivalry. If the failure of the ruler to resolve intra-elite competition produces a rift within the regime, this provides an opportunity for regime change.

In Indonesia's case, the abovementioned collapse of the support mobilizing system occurred as a consequence of the way Suharto had been distributing patronage. In and after the 1980s, Suharto expanded the range of patronage distribution to social elites and co-opted them into the regime through the ruling party Golkar in an attempt to reinforce the government's political basis. As a result, the competition over posts intensified within the regime. Then, in the mid-1990s, the competition over posts was complicated by the issue of the succession of the presidency and created a rift inside the regime, especially within Golkar, because Suharto's distribution pattern became substantially skewed to the group close to his family members and marginalized the group of social elites who had been co-opted into the regime, eventually driving them away from Suharto. This rift inside the regime completely collapsed Suharto's rule as the economic and political crisis unfolded. The consensus on his resignation and establishment of a new political system was formed in parallel with the rapid withdrawal of support for Suharto.

Regime change without a loser

As discussed in Chapter One, the end of personal rule is often associated with the overthrow of a government by mass mobilization or military coup, or defeat in a reckless war started by the ruler. In particular, in personal rule where the ruler depends on violence and patronage distribution is limited in scope, the country degenerates into anarchy, as fear and hatred toward the ruler is exacerbated to breaking point triggering mass mobilization and rioting aimed at overthrowing the government or a blatant power struggle such as the usurpation of governmental authority by the military or a militant group that takes advantage of a power vacuum. If a ruler who has continuously oppressed the people with no mercy becomes a loser in the midst of such mass mobilization or a power struggle, the inevitable consequence is that they will be executed or must flee in exile. Ceauşescu of Rumania and Saddam Hussein of Iraq were executed whereas Batista of Cuba, Mohammad Reza Pahlavi of Iran, Amin of Uganda, Marcos of the Philippines and Jean-Claude Duvalier of Haiti were forced to find refuge in another country. In such cases, the fate of the ruler is to pay for their violent and arbitrary rule with their own life.

In countries under the co-opting type of personal rule, namely Tunisia under the Bourguiba regime, Ivory Coast under the Houphouët regime and Indonesia under the Suharto regime, anti-government, democratic movements did occur towards the end of the regimes. However, none of them constituted mass mobilization on a scale that would paralyze the government or lead to an anarchical situation. In Tunisia, Bourguiba's subordinate, Prime Minister Ben Ali, staged a 'legal coup' using Bourguiba's medical unfitness as grounds to oust him before the nationwide disorder as a result of Bourguiba's oppression of the Islamist groups was able to come to a head (Zartman 1991: 12–13). As for Ivory Coast, the death of Houphouët who was carrying out 'democratization from above' to a limited extent ended his rule and Henri Konan Bédié, who was one of the prominent figures in the ruling party, took over the presidential authority (A. Satō 2000: 38–41). In Indonesia's case, the end of Suharto's rule took the form of his resignation. In the cases of all three countries, personal rule came to an end without the execution or exile of the ruler. In co-opting-type personal rule where the ruler distributes patronage comprehensively to appease the people, fear and hatred toward the ruler do not escalate to breaking point and thus its end takes a different form from other types of personal rule.

One characteristic of the end of the Suharto regime as an example of co-opting-type personal rule was that it constituted regime change without a loser. The resignation upon acceptance of the request from the parliament defended Suharto's honor and respected his will. Therefore, it was an acceptable option for Suharto. From the very beginning of the reformist movement, the reformist forces tried to influence the elites within the regime through dialogue and negotiation in an attempt to avoid a head-on confrontation with the regime side as much as possible. Direct confrontation may result in bloodshed and does not always guarantee success even after heavy casualties. The allied reformist forces and regime elites intently sought a peaceful means to transfer power by prompting the President to resign without making him lose face. At the same time, they demonstrated that they were aiming for a constitutional transfer of power by ensuring they followed parliamentary procedures to gain support from as many regime elites as possible or obtain their unspoken approval. By adopting the strategy of not making Suharto an 'outright loser', the reformist forces could not only avoid a head-on confrontation by providing Suharto with one last escape route but also win as many regime elites as possible over to their side, helping to make the peaceful transfer of power a reality.

Similarly, the fact that the reformist forces were not preoccupied with wresting governmental authority contributed to the smooth political transition. The leaders of the reformist forces allowed Habibie, who was one of Suharto's cronies, to take over the presidential office and also allowed the regime elites who had collaborated with the reformist forces to maintain their power and posts in the government and DPR. Many of the ruling elites who worked under the Suharto regime inherited power not because they held predominant power over the reformist forces but rather due to the fact that their cooperation with them and contribution to the resignation of Suharto were appreciated. If the reformist forces had been obsessed with eliminating ruling elites completely and seizing governmental power themselves, it would have been impossible to form an alliance with the regime elites, and if such an alliance had not existed, a compromise with the hard-liners including Suharto would not have been reached.

The reformist forces offered Suharto an acceptable option of resignation and let the regime elites who cooperated with them inherit power. The strategy of avoiding the creation of a 'loser' brought about a smooth transition accompanied with consensus building.

Implications for the democratization of Indonesia
It has been observed that in some cases of political transition where some of the old ruling elites inherit power, the transfer of power does not always lead to transition to a democratic regime. For instance, in Tunisia and Ivory Coast where the elites of the old regime inherited power at the end of co-opting-type personal rule, despite a temporary emergence of the democratic transition process, the new government changed the rules of the political game to maintain their power during the institutional reform. In these two countries, the failure to ensure fair political competition caused democratization to stall as the new governments manipulated the electoral system with rules that were favorable to the existing ruling party such as single-seat constituency and candidate lists[1]. As arriving at power through elections was no longer an option, the opposition forces resorted to other means to raise a protest or grab power. The government chose not to make a compromise but instead responded with hard-line oppression as the anti-government movement led by the opposition forces gained momentum, and this resulted in a resurgence of authoritative rule. It is only reasonable that if a newly established 'democratic' institution gives the opposition forces no chance to win at all, this will give rise to some sort of resistance that will naturally be formed outside the framework of this institution. It can be said that in these situations

the non-compromising attitude of the elites from the old regime who inherited power caused the democratization process to reach an impasse.

However, there is also no guarantee that the transition to a democratic system definitely takes place when the elites from the old regime are completely removed and a drastic transfer of power by mass mobilization occurs. There have been cases in which the collapse of a government has given rise to an anarchic situation with emergent political actors engaging in intensive power struggles over governmental authority. In other cases the military has launched a coup during a power vacuum. A power struggle or military coup delays the efforts of democratic-minded groups to expand their influence and hinders the broad consensus building toward democratization among elites. Furthermore, in some cases, a segment of the elites from the old regime who were dismissed from government posts as 'losers' have taken reprisal action and caused public security to deteriorate precipitously, shaking the foundation of the newly born government or delaying the establishment of a democratic system. When an intense power struggle or deterioration of public security takes place before institutional competition through the electoral and parliamentary system is established, the democratization process can be stalled as it facilitates the revival of a brute-force approach to conflict resolution, creating a new 'strong man'.

As has been shown above, the tough reality is that the end of personal rule does not always lead to a transition toward democracy. Indonesia is no exception in that democratization certainly did not progress without difficulty. Nevertheless, the end of Suharto's rule did lead to the transition to a democratic system and its journey has never ceased until this day, albeit slowly. I would like to conclude this book by presenting four factors that have enabled Indonesia to undergo democratic transition following the end of personal rule.

Firstly, Indonesia did not experience a major upheaval, a power vacuum or an anarchic situation associated with the collapse of the government. Neither was there an intense leadership struggle among new political actors. This was quite simply the fruit of consensus building between the reformist forces and regime soft-liners. A consensus had been formed, prior to the resignation of Suharto, that Vice President Habibie would take over the presidential office and the regime soft-liners who were involved in collaborating with the reformist forces would inherit governmental power. This prevented the emergence of a power vacuum created by the collapse of the regime. As a result, the policy making process avoided a major disruption and political actors did not have to spend time and effort in a power struggle, enabling Indonesia to concentrate on institution-building to realize liberalization and democratization immediately.

Secondly, in the process of regime change, there was no 'outright winner'. This meant that the new governing elites who took over power did not try to manipulate the rules of the political game to serve their own interests. The reason why Tunisia and Ivory Coast failed to make the end of personal rule an opportunity to transition to a democratic system was because the ruling elites had predominant positions over groups outside the government when they assumed power, and those elites continued to take an uncompromising attitude toward demands for democratization raised from outside the government in their efforts to hold on to political leadership to maintain their superiority. The absence of such situation in Indonesia can be explained by the fact that the regime elites who inherited power and the reformist forces were more or less equal in power and the new government needed to sustain a harmonious relationship with the reformist forces. Since the political base of President Habibie was vulnerable to start with, the government required support and cooperation from the reformist forces to hamper the hard-liner elites from the old regime who were seeking to regain lost ground in the political arena. In order to ensure continuous support and cooperation from the reformist forces, liberalization and democratization needed to be promptly carried out as a concerted effort. This in turn allowed the opinions of the reformist forces to be reflected through institution building in the democratization process.

Thirdly, the absence of an 'outright winner' and 'outright loser' in Indonesia's political change allowed the formation of a political attitude that accepted the rule of democracy—the very concept that the winner/loser position could be reversed through election. In order to establish a democratic system that motivates all political actors to participate, the rules of the political game must give all political forces a chance to win on the next occasion, even if they have lost the current ballot, and the belief that 'their future will be better if they continue to follow the rules of the democratic game' must be shared among all actors (Przeworski 1991: 31, 33). If the group in power refuses to become a loser and give the other side a chance to regain ground, then, the winner-loser relationship becomes fixed and the groups that are not allowed the opportunity to turn the game around will eventually quit it altogether. If this happens, the possibility of the political competition being carried out within the framework of the democratic game diminishes. If the opposition groups try to grab power using non-institutional means, that is violence, then the government will also attempt to suppress them in the same manner. Confrontations and conflicts with violence hamper the creation of the mutual trust relationship required for the establishment of a democratic system even further. However, Indonesia's political transition did not produce an 'outright winner' and 'outright loser', and this became the foundation upon which the political actors came to share an understanding that winning or losing is just a temporary situation. The elites of the new government and reformist forces who did not become the 'outright winners' needed to maintain mutual cooperation and compromise to devise the rules of the new political game. On the other hand, the hard-liner elites of the old regime who did not become the 'outright losers' understood that they had a chance to regain political power within the framework of the new political game. As this form of politics unfolded, Indonesia became prepared to accept the new political game called democracy.

Lastly, parliamentary procedure came to be respected for the first time in the history of Indonesia. Suharto's governance began as he curtailed the role of the legislature and gave their legislative authority to an informal policy-making team consisting of a small number of people. Suitably, the ending of Suharto's rule took place in the parliament that was trying to regain its legislative role. In personal rule characterized by extremely personal governance based on the patron-client relationship, disdain for parliamentary procedures, weak institutions, weakness of the rule of law and the violent resolution of conflicts and confrontations, even if the ruler steps down from political leadership, it is very difficult to completely remove the remnants of such rule. However, the fact that the end of Suharto's rule took place in the parliament, with the support of the reformist movement, can be interpreted as the manifestation of the will of the broad range of the political and social elites who were determined to change the governance system of Indonesia—from rule based on personal relationships to rule by laws and institutions based on parliamentary procedure. Politics based on the patron-client relationship, however, did not come to an end and numerous attempts were made to resolve conflicts and confrontations with violence in Indonesia's democratization process that followed. What made it possible for Indonesia to endure this without reversal to authoritarianism nonetheless was that the political elites came to share the same intention—that is, the bottom line was to solve confrontations and conflicts through institutional means such as elections or deliberation in parliament. Respect for elections and parliament by all political actors is an important step forward in building the rule by law that constitutes the foundation of democracy. This has become embedded in Indonesia over the course of the one and a half decades since the political transition of 1998.

Notes

Chapter 1

1 The name of these regional rebellions is *Pemberontakan PRRI/Permesta*. PRRI means 'the Revolutionary Government of the Republic of Indonesia' and *Permesta* means 'Total struggle'. The commanders of the regional military commands of West and North Sumatra and North and South Sulawesi demanded a...n increase in budget allocation to the regional commands and expressed their sense of vigilance against the soaring influence of the Communist Party in the central government. They also called for a diarchy with President Sukarno and Mohammad Hatta, the latter coming from West Sumatra. They declared the establishment of the counter-government (PRRI) upon the rejection of these demands by the central government. The rebellions were quelled by Armed Forces troops.
2 NASAKOM was a political slogan coined from the first letters of Indonesian words, *nasionalisme* (nationalism), *agama* (religion) and *kommunisme* (communism).
3 Suharto was Javanese, born in 1921. He joined the Defenders of the Homeland (PETA), during the Japanese occupation of Indonesia and later enlisted in the Army in 1945 and participated in the war for independence. He accumulated military credentials as a field commander and was appointed as Commander of the Army Strategic Reserve Command (Kostrad) in 1963. He seized leadership of the Armed Forces following the September 30th Affair of 1965 and received authority pertaining to security and order from President Sukarno based on the Order of March the Eleventh (*Supersemar*) on March 11, 1966 (refer to Note 5). He assumed the office of acting president in March 1967 and became the second Indonesian President in March 1968 and remained in office until he resigned in May 1998. He died in January 2008.
4 *Konfrontasi Malaysia* was a policy of confrontation against the formation of the new Malaysia by merging Singapore and North Borneo, proposed by the Federation of Malaya under the initiative of Britain, its colonial master. President Sukarno opposed the initiative, accusing such an idea as a manifestation of British neocolonialism.
5 The Order of March the Eleventh (*Supersemar*) was a decree mandating Minister/Commander of the Army Suharto to take any measures necessary to restore security and stabilize the political situation. President Sukarno

had no other option but to issue this decree to Suharto given the intensity of anti-PKI and anti-Sukarno demonstrations following the September 30th Affair. There is also a suggestion that the Army threatened Sukarno to force him to draft this document. Nonetheless, the location of the original document has not yet been identified. Suharto ordered the dissolution of the PKI pursuant to the decree. *Supersemar* was approved in the general session of the Provisional People's Consultative Assembly (MPRS), held in June 1966 (Sutjipto 1966 (II): 107), but this did not mean that presidential authority was transferred from Sukarno to Suharto; in fact, Sukarno later formed a cabinet with himself as president. The dual power situation with Sukarno and Suharto lasted until March 1967 when Sukarno was dismissed in a special session of the MPRS (Masuhara 2004: 6–7, 18–19).

6 Nevertheless, Sutowo himself insists that the reason for his dismissal was because he declined requests for financial assistance from Suharto and was not related to the management issues of Pertamina (Karma 2001: 268).

7 Hutchcroft explained the structure of the Philippine's political and economic rule using the analytical concept 'patrimonial oligarchic state' (Hutchcroft 1993; 1998). According to him, the ruling group consisted of landowners and entrepreneurs in the Philippines who squeezed privileges out of bureaucratic institutions and became a strong resistance force against economic reforms that could adversely impact them in terms of securing concessions (Hutchcroft 1998: 52–55). On the other hand, he cited Indonesia under the Suharto regime, particularly in its early years, as an example of a 'patrimonial administrative state' in which bureaucrats and senior government officers held superior power while the entrepreneur class was vulnerable, unorganized and needed patrons within the government to protect their businesses (Hutchcroft 1998: 46–48). He argued that unlike the Philippines, senior government officers had the ability to carry out economic reforms and rational policy was possible in Indonesia (Hutchcroft 1998: 48–51).

8 Well-known studies on the 1998 political change include Shiraishi (1999), Aspinall, Feith and van Klinken (1999), Budiman, Hatley and Kingsbury (1999), Eklöf (1999), Forrester and May (1999), Schwarz (1999), Van Dijk (2001), O'Rourke (2002), Honna (2003), Canonica-Walangitang (2003), Aspinall (2005) and Mietzner (2009).

9 Its first appearance was in Juan J. Linz 'Totalitarian and Authoritarian Regimes', in F. Greenstein and N. Polsby (eds.) *Macropolitical Theory* (1975). The source referred to in this book is found in the version published in 2000 (Linz 2000).

10 However, Sakai wrote that this redistribution policy was increasingly

replaced by symbolic manipulation that actively propagandized Hussein as a symbol of national unity as the Iran–Iraq War continued and resources for distribution were gradually depleted (Sakai 2003: 247, 249–250).
11 Patrick Ziegenhain mentioned the presence of soft-liners within Golkar the night before the 1998 political transition (Ziegenhain 2008: 57–69). Nevertheless, his study does not provide a concrete account of how and why such groups emerged within Golkar and how they managed to cooperate with the reformist forces.

Chapter 2

1 The five political laws passed in 1985 (law on general election, law on the composition of the MPR, DPR and DPRD, law on political parties and Golkar, law on referendum and law on mass organizations) included provisions needed to actualize restrictions on political participation which the Suharto regime had been gradually regulating, including the appointive system of members of the parliaments and restrictions on the number of political parties as well as on political activities in rural areas.
2 On the total assets of the Suharto family including the assets of their foundations, *Time*, *Forbes*, *Newsweek* and *Asiaweek* provided estimations of fifteen billion, forty billion, forty billion and eight billion US dollars respectively, whereas George Aditjondro estimated it at twenty-five billion US dollars (Murai et al. 1999: 56–57). If it was indeed forty billion US dollars, it is four times more than the assets of President Marcos of the Philippines, which is said to have been ten billion US dollars.
3 Other Chinese-Indonesian business groups that were known to be closely associated with the Suharto family included the Sinar Mas Group founded by Eka Cipta Wijaya, the Lippo Group founded by Mochtar Riyadi and the Barito Group founded by Prayogo Pangestu.
4 Based on data aggregated by Yuri Satō, of the Chinese-Indonesian companies closely linked with the Suharto family, Salim, Sinar Mas, Lippo, Nusamba and Barito ranked in the top-performing companies at the end of the Suharto regime, in the first, third, fourth, sixth and seventh position respectively. Except for Suharto's second son Bambang's Bimantara Group, which ranked in the ninth position, all corporate groups within the top ten were Chinese-Indonesian businesses (Y. Satō 2003: 113).
5 At the end of the 1950s, Army Chief of Staff Abdul Haris Nasution proposed the notion of the 'middle way' (*jalan tengah*), which suggested

that the positioning of the Indonesian Armed Forces should be somewhere between the militaries of western countries which served merely as tools of their governments and those of Latin American countries which staged coups to seize control of politics, and that they should be widely involved in nation-building. This notion was theorized under the Suharto regime as a 'Dual function' and constituted grounds for both active and retired military personnel to advance into political posts.

6 *Sumpah Pemuda* of 1928 was a declaration made by a group of young nationalist elites assembled from various parts of the Dutch East Indies, which proclaimed 'one native land, Indonesia', 'one nation, the Indonesian nation' and 'one unifying language, the Indonesian language'.

7 The term '*ulama*' refers to scholars who possess profound knowledge of Islam in the Muslim world. '*Kyai*' refers to *ulama* who lead Islamic boarding schools called '*pesantren*' (traditional Islamic educational institutions) in the island of Java. Both *ulama* and *kyai* not only had religious influence but also had significant political authority in their regions.

8 The Islamic forces demanded of the government that *Kebatinan*, the traditional belief indigenous to Java, be removed from the jurisdiction of the Ministry of Religious Affairs and transferred to the Ministry of Education and Culture, on the grounds that it is not a religion (*Agama*), but a faith (*Kepercayaan*). The government compromised with the Islamic forces and did as they demanded.

9 Richard Tanter (1990: 269–270) and Takashi Shiraishi (1997: 164) both noted that that the government used the memory of terror of the past such as the massacre after the September 30th Affair to maintain security and order.

10 This report was made based on the response given by Chief State Secretary Murdiono to a question in the DPR on September 14, 1988 (Pangaribuan 1995: 32, 44). The exchange rate from dollars to rupiah was one to 1685.7 in 1988 according to the *Ajia Dōkō Nenpō* (Yearbook of Asian Affairs) (1994: 414). If 110.9 billion dollars were the accurate figure, then the annual expenditure would have been approximately 22.2 billion dollars.

11 This categorization is the author's original work. The categorization process included listing the items and descriptions of 'presidential assistance' and 'presidential contribution' (*sumbangsih presiden*) reported in the Armed Forces-owned magazine *Mimbar Kekaryaan ABRI* at fixed intervals during the period from 1971 to 1988.

12 According to Abdulgani-KNAPP's study, the aggregate number of grantees of assistance from this foundation from its creation to 2006 were as follows: 427,780 university students, 889,961 high school students, 13,060 sports

players, 832,500 orphans, 5,972 master's degree holders and 1,160 doctoral degree holders, and the total amount of assistance was 455,261,960,000 rupiah (Abdulgani-KNAPP 2007: 293).

13 According to Abdulgani-KNAPP, the Dakab Foundation's relationship with Golkar ended upon Suharto's resignation from the presidency in 1998 and since then it has refocused its business on financing business loans to small and medium-sized regional enterprises (Abdulgani-KNAPP 2007: 311).

Chapter 3

1 The total number of seats held by the government factions was 167, with the Golkar faction having ninety-two seats and the Armed Forces faction seventy-five. As for the party factions, the total number of seats was 247, with the nationalist faction (such as PNI) holding ninety-three seats, the Islamic faction (such as NU) holding 122 and the Christian faction (such as Parkindo) holding thirty-two. Accordingly, the government factions (167 seats) accounted for 40.3 percent of the 414 seats in the DPR. Prior to the parliamentary reorganization, the proportion of non-party members in the DPR was approximately twenty-three percent since the Golongan Karya faction included party-affiliated members (Masuhara 2004: 21).
2 KOSGORO (Kesatuan Organisasi Serbaguna Gotong-Royong, or United Multipurpose Mutual Assistance Organizations) was originally a cooperative founded in 1957 under the name of Koperasi Simpan Pindjam Gotong-Rojong (Mutual Assistance Cooperative Savings and Loans) (Bangun 1994: 109–125).
3 SOKSI stands for Sentral Organisasi Karyawan Swadiri Indonesia (Central Organization for Indonesian Independent Workers). It was a coordinating body on industrial relations formed in 1960 to compete against SOBSI (Sentral Organisasi Buruh Seluruh Indonesia, or All Indonesia Centre of Labor Organizations), a PKI-affiliated trade union federation (Bangun 1994: 129–156). The members of this organization consisted of manual workers working in foreign corporations and plantations seized by the Armed Forces and advocated industrial harmony against SOBSI, which was fuelling confrontation between employers and employees.
4 MKGR stands for Musyawarah Kekeluargaan Gotong-Royong (Mutual Assistance Families Association) and was established in 1960 (Bangun 1994: 159–178).
5 GAKARI stands for Gabungan Karya Rakyat Indonesia (Indonesian People's Functional Union) (Bangun 1994: 201–217).

6 Ormas Hankam stands for Organisasi Massa Pertahanan Keamanan (Defense and Security Mass Organization) (Bangun 1994: 181–188).
7 Karya Profesi means Professional Function. The original name was Organisasi Profesi (Professional Organization) (Bangun 1994: 191–197).
8 Karya Pembangunan (Development Function) consisted of members of parliament belonging to the Golkar faction (Bangun 1994: 221–243).
9 Julian Boileau examined Golkar within the framework of corporatism theory and argued that it was indeed a corporate party on the basis that it owned a series of functional and occupational organizations (Boileau 1983: 114–121). However, Golkar at that time was not a corporatist organization, as it did not play the role of coordinating the interests of a variety of groups within society and communicating those with the government. William Liddle conducted a study on the HKTI and posed that this kind of functional and occupational organization did play the role of communicating farmers' interests to the government, albeit partially (Liddle 1987: 127–146). However, this was too limited in scope to generally define Golkar's nature as corporatist.

Chapter 4

1 The term '*kadre*' mentioned here originates from the French word *cadre*. This word is used to cover a number of quite divergent situations, such as 'village cadre' (*karakterdes*), and 'national cadre' (*kadre bangsa*). 'Village cadre' refers to 'cells' of the organization which played the role of propagating Golkar's and the government's policies to rural areas through propaganda activities and discussion sessions to increase support for Golkar. 'Functional cadre' (*karaknal*) signifies the 'executives' who took a central role in the Golkar organization. 'National cadre' refers to those who played a commanding role in leading the nation. I will use the expression 'executive' whenever appropriate but use 'cadre' otherwise.
2 The KAMI (Indonesian Student's Action Front) was formed across many universities as a federation of anti-communist student groups against the backdrop of the September 30th Affair. It mobilized anti-communist and anti-Sukarno demonstrations in cooperation with the Armed Forces and played a significant role in the ousting of President Sukarno. While the KAMI's headquarters was in Jakarta where many universities such as the University of Indonesia were located, Bandung in the province of West Java, home of the Bandung Institute of Technology, also became a base for the KAMI's activities. Those student activists who were based in Bandung are called the 'Bandung group'.

3 This is the number recorded in a document prepared by Golkar. Whether Golkar actually had over 30,000,000 members cannot be verified.
4 Nevertheless, their qualities as politicians—how they were untarnished by corruption and asserted their opinions even against people in power—were highly recognized. They made a political comeback in the post-Suharto era, with Sarwono joining the MPR as the elected regional representative of Jakarta in 2004 and Rachmat taking office as the State Minister of the Environment under the Yudhoyono government in the same year.
5 Akbar Tandjung extended his power within the Central Executive Board under Golkar Chairman Sudharmono, gradually gaining Suharto's trust. He was appointed as minister over three consecutive terms: as State Minister for Youth and Sports Affairs in 1988, State Minister for Public Housing in 1993 and again as State Minister for Public Housing in 1998 (until May 1998). After Suharto's fall in May 1998, he was selected as the Golkar Party Chairman and even became the Chair of the DPR.
6 They established business enterprises by forming partnerships with fellow businesspeople with whom they were acquainted. For example, Jusuf Kalla co-founded Bukaka with Fadel Muhammad whereas Fahmi Idris co-founded the Kodel Group with Sugeng Suryadi and Yan Darmadi. Agung Laksono started publication of the magazine *Info Bisnis* with Fadel Muhammad and Abrizal Bakrie and collaborated with Abrizal Bakrie again to launch a private television station AN-teve. A Chinese-Indonesian William Soeryadjaya who founded the Astra Group is known for his active support for *pribumi* entrepreneurs. *Pribumi* corporate groups continued to grow into the 1990s and eventually the Suharto family began forming joint enterprises with *pribumi* entrepreneurs.
7 The Chamber of Commerce and Industry (KADIN) was established in 1968. It remained a rather low-profile organization in the 1970s but started to build its presence in the 1980s. The enrolment of KADIN members into Golkar can be regarded as part of such development. The resumption of trade with China in 1990 came as a result of a strong demand by the KADIN, to which the government gave approval (Gitosardjono 1997: 538–539). Despite its pro-government stance, KADIN members were conscious of independence from the government and this was observable from the defeat of Suharto's brother-in-law Probosutedjo by Sukamdani in the 1982 chairmanship election by vote (Pour 2000: 361–362) as well as the 'upset' of the 1994 chairmanship election in which the candidate (a former military officer) who the government had prearranged to become the chair lost the vote to Abrizal Bakrie (Pour 2000: 364–365).
8 The government's surveillance of and control over the ICMI was evident

in the following events. In May 1991, Emha Ainun Nadjib, who was one of the original members of the ICMI, sought to have the ICMI sponsor a small conference on a development project that involved the issue of the displacement of local residents but was later told by an ICMI superior that the organization would not sponsor such conference. Another incident occurred in May 1992 when other ICMI members tried to hold a seminar on human rights issues. This seminar was cancelled by the government for not having obtained a conference permit (Hefner 1993: 29–30).
9 Well-known bureaucrats who used to be HMI members included former chiefs of the National Food Logistics Agency (Bulog) Bustanil Arifin and Beddu Amang, former State Secretary Saadillah Mursid and former Minister of Finance Mar'ie Muhammad.

Chapter 5

1 This law refers to 'Law No.16 on the Composition and Position of Members of the People's Consultative Assembly (MPR), People's Representative Council (DPR) and Regional Representative Council (DPRD)' of 1969 (*Undang-undang No.16 Tahun 1969 tentang Susunan dan Kedudukan MPR, DPR dan DPRD*) and Law No.2, formulated by amending the aforementioned law in 1985 (*Undang-undang No.2 Tahun 1985 tentang Perubahan atas UU No.16 Tahun 1969 tentang Susunan dan Kedudukan MPR, DPR dan DPRD sebagaimana telah diubah dengan Undang-undang No.5 Tahun 1975*).
2 Article 32 of Law No.2 of 1985 which enumerated the positions and rights of the MPR, DPR and DPRD also provided the DPR with rights to revise bills and express and submit opinions, as well as rights regarding diplomatic protocol and so on.
3 This is an extract from the account given by Mohammad Said who was the head of the East Java branch of Golkar (*Media Karya* Apr. 1991: 37).
4 This process in which the local coordinators reduced the list from 2,000 to 1,200 was newly introduced in the Wahono era (*Tempo* Sept. 14, 1991: 27).
5 An interview with Rachmat Witoelar (conducted in Jakarta on April 9, 2003).
6 This group of the 'Generation of 66' was the Association of Members of the Arief Rahman Hakim Front (*Ikatan Keluarga Laskar Ampera Arief Rachman Hakim*). Along with the Chair Fahmi Idris, Akbar Tandjung attended this meeting as one of the members (*Tempo* Oct. 5, 1991: 22).
7 Anang Adenansi died shortly after the announcement of this list.

8 The 'Great Golkar Family' was conveniently interpreted to justify the involvement of the Armed Forces and Ministry of Home Affairs in Golkar's concerns. When the rivalry between Sudharmono and Murdani became the subject of rampant rumors, the Armed Forces displayed hesitance in endorsing Golkar in the election on the grounds that 'the Armed Forces does not need to support a particular organization because it is an entity independent from all political forces', despite being part of the 'Great Golkar Family'. However, later, when the Armed Forces fielded some of their officers as candidates for heads of local branches and Golkar's chair, their reasoning for nominating military officers who had barely engaged in the organization's activities until then was that 'the Armed Forces is a member of the Great Golkar Family'.

9 This kind of incident was unprecedented in the general session of the MPR under the Suharto regime, in which the proceedings always went according to script. This MPR member was immediately removed from the hall and dismissed from the MPR after the general session ended.

10 The table includes only events that took place particularly between the Armed Forces and Golkar, but in fact there were other incidents of disorder not mentioned here. Fukao (1999: 91–134) provides detailed accounts of these incidents in his work.

11 However, although the selection process was subject to this kind of control, 'upsets' did happen, albeit uncommonly. An incident occurred in the gubernatorial election in the Riau Province in 1985, in which the DPRD elected an accompanying candidate rather than the real candidate. Subsequently, a 'discussion' was held after which the elected accompanying candidate declined the post and the real candidate assumed the gubernatorial office (Sudharmono 1997: 349–354).

12 The shooting incident occurred at Santa Cruz cemetery in Dili, the capital of East Timor on November 12, 1991, under the Indonesian occupation. The Indonesian military troop shot demonstrators who marched at the ceremony for two youths of the independence group killed by the military two weeks prior. The Indonesian government and Amnesty International reported that fifty people were killed. Conversely, East Timor, after independence from Indonesia in 2002, reported that more than 500 people were killed in the massacre.

13 Although the Dual function was formulated as a doctrine in the Second Army Seminar held in August 1966, the 'social function' of the Armed Forces was legislated in Law No.20 of 1982 and as for the 'socio-political function', its formal legislation took place six years later, in Law No.2 of 1988 (*UU No.2 Tahun 1988 tentang Prajurit*) (*Forum Keadilan* Oct. 15, 1992: 72).

Chapter 6

1 The 'Great Armed Forces Family' (*Keluarga Besar Angkatan Bersenjata Republik Indonesia*, KBA) is a concept that covers a group of several military-related organizations led by the Armed Forces including the Veterans' Association, Indonesian Women Armed Forces Corps and FKPPI.

2 The Cipayung Group was composed of an Islamic organization the HMI, a Catholic organization the PMKRI, the Indonesian National Party-affiliated GMNI, a Protestant organization the GMKI and the Islamic, NU-affiliated PMII.

3 For example, in Muhammadiyah, the group led by Amien Rais and Syafii Ma'arif that wanted to maintain a distance from the government and its rival group led by Lukman Harun and Din Syamsuddin which tried to get closer to the government coexisted, although in a competitive relationship. The former remained critical of the Suharto regime while some members of the latter group joined Golkar's Central Executive Board or even became members of parliament as Golkar representatives in the Suharto regime.

4 In the KNPI, a formation team of electors and the government had dictated the designation of the chair post until the chairmanship election in the national congress of November 1993 when the full-scale voting system was introduced for the first time. In the 1993 election, Tubagus Haryono, Maulana Isman and Harris Ali Murfi from the FKPPI, Herman Widyananda from the HMI, Kristiya Kartika from the GMNI and Iqbal Assegaf from the GP Ansor were nominated as candidates (*Media Karya* Oct. 1993: 45–46; *Tempo* Nov. 6, 1993: 22). Tubagus Haryono from the FKPPI emerged victorious in the congress, winning forty out of sixty-four votes (*Forum Keadilan* Nov. 25, 1993: 13).

5 For the election of the chair in the KNPI's national congress in 1996, Islamic youth groups such as the HMI and GP Ansor nominated HMI's Taufik Hidayat as a unified candidate, whereas the FKPPI fielded Maulana Isman jointly with the Pancasila Youth and Panca Marga Youth. The latter won the election (*Tiras* Nov. 14, 1996: 84–85; *Gatra* Nov. 16, 1996: 33).

6 An agreement among the Chairman of Golkar, Commander of the Armed Forces and Minister of Home Affairs to elect Indra Bambang Utoyo as the chair of the AMPI is said to have been made in advance of the AMPI national congress of July 1994 (*Forum Keadilan* July 21, 1994: 18).

7 The Pancasila Youth was a semi-militia organization that pledged their loyalty to Suharto. It acted as an informal apparatus of violence in the Suharto regime, carrying out various operations such as the violent elimination of those deemed by the government to be anti-regime, using its members and the *preman* (petty gang members) they controlled.

8 It was required that bills be presented to and approved and signed by the president for them to be formally enshrined into law, after they were passed in the DPR. Even if a bill was passed in the DPR based on the agreement between the DPR and the government, it did not become a valid law without approval from the president. In fact, there was an incident in which the President refused to sign the broadcasting bill that was passed in the DPR in July 1997, alleging that the bill had flaws (*Tiras* July 21, 1997: 54).

9 '*SK* [Letter of Decision] *DPR RI No.10/DPR RI/III/82-83 tanggal 26 Februari 1983*' specified the DPR's mandate and duties as follows: to make laws and formulate budgets in conjunction with the president, to supervise the enforcement of laws, budget execution and the government's policies, to ratify, or agree to, the declaration of war, peace or a treaty made by the president upon deliberation, to debate on audit results concerning the state's financial situation carried out by the Supreme Audit Board and to execute the resolutions adopted in the MPR (*Tiras* June 23, 1997: 22).

10 The official name of the resolution was '*Ketetapan MPR RI /Nomor V/ MPR/1998 tentang Pemberian Tugas dan Wewenang Khusus kepada Presiden/Mandataris MPR RI dalam Rangka Penyuksesan dan Pengamanan Pembangunan Nasional sebagai Pengamalan Pancasila*', which means MPR Resolution No.5 of 1998 concerning the granting of special duties and authorities to the president in relation to the success and maintenance of national development for the implementation of Pancasila.

Chapter 7

1 Other members included Chief State Secretary Murdiono, Minister of Industry and Trade Tunky Ariwibowo and Economic Advisors to the President Widjojo Nitisastro and Ali Wardhana.

2 This Economic and Financial Resilience Council (DPK-EKU) was composed of the following twelve members: Widjojo Nitisastro acting as the Secretary-General, Director General of Taxes of the Ministry of Finance Fuad Bawazir acting as the Vice-Secretary-General, two coordinating ministers, four ministers, the Governor of the BI and three private sector representatives (Djiwandono 2005: 160).

3 The CBS system ensures the stability of the exchange rate by pegging a currency to a strong currency such as US dollars. However, some pointed out that its introduction in Indonesia was questionable on the grounds that it would require a huge amount of foreign currency to maintain the exchange rate and it would not bring the expected effect without having

the combination of a healthy banking system and low inflation rate (Mann 1998: 158; Djiwandono 2005: 189).
4 Some suggested this was Pieter Gontha. He was a board member of the Bimantara Group owned by the President's second son Bambang (Shiraishi 1999: 73–74; Kenward 2002: 75; Djiwandono 2005: 188).
5 The KAMMI was more strongly pro-Islamic than the KAMI, as exemplified by the participation of representatives of the campus Islamic preaching organization (*lembaga dakwah kampus*) based at universities (*Gatra* Apr. 18, 1998: 64).
6 Epistolary interview with former HMI activist legislator Ade Komaruddin (dated October 4, 2006).
7 According to Ade Komaruddin, he hosted a study group (called RESPOND-EO) in Ciputat, southern Jakarta where the State Institute of Islamic Studies (IAIN) Jakarta, his alma mater, was located on a continuous basis since the late 1980s to provide opportunities for interaction and discussion with young student activists. (From an epistolary interview with Ade Komaruddin, September 18, 2006).
8 Epistolary interview with Ade Komaruddin and Ibrahim Ambong (dated September 18, 2006 and August 9, 2006, respectively).
9 Epistolary interview with Ade Komaruddin (dated September 18, 2006).
10 From Eky Syachrudin's essays *Sang Intel* and *The Triple Crisis* (Syachrudin 2006: 33–37, 38–41). The latter first appeared in *Kompas* (May 16, 1998).
11 The Wednesday Meeting originally started as the 'Ramadhan study group' (*pengajian Ramadhan*) in the fasting month of January 1998 (Hudijono and Thayib 2006: 143–144), but the study group continued after the end of Ramadhan.
12 This was a tax proposed by the Jakarta provincial government to solve road congestion in the center of the capital city. The idea was to make it obligatory for ordinary automobiles to display a sticker that cost 5,000 rupiah to reduce the volume of traffic (*Suara Karya* Apr. 23, 1998).
13 Another MPR special session was held in July 2001 during which President Abdurrahman Wahid was dismissed.
14 The procedure was as follows: the DPR submits a memorandum on two occasions describing the grounds on which the president is in violation of the 1945 Constitution or the GBHN and if the president fails to provide a convincing response to the DPR, then the DPR can convene an MPR special session to hold the president to account. Because of this procedure, presumably it would take around six months from the submission of the first memorandum to the convening of a special session.
15 At that time, there was a rivalry within the Armed Forces between

Commander of the Armed Forces Wiranto and Commander of Kostrad Prabowo. Some studies explain that scheming on the part of Prabowo's side was behind the riots in the hope that he would be able to wrest the leadership of the Armed Force from Wiranto if Suharto was forced to resign by provoking a riot and Vice President Habibie with whom Prabowo had a close relationship was promoted to the position of president (Simanjorang 2008: 229–241). On the other hand, others argue that Prabowo was not in a position to gain anything from the riot but rather made into a scapegoat, labeled as the conspirator behind the events (Zon 2004: 132).

16 Subsequently, the President explained that the indication of the DPR factions' view was sufficient since the factional composition in the DPR reflected its counterpart in the MPR (Sekretariat Jenderal DPR-RI 1998: 19–20).

17 Epistolary interview with Ade Komaruddin (dated September 18, 2006).

18 Epistolary interview with Ade Komaruddin (dated September 18, 2006). Those who signed this petition were the following twenty: Abu Hasan Sazili, Zamharir, Siti Ainomi Lengkong, Usman Ermulan, Azhar Romli, Ariady Achmad, Ferry Mursyidan Baldan, Engkoswara, Eky Syachrudin, Ade Komaruddin, Ganjar Razuni, Priyo Budi Santoso, Hajriyanto Thohari, Muhammad Iqbal Assegaf, Yahya Zaini, Yanto, Ibnu Munzir, Fachri Andi Leluasa, Ibrahim Ambong and Laode Kamaluddin (*Suara Karya* May 19, 1998).

19 One of the episodes that describes the antagonism between them after both parties took their respective offices concerned Kopassus. Wiranto was frustrated that the President had selected an officer for the position of commander of Kopassus nominated by Prabowo (Muchdi) over the rival candidate he backed (I Nyoman Suwisma), while Prabowo was annoyed that Wiranto had raised an objection to his idea of creating a helicopter troop in Kopassus (Simanjorang 2008: 232).

20 The presidential decree concerning the establishment of the KOPKKN was dated May 18. However, Suharto actually only handed this decree to the newly designated Commander and Vice Commander of the KOPKKN Wiranto and Subagyo on the night of May 20. Subagyo claims that it was the night of May 20 that Wiranto and he received the presidential decree from the President (Sukmawati 2004: 176–177). As for Wiranto, although he does not clearly mention the date he received this decree in his memoir, it can be inferred that it was the night of May 20 from his recollection of the situation at the time where he mentioned the resignation of the fourteen cabinet members (Azhari 2003: 82–87).

21 In effect, the establishment of the KOPKKN did not occur. When Habibie

took over the presidency from Suharto, he requested that Wiranto continue in the office of the Armed Forces Commander and Minister of Defense and Security. When shown the presidential decree concerning the establishment of the KOPKKN and asked for his instruction by Wiranto, Habibie directed him to keep the document himself, just as he did to Suharto (Habibie 2006: 79–80). Habibie later dismissed Prabowo as the Kostrad Commander despite their close personal relationship, based on the information from Wiranto that Prabowo was conducting suspicious activities (Habibie 2006: 81–84, 94–95, 100–104).

22 The general meeting of the Central Executive Board of Golkar held on the night of May 18 is mentioned in Gafur (2000: 93–97) and an epistolary interview with Ade Komaruddin (dated September 3, 2006).

23 Although the reformist movement in the business community was more subtle when compared with others, some did voice their support for the reformist movement and removal of the President. For example, Hotasi Nababan launched the 'Solidarity of Professionals for Reform' and started a petition among entrepreneurs to demand the holding of an MPR special session, whereas Arifin Panigoro participated in Amien Rais's MAR. Jusuf Kalla also expressed his full support for the reformist movement. Other entrepreneurs who also made statements in support of the reformist movement include Fadel Muhammad, Laksamana Sukardi, Syarif Tando, Sugeng Suryadi, Sofyan Wanandi and M. S. Hidayat (*Warta Ekonomi* May 25, 1998: 18–23; *Kompas* May 19, 1998). Some of them were the so-called 'Ginandjar boys', *pribumi* entrepreneurs who were close to Coordinating Minister for Economy and Finance Ginandjar.

24 DPR member Ade Komaruddin evacuated his family upon receipt of a threat from an FKPPI member. They returned to the dormitory for DPR members located in Jakarta after their safety was guaranteed by the Chair of the FKPPI Youth Asep Sudjana. (From an epistolary interview with Ade Komaruddin dated September 18, 2006).

25 Vice-Chair of the DPR leadership Syarwan Hamid who represented the Armed Forces faction stated that he supported the request for the President's resignation as a DPR member rather than as a representative of the Armed Forces based on the agreement reached in the DPR leadership (Syam 2008: 110).

26 Nurcholish is said to have told the President at this meeting that if the new organization was going to be a think-tank, then its function would not overlap with the DPR, and also provided advice that the President himself should not chair the committee (*Kompas* May 21, 1998). In addition, Nurcholish suggested a review of the initial proposal that specified the date

of the election as the year 2000 and pushed for an election in three months' time (Gafur 2000: 115).
27 They claimed that the President's reform plan that included rescheduling the election to an earlier date was in violation of the clause that read 'the general election will be held in 2002' in the resolution of the GBHN adopted in the MPR general session in March 1998 (*Kompas* May 21, 1998).
28 Three economic ministers were absent. One of these three was sick and the remaining two were Minister of Industry and Trade Bob Hasan and Minister of Finance Fuad Bawazir who were close to the President (Abeng 2001: 42; Makka 2008: 69; Kartasasmita 2013: 191, epistolary interview with Ary Mardjono dated November 1, 2006).
29 The central bank of Indonesia, the BI, had ceased operation for two days and there were reports of problems with the procurement of food (Makka 2008: 79, 158, 184; Kartasasmita 2013: 191–192).
30 Epistolary interview with Ary Mardjono (dated September 3, 2006) and Makka (2008: 185). President's Suharto's new cabinet was scheduled to be announced on May 21.
31 Although strictly speaking it was not a letter of resignation since it presented an intention to refuse to join the new cabinet, it can be regarded as a de facto resignation as it was highly likely that most economic ministers would be included in the new cabinet which was to be formed the following day.
32 Epistolary interview with Ade Komaruddin (dated September 18, 2006).

Conclusion

1 In Tunisia, President Ben Ali who inherited power from Bourguiba adopted an electoral system that was favorable to the existing major political party. It was a system in which candidates were elected through district candidate lists and winning candidate lists were granted all seats in the districts. Therefore, while candidates from the opposition Islamist party garnered a total of thirty percent of the popular vote, most seats were claimed by the Democratic Constitutional Rally (RCD), a successor party of the former ruling party (Waltz 1995: 59). The Islamist party al-Nahda denounced the election results as fraud and declared war on the government, resorting to armed resistance (Kisaichi 2004: 190), to which the government responded with a hard-line crackdown. In Ivory Coast, Bédié, who became president following the death of Houphouët, tried to introduce a clause which imposed a restriction concerning candidate's nationality to the electoral law to bar his political rival Alassane Dramane Ouattara from participating in the

presidential election, after having made him withdraw from the ruling party, in an attempt to remove him from the political stage. As was the case in Tunisia, the newly formulated election law favored the existing major party as it employed the winner-takes-all system which granted all the seats to the party candidate list with the most votes based on the single-seat constituency system (A. Satō 2005: 105–106). As a result, the country suffered from serious political disorder caused by the return of dictatorship, followed by a coup and then a civil war.

Bibliography

Books and articles in English and Indonesian

Abdulgani-KNAPP, Retnowati (2007) *Soeharto: The Life and Legacy of Indonesia's Second President* (Edisi Bahasa Indonesia), Jakarta: Kata Hasta Pustaka.

Abeng, Tanri (2001) *Indonesia, Inc.: Privatising State-owned Enterprises*, Singapore: Times Academic Press.

Aditjondro, George Junus (1998) *Dari Soeharto ke Habibie, Guru Kencing Berdiri, Murid Kencing Berlari: Kedua Puncak Korupsi, Kolusi, dan Nepotisme Rezim Orde Baru*, Jakarta: Pijar Indonesia.

Ali, Fachri (2003) 'Nurcholish Madjid sebagai "Guru Bangsa"', in A. K. Sukandi *Prof. Dr. Nurcholish Madjid: Jejak Pemikiran dari Pembaharu sampai Guru Bangsa* (Edisi Revisi), Jakarta: Pustaka Pelajar, pp. xxii–xxvii.

Amirmachmud (1987) *H. Amirmachmud, Prajurit Pejuang: Otobiografi*, Jakarta: Panitia Penerbitan Otobiografi Bapak H. Amirmachmud.

Anderson, Benedict O'G. (1983) 'Old state, new society: Indonesia's New Order in comparative historical perspective', *Journal of Asian Studies*, May, XLII(3): 477–496.

Anderson, Benedict O'G. (1990) 'The idea of power in Javanese culture', in *Language and Power: Exploring Political Cultures in Indonesia*, Ithaca: Cornell University Press, pp. 17–77.

Anderson, Benedict O'G. and Ruth T. McVey (with the assistance of Frederick P. Bunnell) (1971) *A Preliminary Analysis of the October 1, 1965, Coup in Indonesia*, Interim Report Series, Ithaca: Modern Indonesia Project Southeast Asia Program, Cornell University.

Anderson, Lisa (1986) *The State and Social Transformation in Tunisia and Libya, 1830–1980*, New Jersey: Princeton University Press.

Anwar, Mohammad Arsjad, Aris Ananta and Ari Kuncoro (eds.) (2007) *Kesan Para Sahabat tentang Widjojo Nitisastro*, Jakarta: Penerbit Buku Kompas.

Aspinall, Edward (2005) *Opposing Suharto: Compromise, Resistance, and Regime Change in Indonesia*, Stanford: Stanford University Press.

Aspinall, Edward, Herb Feith and Gerry van Klinken (1999) *The Last Days of President Suharto*, Clayton: Monash Asia Institute, Monash University.

Azhari, Aidul Fitriciada (2003) *Dari Catatan Wiranto, Jenderal Purnawirawan Bersaksi di Tengah Badai*, Jakarta: IDe Indonesia.

Bachtiar, Harsja W. (1988) *Siapa Dia?, Perwira Tinggi Tentara Nasional Indonesia Angkatan Darat (TNI-AD)*, Jakarta: Djambatan.
Boileau, Julian M. (1983) *Golkar: Functional Group Politics in Indonesia*, Jakarta: Centre for Strategic and International Studies.
Boudreau, Vincent (1999) 'Diffusing democracy? People power in Indonesia and the Philippines', *Bulletin of Concerned Asian Scholars*, October–December, 31(4): 3–18.
Bratton, Michael and Nicolas van de Walle (1994) 'Neopatrimonial regimes and political transitions in Africa', *World Politics*, July, 46: 453–489.
Bratton, Michael and Nicolas van de Walle (1997) *Democratic Experiments in Africa: Regime Transitions in Comparative Perspective*, Cambridge: Cambridge University Press.
Brownlee, Jason (2002) '...And yet they persist: Explaining survival and transition in neopatrimonial regimes', *Studies in Comparative International Development*, Fall, 37(3): 35–63.
Budiman, Arief, Barbara Hatley and Damien Kingsbury (eds.) (1999) *Reformasi: Crisis and Change in Indonesia*, Clayton: Monash Asia Institute, Monash University.
Butarbutar, Benny S. (2003) *Soeyono: Bukan Puntung Rokok*, Jakarta: Ridma Foundation.
Cahyono, Heru (1998) *Pangkopkamtib Jenderal Soemitro dan Peristiwa 15 Januari '74*, Jakarta: Pustaka Sinar Harapan.
Canonica-Walangitang, Resy (2003) *The End of Suharto's New Order in Indonesia*, Frankfurt am Main: Peter Lang.
Chandra, Siddharth and Douglas Kammen (2002) 'Generating reforms and reforming generations: Military politics in Indonesia's democratic transition and consolidation', *World Politics*, October, 55: 96–136.
Chehabi, H. E. and Juan J. Linz (eds.) (1998a) *Sultanistic Regimes*, Baltimore: The Johns Hopkins University Press.
Chehabi, H. E. and Juan J. Linz (1998b) 'A theory of sultanism 1: A type of nondemocratic rule', in H. E. Chehabi and Juan J. Linz (eds.), *Sultanistic Regimes*, Baltimore: The Johns Hopkins University Press, pp. 3–25.
Chehabi, H. E. and Juan J. Linz (1998c) 'A theory of sultanism 2: Genesis and demise of sultanistic regimes', in H. E. Chehabi and Juan J. Linz (eds.), *Sultanistic Regimes*, Baltimore: The Johns Hopkins University Press, pp. 26–48.
Cokro, Heru (2008) *Pendudukan Gedung DPR/MPR: Kesaksian Aktivis Mahasiswa 1998*, Jakarta: Teraju.
Crook, Richard (1989) 'Patrimonialism, administrative effectiveness and economic development in Côte d'Ivoire', *African Affairs*, April, 88(351): 205–228.

Crouch, Harold (1979) 'Patrimonialism and military rule in Indonesia', *World Politics*, July, XXX(14): 571–587.
Crouch, Harold (1988) *The Army and Politics in Indonesia (Revised Edition)*, Ithaca: Cornell University Press.
Danial, Akhmad (2001) 'Ferry Mursyidan Baldan: Menjadi politisi untuk memaknai hidup', in S. S. Suradi, *Sepuluh Anggota DPR Terbaik: Pilihan Wartawan*, Jakarta: Millennium Publisher, pp. 76–96.
Djafar, Zainuddin (2006) *Rethinking the Indonesian Crisis*, Jakarta: Pustaka Jaya.
Djiwandono, J. Soedradjad (2005) *Bank Indonesia and the Crisis: An Insider's Review*, Singapore: Institute of Southeast Asian Studies.
Domínguez, Jorge I. (1998) 'The Batista regime in Cuba', in H. E. Chehabi and Juan J. Linz (eds.), *Sultanistic Regimes*, Baltimore: The Johns Hopkins University Press, pp. 113–131.
Dwipayana, G. and K. H. Ramadhan (1989) *Soeharto, Pikiran, Ucapan, dan Tindakan Saya: Otobiografi seperti Dipaparkan kepada G. Dwipayana dan Ramadhan K. H.*, Jakarta: Citra Lamtoro Gung Persada.
Effendy, Bahtiar (2003) 'Menimbang perjalanan politik Akbar Tandjung', in Deden Ridwan and Muhadjirin, *Membangun Konsensus: Pemikiran dan Praktek Politik Akbar Tandjung*, Jakarta: Pustaka Sinar Harapan, pp. 321–340.
Eisenstadt, S. N. (1973) *Traditional Patrimonialism and Modern Neopatrimonialism*, London: Sage Publications.
Eklöf, Stefan (1999) *Indonesian Politics in Crisis: The Long Fall of Suharto, 1996–98*, Copenhagen: Nordic Institute of Asian Studies (NIAS).
Elson, R. E. (2001) *Suharto: A Political Biography*, Cambridge: Cambridge University Press.
Emmerson, Donald K. (1983) 'Understanding the New Order: Bureaucratic pluralism in Indonesia', *Asian Survey*, November, XXIII(11): 1220–1241.
Emmerson, Donald K. (ed.) (1999) *Indonesia beyond Suharto: Polity, Economy, Society and Transition*, New York: M. E. Shape.
Fauré, Yves-André (1989) 'Côte d'Ivoire: Analysing the Crisis', in Donal B. Cruise O'Brien, John Dunn and Richard Rathbone (eds.), *Contemporary West African States*, Cambridge: Cambridge University Press, pp. 59–73.
Fauré, Yves-André (1993) 'Democracy and realism: Reflections on the Case of Côte d'Ivoire', *Africa*, 63(3): 313–329.
Forrester, Geoff and R. J. May (eds.) (1999) *The Fall of Soeharto*, Singapore: Select Books.
Gafur, Abdul (1985) 'Pembinaan organisasi kepemudaan', *Derap Langkah Generasi Muda Indonesia*, Jakarta: Yayasan Karya Pemuda Indonesia, pp. 133–236.

Gafur, Abdul (2000) *Hari-hari Terakhir Seorang Presiden*, Jakarta: Pustaka Sinar Harapan.
Geddes, Barbara (1999) 'What do we know about democratization after twenty years?', *Annual Review of Political Science*, 2: 115–144.
Gilberg, Trond (1990) *Nationalism and Communism in Romania: The Rise and Fall of Ceausescu's Personal Dictatorship*, Boulder: Westview Press.
Gitosardjono, Sukamdani Sahid (1997) 'Bapak Sudharmono di mata wirausaha swasta', in *Kesan dan Kenangan dari Teman: 70 Tahun H. Sudharmono, S. H.*, Jakarta: Grasindo, pp. 534–539.
Goodwin, Jeff and Theda Skocpol (1989) 'Explaining revolutions in the contemporary third world', *Politics and Society*, December, 17(4): 489–509.
Habibie, Bacharuddin Jusuf (2006) *Detik-detik yang Menentukan: Jalan Panjang Indonesia Menuju Demokrasi*, Jakarta: THC Mandiri.
Hartlyn, Jonathan (1998) 'The Trujillo Regime in the Dominican Republic', in H. E. Chehabi and Juan J. Linz (eds.), *Sultanistic Regimes*, Baltimore: The Johns Hopkins University Press, pp. 85–112.
Hefner, Robert W. (1993) 'Islam, state and civil society: ICMI and the struggle for the Indonesian middle class', *Indonesia*, 56: 1–35.
Hefner, Robert W. (2000) *Civil Islam: Muslims and Democratization in Indonesia*, Princeton: Princeton University Press.
Hisyam, Usamah (ed.) (1999) *Feisal Tandjung, Terbaik untuk Rakyat, Terbaik Bagi ABRI*, Jakarta: Yayasan Dharmapena Nusantara.
Honna, Jun (2003) *Military Politics and Democratization in Indonesia*, London: RoutledgeCurzon.
Hudijono, Anwar and Anshari Thayib (2006) *Darah Guru, Darah Muhammadiyah: Perjalanan Hidup Abdul Malik Fadjar*, Jakarta: Penerbit Buku Kompas.
Huntington, Samuel (1991) *The Third Wave: Democratization in the Late Twentieth Century*, Oklahoma: University of Oklahoma Press.
Hutchcroft, Paul D. (1993) 'Predatory oligarchy, patrimonial state: The politics of private domestic commercial banking in the Philippines', a Dissertation Presented to the Faculty of the Graduate School of Yale University in Candidacy for the Degree of Doctor of Philosophy, May 1993.
Hutchcroft, Paul D. (1998) *Booty Capitalism: The Politics of Banking in the Philippines*, Ithaca: Cornell University Press.
Irsyam, Mahrus (1984) *Ulama dan Partai Politik: Upaya Mengatasi Krisis*, Jakarta: Yayasan Perkhidmatan.
Jackson, Karl D. (1978) 'Bureaucratic polity: A theoretical framework for the analysis of power and communications in Indonesia', in Karl D. Jackson and Lucian W. Pye (eds.) *Political Power and Communications in Indonesia*, Berkeley: University of California Press, pp. 3–22.

Jackson, Robert and Carl G. Rosberg (1982) *Personal Rule in Black Africa: Prince, Autocrat, Prophet, Tyrant*, Berkeley: University of California Press.

Jenkins, David (1984) *Suharto and His Generals: Indonesian Military Politics 1975–1983* (Third Edition), Ithaca: Cornell Modern Indonesia Project.

Karma, Mara (2001) *Ibnu Sutowo, Mengemban Misi Revolusi, sebagai Doktor, Tentara dan Pejuang Minyak Bumi*, Jakarta: Pustaka Sinar Harapan.

Kartasasmita, Ginandjar (1997) 'Pak Dhar guru saya', in *Kesan dan Kenangan dari Teman: 70 Tahun H. Sudharmono, S. H.*, Jakarta: Grasindo, pp. 159–187.

Kartasasmita, Ginandjar (2013) *Managing Indonesia's Transformation: An Oral History*, Singapore: World Scientific Publishing.

Katouzian, Homa (1998) 'The Pahlavi Regime in Iran', in H. E. Chehabi and Juan J. Linz (eds.), *Sultanistic Regimes*, Baltimore: The Johns Hopkins University Press, pp. 182–205.

Kenward, Lloyd R. (2002) *From the Trenches: The First Year of Indonesia's Crisis of 1997/98 as Seen from the World Bank's Office in Jakarta*, Jakarta: Centre for Strategic and International Studies.

King, Dwight (1982) 'Indonesia's New Order as a bureaucratic polity, a neopatrimonial regime or a bureaucratic-authoritarian regime: What differences does it make?', in Benedict Anderson and Audrey Kahin (eds.), *Interpreting Indonesian Politics: Thirteen Contributions to the Debate*, Ithaca: Cornell Modern Indonesian Project, Southeast Asia Program, Cornell University (Interim Reports Series), pp. 104–116.

Kingsbury, Damien (2002) *The Politics of Indonesia* (Second Edition), Melbourne: Oxford University Press.

Kingsbury, Damien (2003) *Power Politics and the Indonesian Military*, London: RoutledgeCurzon.

Laksono, H. R. Agung (2004) *Rumah Terindah untuk Rakyat: Perjalanan dan Pandangan Politik, Menuju Indonesia yang Kita Cita-citakan*, Jakarta: PT Info Jaya Abadi.

Liddle, William (1985) 'Soeharto's Indonesia: Personal rule and political institutions', *Pacific Affairs*, September, 58(1): 68–90.

Liddle, William (1987) 'The politics of shared growth: Some Indonesian cases', *Comparative Politics*, January, 19(2): 127–146.

Liddle, William (1999) 'Indonesia's democratic opening', *Government and Opposition*, 34(1): 94–116.

Linz, Juan J. (1975) 'Totalitarian and authoritarian regimes', in F. Greenstein and N. Polsby (eds.), *Macropolitical Theory* (Handbook of political science, vol. 3), Addison Wesley: Reading Mass, pp. 175–411.

Linz, Juan J. (2000) *Totalitarian and Authoritarian Regimes: With a Major New Introduction*, Boulder: Lynne Rienner Publishers.
Linz, Juan J. and Alfred Stepan (1996) *Problems of Democratic Transition and Consolidation: Southern Europe, South America, and Post-communist Europe*, Baltimore: The Johns Hopkins University Press.
MacIntyre, Andrew (1990) *Business and Politics in Indonesia*, Sydney: Allen & Unwin.
MacIntyre, Andrew (1992) 'Politics and the reorientation of economic policy in Indonesia', in MacIntyre and Jayasuriya (eds.), *The Dynamics of Economic Policy Reform in South-east Asia and the South-west Pacific*, Singapore: Oxford University Press, pp. 138–157.
MacIntyre, Andrew (2003) *The Power of Institutions: Political Architecture and Governance*, Ithaca: Cornell University Press.
Madjid, Nurcholish (2003) 'Sekapur sirih', in Deden Ridwan and Muhadjirin, *Membangun Konsensus: Pemikiran dan Praktek Politik Akbar Tandjung*, Jakarta: Pustaka Sinar Harapan, pp. xvii–xxii.
Makka, A. Makmur (2008) *Sidang Kabinet Terakhir Orde Baru: 12 Jam Sebelum Presiden Soeharto Mundur*, Jakarta: Penerbit Republika.
Mangiang, Masmimar (ed.) (2000) *Lukman Harun dalam Lintasan Sejarah dan Politik*, Jakarta: Yayasan Lukman Harun.
Mann, Richard (1998) *Economic Crisis in Indonesia: The Full Story*, Jakarta: Gateway Books.
Massadiah, Egy (ed.) (1993) *Top Pengusaha Indonesia, 1 dan 2*, Jakarta: Ciptawidya Swara.
McCulloh, Lesley (2003) 'Trifungsi: The role of the Indonesian military in business', in Jörn Brömmelhörster and Wolf-Christian Paes (eds.), *The Military as an Economic Actor: Soldiers in Business*, Hampshire: Palgrave Macmillan, pp. 94–123.
McLeod, Ross H. (1999) 'Indonesia's crisis and future prospects', in Karl D. Jackson (ed.), *Asian Contagion: The Causes and Consequences of a Financial Crisis*, Boulder: Westview Press, pp. 209–240.
Médard, Jean-François (1982) 'The underdeveloped state in tropical Africa: Political clientelism or neo-patrimonialism?', in Christopher Clapham (ed.), *Private Patronage and Public Power: Political Clientelism in the Modern State*, London: Frances Pinter, pp. 162–192.
Mietzner, Marcus (2009) *Military Politics, Islam, and the State in Indonesia: From Turbulent Transition to Democratic Consolidation*, Singapore: Institute of Southeast Asian Studies.
Mochammad, Ade Komaruddin (ed.) (1993) *Pengadilan Sejarah: Otobiografi Soehardiman*, Jakarta: Yayasan Bina Produktivitas.

Murphy, Emma C. (1999) *Economic and Political Change in Tunisia: From Bourguiba to Ben Ali*, London: MacMillan Press (in association with the University of Durham).

Murtopo, Ali (1973) *Dasar-dasar Pemikiran tentang Akselerasi Modernisasi Pembangunan 25 Tahun*, Jakarta: Centre for Strategic and International Studies.

Murtopo, Ali (1974) *Strategi Politik Nasional*, Jakarta: Centre for Strategic and International Studies.

Nicholls, David (1998) 'The Duvalier Regime in Haiti', in H. E. Chehabi and Juan J. Linz (eds.), *Sultanistic Regimes*, Baltimore: The Johns Hopkins University Press, pp. 153–181.

Notosusanto, Nugroho (ed.) (1985) *Tercapainya Konsensus Nasional 1966–1969*, Jakarta: Balai Pustaka.

Notosusanto, Nugroho and Ismail Saleh (1987) *The Coup Attempt of the 'September 30 Movement' in Indonesia* (Second Edition), Jakarta: Headquarters of the Indonesian Armed Forces, Centre for Armed Forces History and Tradition.

O'Donnell, Guillermo and Philippe C. Schmitter (1986) *Transitions from Authoritarian Rule: Tentative Conclusions and Uncertain Democracies*, Baltimore: The Johns Hopkins University Press.

Omar, Irwan and Muhammad Najib (2003) *Putra Nusantara, Son of the Indonesian Archipelago: Muhammad Amien Rais*, Singapore: Stamford Press.

O'Rourke, Kevin (2002) *Reformasi: The Struggle for Power in Post-Soeharto Indonesia*, Sydney: Allen & Unwin.

Pangaribuan, Robinson (1995) *The Indonesian State Secretariat 1945–1993* (translated by Vedi Hadiz), Jakarta: Pustaka Sinar Harapan.

Parikesit, Suparwan G. and Krisna R. Sempurnadjaja (1995) *H. Alamsjah Ratu Perwiranegara: Perjalanan Hidup Seorang Anak Yatim Piatu*, Jakarta: Pustaka Sinar Harapan.

Perthes, Volker (1995) *The Political Economy of Syria under Asad*, New York: I. B. Tauris.

Perthes, Volker (ed.) (2004) *Arab Elites: Negotiating the Politics of Change*, Boulder: Lynne Rienner Publishers.

Pierret, Thomas (2013) *Religion and State in Syria: The Sunni Ulama from Coup to Revolution*, Cambridge: Cambridge University Press.

Pompe, Sebastiaan (2005) *The Indonesian Supreme Court: A Study of Institutional Collapse*, Ithaca: Cornell Southeast Asia Program, Cornell University.

Pour, Julius (2000) *A. A. Baramuli S. H. Menggugat Politik Zaman*, Jakarta: Pustaka Sinar Harapan.
Pradjamanggala, Tatto S. (2000) *Perjalanan*, Jakarta: Pustaka Sinar Harapan.
Prasetyo, Stanley Adi (ed.) (1999) *Golkar Retak?*, Jakarta: Institute Studi Arus Informasi (ISAI).
Prawiro, Radius (1998) *Radius Prawiro: Kiprah, Peran dan Pemikiran*, Jakarta: Grafiti.
Przeworski, Adam (1991) *Democracy and the Market: Political and Economic Reforms in Eastern Europe and Latin America*, Cambridge: Cambridge University Press.
Putnam, Robert (1993) *Making Democracy Work: Civic Traditions in Modern Italy*, Princeton: Princeton University Press.
Ramadhan, K. H. and Sugiarta Sriwibawa (1999) *Demi Bangsa: Liku-liku Pengabdian Prof. Dr. Midian Sirait, dari Guru SR Porsea sampai Guru Besar ITB, Otobiografi*, Jakarta: Pustaka Sinar Harapan.
Ranuwihardjo, Dahlan (1997) '50 tahun sejarah perjuangan HMI turut menegakkan dan membangun Negara Kesatuan Republik Indonesia', in Ramli H. M. Yusuf, *50 Tahun HMI, Mengabdi Republik*, Jakarta: Lembaga Studi Pembangunan Indonesia, pp. 3–15.
Reeve, David (1985) *Golkar of Indonesia: An Alternative to the Party System*, Singapore: Oxford University Press.
Ridwan, Deden and Muhadjirin (2003) *Membangun Konsensus: Pemikiran dan Praktek Politik Akbar Tandjung*, Jakarta: Pustaka Sinar Harapan.
Riggs, Fred W. (1966) *Thailand: The Modernization of a Bureaucratic Polity*, Honolulu: East-west Center Press.
Robison, Richard (1986) *Indonesia: The Rise of Capital*, Sydney: Allen & Unwin.
Robison, Richard and Vedi R. Hadiz (2003) *Reorganizing Power in Indonesia: The Politics of Oligarchy in an Age of Markets*, London: RoutledgeCurzon.
Roth, Guenther (1968) 'Personal rulership, patrimonialism, and empire-building in the new states', *World Politics*, January, 20(2): 194–206.
Ryter, Loren (2001) 'Pemuda Pancasila: The last loyalist free men of Suharto's order?', in Benedict O'G Anderson (ed.), *Violence and the State in Suharto's Indonesia*, Ithaca: Cornell University, Southeast Asia Program Publications.
Salim, Emil (2000) *Kembali ke Jalan Lurus: Esai-esai 1966–99*, Jakarta: AlvaBet.
Schwarz, Adam (1999) *A Nation in Waiting: Indonesia's Search for Stability*, Sydney: Allen & Unwin.
Simanjorang, Raymond R. (ed.) (2008) *Kerusuhan Mei 1998: Fakta, Data dan*

Analisa, Jakarta: Solidaritas Nusa Bangsa dan Asosiasi Penasehat Hukum dan Hak Asasi Manusia Indonesia.

Snyder, Richard (1992) 'Explaining transitions from neopatrimonial dictatorships', *Comparative Politics*, July, 24(4): 379–399.

Snyder, Richard (1998) 'Paths out of Sultanistic regimes: Combining structural and voluntarist perspectives', in H. E. Chehabi and Juan J. Linz (eds.), *Sultanistic Regimes*, Baltimore: The Johns Hopkins University Press, pp. 49–81.

Soesatyo, Bambang (1995) *HIPMI: Gerakan dan Pemikiran*, Jakarta: Info Bisnis.

Sriwidodo, Rayani (2002) *Jenderal dari Pesantren Legok: Memoar 80 Tahun Achmad Tirtosudiro*, Jakarta: Pustaka Jaya.

Stacher, Joshua (2012) *Adaptable Autocrats: Regime Power in Egypt and Syria*, California: Stanford University Press.

Sudharmono (1997) *Sudharmono, S. H., Pengalaman dalam Masa Pengabdian: Sebuah Otobiografi*, Jakarta: Grasindo.

Sukmawati, Carmelia (2004) *Subagyo H. S.: Kasad dari Piyungan*, Jakarta: Aksara Karunia.

Suny, Ismail (2000) 'Keterlibatan Muhammadiyah dalam percaturan politik', in Masmimar Mangiang, (ed.) *Lukman Harun dalam Lintasan Sejarah dan Politik*, Jakarta: Yayasan Lukman Harun, pp. 138–145.

Suryadinata, Leo (1989) *Military Ascendancy and Political Culture: A Study of Indonesia's Golkar*, Athens: Ohio University Center for International Studies.

Sutjipto, S. H. (ed.) (1966) *ABRI Pengemban Suara Hati Nurani Rakjat (keputusan-keputusan sidang umum ke-IV Madjelis Permusjawaratan Rakjat Sementara)*, Djakarta: MATOA.

Syachrudin, Eki (2006) *Moral Politik: Sebuah Refleksi Eki Syachrudin*, Jakarta: LP3ES.

Syam, Firdaus (2008) *Berhentinya Soeharto: Fakta dan Kesaksian Harmoko*, Jakarta: Gria Media Prima.

Tambunan, A. S. S. (1986) *Pemilihan Umum di Indonesia dan Susunan dan Kedudukan MPR, DPR, dan DPRD*, Jakarta: Binacipta.

Tandjung, Akbar (1997) 'Tri Sukses dan Panca Bhakti Golkar: Catatan untuk 70 tahun Pak Dhar', in *Kesan dan Kenangan dari Teman: 70 Tahun H. Sudharmono, S. H.*, Jakarta: Grasindo, pp. 334–340.

Tanter, Richard (1990) 'The totalitarian ambition: Intelligence and security agencies in Indonesia', in Arief Budiman (ed.), *State and Civil Society in Indonesia*, Clayton: Center of Southeast Asian Studies, Monash University, pp. 215–288.

Tempo (1986) *Apa dan Siapa, Sejumlah Orang Indonesia 1985–1986*, Jakarta: Grafitipers.
Thompson, Mark R. (1995) *The Anti-Marcos Struggle: Personalistic Rule and Democratic Transition in the Philippines*, New Haven: Yale University Press.
Thompson, Mark R. (1998) 'The Marcos regime in the Philippines', in H. E. Chehabi and Juan J. Linz (eds.), *Sultanistic Regimes*, Baltimore: The Johns Hopkins University Press, pp. 206–230.
Tim Penyusun IRSED (1999) *Syarwan Hamid: Dari Orde Baru ke Orde Reformasi*, Jakarta: Mutiara Sumber Widya.
Tim Redaksi Tatanusa, Suradji and Pularjono (2001) *Himpunan Beranotasi Ketetapan MPR-RI 1960–2001*, Jakarta: PT Tatanusa.
Tismaneanu, Vladimir (1989) 'Personal power and political crisis in Romania', *Government and Opposition*, Spring, 24(2): 177–198.
Tobing, Jacob (1997) 'Bersama Pak Dhar menjadi anggota DPP Golkar, 1983–1988', in *Kesan dan Kenangan dari Teman: 70 Tahun H. Sudharmono, S. H.*, Jakarta: Grasindo, pp. 394–400.
Tomsa, Dirk (2006) 'The defeat of centralized paternalism: Factionalism, assertive regional cadres, and the long fall of Golkar Chairman Akbar Tandjung', *Indonesia*, April, 81: 1–22.
Tomsa, Dirk (2008) *Party Politics and Democratization in Indonesia: Golkar in the Post-Suharto Era*, London: Routledge.
Tripp, Charles (2000) *A History of Iraq* (Edition 2), Cambridge: Cambridge University Press.
Uhlin, Anders (1997) *Indonesia and the 'Third Wave of Democratization': The Indonesian Pro-Democracy Movement in a Changing World*, New York: St. Martin's Press.
Van Dijk, Kees (2001) *A Country in Despair: Indonesia between 1997 and 2000*, Jakarta: Koninklijk Instituut voor Taal-, Land- En Volkenkunde (KITLV) Press.
Vatikiotis, Michael (1999) 'Romancing the dual function: Indonesia's Armed Forces and the Fall of Soeharto', in Geoff Forrester and R. J. May (eds.), *The Fall of Soeharto*, Singapore: Select Books, pp. 154–166.
Waltz, Susan (1991) 'Clientelism and reform in ben Ali's Tunisia', in I. William Zartman (ed.), *Tunisia: The Political Economy of Reform*, Boulder: Lynne Rienner Publishers, pp. 29–44.
Waltz, Susan (1995) *Human Rights and Reform: Changing the Face of North African Politics*, Berkeley: University of California Press.
Ward, Ken (1974) *The 1971 Election in Indonesia: An East Java Case Study*, Clayton: Monash University, Centre of Southeast Asian Studies.

Weber, Max (1978) *Economy and Society: An Outline of Interpretive Sociology*, edited by Guenther Roth and Claus Wittich, Berkeley: University California Press.
Widoyoko, Danang et al. (2003) *Bisnis Militer Mencari Legitimasi*, Jakarta: Indonesia Corruption Watch.
Wiwoho, B. and Banjar Chaeruddin (1990) *Memori Jenderal Yoga sebagaimana Diceritakan kepada Penulis B. Wiwoho dan Banjar Chaeruddin*, Jakarta: Bina Rena Pariwara.
Wurfel, David (1988) *Filipino Politics: Development and Decay*, Ithaca: Cornell University Press.
Yusuf, Ramli H. M. (1999) *Partai Politik Reformasi dan Masa Depan: 70 Tahun Buya H. Ismail Hasan Metareum, S. H.*, Jakarta: Pustaka Lembaga Studi Pembangunan Indonesia.
Zaghlul, Zarlons (1997) 'Bapak Sudharmono, S. H., figur seorang pemimpin yang patut ditiru keteladanannya', in *Kesan dan Kenangan dari Teman: 70 Tahun H. Sudharmono, S. H.*, Jakarta: Grasindo, pp. 289–297.
Zartman, I. William (1991) 'The conduct of political reform: The path toward democracy', in I. William Zartman (ed.), *Tunisia: The Political Economy of Reform*, Boulder: Lynne Rienner Publishers, pp. 9–28.
Ziegenhain, Patrick (2008) *The Indonesian Parliament and Democratization*, Singapore: ISEAS.
Zon, Fadli (2004) *Politik Huru-hara Mei 1998*, Jakarta: Institute for Policy Studies.

Books and articles in Japanese

Aoyama, Hiroyuki (2001) '"Jumurūkīya" e no michi (1)—Basshāru aru-Asado seiken no seiritsu' (The path to Jumulūkīya Part 1—The establishment of the Bashshār al-Asad regime), *Gendai no Chūtō* (The Contemporary Middle East), 31: 13–37.
Aoyama, Hiroyuki (2002) '"Jumurūkīya" e no michi (2)—Basshāru aru-Asado ni yoru zettai shidōsei no kengen' (The path to Jumulūkīya Part 2), *Gendai no Chūtō* (The Contemporary Middle East), 32: 35–65.
Aoyama, Hiroyuki (2004) 'Bāsu shugi ni okeru "jiyū" to "minshushugi"' ('Freedom' and 'democracy' in Ba'athism). *Chiiki Kenkyu* (Area Studies), April, 6(1): 31–45.
Aoyama, Hiroyuki (2012) *Konmeisuru Siria—Rekishi to Seijikozo kara Yomitoku* (Syria in confusion—a perspective of history and political structure), Tokyo: Iwanami Shoten.

Aramaki, Kenji (1999) *Ajia Tsūka Kiki to IMF: Gurōbarizēshon no Hikari to Kage* (The Asian currency crisis and the IMF: The light and shade of globalization), Tokyo: Nihon Keizai Hyōron Sha.

Aramaki, Kenji (2002) 'Indoneshia kiki to IMF kaikaku' (Indonesian crisis and IMF reform), in Ikuo Kuroiwa (ed.), *Ajia Tsūka Kiki to Enjo Seisaku—Indoneshia no Kadai to Tenbō* (The Asian currency crisis and aid policy—Issues and prospects for Indonesia), Chiba: Institute of Developing Economies.

Endō, Mitsugi (2006a) 'Somaria ni okeru Shiado Bāre taisei towa nandatta no ka—"Houkai kokka" to iu seiji shakai jōkyō wo unda seiji rikigaku wo megutte' (Re-examination of the Siad Barre regime in Somalia—Notes on the political dynamics that led society and politics to the 'fallen state'), in Akira Satō (ed.), *Afurika no 'kojin shihai' saikō—Kyōdō kenkyūkai chūkan hōkoku* ('Personal rule' in Africa reconsidered—Joint research interim report), Chiba: Institute of Developing Economies, pp 21–57.

Endō, Mitsugi (2006b) 'Minshushugi wo motarasanai "minshuka"?—1990-nen dai ikō no Afurika ni okeru seiji hendō to sono hyōka wo megutte' ('Democratization' without democracy?—Evaluating political change in Africa since the 1990s), in Keiichi Tsunekawa (ed.), *Minshushugi aidentitī—Shinkō demokurashī no keisei* (Democratic identity—Formation of new democracies), Tokyo: Waseda University Press, pp. 51–72.

Fujiwara, Kiichi (1994) 'Seifuto to zaiyato—Tōnan Ajia ni okeru seifutō taisei' (The government party and the opposition party—Government party regimes in Southeast Asia), in Yoshiyuki Hagiwara (ed.), *Kōza gendai Ajia 3: Minshuka to keizaihatten* (Contemporary Asia 3: Democratization and economic development), Tokyo: University of Tokyo Press, pp. 229–269.

Fujiwara, Kiichi (1996) 'Kanryo to kaihatsu—Keizaihatten no seijiteki jōken ni tsuite' (Bureaucrats and development—The search for the political conditions of economic growth), in Ikuo Iwasaki and Yoshiyuki Hagiwara (eds.), *ASEAN shokoku no kanryōsei* (The Bureaucracy in ASEAN countries), Tokyo: Institute of Developing Economies, pp. 195–224.

Fukao, Yasuo (1995) 'Kaihatsu taisei ka no Indoneshia Chiho Gikai—Sono genjō to shakai keizaiteki haikei no ichikōsatsu' (Local assemblies under the Soeharto regime in Indonesia—A study on its conditions and socioeconomic background), *Ajia Daigaku Daigakuin keizaigaku kenkyū ronshu* (Asia University, Graduate School journal of economics), 19: 103–135.

Fukao, Yasuo (1999) 'Chuō erīto no naibu tairitsu to shūchiji senkyo—1990-nendai zenhan Indoneshia no jirei' (Internal conflict of central elites and gubernatorial elections—A case of Indonesia in the first half of the 1990s). *Ajia Daigaku kokusai kankei kiyō* (Journal of international relations, Asia University), February, 8(2): 91–134.

Honna, Jun (2002) 'Shihai kara Sanka e—Minshuka tekiou no kokugun seiji' (From dominance to participation: Military politics of democratic adaptation), in Yuri Satō (ed.), *Minshuka jidai no Indoneshia—Seiji keizai hendō to seido kaikaku* (Democratizing Indonesia—Politics and economy in historical perspective), Chiba: Institute of Developing Economies, pp. 139–198.

Igarashi, Seiichi (2007) 'Marukosu taisei houkai katei ni okeru shimin shakai no jissou—Minshuka wo meguru hegemonī tousou ni chakumoku shite' (The anatomy of civil society during the dismantling process of the Marcos regime—Focusing on the hegemonic struggles over democratization), *Ajia Kenkyū* (Asian studies), January, 53(1): 37–57.

Iwasaki, Ikuo (1994) 'ASEAN shokoku no kaihatsu taisei ron' (Development-oriented authoritarian regimes in ASEAN countries), in Ikuo Iwasaki (ed.), *Kaihatsu to seiji: ASEAN shokoku no kaihatsu taisei* (Development and politics: A study of development-oriented authoritarian regimes in ASEAN countries), Tokyo: Institute of Developing Economies, pp. 3–48.

Kanō, Hiroyoshi (1987) 'Indoneshia no seiji taisei to gyōsei kikō' (Political system and bureaucracy in Indonesia), in Yoshiyuki Hagiwara and Eiji Murashima (eds.), *ASEAN shokoku no seiji taisei* (Political systems of ASEAN countries), Tokyo: Institute of Developing Economies, pp. 23–52.

Kanō, Hiroyoshi (1996) 'Indoneshia no kanryōsei—Kōmuin seido wo chūshin ni' (The Bureaucracy in Indonesia), in Ikuo Iwasaki and Yoshiyuki Hagiwara (eds.), *ASEAN shokoku no kanryōsei* (The Bureaucracy in ASEAN countries), Tokyo: Institute of Developing Economies, pp. 5–46.

Kanō, Hiroyoshi (2004) *Gendai Indoneshia keizaishi ron—Yushutsu keizai to nōgyō mondai* (Contemporary Indonesian economic history—Export economy and agricultural problem), Tokyo: University of Tokyo Press.

Kawamura, Koichi (2002) '1945-nen kenpō no seijigaku—Minshuka no seiji seido ni taisuru inpakuto' (Politics of the 1945 Constitution—Democratization and its impact on political institutions), in Yuri Satō (ed.), *Minshuka jidai no Indoneshia—Seiji keizai hendō to seido kaikaku* (Democratizing Indonesia—Politics and economy in historical perspective), Chiba: Institute of Developing Economies, pp. 33–97.

Kisaichi, Masatoshi (2004) *Kita Afurika Isuramu shugi undō no rekishi* (History of Islamist movements in North Africa), Tokyo: Hakusuisha.

Komatsu, Masaaki (2002) 'Keizai seisaku kettei mekanizumu to keizai seisaku no kadai' (Economic policy-making mechanism and the problems of economic policy), in Ikuo Kuroiwa (ed.), *Ajia tsūka kiki to enjo seisaku—Indoneshia no kadai to tenbō* (The Asian currency crisis and aid policy—Issues and prospects for Indonesia), Chiba: Institute of Developing Economies, pp. 61–91.

Kurasawa, Aiko (2006) *Indoneshia—Isurāmu no kakusei* (Indonesia—Awakening of Islam), Tokyo: Yōsensha.

Maotani, Sakae (2000) *Gendai Indoneshia no kaihatsu to seiji shakai hendō* (Development and political and social change in contemporary Indonesia), Tokyo: Keiso Shobo.

Masuhara, Ayako (1998) 'Indoneshia kokugun no jinji seisaku—Shōkōdan no tōsei wo tsūjita seiken kiban no anteika' (Personal policy in the Indonesian military—Stabilization of the government by control of officer corps)', *Ajia Keizai* (Asian Economies), April, 39(4): 21–46.

Masuhara, Ayako (2004) 'Indoneshia-Suharuto taisei shoki no daitōryō to zantei kokumin kyōgikai' (MPRS and the presidents in the early years of the Suharto regime), *Ajia Keizai* (Asian Economies), October, 45(10): 2–23.

Masuhara, Ayako (2005) 'Indoneshia Suharuto taiseiki ni okeru Gorukaru giin—Giin dēta no bunseki ni motozuite' (Profiles of Golkar members in the Indonesian Parliament under the Suharto regime—An analysis of the personal data of the People's Representative Council (DPR), 1971–1998), *Ajia chiiki bunka kenkyū* (Komaba Journal of Asian Studies), (Asian Area Studies, University of Tokyo), March, 1: 38–67.

Masuhara, Ayako (2007) *Suharuto taiseika ni okeru yotō Gorukaru no henyō to Indoneshia no seiji hendō—Yokusan gata kojin shihai to sono seijiteki ikō* (Transformation of the ruling party Golkar and political change under the Suharto regime in Indonesia—Co-opting-type personal rule and its political transition), doctoral thesis, Department of Advanced Social and International Studies, Graduate School of Arts and Sciences, University of Tokyo.

Mihira, Norio (1995) 'Makuro keizai no seika' (The macro economic framework and its performance), in Akio Yasunaka and Norio Mihira (eds.), *Gendai Indoneshia no seiji to keizai* (Thirty years of the Soeharto government: Its political and economic performance), Tokyo: Institute of Developing Economies, pp. 193–272.

Miichi, Ken (2004) *Indoneshia: Isurāmu Shugi no Yukue* (Indonesia: The fate of Islamism), Tokyo: Heibonsha.

Murai, Yoshinori, Saeki Natsuko, Yasuyuki Kubo and Tomoko Mase (1999) *Suharuto famirī no chikuzai* (The Suharto family's accumulation of wealth), Tokyo: Komonzu.

Nakamura, Mitsuo (1994) 'Indoneshia ni okeru shin chūkansō no keisei to Isurāmu no shuryūka—Musurimu Chishikijin Kyōkai kessei no shakaiteki haikei' (Emergence of the new middle class and mainstreaming of Islam in Indonesia—Social context of the establishment of the Association of Islamic Intellectuals), in Yoshiyuki Hagiwara (ed.), *Kōza gendai Ajia 3:*

Minshuka to keizaihatten (Contemporary Asia 3: Democratization and economic development), Tokyo: University of Tokyo Press, pp. 271–306.

Ōgata, Toshiyuki (1994) 'Indoneshia ni okeru kaihatsu taisei no keisei katei: 1971-nen sōsenkyo to 85-nen sōsenkyohō no igi' (The formation of the Suharto regime in Indonesia: The role of the 1971 general election and 1985 election amendment law), in Ikuo Iwasaki (ed.), *Kaihatsu to seiji: ASEAN shokoku no kaihatsu taisei* (Development and politics: A study of development-oriented authoritarian regimes in ASEAN countries), Tokyo: Institute of Developing Economies, pp. 141–198.

Ōgata, Toshiyuki (1996) 'Gorukaru—Suharuto to kokugun no hazama de' (Golkar—Under Soeharto and Army), in Akio Yasunaka and Norio Mihira (eds.), *Gendai Indoneshia no seiji to keizai* (Thirty years of the Soeharto government: Its political and economic performance), Tokyo: Institute of Developing Economies, pp. 143–192.

Omura, Keiji (ed.) (1998) *Suharuto taisei no shūen to Indoneshia no shinjidai: Kinkyū ripōto* (The end of the Suharto regime and the new era of Indonesia: Urgent report), Tokyo: Institute of Developing Economies.

Sakai, Keiko (2002) *Iraku to Amerika* (Iraq and America), Tokyo: Iwanami Shinsho.

Sakai, Keiko (2003) *Fusein-Iraku seiken no shihai kouzou* (The ruling structure of the Hussein regime in Iraq), Tokyo: Iwanami Shoten.

Sakumoto, Naoyuki (2003) 'Indoneshia no minshuka katei to kenpō seido' (Democratization process and the constitutional system in Indonesia), in Naoyuki Sakumoto and Shinya Imaizumi (eds.), *Ajia no minshuka katei to hō—Firipin, Tai, Indoneshia no hikaku* (Democratization process and law in Asia: Comparison of the Philippines, Thailand and Indonesia), Chiba: Institute of Developing Economies, pp. 69–96.

Satō, Akira (2000) 'Kōtodivowāru no seiji kiki' (Political crisis of the Ivory Coast), *Ajiken wārudo torendo* (Ajiken world trends), October, 61: 34–41.

Satō, Akira (2004) 'Kōtodivowāru ni okeru shinkasansei no henka henshitsu—1990-nen igoki no seiji bunseki ni mukete' (Changes and transformation of neopatrimonialism in the Ivory Coast: Toward political analysis of the period from 1990), in Miwa Tsuda (ed.), *Afurika shokoku no 'minshuka' saikō—Kyōdō kenkyūkai chūkan hōkoku* ('Democratization' in African countries reconsidered—Joint research interim report), Chiba: Institute of Developing Economies, pp. 71–104.

Satō, Akira (2005) 'Seiken koutai to shōsūsha no gēmu—Kōtodivowāru no "minshuka" no kiketsu' (Regime change and the game of the few—Outcomes of the 'democratization' of Côte d'Ivoire), *Ajia Keizai* (Asian Economies), November and December, XLVI-11(12): 98–125.

Satō, Akira (2006) '"Tōchisha" saikō toiu mondai ishiki to kanōsei—jo ni kaete' (Introduction—Framework of inquiry about rethinking 'rulers' and possibilities of future studies), in Akira Satō (ed.), *Afurika no 'kojin shihai' saikō—Kyōdō kenkyūkai chūkan hōkoku* ('Personal rule' in Africa reconsidered—Joint research interim report), Chiba: Institute of Developing Economies, pp. 9–20.

Satō, Yuri (1992) 'Sarimu gurūpu—Tōnan ajia saidai no konguromaritto no hatten to kōdō genri' (The Salim Group—The development and behavior of the largest conglomerate in Southeast Asia), *Ajia Keizai* (Asian Economies), March, XXXIII-3: 54–86.

Satō, Yuri (2003) 'Indoneshia no sarimu—Seishō, konguromaritto, soshite kaitai e' (Indonesia's Salim—From *cukong* to conglomerate and dissolution), in Ikuo Iwasaki (ed.), *Ajia no kigyōka* (Entrepreneurs in Asia), Tokyo: Tōyō Keizai Shinpōsha, pp. 79–132.

Shiraishi, Takashi (1992) *Indonesia—Kokka to seiji* (State and politics in Indonesia), Tokyo: Libroport.

Shiraishi, Takashi (1997) *Sukaruno to Suharuto—Idainaru Indoneshia wo mezashite* (Sukarno and Suharto—Seeking a greater Indonesia), Tokyo: Iwanami Shoten.

Shiraishi, Takashi (1999) *Hōkai: Indoneshia wa doko e iku* (Collapse: Whither Indonesia?), Tokyo: NTT Publishing.

Shutō, Motoko (1993) 'Indoneshia no seitō seiji' (Party politics in Indoensia), in Eiji Murashima, Ikuo Iwasaki and Yoshiyuki Hagiwara (eds), *ASEAN shokoku no seitō seiji* (Party politics in the ASEAN countries), Tokyo: Institute of Developing Economies, pp. 3–48.

Suehiro, Akira (2002) 'Sōsetsu' (General introduction), in Akira Suehiro (ed.), *Iwanami koza Tonan Ajia shi 9: 'Kaihatsu' no jidai to 'mosaku' no jidai* (Iwanami series of Southeast Asian history 9: The age of 'development'), Tokyo: Iwanami Shoten, pp. 1–30.

Takahashi, Muneo (1996) 'Kokumin tōgō to panchashira' (National integration and Pancasila), in Akio Yasunaka and Norio Mihira (eds.), *Gendai Indoneshia no seiji to keizai* (Thirty years of the Soeharto government: Its political and economic performance), Tokyo: Institute of Developing Economies, pp. 53–94.

Takeda, Yasuhiro (2001) *Minshuka no hikaku seiji—Higashi Ajia shokoku no taisei hendō katei* (Comparative politics of democratization—Regime transitions in East Asia), Kyoto: Minerva Shobo.

Tsunekawa, Keiichi (2006a) 'Minshushugi taisei no chōkiteki jizoku no jouken—Minshuka no funsō riron ni mukete' (Explaining long-term endurance of democratic regimes—Toward a conflict theory of democratization), in

Keiichi Tsunekawa (ed.), *Minshushugi aidentitī—Shinkō demokurashī no keisei* (Democratic identity—Formation of new democracies), Tokyo: Waseda University Press, pp. 1–23.

Tsunekawa, Keiichi (2006b) 'Minshushugi taisei no chōkiteki jizoku' (Long-term endurance of democratic regimes), in Keiichi Tsunekawa (ed.), *Minshushugi aidentitī—Shinkō demokurashī no keisei* (Democratic identity—Formation of new democracies), Tokyo: Waseda University Press, pp. 165–173.

Umezawa, Tatsuo (1992) *Suharuto Taisei no Kouzou to Henyō* (Suharto regime: Its basic structure and the recent transformation), Tokyo: Institute of Developing Economies.

Yasunaka, Akio (1996) 'Suharuto "shin chitsujo" taisei saikō—Seijiteki kindaika no kiseki' (Soeharto's 'New Order' reconsidered), in Akio Yasunaka and Norio Mihira (eds.), *Gendai Indoneshia no seiji to keizai* (Thirty years of the Soeharto government: Its political and economic performance), Tokyo: Institute of Developing Economies, pp. 23–52.

Government and legislature documents

Bantuan Pembangunan (1987?) *Bantuan Pembangunan: 1. Bantuan Presiden, 2. Yayasan Dharma Bhakti Sosial, 3. Yayasan Amal Bhakti Muslim Pancasila, 4. Yayasan Beasiswa Supersemar*, Jakarta.

Departemen Keuangan, *Nota Keuangan dan Rancangan Anggaran Pendapatan dan Belanja Negara*, Jakarta: Departemen Keuangan.

Kantor Menteri Negara Pemuda dan Olahraga (1992) *Direktori Organisasi Pemuda Indonesia*, Jakarta: Kantor Menteri Negara Pemuda dan Olahraga.

Lembaga Pemilihan Umum (1971) *Memperkenalkan Anggota-anggota Dewan Perwakilan Rakyat Hasil Pemilihan Umum 1971*, Jakarta: LPU.

Lembaga Pemilihan Umum (1978) *Buku Pelengkap IV Pemilihan Umum 1977: Ringkasan Riwayat Hidup dan Riwayat Perjuangan Anggota Majelis Permusyawaratan Rakyat Hasil Pemilihan Umum Tahun 1977, Buku I*, Jakarta: LPU.

Lembaga Pemilihan Umum (1983) *Buku Pelengkap V Pemilihan Umum 1982: Ringkasan Riwayat Hidup dan Riwayat Perjuangan Anggota Dewan Perwakilan Rakyat Hasil Pemilihan Umum Tahun 1982*, Jakarta: LPU.

Lembaga Pemilihan Umum (1987) *Buku Pelengkap VIII Pemilihan Umum 1987: Ringkasan Riwayat Hidup dan Riwayat Perjuangan Anggota Dewan Perwakilan Rakyat Hasil Pemilihan Umum Tahun 1987*, Jakarta: LPU.

Lembaga Pemilihan Umum (1993) *Buku Pelengkap VIII Pemilihan Umum 1992: Ringkasan Riwayat Hidup dan Riwayat Perjuangan Anggota Dewan Perwakilan Rakyat Hasil Pemilihan Umum Tahun 1992*, Jakarta: LPU.

Lembaga Pemilihan Umum (1997a) *Buku Pelengkap XIII Pemilihan Umum 1997: Ringkasan Riwayat Hidup dan Riwayat Perjuangan Anggota Dewan Perwakilan Rakyat Hasil Pemilihan Umum Tahun 1997*, Jakarta: LPU.

Lembaga Pemilihan Umum (1997b) *Buku Lampiran V Pemilihan Umum 1997: Hasil Pemilihan Umum Anggota Dewan Perwakilan Rakyat Tahun 1997, Jilid 6*, Jakarta: LPU.

Sekretariat Jenderal DPR-RI (1997) *Himpunan Surat Keputusan Pimpinan DPR-RI No. 1-48 Tahun 1997–1998*, Jakarta: Sekretariat Jenderal DPR-RI, Pusat Pengkajian dan Pelayanan Informasi Bidang Dokumentasi.

Sekretariat Jenderal DPR-RI (1998) *DPR-RI dalam Menyikapi Proses Reformasi dan Berhentinya Presiden Soeharto*, Jakarta: Sekretariat Jenderal DPR-RI.

Sekretariat Jenderal MPR-RI (1998) *Buku Ketiga Jilid 12: Risalah Rapat Panitia Ad Hoc II (Non GBHN)*, Jakarta: Sekretariat Jenderal MPR.

Skarwil II (1974) *Perumusan Kompilasi Jawaban Checklist dan Data dari Pakokarda Tk. II Se-Wilayah II*, Jakarta: Departemen Pertahanan Keamanan, Staf Kekaryaan Wilayah II.

Skarwil II (1976) *Keadaan dan Kegiatan Parpol sampai dengan Akhir Desember 1976 di Wilayah-II*, Jakarta: Departemen Pertahanan Keamanan, Staf Kekaryaan Wilayah II.

Golkar documents

Bangun, Roberto (ed.) (1994) *Kenang-kenangan Sekber Golkar - KINO - Golkar dari Mukernas ke Munas-V Golkar: Sejarah Kepeloporan, Pembaruan dan Pembangunan Politik*, Jakarta.

Dewan Pimpinan Pusat Golkar (1978) *Laporan Pertanggungjawaban DPP Golkar Periode 1973–1978 kepada Musyawarah Nasional II Golongan Karya*, Jakarta: DPP Golkar.

Dewan Pimpinan Pusat Golkar (1980) *Penlat Kader*, Jakarta: DPP Golkar.

Dewan Pimpinan Pusat Golkar (1984) *20 Tahun Golkar, 20 Oktober 1964—20 Oktober 1984*, Jakarta: DPP Golkar.

Dewan Pimpinan Pusat Golkar (1988a) *Lampiran Pertanggungjawaban DPP-Golkar Masa Bakti 1983–1988*, Jakarta: DPP Golkar.

Dewan Pimpinan Pusat Golkar (1988b) *Anak Lampiran LXXVIII S/D CV dari Lampiran Pertanggungjawaban DPP Golkar Masa Bhakti 1983–1988*, Jakarta: DPP Golkar.

Dewan Pimpinan Pusat Golkar (1989) *Memperingati 25 Tahun Golongan Karya*, Jakarta: DPP Golkar.
Dewan Pimpinan Pusat Golkar (1994) *30 Tahun Golkar*, Jakarta: DPP Golkar.
Panitia Raker Golkar 1972 (1972) *Bahan-bahan Komisi A Raker Golkar 1972*, Jakarta: Panitia Raker Golkar 1972.
Sekretariat Bersama Golkar (1968) *Peranan Sekretariat Bersama Golongan Karya dalam Pembangunan*, Jakarta: Biro Humas Sekber Golkar.
Sekretariat Bersama Golkar (1969) *Partisipasi Sekber Golkar dalam Repelita*, Jakarta: Biro Humas Sekber Golkar.
Sekretariat Bersama Golkar (1970) *Rapat Kerdja Bapilu Sekber Golkar Seluruh Indonesia di Tjibogo, September 1970*, Jakarta: Sekber Golkar.

Newspapers, magazines and other periodicals

Ajia Dōkō Nenpō (Yearbook of Asian Affairs)
Asiaweek
Far Eastern Economic Review
Forum Keadilan
Gatra
Info Bisnis
Kompas
Majalah Tokoh Indonesia
Media Karya
Military Balance
Mimbar Kekaryaan ABRI
Suara Karya
Swasembada
Tempo
Tiras
Warta Ekonomi

Name Index

Achmad, Marzuki, 212
Adenansi, Anang, 99, 133, 136–137, 139–140, 142, 249
al-Asad, Bashar, 33–34
al-Asad, Hafiz, 25, 29, 32–33, 35
Ali, Ben, 237, 256
Ambong, Ibrahim, 177, 254
Amin, Idi, 25, 29, 31, 237
Amirmachmud, 47, 82–83, 150
Arifin, Bustanil, 74
Assegaf, Muhammad Iqbal, 120, 177, 205, 251, 254

Bakrie, Abrizal, 108–110, 114–115, 123, 126, 248
Baldan, Ferry Mursyidan, 107, 126, 165, 177, 205–206, 220, 254
Batista, 14, 19, 29–30, 237
Batubara, Cosmas, 82, 84, 86, 104, 106
Bawazir, Fuad, 182, 194–195, 213, 252, 256
Bédié, Henri Konan, 237, 256
Bourguiba, Habib, 29, 34, 36, 237, 256

Ceauşescu, Nicolae, 25, 29, 237

Danutirto, Haryanto, 128, 133, 182
Darusman, Marzuki, 107, 135, 137, 139–140, 142, 170
Djiwandono, Soedradjad, 190–195
Duvalier, François, 19, 25, 29, 32
Duvalier, Jean-Claude, 29, 32, 237

Fadjar, Malik, 198, 206–207

Gafur, Abdul, 90, 106, 164, 166–167, 169, 198, 204, 209, 220, 222, 227–228
Gie, Kwik Kian, 143
Gitosardjono, Sukamdani Sahid, 116, 248

Habibie, Bacharuddin Jusuf, 13, 48, 122, 128, 142, 154–156, 168, 172–173, 180–183, 190–191, 201, 214, 225, 229–230, 238–240, 254–255
Hamid, Syarwan, 172–173, 204, 208, 230, 255
Harmoko, 91, 156–159, 167, 169, 171–174, 179–182, 186, 202, 204, 211–212, 215, 218, 220, 227–228, 232
Hartas, Harsudiono, 156–157
Hartono, 63, 172–173, 178–180, 182, 197–198, 201–202, 210, 230
Harun, Lukman, 120–121, 139, 198, 205, 251
Hasan, Bob, 51, 182, 196, 256
Houphouët-Boigny, Félix, 25, 27, 29, 34, 36, 237, 256
Hussein, Saddam, 25–27, 29, 32, 34, 237

Ibrahim, Marwah Daud, 122–123, 168, 182
Idris, Fahmi, 111, 115, 123, 126,

168–169, 182, 198, 207, 220, 228, 248–249
Isman, Hayono, 166

Kalla, Jusuf, 108, 111, 114–115, 123, 126, 228, 248, 255
Kamaluddin, Laode, 254
Kamarulzaman, Rambe, 107, 126, 167, 169, 209
Kartasasmita, Ginandjar, 111, 114, 146, 180, 190–191, 195, 217, 233, 255
Komaruddin, Ade, 107, 123, 126, 177, 205, 220, 233, 254
Kumolo, Tjahjo, 164
Kusumaatmadja, Sarwono, 98–99, 104, 106, 120, 131, 146, 248

Laksono, Agung, 108, 110, 115–116, 132–133, 164, 167, 182, 200–202, 248
Lion, Liem Sioe, 50–51, 72, 244

Madjid, Nurcholish, 127, 197–198, 203, 206–207, 219–220, 224, 228, 231, 255
Mangkusubroto, Kuntro, 195, 212–213
Marcos, Ferdinand, 10, 12, 29–30, 237, 244
Mardjono, Ary, 169, 182, 227–228, 233, 256
Megawati, Sukarnoputri, 71
Memet, Yogi Suwardi, 153, 156
Metareum, Ismail Hasan, 127, 204–205, 218
Muarif, Syamsul, 107, 123, 126, 205, 207
Muhammad, Fadel, 110–111, 114–115, 123, 168–169, 220, 248, 255

Muhammad, Mar'ie, 80, 190–195, 249
Murdani, Benny, 47–48, 62–63, 96, 145, 154, 250
Murfi, Harris Ali, 163–164, 251
Murtono, Amir, 83–86, 90–91
Murtopo, Ali, 47–48, 62, 79, 82–85, 87–88, 104, 163

Nadjib, Emha Ainun, 231, 249
Napitupulu, David, 82, 84, 86, 91, 99, 104, 106
Nasution, Abdul Haris, 61, 244
Nitisastro, Widjojo, 49, 114, 191, 233, 252

Oesman, Oetojo, 86, 99, 132–133

Pahlavi, Mohammad Reza, 25, 29, 237
Pakpahan, Mochtar, 68, 71
Paloh, Surya Dharma, 113, 126
Panigoro, Arifin, 114, 233, 255
Prawiro, Radius, 49, 80
Probosutedjo, 50, 72, 193, 248

Rahardjo, Dawam, 122, 127, 179
Rais, Amien, 120–121, 128, 179, 183, 197–198, 200, 206, 216, 222, 225, 251
Rudini, 153, 156
Rukmana, Siti Hardiyanti see 'Tutut'

Sabirin, Syahril, 195, 233
Sadikin, Ali, 61, 207
Salim, Emil, 49, 121, 191, 197–198, 204, 209, 215, 233
Sambuaga, Theo, 107, 123, 167, 169, 182, 202
Santoso, Priyo Budi, 122, 205, 213, 254

Sasono, Adi, 122, 127–128, 179, 182–183, 200, 214
Sazili, Abu Hasan, 107, 125, 205–206, 208, 254
Sirait, Midian, 83, 85–87, 104
Soedradjad see 'Djiwandono'
Sokowati, 80–81, 83–84
Somoza, 14
Subagyo, 172, 199, 217, 225–227, 254
Subianto, Prabowo, 225–227, 254–255
Sudharmono, 47–48, 62–63, 80, 94–95, 97–102, 114, 116, 118, 132, 137–138, 145–147, 150, 168, 248, 250
Sudiro, Irsyad, 133, 167, 205, 207–209, 211, 229
Sudradjat, Edi, 63, 146, 156–157, 173
Sugama, Yoga, 163, 167
Sugandhi, R. H., 80, 91, 99, 146
Sugomo, Bambang Riyadi, 163, 167, 170, 173, 193
Suhardiman, 90
Suharto, 7–8, 29, 34–36, 41, 45, 47–48, 50–51, 53, 56, 61–63, 69–72, 74, 97, 138–141, 150, 170, 180, 186, 189–190, 193–195, 201, 209–211, 217–219, 226–227, 230–233, 236, 238–239, 242, 254 see also Subject Index
Sukarno, 6–8, 77–79, 85, 87, 242–243, 247
Sumitro, 48, 61–62, 135
Suryosumarno, Yapto, 170
Sutowo, Ibnu, 11, 49, 60, 112, 114, 163, 167, 243
Sutowo, Ponco, 112, 114, 126, 132–133, 163–164, 167, 170
Sutrisno, Try, 146, 155–156, 173, 180–181

Syafruddin, Eky, 125, 177, 205–207, 212, 220–221, 228, 254
Syamsuddin, Din, 121, 127, 168, 182, 198, 209, 251

Tandjung, Akbar, 97–99, 105–106, 123, 125, 127, 131, 146, 164–166, 168–169, 178, 181, 198, 207, 220, 233, 248–249
Tandjung, Feisal, 63, 156–157, 172–173, 198, 230, 233
Tawari, Mohammad Yamin, 107, 126, 206
Thohari, Hajriyanto, 205, 254
Tirtosudiro, Achmad, 183, 207, 214–215, 233
Tobing, Jacob, 83, 96, 99, 104, 132–133
Tommy, Suharto, 74, 163
Trihatmodjo, Bambang, 74, 163, 167, 169, 170, 253
Trujillo, 19
Tutut, 74, 163, 167, 169, 171–173, 178–179, 181–182, 196, 200

Utoyo, Indra Bambang, 162, 164–165, 167, 169–170, 227–229, 251

Wahid, Abdurrahman, 207, 253
Wahono, 131–133, 135, 137–140, 142, 155–156
Wanandi, Jusuf, 82, 84, 86, 91, 99, 104, 106
Wanandi, Sofyan, 195, 255
Wiranto, 199, 208, 217, 223, 225–227, 254–255
Witoelar, Rachmat, 98–99, 104, 106, 132–135, 139–140, 142, 248
Yudhoyono, Susilo Bambang, 199, 208, 219–220, 224, 248

Yudohusodo, Siswono, 98–99, 112, 114–115, 123, 131, 228
Yusuf, Slamet Effendy, 119–121, 123, 127, 132–133, 202, 205, 207–208, 229
Zaini, Yahya, 107, 126, 254

Subject Index

Advisory Board see 'Golkar'
All Indonesian Labor Federation (FBSI, renamed SPSI in 1985), 68, 88, 90–91, 99, 133, 167
All-Indonesian Fishermen's Association (HNSI), 88, 90, 167
Amal Bakti Muslim Pancasila Foundation, 74–75
AMPI see 'Indonesian-Renewal Youth Generation'
Ansor Youth Movement (GP Ansor), 120, 124, 127, 132–133, 165–166, 169, 173, 175, 177–178, 205, 221, 251
Armed Forces, 8, 15, 46, 53, 55–63, 78, 87, 130, 144, 147–148, 153, 155, 157–158, 199–201, 216, 223–225, 245
  Armed Forces faction, 135, 140–141, 146, 149–153, 156, 204, 230, 246, 255
Association of Islamic Intellectuals (ICMI), 119, 121–122, 126–128, 154, 167–168, 175, 177–183, 198, 205, 207, 214–215, 220, 229, 233, 248–249

BAKIN see 'State Intelligence Agency'
Bandung group, 98–99, 104, 106, 132–133, 247
Bank of Indonesia (BI), 189–195, 252, 256
BAPILU see 'Golkar'

Bulog see 'National Food Logistics'

cadre cultivation, 89, 97–98, 101–103, 115–116, 247
CBS see 'Currency Board System'
Central Executive Board of Golkar see 'Golkar'
Chamber of Commerce and Industry (KADIN), 109–112, 115–116, 127, 133, 168, 248
Chinese-Indonesian entrepreneur, 50–52, 60, 74, 244 see also 'entrepreneur'
Cipayung Group, 105, 162, 251
consensus building, 17, 40, 189, 215, 238–239
co-opting-type personal rule, 2, 3, 5, 29, 31, 34, 36–39, 189, 236–238 see also 'personal rule'
corruption, 9, 27, 52, 60, 196
Council for Islamic Dakwah (MDI), 90–91, 99, 118, 132–133, 139, 177
currency crisis, 14, 36, 189, 191–192, 200
Currency Board System (CBS), 194–195, 252

Dakab Foundation, 74–75, 101, 246
Darul Islam, 66
defense budget, 49, 53–55, 60, 62
democratization, 238–241
development, 10–11, 71
developmental dictatorship, 10

dialogue, 17, 39–40, 199–202, 204–205, 224
Dili incident, 154, 250
dividing-type personal rule, 29, 31–37
  see also 'personal rule'
DPR see 'People's Representative Council'
DPRD see 'Regional Representative Councils'
Dual function, 155, 245, 250

election, 42, 94–95, 162, 174
  1971 election, 42, 78, 81–83, 123
  1977 election, 123
  1982 election, 123
  1987 election, 97, 117, 123, 129–130, 145, 161–162
  1992 election, 117, 123, 136–137, 140–141, 166
  1997 election, 117, 123, 162, 173–178
entrepreneur, 51, 99, 109, 117, 167–168, 207
  Chinese-Indonesian entrepreneur, 50–52, 60, 74, 244
  pribumi entrepreneur, 98, 103, 108–117, 123, 126–127, 163, 180, 248, 255

FBSI see 'All Indonesian Labor Federation'
five political laws, 67, 70–71, 135, 186, 203, 208–211, 219, 231, 244
FKPPI (Armed Forces Son's and Daughter's Communication Forum), 110–113, 132–133, 160–170, 173, 175–178, 180–182, 227, 229–230, 251, 255 see also 'Armed Forces'
FKPPI Youth, 170

Floating Mass, 85
foundation, 50, 60, 71–72, 74, 244–245

'Generation of 45', 96
'Generation of 66', 64, 105, 141–142, 198, 206–207, 228, 249
Golkar, 38–40, 77, 83, 88–89, 141, 177, 220
  Advisory Board of Golkar, 45, 84, 92–93, 100, 132, 140, 142–143, 157, 215, 228
  Central Executive Board of Golkar, 79–80, 84–86, 91–93, 98–100, 103, 108–113, 132–133, 138, 166–169, 173, 181, 209, 227–228, 255
  General Election Controlling Body (BAPILU) of Golkar, 82–84, 104
  Golkar faction, 79, 81, 136, 139, 148–149, 151–153, 155, 159, 185–187, 202, 204–205, 207–209, 211–213, 221, 223, 227–229, 232, 246
  independence of Golkar, 129–130, 132, 139, 143–145, 158–159
  Golkar National Congress, 85
    1978, 90, 92–93
    1983, 97–98
    1988, 131–132
    1993, 157, 166
  Sekber Golkar, 78–83
GP Ansor see 'Ansor Youth Movement'
Great Armed Forces Family, 161, 163, 170, 251
Great Golkar Family, 144–145, 158, 181, 250
Group of Twenty, 221, 228–229
gubernatorial election, 153, 250
Guidance on Understanding and

Implementing Pancasila (P 4), 65–66, 118
Guided Democracy, 6, 67, 78
GUPPI see 'Islamic Education Reform Endeavour Movement'

hard-liner, 189, 230, 238, 241
HIPMI see 'Young Indonesian Entrepreneurs' Association'
HKTI see 'Indonesian Farmers' Harmony Association'
HMI see 'Islamic Students' Association'
HNSI see 'All-Indonesian Fishermen's Association'

ICMI see 'Association of Islamic Intellectuals'
IMF, 48, 192–195
individual membership system, 101–102
Indonesian Communist Party (PKI), 6–8, 77–78, 87, 217, 246
Indonesian Democratic Party (PDI), 14, 16, 42, 71, 88, 177
PDI faction, 204–205
Indonesian Farmers' Harmony Association (HKTI), 88, 90, 133, 247
Indonesian Islamic Student Movement (PMII), 124, 251
Indonesian Muslims' Party (PMI), 42
Indonesian Renewal Youth Generation (AMPI), 64, 90, 105–106, 108, 110, 115, 124, 162–166, 173, 176, 251
Indonesian Student's Action Front (KAMI), 64, 98, 104, 196, 247, 253
Islamic Education Reform Endeavour Movement (GUPPI), 90–91, 99, 117–118, 133, 168
Islamic Students' Association (HMI), 89–90, 98–99, 105–106, 123–128, 162–169, 173, 175, 177–178, 198, 201, 205–206, 208–209, 220–221, 229, 233, 249, 251
isolated-type personal rule, 29–3, 36
see also 'personal rule'

Jakarta riots, 216–217, 224, 235

KADIN see 'Chamber of Commerce and Industry'
KAHMI (Alumni of the Islamic Students' Association), 124, 169, 215
KAMI see 'Indonesian Student's Action Front'
KAMMI (Indonesian Muslim Students' Action Front), 196, 221, 253
KBA see 'Great Armed Forces Family'
Kebatinan, 46, 65, 67, 119, 245
Khittah 1926, 119
KINO (Basic Organizational Units), 79, 81–84, 90, 92, 101, 146
KNPI see 'National Committee of Indonesian Youth'
Kopkamtib (Operational Command for the Restoration of Security and Order), 7–8, 25, 217
KOPKKN (Operational Command for National Alertness and Safety), 217–218, 225–227, 254–255
KOSGORO (United Multipurpose Mutual Assistance Organizations), 80–82, 84, 86, 88, 91, 99, 110, 133, 167, 246

Malari incident, 62, 64, 90, 104
MAR see 'People's Mandate Council'
Marsinah incident, 71
MDI see 'Council for Islamic Dakwah'
MKGR (Mutual Assistance Families Association), 80–82, 84, 91, 99, 133, 167, 246
monoloyalty, 44
MPR see 'People's Consultative Assembly'
Muhammadiyah, 65, 96, 118–119, 121, 139, 169, 177, 198, 205–206, 220, 251
Muhammadiyah Youth, 120, 124, 127, 165–166, 168–169, 173, 178, 205, 221
Mukhabarat, 25, 32
mysterious shooting, 69–70

Nahdlatul Ulama (NU), 42, 65, 96, 118–119, 139, 169, 177, 207, 217, 219, 225–226, 232, 246, 251
NASAKOM (Nationalism, Religion and Communism), 6, 77, 242
National Committee of Indonesian Youth (KNPI), 64, 88–90, 105–106, 108, 124, 162–166, 176, 251
National Congress see 'Golkar'
National Food Logistics (Bulog), 10, 60, 74, 99, 183, 249
nepotism, 192, 196
normalization of campus life (NKK), 64, 108
NU see 'Nahdlatul Ulama'

openness, 12, 129, 134–135, 140–141, 153
Order of March the Eleventh (Supersemar), 8, 242–243

P 4 see 'Guidance on Understanding and Implementing Pancasila'
pacted transition, 20–21, 189, 235
Panca Marga Youth, 166, 173, 230, 251
Pancasila, 85
Pancasila as the sole principle, 65–67, 95, 118, 135
Pancasila industrial relations, 67–68
Pancasila journalism, 67–68
Pancasila Youth, 166, 170, 173, 176, 230, 251
patrimonialism, 9–10, 12, 18–20, 22, 33
patron-client relationship, 9, 18, 22, 26, 35, 48, 241
patronage, 29
patronage distribution, 28, 30–33, 35–40, 61, 63, 188, 236
economic patronage, 9, 26–27, 48, 50–52
distributing patronage, 34, 237
political patronage, 9, 26, 45, 56–59, 183
PDI see 'Indonesian Democratic Party'
People's Consultative Assembly (MPR), 41–42, 46, 142, 154–155, 179, 204, 250
MPR-appointed seat, 42, 203, 210
MPR general session, 43, 66, 97, 132, 156, 186, 256
1988, 145–146
MPR special session, 214–215, 218–220, 222, 229–230, 232–233, 253, 255
People's Mandate Council (MAR), 216–217, 255
People's Representative Council (DPR), 41–43, 46, 134–136, 141, 143, 174, 178, 183–186, 202, 204,

207–210, 213, 215, 219, 221–222, 231, 233–234, 246, 252–255
empowerment of DPR, 202–203, 223, 235
DPR leadership, 204–205, 209, 218, 222–223, 227–230, 232, 255
DPR-appointed seat, 203, 210
personal rule, 2, 13, 15, 17–24, 26–29, 41, 235, 240–241
co-opting type, 3, 29, 31, 34, 36–39, 189, 236–238
dividing-type, 29, 31–34
isolated-type, 29–30
terrorizing-type, 28–32
personalist dictatorship see 'personal rule'
personnel policy, 46–48, 56, 141
Pertamina, 10–11, 49, 60, 114, 163, 191, 243
Petrus incident see 'mysterious shooting'
PKI see 'Indonesian Communist Party'
PMII see 'Indonesian Islamic Student Movement'
political change, 17, 38–39
political patronage, 9, 26, 45, 56–59, 183 see 'patronage'
political transition, 238, 241, 244 see also 'transition'
PPP see 'United Development Party'
President's family, 192 see also 'Suharto family'
President's resignation, 218, 222–223, 227–228 see also 'Suharto's resignation'
presidential assistance (banpres), 27, 50, 71–73, 118, 245
Presidential Decision 10 (Keppres 10), 108, 111, 114

pribumi, 51
pribumi entrepreneur, 98, 103, 108–117, 123, 126–127, 163, 180, 248, 255 see also 'entrepreneur'

reform, 196, 210
total reform, 218
Reform Committee, 230–232
reformist force, 16–17, 39–40, 188–189, 196–197, 199, 202, 204–206, 209, 211, 218–219, 223–224, 230, 233, 235, 238–240, 244, 255
regime change, 17, 236, 239
Regional Representative Councils (DPRD), 147–149
Regulation of the Ministry of Home Affairs No.12, (Permen 12), 82
resignation of the President see 'Suharto's resignation'
reward, 23–24, 26, 28

SARA (Ethnicity, Religion, Race and Inter-group Relations), 68
SAVAK (Organization of Intelligence and National Security), 25
Securitate, 25
September 30th Affair, 7, 25, 63, 70, 87, 245
SOBSI (All Indonesia Centre of Labor Organizations), 67, 246
soft-liner, 16–17, 20–21, 37–40, 189, 205, 235, 239, 244
SOKSI (Central Organization for Indonesian Independent Workers), 80–82, 84, 86, 88, 90–91, 99, 133, 167–168, 246
SPSI see 'All Indonesian Labor Federation'
State Intelligence Agency (BAKIN), 25, 91, 104, 163, 167

student activist, 63, 69, 91, 98–99, 103–106, 123, 132–133, 167–168
Suharto see also Name Index
Suharto family, 13, 40, 50–52, 60, 68, 194, 244 see also 'President's family'
Suharto regime, 9–10, 12, 14, 25, 37, 41, 237
Suharto's resignation, 15–17, 39–40, 188, 215–217, 220–221, 223, 225, 229–230, 232–235 see also 'President's resignation'
Suharto's succession, 178–179, 181, 188
sultanistic regime, 2, 14–15, 17–23, 31
Supersemar see 'Order of March the Eleventh'
Supreme Court (MA), 41, 44–45, 203

Tanah Abang group, 99, 104–106, 133
Tanjung Priok incident, 69–71
terrorizing-type personal rule, 28–32, 34, 36 see also 'personal rule'
Tonton Macoute, 25, 32
total reform, 218 see also 'reform'
transition, 239–240
political transition, 238, 241, 244
Tri Sakti University incident, 216, 219, 225

United Development Party (PPP), 42, 65–66, 88, 96, 118–119, 127, 177
PPP faction, 185–186, 204–205, 208, 212

vengeance, 23–26, 28–34, 63, 69–70

Wednesday Meeting, 206–207, 219, 228, 253

Young Indonesian Entrepreneurs' Association (HIPMI), 108–114, 116, 126–127, 133, 162, 164, 167